Lecture Notes in Computer Science   11527

Commenced Publication in 1973
Founding and Former Series Editors:
Gerhard Goos, Juris Hartmanis, and Jan van Leeuwen

More information about this series at http://www.springer.com/series/7410

Shlomi Dolev · Danny Hendler ·
Sachin Lodha · Moti Yung (Eds.)

Cyber Security Cryptography and Machine Learning

Third International Symposium, CSCML 2019
Beer-Sheva, Israel, June 27–28, 2019
Proceedings

 Springer

Editors
Shlomi Dolev
Ben-Gurion University of the Negev
Beer-Sheva, Israel

Danny Hendler
Ben-Gurion University of the Negev
Beer-Sheva, Israel

Sachin Lodha
Tata Consultancy Services
Mumbai, India

Moti Yung
Columbia University and Google
New York, NY, USA

ISSN 0302-9743   ISSN 1611-3349 (electronic)
Lecture Notes in Computer Science
ISBN 978-3-030-20950-6   ISBN 978-3-030-20951-3 (eBook)
https://doi.org/10.1007/978-3-030-20951-3

LNCS Sublibrary: SL4 – Security and Cryptology

This Springer imprint is published by the registered company Springer Nature Switzerland AG
The registered company address is: Gewerbestrasse 11, 6330 Cham, Switzerland

Preface

CSCML, the International Symposium on Cyber Security Cryptography and Machine Learning, is an international forum for researchers, entrepreneurs, and practitioners in the theory, design, analysis, implementation, or application of cyber security, cryptography, and machine learning systems and networks, and, in particular, of conceptually innovative topics in these research areas.

Information technology has become crucial to our everyday lives, an indispensable infrastructure of our society and therefore a target for attacks by malicious parties. Cyber security is one of the most important fields of research today because of these developments. Two of the (sometimes competing) fields of research, cryptography and machine learning, are the most important building blocks of cyber security.

Topics of interest for CSCML include: cyber security design; secure software development methodologies; formal methods, semantics, and verification of secure systems; fault tolerance, reliability, availability of distributed secure systems; game-theoretic approaches to secure computing; automatic recovery self-stabilizing, and self-organizing systems; communication, authentication and identification security; cyber security for mobile and Internet of Things; cyber security of corporations; security and privacy for cloud, edge, and fog computing; cryptocurrency; Blockchain; cryptography; cryptographic implementation analysis and construction; secure multi-party computation; privacy-enhancing technologies and anonymity; post-quantum cryptography and security; machine learning and Big Data; anomaly detection and malware identification; business intelligence and security; digital forensics, digital rights management; trust management and reputation systems; and information retrieval, risk analysis, DoS.

The Third CSCML took place during June 27–28, 2019, in Beer-Sheva, Israel. This year the conference was organized in cooperation with the International Association for Cryptologic Research (IACR) and selected papers will appear in a dedicated special issue in the journal *Information and Computation*.

This volume contains 18 contributions selected by the Program Committee and ten brief announcements. All submitted papers were read and evaluated by Program Committee members, assisted by external reviewers. We are grateful to the EasyChair system in assisting the reviewing process.

The support of Ben-Gurion University of the Negev (BGU), in particular the BGU-NHSA, BGU Lynne and William Frankel Center for Computer Science, the BGU Cyber Security Research Center, Oracle, ATSMA, the Department of Computer Science, Tata Consultancy Services, IBM and BaseCamp, is also gratefully acknowledged.

March 2019

Danny Hendler
Moti Yung
Shlomi Dolev
Sachin Lodha

Organization

CSCML, the International Symposium on Cyber Security Cryptography and Machine Learning, is an international forum for researchers, entrepreneurs, and practitioners in the theory, design, analysis, implementation, or application of cyber security, cryptography, and machine learning systems and networks, and, in particular, of conceptually innovative topics in the scope.

Founding Steering Committee

Orna Berry	DELLEMC, Israel
Shlomi Dolev (Chair)	Ben-Gurion University, Israel
Yuval Elovici	Ben-Gurion University, Israel
Bezalel Gavish	Southern Methodist University, USA
Ehud Gudes	Ben-Gurion University, Israel
Jonathan Katz	University of Maryland, USA
Rafail Ostrovsky	UCLA, USA
Jeffrey D. Ullman	Stanford University, USA
Kalyan Veeramachaneni	MIT, USA
Yaron Wolfsthal	IBM, Israel
Moti Yung	Columbia University and Google, USA

Organizing Committee

General Chairs

Shlomi Dolev	Ben-Gurion University of the Negev
Sachin Lodha	Tata Consultancy Services

Program Chairs

Danny Hendler	Ben-Gurion University of the Negev
Moti Yung	Columbia University and Google

Organizing Chairs

Timi Budai	Ben-Gurion University of the Negev
Simcha Mahler	Ben-Gurion University of the Negev

Program Committee

Ittai Abraham	VMware., Israel
Adi Akavia	Tel Aviv Yaffo Academic College, Israel
Amir Averbuch	Tel Aviv University, Israel
Silvia Bonomi	Sapienza University of Rome, Italy

Anat Bremler-Barr	IDC Herzliya, Israel
Emilio Coppa	PSapienza University of Rome, Italy
Antonella Del Pozzo	CEA List, France
Itai Dinur	Ben-Gurion University, Israel
Orr Dunkelman	University of Haifa, Israel
Karim El Defrawy	SRI International, USA
Bezalel Gavish	Southern Methodist University, USA
Niv́ Gilboa	Ben-Gurion University, Israel
Ehud Gudes	Ben-Gurion University, Israel
Shay Gueron	University of Haifa, Israel
Danny Hendler (Co-chair)	Ben-Gurion University, Israel
Stratis Ioannidis	Northeastern University, USA
Gene Itkis	MIT Lincoln Laboratory, USA
Bhavana Kanukurthi	IISc, India
Ben Kreuter	Google, USA
Mark Last	Ben-Gurion University, Israel
Ximing Li	South China Agricultural University, China
Yin Li	Fudan University, China
Avi Mendelson	Technion, Israel
Aikaterini Mitrokosta	Chalmers University of Technology, Sweden
Kobbi Nissim	Georgetown University, USA and Ben-Gurion University, Israel
Yossi Oren	Ben-Gurion University, Israel
Chandrasekaran Pandurangan	IIT Madras, India
Haim Permuter	Ben-Gurion University, Israel
Giuseppe Persiano	Università degli Studi di Salerno, Italy
Benny Pinkas	Bar Ilan University, Israel
Christian Riess	FAU, Germany
Or Sattath	Ben-Gurion University, Israel
Elad M. Schiller	Chalmers University of Technology, Sweden
Galina Schwartz	UC Berkeley, USA
Gil Segev	Hebrew University, Israel
Paul Spirakis	University of Liverpool, UK and University Patras, Greece
Kannan Srinathan	IIIT, India
Uri Stemmer	Ben-Gurion University, Israel
Ari Trachtenberg	Boston University, USA
Philippas Tsigas	Chalmers University of Technology, Sweden
Doug Tygar	UC Berkeley, USA
Kalyan Veeramachaneni	MIT LIDS, USA
Colin Wilmott	Nottingham Trent University, UK
Rebecca Wright	Rutgers University, USA
Moti Yung (Co-chair)	Columbia University and Google, USA

Additional Reviewers

Luigi Catuogno
Eran Lambooij
Calvin Newport
Moshe Shechner
Nadav Voloch
Yu Zhang

Sponsors

Contents

Jamming Strategies in Covert Communication

Ori Shmuel[(⊠)], Asaf Cohen, and Omer Gurewitz

Ben Gurion University of the Negev, Beersheba, Israel
{shmuelor,coasaf,gurewitz}@bgu.ac.il

Abstract. Consider the communication problem where Alice tries to send a message towards Bob while trying to conceal the presence of communication from a watchful adversary, Willie, which tries to determine if a transmission took place or not. Under the basic settings, where all variables are known to Willie, the total amount of information bits that can be transmitted covertly and reliably in n independent channel uses is $O(\sqrt{n})$ (a.k.a the square-root law). Thus, the resulting rate is $O(\sqrt{n}/n)$ which goes to zero as $n \to \infty$. However, when a jammer is present and assists Alice by creating uncertainty in Willie's decoder, this transmission may have a strictly positive rate.

In this work, we consider the case where the jammer is equipped with multiple antennas. We analyze this case and present transmission strategies for the jammer in order to maximize his assistance to Alice, in terms of maximizing a ratio between Willie's and Bob's noise variances. Specifically, the analysis is performed for the cases were Bob is equipped with multiple antennas and employs a linear receiver. Our results indicate that the jammer's transmission strategy is to perform beamforming towards a single direction which depends on the channel coefficients of both the legitimate receiver and the adversary. However, in case Bob is able to cancel the jammer's interference completely, then the jammer's strategy becomes independent and may be set according to the channel coefficients of the adversary alone.

Keywords: Covert communication · MIMO · Jamming

1 Introduction

The demands for privacy and security of information have become a dominant factor in the design of many communication systems. These demands can be categorized into two broad requirements. The first is preventing an adversary from determining the content of the transmission (or changing it) while the other is preventing the *detection of the transmission in the first place* (up to a certain probability of detection) which is more restrictive in nature. In this work, we concentrate on the latter, which is also known as Low Probability of Detection (LPD) or covert communication. In covert communication, Alice wishes to communicate with Bob while keeping the transmission hidden from a watchful

© Springer Nature Switzerland AG 2019
S. Dolev et al. (Eds.): CSCML 2019, LNCS 11527, pp. 1–15, 2019.
https://doi.org/10.1007/978-3-030-20951-3_1

adversary, Willie. In order to do so, Alice must construct a transmission scheme which will enable her to remain within the margin of uncertainty at Willie's detector. In fact, for Additive White Gaussian Noise (AWGN) channels, it was shown in [1] that Alice can transmit $O(\sqrt{n})$ bits in n channel uses (a.k.a the square root law) due to the noise Willie endures. This problem was extended to other types of communication channels, e.g., binary symmetric, discrete memoryless and multiple access channels in [2–5], respectively. These works presented similar results for the total transmission rate that can be achieved i.e., $O(\sqrt{n}/n)$, which goes to zero as $n \to \infty$.

The concept of hiding information from possible detection relates to steganography which deals with hiding information in legitimate objects such as digital images, audio or text [6]. Specifically, by using the statistical properties of the legitimate objects, specific symbols may be modified in order to hide a steganographic message. In fact, under certain assumptions, similar behaviour for the total amount of covert information that can be concealed (or transmitted in our case) from Willie can be described also by the square root law in steganography [6, Chap. 13]. The difference lies in the fact that in steganography one uses a legitimate signal to hide the information whereas in covert communication one uses the channel noise to hide the information. Note that in covert communication the presence of information is concealed in the noise and therefore unknown as opposed to using noise to hide a massage but with the knowledge of its existence (e.g., [7,8]).

When Willie suffers from additional uncertainty in his received noise power, besides his own noise variance, it was shown in subsequent works that $O(n)$ covert and reliable bits can be transmitted in n channel uses, namely, a strictly positive rate [9–11]. The uncertainty may be a result of inaccurate knowledge of Willie's own noise or a result of an active node which causes confusion at Willie's side (e.g., a jammer that varies his noise power randomly).

The limits of covert communication in a multiple-antenna setting were first established in [12]. Therein, it was shown that in case Alice is equipped with multiple antennas, her best strategy is to perform beamforming towards Bob, which results with a constant gain to the square root law (i.e., the scaling law remains the same) by the number of independent paths between her and Bob. However, the case where such a communication channel includes a jammer which is equipped with multiple antennas is still open and remains unclear under various settings. For example, the knowledge the jammer possesses on the channel coefficients, and his preference on which user to assist, may affect his strategy, and the resulting rates, significantly. Thus, in a previous work[1], we analyzed the effect of multiple antennas at the jammer on covert communication and obtained the optimal transmission strategy for the jammer while helping Alice and Bob for the case which Bob is equipped with a single antenna.

In this work, we extend the settings and assume that Bob is equipped with multiple antennas as well. Accordingly, we analyze the system and try to deter-

---

[1] The mentioned work is currently under peer review for the ISIT 2019 conference at the time of submission of this paper.

mine whether the fact that Bob possess multiple antennas affect the jammer's transmission strategy while helping Alice and Bob. We further assume that Bob uses a linear receiver, with contrast to the existing literature on covert communication which assumes that Bob performs ML decoding. This assumption addresses the nowadays practical demands for receiver complexity; moreover, it can provide interesting insights on the transmission and detection strategies of the jammer and Bob.

This work contribution is built on previous results which appear in this paper as well. Specifically, we provide a criterion for Alice's transmission power as a function of the jammer assistance transmission strategy. This criterion promises that the system is covert; that is, Willie has nothing better to do besides guessing if communication occurred or not. We then describe Bob's received SNR for the case of a single and multiple antennas as a function of this strategy and transmission powers. Then, given that the system is covert, we examine the strategies of the jammer and Bob which maximize both Alice's allowed transmission power and Bob's received SNR. The resulting optimization problem for the case which Bob is equipped with a single antenna has a closed-form solution which is given in this paper. However, when Bob has multiple antennas the optimization problem of Bob and the jammer results in complicated global optimization. We thus relax it and provide sub optimal transmitting and detection strategies for the jammer and Bob, respectively.

2   System Model

We consider a system in which Alice ("a" in the channel coefficients notation) wishes to communicate covertly with Bob ("b") while Willie's ("w") awareness of this communication remains uncertain. In addition, we assume that there is a third participant, the jammer ("j"), which may assist either Alice and Bob or Willie, depending on the side he takes and the knowledge he possesses. This model is depicted in Fig. 1. In our settings, we assume that Alice and Willie are equipped with a single antenna, while Bob and the jammer are equipped with M and N antennas, respectively. Further more, as mentioned in the introduction, we assume that Bob employs a linear receiver. The channel between all participates is subject to block fading and AWGN. In this setting, Willie tries to detect whether transmission by Alice was made or not, by performing a statistical hypothesis test on his received signal. The null hypothesis $\mathcal{H}_0$ means that no transmission was made by Alice, while the hypothesis $\mathcal{H}_1$ suggests otherwise. Throughout, lower case letters represent random variables, bold lower case represent random vectors, and bold upper case represent random matrices. Thus, under each of the hypotheses, the received signals at Bob and Willie in the $i - th$ channel use is

$$
\begin{aligned}
\mathcal{H}_1: \quad & \mathbf{y}_b[i] = x[i]\mathbf{h}_{ab} + \mathbf{H}_{jb}\mathbf{v}[i] + \mathbf{n}_b[i] \\
& y_w[i] = x[i]h_{aw} + \mathbf{v}[i]^T\mathbf{h}_{jw} + n_w[i] \\
\mathcal{H}_0: \quad & \mathbf{y}_b[i] = \mathbf{H}_{jb}\mathbf{v}[i] + \mathbf{n}_b[i] \\
& y_w[i] = \mathbf{v}[i]^T\mathbf{h}_{jw} + n_w[i],
\end{aligned}
\tag{1}
$$

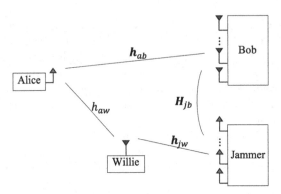

Fig. 1. A Covert communication model, where an independent jammer assists the communication between Alice and Bob by transmitting AN.

where $x[i]$ is the complex symbol transmitted by Alice in the $i-th$ channel use, with average power P_a (i.e., $\mathbb{E}[|x[i]|^2] = P_a$) and $\mathbf{v}[i] = (v_1[i], v_2[i], ..., v_N[i])^T$ is the vector transmitted by the jammer at the $i-th$ channel use, with a covariance matrix $\boldsymbol{\Sigma} = \mathbb{E}[\mathbf{v}[i]\mathbf{v}[i]^\dagger]$ and total power P_j.

The channel coefficients between Alice, Willie and Bob are $h_{aw} \in \mathbb{C}$ and $\mathbf{h}_{ab} \in \mathbb{C}^M$, respectively. $\mathbf{h}_{jw} \in \mathbb{C}^N$ and $\mathbf{H}_{jb} \in \mathbb{C}^{M \times N}$ are the channel coefficients from the jammer to Willie and Bod, respectively. These channel coefficients are originated from a zero mean complex Gaussian distribution with unit variance and are considered to be fixed for the period of n channel uses (a slot). This is a common channel model for slowly varying fading channels (block fading channels). We assume that Bob possesses the knowledge of $\mathbf{h}_{ab}$ and $\mathbf{H}_{jb}$ and Willie possesses the knowledge of h_{aw} and $\mathbf{h}_{jw}$. In addition, both Bob and Willie endure complex additive Gaussian noise denoted by $\mathbf{n}_b \sim \mathcal{CN}(0, \sigma_b^2 \mathbf{I}_M)$ and $n_w \sim \mathcal{CN}(0, \sigma_w^2)$. The above assumptions concerning the channel coefficients, follow similar assumptions in the covert communication literature.

This paper focuses on the achieving a positive covert rate. Thus, we assume that the jammer assists Alice to create uncertainty at Willie's decoder continuously, regardless of whether or not Alice transmits (Similarly to [11]). We note that the case where the jammer assists Willie is out of this paper's scope, and may be considered as future work. The jammer's assistance comes in the form of Artificial Noise (AN) with a randomly varying total power P_j while using his multiple antennas. This is due to the assumption that the jammer does not coordinate with Alice. In case the jammer and Alice are coordinating, the jammer can lower his noise when Alice is transmitting and increase it back up when she is not. This keeps Willie unaware of the changes in the noise power level while improving Bob reception when a transmission takes place. As this is not the case here, the jammer must create uncertainty with respect to the noise power at Willie's decoder so that the transmission power by Alice can be concealed in the AN [10,11,13]. Hence, the transmitted vector by the jammer is $\mathbf{v}[i] \sim \mathcal{CN}(0, \boldsymbol{\Sigma})$ where the total power P_j is a r.v. which is allocated according to Σ. Specifically, following similar assumptions as in [11,13], we assume that P_j is a uniform r.v. on $[0, P_{max}]$ with the probability density function (pdf) given by,

$$f_{P_j}(x) = \begin{cases} \frac{1}{P_{max}} & \text{if } 0 \leq x \leq P_{max} \\ 0 & \text{otherwise} , \end{cases} \tag{2}$$

and it's redrawn for every n channel uses independently. This way, even if Willie correctly estimates the power on the channel during n channel uses, he has no way of knowing whether it is the result of solely the jammer, or does it include Alices's transmission. The next block has independent drawings. We also note that in case Willie had not known the channel coefficients, the jammer could have used a noise distribution with constant variance, since the uncertainty would arise from the random channel coefficients [11].

The jammer allocates its power P_j in each slot according to the covariance matrix Σ. This allocation is constructed in a way that assists Alice as much as possible. That is, the jammer may direct his AN towards certain directions with different powers. The magnitude of this division is represented by the vector $\boldsymbol{\xi} = (\xi_1, ..., \xi_N)^T$ such that $\sum_{l=1}^{N} \xi_l = 1$. That is, $P_j \boldsymbol{\xi}$ is the singular values vector of the covariance matrix Σ, where the corresponding eigenvectors represent the directions for this power allocation. Let us also denote $\mathbf{X}$ to be a diagonal matrix with $\boldsymbol{\xi}$ as its elements.

Similar to previous works on covert communication [1,10,11,13], we assume that Alice and Bob share a codebook which is not revealed to Willie; however, Willie knows its statistics. This codebook is generated by independently drawing symbols from a zero-mean complex Gaussian distribution with variance P_a and it is assumed to be used only once. When Alice wishes to transmit, she picks a codeword and transmits its n symbols as the sequence $\{x[i]\}_{i=1}^{n}$.

2.1 Covert Criteria

Upon receiving the vector $\mathbf{y}_w$, Willie performs hypothesis testing in order to determine if transmission by Alice took place or not. That is, he tries to distinguish between the two hypothesis $\mathcal{H}_0$ and $\mathcal{H}_1$. Accordingly, Willie seeks to minimize his probability of error which is a function of the probability of Miss Detection (P_{MD}) in case a transmission occurred and the probability of False Alarm (P_{FA}) in case a transmission did not occurred. That is,

$$\mathbb{P}_e = pP_{MD} + (1-p)P_{FA}, \tag{3}$$

where p is the a priori probability that Alice transmitted a message $(\mathcal{H}_1)$. According to [11], $\mathbb{P}_e \geq \min\{p, 1-p\}(P_{MD} + P_{FA})$. Thus, we define the following criteria for covert communication, which eventually will define Alice's transmission power, as

$$P_{MD} + P_{FA} \geq 1 - \epsilon, \tag{4}$$

where $\epsilon > 0$ is the covertness requirement ([1]). That is, as long as (4) hold for a given ϵ, the transmission is considered covert. Note also that this criterion is reasonable for the following reason. Willie can easily choose a strategy with $P_{FA} = 0$ and $P_{MD} = 1$, by simply declaring $\mathcal{H}_0$ at all times, regardless of his channel measurements. Analogously, $P_{FA} = 1$ and $P_{MD} = 0$ are achieved by always declaring $\mathcal{H}_1$. Requiring $P_{MD} + P_{FA} \geq 1 - \epsilon$ is therefore equivalent to forcing Willie to only time-share between these two trivial strategies, hence if $P_{MD} + P_{FA} \geq 1 - \epsilon$, Willie is as ignorant as an adversary without any data at all.

The optimal test for Willie to distinguish between $\mathcal{H}_0$ and $\mathcal{H}_1$ and minimize its probability of error is to apply the Neyman-Pearson criterion, resulting with the likelihood ratio test:

$$\frac{\prod_{i=1}^{n} \mathbb{P}_1}{\prod_{i=1}^{n} \mathbb{P}_0} \underset{\mathcal{H}_0}{\overset{\mathcal{H}_1}{\underset{<}{>}}} \frac{1-p}{p}, \tag{5}$$

where $\mathbb{P}_0$ and $\mathbb{P}_1$ are the probability distributions of Willie's observation in a single channel use under the hypotheses $\mathcal{H}_0$ and $\mathcal{H}_1$, respectively. Note that we may write the joint distribution as a multiplicative of the marginal distributions since the channel uses are $i.i.d.$ In particular, under $\mathcal{H}_0$ and given P_j, $\mathbb{P}_0$ is distributed as $\mathcal{CN}(0, \sigma_w^0)$, and under $\mathcal{H}_1$ and given P_j, $\mathbb{P}_1$ is distributed as $\mathcal{CN}(0, \sigma_w^1)$ where,

$$\begin{aligned} \sigma_w^0 &= \sigma_w^2 + \mathbf{h}_{jw}^\dagger \boldsymbol{\Sigma} \mathbf{h}_{jw}, \\ \sigma_w^1 &= \sigma_w^2 + \mathbf{h}_{jw}^\dagger \boldsymbol{\Sigma} \mathbf{h}_{jw} + P_a h_{aw}^2. \end{aligned} \tag{6}$$

The terms in the last line above reflect the self noise power of Willie, the received AN power and the transmission power of Alice, respectively. Eventually, the optimal ratio test Willie preforms is an energy test on the average received power. Specifically, the average received power, $P_w^{r_{av}}$, is compared with a threshold η,

$$P_w^{r_{av}} \triangleq \frac{1}{n} \sum_{i=1}^{n} |y_w[i]|^2 \underset{\mathcal{H}_0}{\overset{\mathcal{H}_1}{\underset{<}{>}}} \eta. \tag{7}$$

This was shown in [11] by using Fisher-Neyman factorization and likelihood ratio ordering techniques. One can realize that, given P_j, the average received power $P_w^{r_{av}}$ is a Gamma r.v. with parameters $k = n$ and $\theta = \frac{\sigma_w^i}{n}$ for $i = 0, 1$, i.e. $P_w^{r_{av}} \sim \Gamma(n, \frac{\sigma_w^i}{n})$.

In this work, we wish to check the effect of multiple antennas and CSI at the jammer on covert communication. Therefore, in the next sections, we describe this effect on Alice's transmission power, which is linked to Willies ability to detect transmission, and on Bob received SNR and the jammer's transmission strategy. Specifically, we provide a criterion for a strictly positive covert rate, discuss the received SNR at Bob while assuming $M = 1$ and $M > 1$ antennas. Finally, we present the transmission strategies the jammer takes in order to assist Alice as much as possible.

3   Covert Criteria Compliance

In covert communication, Alice wishes to maximize the ambiguity of Willie concerning her transmission. That is, she would like to make $P_{MD} + P_{FA}$ as close as possible to 1. In other words, Alice would like to set her power P_a appropriately (codebook construction) such that for a fixed $\epsilon > 0$ the criteria $P_{MD} + P_{FA} \geq 1 - \epsilon$ holds.

   In the following lemma we present a positive achievable rate for Alice codebook such that the system is considered covert ((4) holds) under our model.

Lemma 1. *Under the model of block fading AWGN model, where there is a jammer with N antennas who transmit AN with covariance matrix $\Sigma = P_j \mathbf{V}\mathbf{X}\mathbf{V}^\dagger$, as long as Alice transmits with power*

$$P_a = \frac{\epsilon P_{max}}{4h_{aw}^2} \mathbf{h}_{jw}^\dagger \mathbf{V}\mathbf{X}\mathbf{V}^\dagger \mathbf{h}_{jw}, \tag{8}$$

the system is covert and Alice can transmit with positive rate, i.e., (4) applies and Willie is unable to decided if transmission occurred.

Proof. As mentioned above, Willie compares $P_w^{r_{av}}$ to a threshold η; however, this threshold depends on the distribution of P_j and thus may be optimized by Willie. The following analysis will show that for any optimal threshold τ that Willie set for himself, there exist a construction by Alice such that (4) holds. Specifically, we bound each of the probabilities P_{MD} and P_{FA} for a given value of P_j and average it on all possible values of P_j resulting with the necessary conditions for covertness. This proof's steps are constructed similarly to arguments presented in [11] which were modified to suit the jammer's antennas. Let us begin with the false alarm probability P_{FA} given P_j, i.e.,

$$P_{FA}(P_j) = P_r(P_w^{r_{av}} \geq \tau | \mathcal{H}_0, P_j). \tag{9}$$

Recall that $P_w^{r_{av}} \sim Gamma(n, \frac{\sigma_w^0}{n})$, thus, the expected value of $P_w^{r_{av}}$ is σ_w^0. Accordingly, we may describe the probability of $P_w^{r_{av}}$ to exist around its expected value. Let $\epsilon > 0$ be a fixed small constant. Then, there exist $\delta^0(\epsilon) > 0$ such that

$$P_r(\sigma_w^0 - \delta^0 \leq P_w^{r_{av}} \leq \sigma_w^0 + \delta^0) > 1 - \frac{\epsilon}{2},$$

Since

$$P_r(P_w^{r_{av}} \geq \sigma_w^0 - \delta) \geq P_r(P_w^{r_{av}} \geq \sigma_w^0 - \delta^0)$$
$$> P_r(\sigma_w^0 - \delta^0 \leq P_w^{r_{av}} \leq \sigma_w^0 + \delta^0),$$

for some $\delta(\epsilon) \geq \delta^0(\epsilon)$, then for any $\tau < \sigma_w^0 - \delta(\epsilon)$ we have

$$P_r(P_w^{r_{av}} \geq \tau | \mathcal{H}_0, P_j) > 1 - \frac{\epsilon}{2}. \tag{10}$$

Similarly for P_{MD} given P_j, i.e.,

$$P_{MD}(P_j) = P_r(P_w^{rav} \leq \tau | \mathcal{H}_1, P_j), \tag{11}$$

$P_w^{rav} \sim Gamma(n, \frac{\sigma_w^1}{n})$ with expected value equal to σ_w^1 we have

$$P_r(\sigma_w^1 - \delta^1 \leq P_w^{rav} \leq \sigma_w^1 + \delta^1) > 1 - \frac{\epsilon}{2}.$$

for some $\epsilon > 0$ and $\delta^1(\epsilon) > 0$. Again, since

$$P_r(P_w^{rav} \leq \sigma_w^1 + \delta) \geq P_r(P_w^{rav} \leq \sigma_w^1 + \delta^1)$$
$$> P_r(\sigma_w^0 - \delta^1 \leq P_w^{rav} \leq \sigma_w^0 + \delta^1),$$

for some $\delta(\epsilon) \geq \delta^1(\epsilon)$, then for any $\tau > \sigma_w^1 + \delta(\epsilon)$ we have

$$P_r(P_w^{rav} \leq \tau | \mathcal{H}_1, P_j) > 1 - \frac{\epsilon}{2}. \tag{12}$$

Let us define the set of intervals $\mathcal{P} = \{P_j : \sigma_w^0 - \delta < \tau < \sigma_w^1 + \delta\}$ and let $\delta(\epsilon) = \max\{\delta^0(\epsilon), \delta^1(\epsilon)\}$. Thus, for all $P_j \notin \mathcal{P}$ we have,

$$P_{MD}(P_j) + P_{FA}(P_j) \geq 1 - \frac{\epsilon}{2}.$$

We may compute $P_r(\mathcal{P})$ by rewiriting (6) while using the SVD of Σ in order to express P_j as follows,

$$\sigma_w^0 = \sigma_w^2 + P_j \mathbf{h}_{jw}^\dagger \mathbf{V} \mathbf{X} \mathbf{V}^\dagger \mathbf{h}_{jw},$$
$$\sigma_w^1 = \sigma_w^2 + P_j \mathbf{h}_{jw}^\dagger \mathbf{V} \mathbf{X} \mathbf{V}^\dagger \mathbf{h}_{jw} + P_a h_{aw}^2. \tag{13}$$

Since P_j is a uniform r.v.

$$P_r(\mathcal{P}) = P_r \left(\frac{\tau - \sigma_w^2 - P_a h_{aw}^2 - \delta}{\mathbf{h}_{jw}^\dagger \mathbf{V} \mathbf{X} \mathbf{V}^\dagger \mathbf{h}_{jw}} \leq P_j \leq \frac{\tau - \sigma_w^2 + \delta}{\mathbf{h}_{jw}^\dagger \mathbf{V} \mathbf{X} \mathbf{V}^\dagger \mathbf{h}_{jw}} \right)$$
$$= \frac{P_a h_{aw}^2 + 2\delta}{P_{max} \mathbf{h}_{jw}^\dagger \mathbf{V} \mathbf{X} \mathbf{V}^\dagger \mathbf{h}_{jw}}.$$

Therefore, if we set $P_a = \frac{\epsilon P_{max}}{4 h_{aw}^2} \mathbf{h}_{jw}^\dagger \mathbf{V} \mathbf{X} \mathbf{V}^\dagger \mathbf{h}_{jw}$ and $\delta(\epsilon) = \frac{\epsilon P_{max}}{8} \mathbf{h}_{jw}^\dagger \mathbf{V} \mathbf{X} \mathbf{V}^\dagger \mathbf{h}_{jw}$, we are left with

$$P_r(\mathcal{P}) = \frac{\epsilon}{2}.$$

Considering all the above in order we have,

$$P_{MD} + P_{FA} = \mathbb{E}_{P_j}[P_{MD}(P_j) + P_{FA}(P_j)]$$
$$\geq \mathbb{E}_{P_j}[P_{MD}(P_j) + P_{FA}(P_j)|\mathcal{P}^c] P_r(\mathcal{P}^c) \tag{14}$$
$$> 1 - \epsilon.$$

The above shows that as long as Alice transmits with power $P_a = \frac{\epsilon P_{max}}{4 h_{aw}^2} \mathbf{h}_{jw}^\dagger \mathbf{V} \mathbf{X} \mathbf{V}^\dagger \mathbf{h}_{jw}$ the system is covert. The rate of Alice can be obtained by using P_a in Bob's SNR which can be lower bounded by a constant providing a positive rate.

For the case where the jammer has no knowledge on the channel coefficients, the best he can do is to distribute his power equally and independently between his antennas, i.e., $\boldsymbol{\Sigma} = (P_j/N)\mathbf{I}$. Accordingly, we have the following corollary,

Corollary 1. *In case the jammer has no CSI, and he allocates the power equally between his antennas, i.e., $\xi_l = \frac{1}{N}$, then,*

$$P_a = \frac{\epsilon P_{max} \|\mathbf{h}_{jw}\|^2}{4N h_{aw}^2}. \tag{15}$$

4 Detection at Bob

In Sect. 3, we constructed a criterion for Alice's transmission power (P_a) such that the system is covert. Accordingly, since the power is positive and does not go to zero with n, there exists a rate R for which Bob can decode successfully with a probability of error that goes to zero. This rate can be attained by using capacity achieving codes for AWGN channels, and is eventually a function of Bob's SNR. In what follows we describe Bob's received SNR; first for the case which Bob has a single antenna and second for the case of multiple antennas.

4.1 Bob's Antennas $M = 1$

We first describe Bob's SNR for the simple case where he posses a single antenna (i.e., $M = 1$). This will help us focus only on the jammer's strategy. Thus, in case Alice transmitted, the received SNR of Bob, given the CSI, h_{ab}, and $\mathbf{H}_{jb}$ which is, in this case, a single column matrix denoted as $\mathbf{h}_{jb}$, is given as follows:

$$SNR_b^1 = \frac{P_a h_{ab}^2}{\mathbf{h}_{jb}^{\dagger} \boldsymbol{\Sigma} \mathbf{h}_{jb} + \sigma_b^2} = \frac{P_a h_{ab}^2}{P_j \mathbf{h}_{jb}^{\dagger} \mathbf{V} \mathbf{X} \mathbf{V}^{\dagger} \mathbf{h}_{jb} + \sigma_b^2}. \tag{16}$$

We will use (16) as our target function for the maximization problem in Sect. 5. Note that this function depends also on the covariance matrix of the AN signal (i.e., the jammer strategy) which we will optimize also in the maximization.

4.2 Bob's Antennas $M > 1$

When Bob possess multiple antennas (i.e., $M > 1$), he can take an active part in the communication. For example, by steering his antennas away form the jammer. In fact, even if Bob does not have the channel coefficients from the jammer, he can improve his SNR using a bigger antenna array. As mentioned in Sect. 2, we assume Bob employs a linear receiver. That is, Bob preforms a linear operation on the received signal which eventually increases his received SNR. In other words, Bob projects the received vector onto a subspace which on one hand diminishes the effect of the AN from the jammer and on the other intensifies Alice's transmission. Specifically, Bob performs the following on the received signal

$$\mathbf{c}^T \mathbf{y}_b[i] = x[i]\mathbf{c}^T \mathbf{h}_{ab} + \mathbf{c}^T \mathbf{H}_{jb}\mathbf{v}[i] + \mathbf{c}^T \mathbf{n}_b[i], \tag{17}$$

where $\mathbf{c}$ is the linear filter. Accordingly, the received SNR of Bob for a general linear filter is

$$\frac{P_a(\mathbf{c}^\dagger \mathbf{h}_{ab})^2}{\mathbf{c}^\dagger \left(\mathbf{H}_{jb}^\dagger \boldsymbol{\Sigma} \mathbf{H}_{jb} + \sigma_b^2 \mathbf{I}\right) \mathbf{c}}. \tag{18}$$

We will use (18) when we consider the global maximization for the SNR for the case of multiple antennas at Bob also in Sect. 5.

5   The Jammer's Strategies

If the jammer possess knowledge of the channel state, he may use it to assist either Alice and Bob or Willie. The jammer assistance, when using his CSI, is reflected by the covariance matrix $\boldsymbol{\Sigma}$, according to the player he wishes to assist. This power allocation affects the transmission power Alice can use, the received SNR's side at Bob and Willie's ability to detect the communication.

In this work, we assume the jammer assists Alice. Hence, the jammer should construct his covariance matrix $\boldsymbol{\Sigma}$ in a way that enables Alice to increase her transmission power while still being covert, while reducing the AN at Bob in order to have a higher achievable rate. Recall that $\boldsymbol{\Sigma} = P_j \mathbf{V}\mathbf{X}\mathbf{V}^\dagger$. Thus, the jammer essentially needs to design the diagonal matrix $\mathbf{X}$ and the unitary matrix $\mathbf{V}$ appropriately. In what follows, we describe the jammer's strategies for the case which Bob posses a single antenna and for the case of multiple antennas.

5.1   The Case Where $M = 1$

Following the expressions for Alice's power to ensure covertness, and Bob's SNR (Eqs. (8) and (16), respectively). We may express an optimization problem for Bob's SNR by employing (8) in to (16) as follows,

$$\max_{\mathbf{V},\mathbf{X}} \frac{\left(\frac{\epsilon P_{max}}{4h_{aw}^2}\mathbf{h}_{jw}^\dagger \mathbf{V}\mathbf{X}\mathbf{V}^\dagger \mathbf{h}_{jw}\right)h_{ab}^2}{P_j \mathbf{h}_{jb}^\dagger \mathbf{V}\mathbf{X}\mathbf{V}^\dagger \mathbf{h}_{jb} + \sigma_b^2},$$

$$s.t. \quad 0 \le \xi_l \le 1 \text{ and, } \sum_{l=1}^N \xi_l = 1. \tag{19}$$

Note that $\mathbf{V}\mathbf{X}\mathbf{V}^\dagger$ influence on both the enumerator and the denominator differently with respect to the vectors $\mathbf{h}_{jw}$ and $\mathbf{h}_{jb}$. Note also, since the system is covert, we are only interested in maximizing Bob's SNR as it dictates the rate eventually. The following is our main result.

Theorem 1. *The optimal solution for the maximization problem in* (23) *is the following power allocation,*

$$\Sigma = P_j \mathbf{v}^* \mathbf{v}^{*\dagger}, \tag{20}$$

where

$$\mathbf{v}^* = \frac{(\mathbf{h}_{jb}\mathbf{h}_{jb}^\dagger + \sigma\mathbf{I})^{-\frac{1}{2}}\mathbf{q}^*}{\|(\mathbf{h}_{jb}\mathbf{h}_{jb}^\dagger + \sigma\mathbf{I})^{-\frac{1}{2}}\mathbf{q}^*\|} \tag{21}$$

and $\mathbf{q}^*$ *is the eigenvector which corresponds to the highest eigenvalue of the matrix*

$$(\mathbf{h}_{jb}\mathbf{h}_{jb}^\dagger + \sigma\mathbf{I})^{-\frac{1}{2}}(\mathbf{h}_{jw}\mathbf{h}_{jw}^\dagger)(\mathbf{h}_{jb}\mathbf{h}_{jb}^\dagger + \sigma\mathbf{I})^{-\frac{1}{2}}. \tag{22}$$

Proof. This Proof follows similar steps as in an analytical derivation of the maximization problem performed in [14]. We can simplify (19) as follows,

$$
\begin{aligned}
\max_{\mathbf{V},\mathbf{X}} & \frac{\left(\frac{\epsilon P_{max}}{4h_{aw}^2}\mathbf{h}_{jw}^\dagger \mathbf{V}\mathbf{X}\mathbf{V}^\dagger \mathbf{h}_{jw}\right)h_{ab}^2}{P_j\mathbf{h}_{jb}^\dagger \mathbf{V}\mathbf{X}\mathbf{V}^\dagger \mathbf{h}_{jb} + \sigma_b^2} \\
&= C\frac{P_{max}}{P_j}\max_{\mathbf{V},\mathbf{X}}\frac{\mathbf{w}^\dagger \mathbf{X}\mathbf{w}}{\mathbf{b}^\dagger \mathbf{X}\mathbf{b} + \sigma},
\end{aligned} \tag{23}
$$

where $C = \epsilon h_{ab}^2 / 4h_{aw}^2$, $\sigma = \frac{\sigma_b^2}{P_j}$, $\mathbf{w} = \mathbf{V}^\dagger \mathbf{h}_{jw}$ and $\mathbf{b} = \mathbf{V}^\dagger \mathbf{h}_{jb}$. The maximization function in (23) can be written as

$$\frac{\mathbf{w}^\dagger \mathbf{X}\mathbf{w}}{\mathbf{b}^\dagger \mathbf{X}\mathbf{b} + \sigma} = \frac{\sum_{l=1}^N \xi_l w_l^2}{\sum_{l=1}^N \xi_l b_l^2 + \sigma}. \tag{24}$$

Let us assume $\boldsymbol{\xi}^*$ is the optimal power allocation for fixed $\mathbf{w}$ and $\mathbf{b}$. We examine two indices i and j in $\boldsymbol{\xi}^*$ which have power allocation (ξ_i, ξ_j) such that $\xi_i + \xi_j = P_{ij}$. We will show first that either $\xi_i = P_{ij}$ or $\xi_j = P_{ij}$ must occur, hence, eventually, the optimal power allocation is a unit vector (since this is true for each pair of indices). Then, we will find the corresponding direction (eigenvector) of the AN power.

The optimization problem on $\boldsymbol{\xi}$ can be written as follows,

$$
\begin{aligned}
\max_{\boldsymbol{\xi}} & f(\boldsymbol{\xi}) \\
&\triangleq \max_{\boldsymbol{\xi}} \frac{\sum_{l=1}^N \xi_l w_l^2}{\sum_{l=1}^N \xi_l b_l^2 + \sigma} \\
&= \max_{\boldsymbol{\xi}} \frac{\sum_{l\neq i,j} \xi_l w_l^2 + w_i^2\xi_i + w_j^2\xi_j}{\sum_{l\neq i,j} \xi_l b_l^2 + b_i^2\xi_i + b_j^2\xi_j + \sigma} \\
&= \max_{\boldsymbol{\xi}} \frac{\sum_{l\neq i,j} \xi_l w_l^2 + w_i^2\xi_i + w_j^2(P_{ij} - \xi_i)}{\sum_{l\neq i,j} \xi_l b_l^2 + b_i^2\xi_i + b_j^2(P_{ij} - \xi_i) + \sigma} \\
&= \max_{\boldsymbol{\xi}} \frac{\sum_{l\neq i,j} \xi_l w_l^2 + \xi_i(w_i^2 - w_j^2) + w_j^2 P_{ij}}{\sum_{l\neq i,j} \xi_l b_l^2 + \xi_i(b_i^2 - b_j^2) + b_j^2 P_{ij} + \sigma}
\end{aligned} \tag{25}
$$

The derivative according to ξ_i shows that the function $f(\boldsymbol{\xi})$ is either monotonically increasing or monotonically decreasing with ξ_i depending on the sign of

$$(w_i^2 - w_j^2)\left(\sum_{l \neq i,j} \xi_l b_l^2 + \sigma + b_j^2 P_{ij}\right) - (b_i^2 - b_j^2)\left(\sum_{l \neq i,j} \xi_l w_l^2 + w_j^2 P_{ij}\right).$$

Thus, for every two indices i, j, if $f(\boldsymbol{\xi})$ is monotonically decreasing ξ_i can be minimized by setting $\xi_j = P_{ij}$. On the other hand if $f(\boldsymbol{\xi})$ is monotonically increasing ξ_i can be maximized by setting $\xi_j = 0$. Thus, we conclude that the optimal power allocation is a unit vector, which essentially means that the optimal strategy is to allocate all the power of the jammer towards a single direction.

In order to find this direction, which is the corresponding eigenvector $\mathbf{v}$, we may write the unit rank $\boldsymbol{\Sigma}$ as $\boldsymbol{\Sigma} = P_j \mathbf{v}\mathbf{v}^\dagger$. Note that $\mathbf{v}$ is constrained to have a unit norm, i.e., $\mathbf{v}^\dagger\mathbf{v} = 1$. Returning to the maximization problem in (23), we have,

$$C\frac{P_{max}}{P_j}\max_{\mathbf{V},\mathbf{X}}\frac{\mathbf{h}_{jw}^\dagger\mathbf{V}\mathbf{X}\mathbf{V}^\dagger\mathbf{h}_{jw}}{\mathbf{h}_{jb}^\dagger\mathbf{V}\mathbf{X}\mathbf{V}^\dagger\mathbf{h}_{jb} + \sigma} \tag{26}$$

$$= C\frac{P_{max}}{P_j}\max_{\mathbf{v}}\frac{\mathbf{h}_{jw}^\dagger\mathbf{v}\mathbf{v}^\dagger\mathbf{h}_{jw}}{\mathbf{h}_{jb}^\dagger\mathbf{v}\mathbf{v}^\dagger\mathbf{h}_{jb} + \sigma\mathbf{v}^\dagger\mathbf{v}} \tag{27}$$

$$= C\frac{P_{max}}{P_j}\max_{\mathbf{v}}\frac{\mathbf{v}^\dagger\mathbf{h}_{jw}\mathbf{h}_{jw}^\dagger\mathbf{v}}{\mathbf{v}^\dagger\mathbf{h}_{jb}\mathbf{h}_{jb}^\dagger\mathbf{v} + \sigma\mathbf{v}^\dagger\mathbf{v}} \tag{28}$$

$$= C\frac{P_{max}}{P_j}\max_{\mathbf{v}}\frac{\mathbf{v}^\dagger\mathbf{h}_{jw}\mathbf{h}_{jw}^\dagger\mathbf{v}}{\mathbf{v}^\dagger(\mathbf{h}_{jb}\mathbf{h}_{jb}^\dagger + \sigma\mathbf{I})\mathbf{v}} \tag{29}$$

$$= C\frac{P_{max}}{P_j}\max_{\mathbf{v}}\frac{\mathbf{v}^\dagger\mathbf{W}\mathbf{v}}{\mathbf{v}^\dagger\mathbf{B}\mathbf{v}} \tag{30}$$

where, $\mathbf{W} = \mathbf{h}_{jw}\mathbf{h}_{jw}^\dagger$, and, $\mathbf{B} = \mathbf{h}_{jb}\mathbf{h}_{jb}^\dagger + \sigma\mathbf{I}$. The above maximiztion problem is also known as the Rayleigh quotient [15] when we denote $\mathbf{q} = \mathbf{B}^{1/2}\mathbf{v}$ and rewrite the maximization function above as

$$\frac{\mathbf{v}^\dagger\mathbf{W}\mathbf{v}}{\mathbf{v}^\dagger\mathbf{B}\mathbf{v}} = \frac{\mathbf{q}^\dagger\mathbf{B}^{-1/2}\mathbf{W}\mathbf{B}^{-1/2}\mathbf{q}}{\mathbf{q}^\dagger\mathbf{q}}. \tag{31}$$

The optimal solution $\mathbf{q}^*$ for the Rayleigh quotient problem is the eigenvector which corresponds to the highest eigenvalue of the matrix $\mathbf{B}^{-1/2}\mathbf{W}\mathbf{B}^{-1/2}$. Accordingly, the optimal $\mathbf{v}$ is thus,

$$\mathbf{v}^* = \frac{\mathbf{B}^{-\frac{1}{2}}\mathbf{q}^*}{\|\mathbf{B}^{-\frac{1}{2}}\mathbf{q}^*\|} = \frac{(\mathbf{h}_{jb}\mathbf{h}_{jb}^\dagger + \sigma\mathbf{I})^{-\frac{1}{2}}\mathbf{q}^*}{\|(\mathbf{h}_{jb}\mathbf{h}_{jb}^\dagger + \sigma\mathbf{I})^{-\frac{1}{2}}\mathbf{q}^*\|}. \tag{32}$$

We conclude that the optimal direction $\mathbf{v}^*$ of the AN depends on both channel vectors $\mathbf{h}_{jw}$ and $\mathbf{h}_{jb}$. Though it is not clear from the expression in (32) for $\mathbf{v}^*$, what is the specific AN transmission direction, one can gain intuition on the direction from Eq. (28). Specifically, it is clearly seen that $\mathbf{v}^*$ on one hand should be close to the direction of Willie, i.e., to maximize the projection on $\mathbf{h}_{jw}$, while on the other hand it should be orthogonal to Bob as much as possible, i.e., minimize the projection on $\mathbf{h}_{jb}$.

5.2   The Case Where $M > 1$

In this subsection, we present a sub-optimal strategy for the jammer which follows a specific scheme that Bob employs when using his multiple antennas. That is, assuming the system is covert (i.e. Alice is transmitting with the power given in (8)) we present a sub-optimal solution for the optimization problem for Bob and the jammer strategies which maximize the covert rate.

Recall that Bob possess a linear receiver and thus he preforms a linear function on the received signal. Accordingly, following the SNR expression in (18), we may write the global optimization problem for maximizing Bob's SNR by employing (8) in to (18) as follows

$$\max_{\mathbf{V},\mathbf{X},\mathbf{c}} \frac{\left(\frac{\epsilon P_{max}}{4h_{aw}^2}\mathbf{h}_{jw}^{\dagger}\mathbf{V}\mathbf{X}\mathbf{V}^{\dagger}\mathbf{h}_{jw}\right)(\mathbf{c}^{\dagger}\mathbf{h}_{ab})^2}{\mathbf{c}^{\dagger}\left(\mathbf{H}_{jb}^{\dagger}\boldsymbol{\Sigma}\mathbf{H}_{jb} + \sigma_b^2\mathbf{I}\right)\mathbf{c}}$$

$$s.t. \quad 0 \leq \xi_l \leq 1 \text{ and, } \sum_{l=1}^{N}\xi_l = 1. \tag{33}$$

Note that $\mathbf{c}$ should be chosen with $\boldsymbol{\Sigma}$ together; this complicates the optimization problem greatly. Therefore, we relax the optimization problem and provide a suboptimal scheme for Bob and the jammer in the following subsection. The global solution for the optimization problem is left for future work.

Nulling Towards the Jammer. When Bob posses the complete knowledge of the channel between him and the jammer his detector may cancel the additional AN by projecting the received vector onto the null-space of $\mathbf{H}_{jb}$. Specifically, Bob projects the received vector $\mathbf{y}_b[i]$ at the $i-th$ channel use onto a subspace spanned by a unitary matrix $\mathbf{Q}$ which is the null space of $\mathbf{H}_{jb}$, i.e., $\mathbf{Q} = nullspace(\mathbf{H}_{jb}^T)$. So basically, in order to cancel the AN and retrieve the massage from Alice, Bob multiplies the vector $\mathbf{c}$ with $\mathbf{y}_b[i]$ where $\mathbf{c}$ is some row in $\mathbf{Q}$ (w.l.o.g let us assume that it is the first raw of $\mathbf{Q}$, however one can choose the raw which is closest to the direction of Bob from Alice). That is, we have

$$\begin{aligned}\mathbf{c}^T\mathbf{y}_b[i] &= x[i]\mathbf{c}^T\mathbf{h}_{ab} + \mathbf{c}^T\mathbf{H}_{jb}\mathbf{v}[i] + \mathbf{c}^T\mathbf{n}_b[i] \\ &= x[i]\mathbf{c}^T\mathbf{h}_{ab} + \mathbf{c}^T\mathbf{n}_b[i].\end{aligned} \tag{34}$$

Note that this is a suboptimal strategy for Bob since $\mathbf{c}$ was chosen without considering the channel between Alice and Bob. That is, the choice of $\mathbf{c}$ may be bad after all to the total SNR since $\mathbf{c}$ may reduce the inner product with $\mathbf{h}_{ab}$ at the enumerator. Nevertheless, we may write the optimization problem for Bob's SNR as follows

$$\max_{\mathbf{V},\mathbf{X}} \frac{\left(\frac{\epsilon P_{max}}{4h_{aw}^2}\mathbf{h}_{jw}^{\dagger}\mathbf{V}\mathbf{X}\mathbf{V}^{\dagger}\mathbf{h}_{jw}\right)(\mathbf{c}^T\mathbf{h}_{ab})^2}{\sigma_b^2\|\mathbf{c}\|^2} \tag{35}$$

$$s.t. \quad 0 \le \xi_l \le 1 \text{ and, } \sum_{l=1}^{N}\xi_l = 1.$$

Since $\mathbf{c}$ depends only on the channel matrix $\mathbf{H}_{jb}$ the solution for the maximization problem is given in the following theorem.

Theorem 2. *The optimal solution for the maximization problem in* (35) *is the following power allocation,*

$$\Sigma = P_j\mathbf{v}^*\mathbf{v}^{*\dagger}, \tag{36}$$

where

$$\mathbf{v}^* = \frac{\mathbf{h}_{jw}}{\|\mathbf{h}_{jw}\|} \tag{37}$$

Proof. Since Bob cancels the received AN from the jammer, the maximization problem in (35) reduces to

$$\max_{\mathbf{V},\mathbf{X}}\mathbf{h}_{jw}^{\dagger}\mathbf{V}\mathbf{X}\mathbf{V}^{\dagger}\mathbf{h}_{jw}. \tag{38}$$

With similar arguments as in the proof of Theorem 1, for any $\mathbf{V}$, the power allocation should be for a single direction only. That is, $\boldsymbol{\xi}$ is a unit vector. Thus, the maximization reduces to

$$\max_{\mathbf{V}}\mathbf{h}_{jw}^{\dagger}\mathbf{v}\mathbf{v}^{\dagger}\mathbf{h}_{jw}$$
$$= \max_{\mathbf{V}}\|\mathbf{h}_{jw}^{\dagger}\mathbf{v}\|^2. \tag{39}$$

The maximum is attained when $\mathbf{v}$ is collinear to $\mathbf{h}_{jw}$ and since $\mathbf{v}$ is constrained to have a unit norm, i.e., $\mathbf{v}^{\dagger}\mathbf{v} = 1$, the optimal direction is

$$\mathbf{v}^* = \frac{\mathbf{h}_{jw}}{\|\mathbf{h}_{jw}\|}. \tag{40}$$

Theorem 2 essentially shows that when Bob is able to cancel the AN in any way, the jammer should transmit his AN towards Willie without degrading the covert rate between Alice and Bob.

6   Conclusion

This work engages the problem of covert communication under the assumption that there exists a jammer with multiple antennas which helps Alice and Bob to communicate covertly and reliably by transmitting AN to confuse Willie and increase his detector's uncertainty. Specifically, the detection and transmission strategies for Bob and the jammer were examined. The transmission strategy of the jammer is reflected by the covariance matrix of the AN signal, i.e. the directions and power allocation of the AN transmission. On the other hand, the detection strategy of Bob is reflected by the linear filter he chooses to perform. In case Bob has a single antenna the optimal strategy for the jammer is given whereas for the case Bob is equipped with multiple antennas sub-optimal strategies for Bob and the jammer are given. As future work, we intend to obtain the optimal strategies when Bob is equipped with multiple antennas.

References

1. Bash, B.A., Goeckel, D., Towsley, D.: Limits of reliable communication with low probability of detection on AWGN channels. IEEE J. Sel. Areas Commun. **31**(9), 1921–1930 (2013)
2. Che, P.H., Bakshi, M., Jaggi, S.: Reliable deniable communication: hiding messages in noise. In: 2013 IEEE International Symposium on Information Theory Proceedings (ISIT), pp. 2945–2949. IEEE (2013)
3. Wang, L., Wornell, G.W., Zheng, L.: Fundamental limits of communication with low probability of detection. IEEE Trans. Inf. Theory **62**(6), 3493–3503 (2016)
4. Bloch, M.R.: Covert communication over noisy channels: a resolvability perspective. IEEE Trans. Inf. Theory **62**(5), 2334–2354 (2016)
5. Arumugam, K.S.K., Bloch, M.R.: Keyless covert communication over multiple-access channels. In: 2016 IEEE International Symposium on Information Theory (ISIT), pp. 2229–2233. IEEE (2016)
6. Fridrich, J.: Steganography in Digital Media: Principles, Algorithms, and Applications. Cambridge University Press, Cambridge (2009)
7. Alpern, B., Schneider, F.B.: Key exchange using 'keyless cryptography'. Inf. Process. Lett. **16**(2), 79–81 (1983)
8. Yung, M.M.: A secure and useful "keyless cryptosystem". Inf. Process. Lett. **21**(1), 35–38 (1985)
9. Che, P.H., Bakshi, M., Chan, C., Jaggi, S.: Reliable deniable communication with channel uncertainty. In: 2014 IEEE Information Theory Workshop (ITW), pp. 30–34. IEEE (2014)
10. Lee, S., Baxley, R.J., Weitnauer, M.A., Walkenhorst, B.: Achieving undetectable communication. IEEE J. Sel. Top. Signal Process. **9**(7), 1195–1205 (2015)
11. Sobers, T.V., Bash, B.A., Guha, S., Towsley, D., Goeckel, D.: Covert communication in the presence of an uninformed jammer. IEEE Trans. Wirel. Commun. **16**(9), 6193–6206 (2017)
12. Abdelaziz, A., Koksal, C.E.: Fundamental limits of covert communication over MIMO AWGN channel, arXiv preprint arXiv:1705.02303 (2017)
13. Shahzad, K., Zhou, X., Yan, S., Hu, J., Shu, F., Li, J.: Achieving covert wireless communications using a full-duplex receiver. IEEE Trans. Wirel. Commun. **17**(12), 8517–8530 (2018)
14. Shafiee, S., Ulukus, S.: Achievable rates in Gaussian MISO channels with secrecy constraints. In: IEEE International Symposium on Information Theory, ISIT 2007, pp. 2466–2470. IEEE (2007)
15. Horn, R.A., Johnson, C.R.: Matrix Analysis, vol. 37. Cambridge University Press, New York (1985)

Linear Cryptanalysis Reduced Round
of Piccolo-80

Tomer Ashur[1,2], Orr Dunkelman[3], and Nael Masalha[3(✉)]

[1] Department of Electrical Engineering, ESAT/COSIC, KU Leuven, Leuven, Belgium
[2] iMinds, Leuven, Belgium
[3] Department of Computer Science, University of Haifa, Haifa, Israel
nael.masalha@hotmail.com

Abstract. Piccolo is a 64-bit lightweight block cipher suitable for constrained environments such as wireless sensor networks. In this paper we evaluate the security of Piccolo-80 against linear cryptanalysis, we present a 6-round linear approximation of Piccolo-80 with probability $1/2 + 2^{-29.04}$. We use this approximation to attack 7-round Piccolo-80 (with whitening keys) with data complexity of 2^{61} known plaintexts and time complexity of 2^{61}. Its extension to an 8-round attack merely increases the time complexity to 2^{70}. This is the best linear attack against Piccolo-80 and it is also applicable to Piccolo-128 as the difference between the two variates is only the number of rounds and the key schedule algorithm. Moreover, we show that the bias in the approximation of the F-function, in some cases, is related to the MSB of the input. We utilize this relation to efficiently extract the MSBs of the whitening keys in the first round.

Keywords: Piccolo · Linear cryptanalysis

1 Introduction

Due to the continuously evolving technology of constrained hardware devices, such as RFID tags and wireless sensor nodes, there is a huge demand to provide cryptographic security to such resource-constrained devices. As a result, new lightweight block ciphers suitable for such devices have been studied and Piccolo was proposed in CHES 2011 [16].

Piccolo is a 64-bit lightweight block cipher, it supports 80- and 128-bit secret keys. According to the length of the secret key, they are denoted Piccolo-80 and Piccolo-128, respectively. The respective number of rounds of Piccolo-80 and Piccolo-128 is 25 and 31. The iterative structure of Piccolo is a variant of generalized Feistel networks and has 4 branches, each of 16 bits. Its security was evaluated against several cryptanalytic techniques, such as Meet-in-the-Middle (MITM) [7], biclique [6], and impossible differential [3]. In this paper we evaluate the security of Piccolo-80 against linear cryptanalysis, and show a 7-round attack, on the full first 7 rounds (i.e. with whitening keys) of Piccolo-80, using

© Springer Nature Switzerland AG 2019
S. Dolev et al. (Eds.): CSCML 2019, LNCS 11527, pp. 16–32, 2019.
https://doi.org/10.1007/978-3-030-20951-3_2

6-round linear approximation, with data complexity of 2^{61} known plaintexts, and time complexity of 2^{61}. We then extend this attack to 8-round, with data complexity of 2^{61} known plaintexts, and time complexity of 2^{70}. We experimentally verified the attack on the *first two rounds* and the *first four rounds*. We also show that one can use conditional linear cryptanalysis [5] to attack Piccolo. We found that the bias in the approximation of the F-function might be related to the MSB of the input, thus we can increase the bias of the 6-round linear approximation by discarding plaintexts that have specific values of the bits that go to the MSBs of the F-functions in the first round.

Linear cryptanalysis is considered one of the most powerful cryptanalysis techniques. It was introduced by Matsui in [12] as an attack on the full 16-round DES, and later, an improved version is successfully applied to recover the key of the full 16-round DES [13]. Linear cryptanalysis studies statistical linear relations between bits of the plaintext, the ciphertext and the key. These relations are used to compute values of bits of the key, when enough plaintexts and their corresponding ciphertexts are known.

This paper is organized as follows. In Sect. 2, we briefly introduce the structure of Piccolo. In Sect. 3 we review the related work. The 7-round and 8-round linear attacks on Piccolo-80 are presented in Sect. 4. We report the experimental verification of our results in Sect. 5. Finlay, Sect. 6 concludes the paper.

2   A Brief Description of Piccolo

Before presenting the structure of Piccolo-80 and Piccolo-128, we give the following notations which are used throughout this paper:

$|A|$:   The bit length of A.
$A|B$:   The concatenation of A and B.
A^L: The left half of A.
A^R: The right half of A.
$A[i]$:   The ith bit of A.
$A[i, j, \ldots, k]$: $A[i] \oplus A[j] \oplus \ldots \oplus A[k]$.

Piccolo is a 64-bit block cipher supporting 80- and 128-bit keys. As shown in Fig. 1, the structure of Piccolo is a variant of generalized Feistel networks. The 80- and 128-bit key variates are referred to as Piccolo-80 and Piccolo-128, respectively. The difference between the two key modes lies in the number of rounds and the key schedule. The number of rounds is $r = 25$ for Piccolo-80 and $r = 31$ for Piccolo-128.

The data processing part takes a 64-bit block $X \in \{0,1\}^{64}$, four 16-bit whitening keys $wk_i \in \{0,1\}^{16}$ ($0 \leq i < 4$) and $2r$ 16-bit round subkeys $rk_i \in \{0,1\}^{16}$ ($0 \leq i < 2r$) as inputs, and outputs a 64-bit block $Y \in \{0,1\}^{64}$.

Let $P = (P_0, P_1, P_2, P_3)$ be a 64-bit plaintext, where $P_i \in \{0,1\}^{16}$ ($0 \leq i < 3$), and let (wk_0, wk_1) be a prewhitening key, then the input value $I_0 = (I_{0,0}, I_{0,1}, I_{0,2}, I_{0,3})$ of round 0 is computed as follows:

$$I_{0,0} = P_0 \oplus wk_0, I_{0,1} = P_1, I_{0,2} = P_2 \oplus wk_1, I_{0,3} = P_3.$$

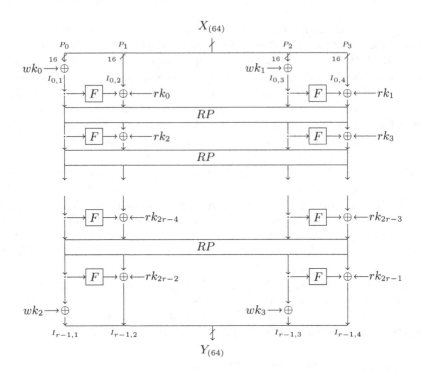

Fig. 1. The structure of Piccolo

To generate I_{i+1} from I_i ($i = 0, ..., r - 2$), each round is composed of two F-functions $F : \{0, 1\}^{16} \rightarrow \{0, 1\}^{16}$ and a round permutation $RP : \{0, 1\}^{64} \rightarrow \{0, 1\}^{64}$.

The F-functions consists of two S-box layers separated by diffusion matrix (see Fig. 2). The S-box layer consists of four 4-bit bijective S-boxes S. The round permutation RP (see Fig. 3) takes a 64-bit input value $X = (x_0, x_1, x_2, x_3, x_4, x_5, x_6, x_7)$ and generates a 64-bit output value $Y = (x_2, x_7, x_4, x_1, x_6, x_3, x_0, x_5)$.

The 64-bit ciphertext $C = (C_0, C_1, C_2, C_3)$, where $C_i \in \{0, 1\}^{16}$ ($0 \le i < 3$), is generated as follows:

$$C_0 = I_{r-1,0} \oplus wk_2, \quad C_1 = F(I_{r-1,0}) \oplus I_{r-1,1} \oplus wk_{2r},$$
$$C_2 = I_{r-1,2} \oplus wk_3, \quad C_3 = F(I_{r-1,2}) \oplus I_{r-1,3} \oplus wk_{2r+1}.$$

The key schedule of Piccolo-80 is simple. First, the 80-bit secret key K is defined as follows. Let $k_j = (k_j^L, k_j^R)$ ($j = 0, 1, 2, 3, 4$), where $k_j \in \{0, 1\}^{16}$, $k_j^L \in \{0, 1\}^8$ and $k_j^R \in \{0, 1\}^8$.

$$K = (k_0, k_1, k_2, k_3, k_4).$$

Four whitening keys (wk_0, wk_1, wk_2, wk_3) and 25 round keys (rk_{2i}, rk_{2i+1}) are generated as follows ($i = 0, 1, ..., 24$). Let (con_{2i}^{80}) and (con_{2i+1}^{80}) be 16-bit round constants.

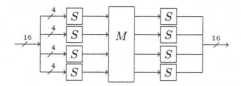

Fig. 2. The F function of Piccolo

$X_{(64)}$

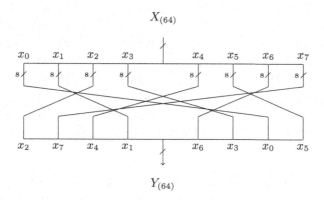

$Y_{(64)}$

Fig. 3. The round permutation (RP) of Piccolo

- The whitening keys are

$$wk_0 = k_0^L||k_1^R, wk_1 = k_1^L||k_0^R,$$
$$wk_2 = k_4^L||k_3^R, wk_3 = k_3^L||k_4^R.$$

- The round keys are

$$(rk_{2i}, rk_{2i+1}) = (con_{2i}^{80}, con_{2i+1}^{80}) \oplus \begin{cases} (k_2, k_3), (i \bmod 5) \equiv 0 \ or \ 2, \\ (k_0, k_1), (i \bmod 5) \equiv 1 \ or \ 4, \\ (k_4, k_4), (i \bmod 5) \equiv 3, \end{cases}$$

$$(con_{2i}^{80}|con_{2i+1}^{80}) = (c_{i+1}|c_0|c_{i+1}|\{00\}_2|c_{i+1}|c_0|c_{i+1}) \oplus \{0f1e2d3c\}_{16}$$

where c_i is a 5-bit representation of i, e.g., $c_{13} = \{01101\}_2$. The key schedule of Piccolo-128 is very similar, the interested reader is referred to [16].

3   Previous Analysis of Piccolo

Several cryptanalytic results on Piccolo were previously proposed. First, the designers of Piccolo evaluated its security against various attacks and attacked Piccolo-80 up to 17 rounds and Piccolo-128 up to 21 rounds by using related-key attacks [16]. In addition, they used a Meet-in-the-Middle (MITM) attack on 14-round Piccolo-80 and a 21-round Piccolo-128 without whitening keys.

Table 1. Summary of attacks on Piccolo-80 in the single-key model

Method	Rounds	Whitening keys pre/post	Data	Time
Imp. Diff. [1]	13	None	$2^{43.25}$ CP	$2^{69.7}$
RK Diff. [14]	14	None	$2^{68.19}$ CP	$2^{68.19}$
MITM [10]	14	None	2^{64} KP	2^{73}
MITM [17]	14	None	2^{48} KP	$2^{75.39}$
Biclique [18]	25	Pre	2^{48} CP	$2^{78.95}$
Biclique [11]	25	Both	2^{48} CP	$2^{79.13}$
Linear [Sect. 4.3]	7	Both	2^{61} KP	2^{61}
Linear [Sect. 4.4]	8	Both	2^{61} KP	2^{70}
Conditional linear [Sect. 4.5]	2	Pre	2^{14} CP	2^{14}
Conditional linear [Sect. 4.6]	8	Both	2^{54} CP	2^{54}

CP: Chosen Plaintext, KP: Known Pliantext, RK: Related Key, MITM: Meet in the Middle

Related-key differential attack on 14-round Piccolo-80 and 21-round Piccolo-128 without whitening keys, are introduced in [14]. The data and time complexities of the attack against Piccolo-80 are $2^{68.19}$ and $2^{68.19}$, respectively, and against Piccolo-128 are $2^{117.77}$ and $2^{117.77}$, respectively.

A Meet-in-the-Middle (MITM) attack on 14-round Piccolo-80 and a 17-round Piccolo-128 without whitening keys, are also proposed in [17]. The data and time complexities of the attack against Piccolo-80 are 2^{48} and $2^{75.39}$, respectively, and against Piccolo-128 are 2^{48} and $2^{126.87}$, respectively.

Biclique cryptanalysis [6] of the full Piccolo-80 without postwhitening keys and a 28-round Piccolo-128 without prewhitening keys was introduced in [18]. These attacks are with data complexity of 2^{48} and 2^{24} chosen ciphertexts, and with time complexity of $2^{78.95}$ and $2^{126.79}$ encryptions, respectively. Later, biclique cryptanalysis of the full round Piccolo-80 and Piccolo-128 was introduced in [11]. These attacks have data complexity of 2^{48} and 2^{24} chosen ciphertexts, and with time complexity of $2^{79.13}$ and $2^{127.35}$ encryptions.

Impossible differential cryptanalysis [3] on Piccolo without whitening keys, is introduced in [1], 12-round and 13-round impossible differential attack on Piccolo-80 and 15-round attack on Piccolo-128. The data and time complexity of the attack against Piccolo-80 is $2^{36.34}$ and $2^{55.18}$ for 12-round and $2^{43.25}$ and $2^{69.7}$ for 13-round. The data and time complexity for 15-round cryptanalysis of Piccolo-128 are $2^{58.7}$ and $2^{125.4}$, respectively.

Multidimensional zero-corellation linear cryptanalysis on Piccolo-128 without whitening keys, was introduced in [9], with 13-round, 14-round and 15-round. The data complexities are $2^{56.8}$, $2^{52.43}$, and $2^{55.6}$, respectively, and time complexities are $2^{117.2}$, $2^{123.09}$, and $2^{126.55}$, respectively. Table 1 shows our results along with the previous cryptanalysis results in the single-key model on Piccolo-80.

4   A Linear Attack on Reduced Round of Piccolo-80

We now introduce a linear approximation of 6 rounds of Piccolo. First, we construct a linear approximation of the F-function, then we use it to create a 6-round linear approximation.

4.1   Linear Approximation of the F-Function

We start by studying the linear approximation of the F-function. Our approach is to treat the F-function as a black box, i.e., to ignore the internal description of the S-box layers and the diffusion matrix M, and to handle the F-function as a 16-bit S-box. This approach solves any dependency issue between the first layer of S-boxes to the second layer, making the analysis more accurate than merely choosing the number of active S-boxes. The linear approximations of the F-function were found by iterating all the input and output masks. Table 2 lists the highest bias entries of the linear approximations table of the F-function.

4.2   Linear Approximation of 6 Round Piccolo-80

We now extend the linear approximation of the F-function to 6-round linear approximation by concatenating linear approximations, as described in [12] and [2]. Namely, we try to minimize the number of active F-functions as much as possible.

Figure 4 describes a 6-round linear approximation. The input mask of the approximation is $\lambda_p = 0008\ 0000\ D301\ 0029_x$ and the output mask is $\lambda_c = 202F\ D308\ 5554\ 0001_x$. This approximation contains 6 active F-functions.

Table 2. High bias linear approximations of the F-function

Linear approximation of F	Bias
$0029_x \rightarrow 8808_x$	2^{-5}
$2229_x \rightarrow 0008_x$	2^{-5}
$2922_x \rightarrow 0800_x$	2^{-5}
$1022_x \rightarrow 0088_x$	2^{-5}
$9022_x \rightarrow 0088_x$	2^{-5}
$4046_x \rightarrow 8900_x$	2^{-5}
$C046_x \rightarrow 8900_x$	2^{-5}
$2222_x \rightarrow 8888_x$	-2^{-5}
$2430_x \rightarrow 0608_x$	-2^{-5}
$8862_x \rightarrow 000D_x$	$2^{-5.2}$
$A862_x \rightarrow 000D_x$	$2^{-5.2}$

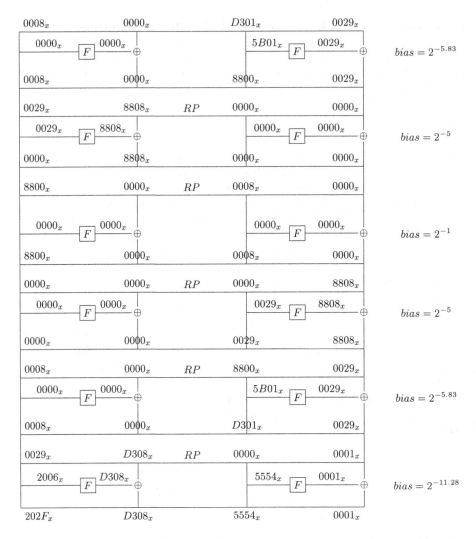

Fig. 4. A 6-round linear approximation of Piccolo-80 with bias $= 2^{-29.04}$

The first round contains one active F-function with the linear approximation $(5B01_x \to 0029_x)$ and a bias of $2^{-5.83}$. The second round contains one active F-function with linear approximation $(0029_x \to 8808_x)$ and a bias of 2^{-5}. There are no active F-functions in the third round. The fourth round is similar to the second one with exchanged active and non-active F-functions. The fifth round is the same as the first one. The sixth round contains two active F-functions, the left one with linear approximation $(2006_x \to D308_x)$ and a bias of $2^{-6.5}$ and the right active F-function with linear approximation $(5554_x \to 0001_x)$ and a bias of $2^{-5.87}$. Figure 4 shows the bias of each round in the right side, based on the

Pilling-up Lemma [12], we conclude that the total bias of this approximation is $2^{-29.04}$.

The 6 round linear approximation was built by applying the linear approximation $(0029_x \rightarrow 8808_x)$, which has maximal bias, to the left side F-function in the second round, and leaving the right side F-function inactive. Then, we extended it up to the first round, by searching the highest biased linear approximation of the F-function with output mask (0029_x). The third round is trivial as it includes no active F-functions. The fourth and fifth rounds are mirror to the second and first rounds. In the sixth round, we searched for the highest biased linear approximations of the F-function with output mask $(D308_x)$, for the left side F-functions, and 0001_x for the right side F-function.

Equations (1) and (2) describe the linear relation between plaintext, ciphertext and round subkey bits for the first 6 rounds of Piccolo. The bias of Eq. (1) is $2^{-29.04}$. Equation (3) assumes that the xor of the key bits involved in the linear approximation, but not contained in wk_2 and wk_3 equals 0. This assumption only affects the bias sign.

$$\sum_k = P[0,3,5,16,24,25,28,30,31,51] \oplus \tag{1}$$
$$C[0,18,20,22,24,26,28,30,35,40,41,44,46,47,48,49,50,51,53,61]$$

$$\sum_k = k_1^L[0,1,4,6,7] \oplus k_0^R[0,3] \oplus k_3^R[0,3,5] \oplus k_0^L[3,7] \oplus k_4^L[3,7] \oplus k_4^R[3] \oplus \tag{2}$$
$$k_1^R[5] \oplus k_2^L[0,1,4,6,7] \oplus k_2^R[3]$$

$$0 = k_1^L[0,1,4,6,7] \oplus k_0^R[0,3] \oplus k_0^L[3,7] \oplus k_1^R[5] \oplus k_2^L[0,1,4,6,7] \oplus k_2^R[3] \tag{3}$$

4.3   A Linear Attack on 7 Rounds of Piccolo-80

According to [12], once an $(n-1)$-round linear approximation is discovered for a given cipher, it is conceivable to attack the cipher by recovering bits of the nth round subkey. In our case, we extract bits from the whitening keys wk_2 and wk_3 in the seventh round, see Fig. 5. We shall refer to the subkeys to be recovered from the seventh round as the *target partial subkeys*.

The bias of the linear approximation, described in Fig. 4, is $2^{-29.04}$, therefore, according to [15], the attack requires 2^{61} plaintext/ciphertext pairs, in order to retrieve the maximum-biased key, with 98% success rate. The basic algorithm of the attack, described in Algorithm 1, is based on the basic M2 algorithm of [12].

Algorithm 1. Basic Attack Procedure

```
1: Data: {(p_i, c_i)}
2: Result: wk_2 and wk_3
3:
4: wk_2 ← 0
5: wk_3 ← 0
6: max_bias ← 0
7:
8: for each candidate_wk_2, candidate_wk_3 ∈ {0,1}^16 do
9:     current_bias ← 0
10:    for each pair (p_i, c_i) do
11:        Decrypt c_i and find A, B, C, D (described in Figure 5)
12:        if Equation 1 holds then
13:            Increment current_bias by 1
14:        else
15:            Decrement current_bias by 1
16:        end if
17:    end for
18:    if |current_bias| ≥ max_bias then
19:        wk_2 ← candidate_wk_2
20:        wk_3 ← candidate_wk_3
21:        max_bias ← |current_bias|
22:    end if
23: end for
24:
25: Output wk_2 and wk_3
```

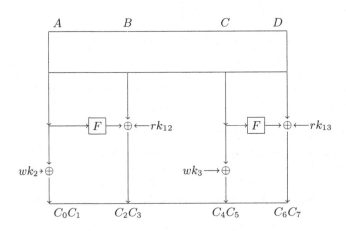

Fig. 5. Decryption of the seventh round

The time complexity of this algorithm is the time needed to partially decrypt 2^{61} ciphertexts under 2^{32} subkeys for one round. Thus, the total time complexity is about $\frac{1}{7} \cdot 2^{61} \cdot 2^{32} \approx 2^{90.19}$ Piccolo encryptions, with data complexity of 2^{61}

plaintexts, and 2^{61} memory for plaintexts. Obviously, in the case of Piccolo-80 this time complexity is greater than that of exhaustive search. A better algorithm in terms of time complexity is based on the algorithm described in [4], this algorithm utilizes that, in the naive Algorithm 1, for each ciphertext we look only on 32 bits, and decrypt many times the same value under the same key. The resulting algorithm is given as Algorithm 2.

Algorithm 2. Improved Attack Procedure

1: **Data:** $\{(p_i, c_i = c_0^i c_1^i | c_2^i c_3^i | c_4^i c_5^i | c_6^i c_7^i)\}$
2: **Result:** wk_2 and wk_3
3:
4: Initialize an array A of 2^{32} counters.
5:
6: **for** each pair (p_i, c_i) **do**
7:     $parity \leftarrow p_i[0..63] \oplus c_2^i c_3^i[0..15] \oplus c_6^i c_7^i[0..15]$
8:     **if** $parity = 0$ **then**
9:         Increment $A[c_0^i c_1^i | c_4^i c_5^i]$ by 1
10:     **else**
11:         Decrement $A[c_0^i c_1^i | c_4^i c_5^i]$ by 1
12:     **end if**
13: **end for**
14:
15: $wk_2 \leftarrow 0$
16: $wk_3 \leftarrow 0$
17: $max\_bias \leftarrow 0$
18:
19: **for** each $candidate\_wk_2, candidate\_wk_3 \in \{0,1\}^{16}$ **do**
20:     $current\_bias \leftarrow 0$
21:     **for** each $c_0^i c_1^i | c_4^i c_5^i$ **do**
22:         Decrypt $c_0^i c_1^i$ and calculate the left F-function parity.
23:         Decrypt $c_4^i c_5^i$ and calculate the right F-function parity.
24:         **if** Equation 1 holds **then**
25:             Increment $current\_bias$ by $A[c_0^i c_1^i | c_4^i c_5^i]$
26:         **else**
27:             Decrement $current\_bias$ by $A[c_0^i c_1^i | c_4^i c_5^i]$
28:         **end if**
29:     **end for**
30:     **if** $|current\_bias| \gtrsim max\_bias$ **then**
31:         $wk_2 \leftarrow candidate\_wk_2$
32:         $wk_3 \leftarrow candidate\_wk_3$
33:         $max\_bias \leftarrow |current\_bias|$
34:     **end if**
35: **end for**
36:
37: Output wk_2 and wk_3

The time complexity of this algorithm is the time needed to partially decrypt 2^{32} ciphertexts under 2^{32} subkeys for one round. Thus, the total time complexity is about $\frac{1}{7} \cdot 2^{32} \cdot 2^{32} \approx 2^{61.19}$ Piccolo encryptions, with data complexity of 2^{61} plaintexts, and memory of 2^{32} counters. We further improve the time complexity of the analysis phase, to $32 \cdot 2^{32} = 2^{37}$, using the fast Fourier transform, suggested in [8], to speed up the computation of the bias for every subkey candidate. Thus, the total time complexity of the algorithm is 2^{61}. The matrix C, in our case, is defined by the following function:

$$C(wk_2|wk_3, c_0c_1|c_4c_5) = parity(F(wk_2|wk_3 \oplus c_0c_1|c_4c_5))$$

According to proposition 1 and demonstration 1 in [8], C is $level$-32 circulant with type $\underbrace{(2, 2, ..., 2)}_{32 \text{ times}}$, thus we can use the fast algorithm to achieve the improved analysis time. While this seems a futile improvement (form $2^{61.19}$ to 2^{61}) it is used in 8-round attack described next, where it saves a lot.

4.4   A Linear Attack on 8 Rounds of Piccolo-80

We now present the attack on the first eight rounds and extract the key bits of the four whitening keys wk_0, wk_1, wk_2 and wk_3. Equation 1, is used as a relation between input bits of the second round to output bits of the seventh round. The attack is described in Algorithm 3.

The time complexity of this algorithm is the time needed to partially encrypt 2^{32} plaintexts under 2^{32} subkeys for one round and partially decrypt 2^{32} ciphertexts under 2^{32} subkeys for one round. Thus, the total time complexity is about $\frac{2}{8} \cdot 2^{64} \cdot 2^{64} \approx 2^{128}$ encryptions, with data complexity of 2^{61} plaintexts, and memory of 2^{64} counters. We further improve the time complexity of the analysis phase to $64 \cdot 2^{64} = 2^{70}$, using the fast Fourier transform. The matrix C, in this case, is defined by the following function:

$$C(wk_0|wk_1|wk_2|wk_3, p_0p_1|p_4p_5|c_0c_1|c_4c_5) = parity(F(wk_0|wk_1|wk_2|wk_3 \oplus p_0p_1|p_4p_5|c_0c_1|c_4c_5))$$

The matrix C is $level$-64 circulant with type $\underbrace{(2, 2, ..., 2)}_{64 \text{ times}}$.

4.5   Input MSB of the F-Function as a Partitioning Distinguisher

While studying the linear behavior of the F-function in Sect. 4.1, we observed that in part of the linear approximations, the bias is influenced by the most significant bit MSB of the input. For example, the bias of the approximation $(5B01_x \rightarrow 0029_x)$, described in the first round of Fig. 4, equals $2^{-5.83}$. Now we divide the input of the F-function into two disjoint sets, the first set includes input values whose MSB equals 0 and the second set includes input values whose MSB equals 1. Recalculating the bias of $(5B01_x \rightarrow 0029_x)$, for each one of the input sets, gives bias $2^{-5.01}$ and $2^{-8.38}$, respectively. The total bias equals to the

---

Algorithm 3. 8-Round Attack Procedure

1: **Data:** $\{(p_i = p_0^i p_1^i | p_2^i p_3^i | p_4^i p_5^i | p_6^i p_7^i, c_i = c_0^i c_1^i | c_2^i c_3^i | c_4^i c_5^i | c_6^i c_7^i)\}$

2: **Result:** wk_0, wk_1, wk_2 and wk_3

3:

4: Initialize an array A of 2^{64} counters.

5:

6: **for** each pair (p_i, c_i) **do**

7:     $parity \leftarrow p_2^i p_3^i[0..15] \oplus p_6^i p_7^i[0..15] \oplus c_2^i c_3^i[0..15] \oplus c_6^i c_7^i[0..15]$

8:     **if** $parity = 0$ **then**

9:         Increment $A[p_0^i p_1^i | p_4^i p_5^i | c_0^i c_1^i | c_4^i c_5^i]$ by 1

10:     **else**

11:         Decrement $A[p_0^i p_1^i | p_4^i p_5^i | c_0^i c_1^i | c_4^i c_5^i]$ by 1

12:     **end if**

13: **end for**

14:

15: $wk_0 \leftarrow 0$

16: $wk_1 \leftarrow 0$

17: $wk_2 \leftarrow 0$

18: $wk_3 \leftarrow 0$

19: $max\_bias \leftarrow 0$

20:

21: **for** each $candidate\_wk_0, candidate\_wk_1, candidate\_wk_2, candidate\_wk_3 \in \{0,1\}^{16}$ **do**

22:     $current\_bias \leftarrow 0$

23:     **for** each $p_0^i p_1^i | p_4^i p_5^i | c_0^i c_1^i | c_4^i c_5^i$ **do**

24:         Encrypt $p_0^i p_1^i$ and calculate the left F-function parity.

25:         Encrypt $p_4^i p_5^i$ and calculate the right F-function parity.

26:         Decrypt $c_0^i c_1^i$ and calculate the left F-function parity.

27:         Decrypt $c_4^i c_5^i$ and calculate the right F-function parity.

28:         **if** Equation 1 holds **then**

29:             Increment $current\_bias$ by $A[p_0^i p_1^i | p_4^i p_5^i | c_0^i c_1^i | c_4^i c_5^i]$

30:         **else**

31:             Decrement $current\_bias$ by $A[p_0^i p_1^i | p_4^i p_5^i | c_0^i c_1^i | c_4^i c_5^i]$

32:         **end if**

33:     **end for**

34:     **if** $|current\_bias| \gtrsim max\_bias$ **then**

35:         $wk_0 \leftarrow candidate\_wk_0$

36:         $wk_1 \leftarrow candidate\_wk_1$

37:         $wk_2 \leftarrow candidate\_wk_2$

38:         $wk_3 \leftarrow candidate\_wk_3$

39:         $max\_bias \leftarrow |current\_bias|$

40:     **end if**

41: **end for**

42:

43: Output wk_0, wk_1, wk_2 and wk_3

Table 3. Bias as a function of input's MSB

Linear approximation of F	Toatal bias	Bias when MSB = 0	Bias when MSB = 1
$5B01_x \rightarrow 0029_x$	$2^{-5.83}$	$2^{-5.01}$	$2^{-8.38}$
$9022_x \rightarrow 0088_x$	$2^{-5.01}$	$2^{-6.05}$	$2^{-4.44}$
$1022_x \rightarrow 0088_x$	$2^{-5.01}$	$2^{-6.05}$	$-2^{-4.44}$
$4046_x \rightarrow 8900_x$	$2^{-5.01}$	$2^{-5.44}$	$2^{-4.71}$
$C046_x \rightarrow 8900_x$	$2^{-5.01}$	$2^{-5.44}$	$-2^{-4.71}$
$62A6_x \rightarrow 0D00_x$	$2^{-5.21}$	$2^{-4.87}$	$2^{-5.71}$
$E2A6_x \rightarrow 0D00_x$	$2^{-5.21}$	$2^{-4.87}$	$-2^{-5.71}$
$662A_x \rightarrow 00D0_x$	$2^{-5.21}$	$2^{-4.87}$	$2^{-5.71}$

average of the other two biases. Table 3 lists several such linear approximations of the F-function.

Utilizing this behavior, the first round of Piccolo can be attacked to extract the MSB of the whitening keys wk_0 or wk_1. For simplicity, we assume that the first round contains only one active F-function on the right side with biases ϵ_{min} for the input set whose MSB equals 1 and ϵ_{max} for the input set whose MSB equals 0. Assuming we have $O(1/(|\epsilon_{max}| - |\epsilon_{min}|)^2)$ pairs of chosen plaintexts, with $X_4[7] = 0$, and their corresponding ciphertexts, we calculate the bias using the linear approximation of the first round, if the observed bias is greater than $\epsilon_{min} + |\epsilon_{max} - \epsilon_{min}|/2 - 2 \cdot \sigma$, then we conclude that $X_4[7] \oplus wk_1[15] = 0$ and $wk_1[15] = 0$, otherwise, we conclude that $X_4[7] \oplus wk_1[15] = 1$ and $wk_1[15] = 1$. As an example, we show how to attack the first round, using the linear approximation described in Fig. 6 and extract $wk_1[15]$. The input to the active F-function is $X_4X_5 \oplus wk_1$, this implies that the MSB input to F-function is $X_4[7] \oplus wk_1[15]$. Assuming that we have 2^{12} pairs of chosen plaintexts, with $X_4[7] = 0$, we calculate the bias according to Eq. 4, if the received bias is greater than $2^{-8.38} + (2^{-5.03} - 2^{-8.38})/2 - 2 \cdot 2^{-1} \cdot 2^{-6} \approx 2^{-7.65}$, then we conclude that $X_4[7] \oplus wk_1[15] = 0$ and $wk_1[15] = 0$, otherwise, we conclude that $wk_1[15] = 1$.

$$P[0, 3, 5, 16, 24, 25, 28, 30, 31, 51] \oplus C[0, 3, 5, 27, 31, 51] = 0 \qquad (4)$$

4.6 Extracting the MSB Values of the Whitening Keys wk_0 and wk_1

We now use the behavior described in Sect. 4.5, to extend the linear attack described in Sect. 4.3 and extract the MSBs of the whitening keys wk_0 and wk_1. We divide the input of the F-functions in the first round into four disjoint sets, according to the MSB values {00,01,10,11}, and recalculate the bias values {$\epsilon_0, \epsilon_1, \epsilon_2, \epsilon_3$} of the linear approximation, for each one of the sets. For example, the bias of the 6-round linear approximation described in Fig. 4 is $2^{-27.3}$ when the MSB of the right F-function input equals 0, and $2^{-34.04}$ when the MSB of

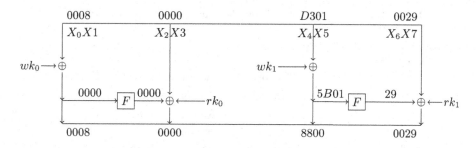

Fig. 6. Extracting MSB of whitening key wk_1

the input equals 1. There are only two values of the bias because there is only one active F-function in this case. The same attack used in Sect. 4.5 can be used to extract the MSB of wk_1.

5 Experimental Verification of a Reduced-Round Attack

In this section we describe the experimental verification of our proposed attacks, which ran on a single core of an Intel Xeon Platinum 8170 CPU, with 2.10 GHz frequency and 125 GB RAM. The attack program is based on C++11, compiled by g++ (GCC) version 5.4.0, running on Ubuntu 16.04.5 LTS.

5.1 Partial Verification of 2 Rounds and 4 Rounds Linear Attack

We start with the experimental verification of a reduced-round versions of the attack described in Sect. 4.3. The attack versions are based on 1-round and 3-round linear approximations, described in Fig. 4, with an additional round for key recovery. This is a partial verification of the attack, as we only compute wk_2 in case of 2 rounds and wk_3 in case of 4 rounds. We repeated each version with three different values of plaintext/ciphertext pairs, and for each value it was verified by 100 random keys. Table 4 summarizes the results of the attack on the first two and the first four rounds.

5.2 Verification of MSB as a Partitioning Distinguisher

We now show the experimental verification results for the attack described in Sect. 4.5. Table 5 summarizes the results of the attack on two different linear approximations of the F-function. The experiment consisted of 2^8 random keys, and for each key we tried variable number of plaintexts/ciphertexts.

Table 4. Summary of 2 and 4 rounds attack verification (100 trials)

Rounds	Plaintexts/Ciphertexts (per key)	Attack time		Success rate %	
		Algorithm 1	Algorithm 2	Actual	Expected [15]
2	$2^{13.66}$	15 min	32 min	28	25
2	$2^{14.66}$	31 min	34 min	84	71
2	$2^{15.66}$	62 min	35 min	99.60	98
4	$2^{21.66}$	70.6 h	23 min	36	25
4	$2^{22.66}$	138.4.1 h	23 min	87.50	69
4	$2^{23.66}$	282.5 h	23 min	99.21	98

Exhuastive search time for two rounds is 1.18 h and for four rounds is 2.11 h

Table 5. Summary of MSB partitioning distinguisher attack verification (256 trials)

Linear approximation of F	Low bias ϵ_{min}	High bias ϵ_{max}	Plaintexts/ Ciphertexts (per key)	Success rate of guessing MSB of wk_1
$5B01_x \rightarrow 0029_x$	$2^{-8.38}$	$2^{-5.01}$	2^{12}	56.01%
$5B01_x \rightarrow 0029_x$	$2^{-8.38}$	$2^{-5.01}$	2^{13}	83.43%
$5B01_x \rightarrow 0029_x$	$2^{-8.38}$	$2^{-5.01}$	2^{14}	96.56%
$5B01_x \rightarrow 0029_x$	$2^{-8.38}$	$2^{-5.01}$	2^{15}	100%
$662A_x \rightarrow 00D0_x$	$2^{-5.71}$	$2^{-4.87}$	2^{12}	63.35%
$662A_x \rightarrow 00D0_x$	$2^{-5.71}$	$2^{-4.87}$	2^{13}	75.78%
$662A_x \rightarrow 00D0_x$	$2^{-5.71}$	$2^{-4.87}$	2^{14}	89.91%
$662A_x \rightarrow 00D0_x$	$2^{-5.71}$	$2^{-4.87}$	2^{16}	98.89%

6   Conclusion

In this paper, we proposed linear cryptanalysis of the lightweight block cipher Piccolo-80. We attacked seven and eight rounds of Piccolo-80 using a 6-round linear approximation with bias $2^{-29.04}$. The 7-round attack requires data complexity of 2^{61} known plaintexts. The time complexity is 2^{61} and memory complexity of 2^{32}. The 8-round attack requires data complexity of 2^{61} known plaintexts. The time complexity is 2^{70} and memory complexity of 2^{64}. The attack was verified on reduced versions of two and four rounds of Piccolo-80. In addition, we showed that the F-function bias might be related to the MSB of the input, and presented an attack that uses this property to extract the MSB's of the whitening keys wk_0 and wk_1.

References

1. Azimi, S.A., Ahmadian, Z., Mohajeri, J., Aref, M.R.: Impossible differential cryptanalysis of piccolo lightweight block cipher. In: 2014 11th International ISC Conference on Information Security and Cryptology (ISCISC), pp. 89–94. IEEE (2014)
2. Biham, E.: On Matsui's linear cryptanalysis. In: De Santis, A. (ed.) EUROCRYPT 1994. LNCS, vol. 950, pp. 341–355. Springer, Heidelberg (1995). https://doi.org/10.1007/BFb0053449
3. Biham, E., Biryukov, A., Shamir, A.: Cryptanalysis of skipjack reduced to 31 rounds using impossible differentials. In: Stern, J. (ed.) EUROCRYPT 1999. LNCS, vol. 1592, pp. 12–23. Springer, Heidelberg (1999). https://doi.org/10.1007/3-540-48910-X_2
4. Biham, E., Dunkelman, O., Keller, N.: Linear cryptanalysis of reduced round serpent. In: Matsui, M. (ed.) FSE 2001. LNCS, vol. 2355, pp. 16–27. Springer, Heidelberg (2002). https://doi.org/10.1007/3-540-45473-X_2
5. Biham, E., Perle, S.: Conditional linear cryptanalysis - cryptanalysis of DES with less than 242 complexity. IACR Trans. Symmetric Cryptol. **2018**(3), 215–264 (2018)
6. Bogdanov, A., Khovratovich, D., Rechberger, C.: Biclique cryptanalysis of the Full AES. In: Lee, D.H., Wang, X. (eds.) ASIACRYPT 2011. LNCS, vol. 7073, pp. 344–371. Springer, Heidelberg (2011). https://doi.org/10.1007/978-3-642-25385-0_19
7. Bogdanov, A., Rechberger, C.: A 3-subset meet-in-the-middle attack: cryptanalysis of the lightweight block cipher KTANTAN. In: Biryukov, A., Gong, G., Stinson, D.R. (eds.) SAC 2010. LNCS, vol. 6544, pp. 229–240. Springer, Heidelberg (2011). https://doi.org/10.1007/978-3-642-19574-7_16
8. Collard, B., Standaert, F.-X., Quisquater, J.-J.: Improving the time complexity of Matsui's linear cryptanalysis. In: Nam, K.-H., Rhee, G. (eds.) ICISC 2007. LNCS, vol. 4817, pp. 77–88. Springer, Heidelberg (2007). https://doi.org/10.1007/978-3-540-76788-6_7
9. Fu, L., Jin, C., Li, X.: Multidimensional zero-correlation linear cryptanalysis of lightweight block cipher Piccolo-128. Secur. Commun. Netw. **9**(17), 4520–4535 (2016)
10. Isobe, T., Shibutani, K.: Security analysis of the lightweight block ciphers XTEA, LED and Piccolo. In: Susilo, W., Mu, Y., Seberry, J. (eds.) ACISP 2012. LNCS, vol. 7372, pp. 71–86. Springer, Heidelberg (2012). https://doi.org/10.1007/978-3-642-31448-3_6
11. Jeong, K., Kang, H., Lee, C., Sung, J., Hong, S.: Biclique cryptanalysis of lightweight block ciphers present, piccolo and LED. IACR Cryptology ePrint Archive **2012**, 621 (2012)
12. Matsui, M.: Linear cryptanalysis method for DES cipher. In: Helleseth, T. (ed.) EUROCRYPT 1993. LNCS, vol. 765, pp. 386–397. Springer, Heidelberg (1994). https://doi.org/10.1007/3-540-48285-7_33
13. Matsui, M.: The first experimental cryptanalysis of the data encryption standard. In: Desmedt, Y.G. (ed.) CRYPTO 1994. LNCS, vol. 839, pp. 1–11. Springer, Heidelberg (1994). https://doi.org/10.1007/3-540-48658-5_1
14. Minier, M.: On the security of *Piccolo* lightweight block cipher against related-key impossible differentials. In: Paul, G., Vaudenay, S. (eds.) INDOCRYPT 2013. LNCS, vol. 8250, pp. 308–318. Springer, Cham (2013). https://doi.org/10.1007/978-3-319-03515-4_21

15. Selçuk, A.A.: On probability of success in linear and differential cryptanalysis. J. Cryptology **21**(1), 131–147 (2008)
16. Shibutani, K., Isobe, T., Hiwatari, H., Mitsuda, A., Akishita, T., Shirai, T.: *Piccolo*: an ultra-lightweight blockcipher. In: Preneel, B., Takagi, T. (eds.) CHES 2011. LNCS, vol. 6917, pp. 342–357. Springer, Heidelberg (2011). https://doi.org/10. 1007/978-3-642-23951-9_23
17. Tolba, M., Abdelkhalek, A., Youssef, A.M.: Meet-in-the-middle attacks on reduced round piccolo. In: Güneysu, T., Leander, G., Moradi, A. (eds.) LightSec 2015. LNCS, vol. 9542, pp. 3–20. Springer, Cham (2016). https://doi.org/10.1007/978-3-319-29078-2_1
18. Wang, Y., Wu, W., Yu, X.: Biclique cryptanalysis of reduced-round piccolo block cipher. In: Ryan, M.D., Smyth, B., Wang, G. (eds.) ISPEC 2012. LNCS, vol. 7232, pp. 337–352. Springer, Heidelberg (2012). https://doi.org/10.1007/978-3-642-29101-2_23

Continuous Key Agreement
with Reduced Bandwidth

Nir Drucker[1,2(✉)] and Shay Gueron[1,2]

[1] University of Haifa, Haifa, Israel
[2] Amazon, Seattle, USA
drucker.nir@gmail.com, shay@math.haifa.ac.il

Abstract. Continuous Key Agreement (CKA) is a two-party procedure used by Double Ratchet protocols (e. g., Signal). This is a continuous and synchronous protocol that generates a fresh key for every sent/received message. It guarantees forward secrecy and post-compromise security. Alwen et al. have recently proposed a new KEM-based CKA construction where every message contains a ciphertext and a fresh public key. This can be made quantum-safe by deploying a quantum-safe KEM. They mention that the bandwidth can be reduced when using an ElGamal KEM (which is not quantum-safe). In this paper, we generalized their approach by defining a new primitive, namely Merged KEM (MKEM). This primitive merges the key generation and the encapsulation steps of a KEM. This is not possible for every KEM and we discuss cases where a KEM can be converted to an MKEM. One example is the quantum-safe proposal BIKE1, where the BIKE-MKEM saves 50% of the communication bandwidth, compared to the original construction. In addition, we offer the notion and two constructions for hybrid CKA.

Keywords: Double Ratchet protocol · Continuous Key Agreement · Post Quantum Cryptography · Code-based cryptography · BIKE

1 Introduction

Double Ratchet (DR) protocols (e. g., Signal [16]) are used to secure instant messaging applications such as WhatsApp [3], Skype [14], Facebook Messenger [1], and Google Allo [15]. Several formal security analyses of the DR protocol and its variants are given in [4,6,10,11,13,17], focusing on slightly different sets of security properties. For example, according to [4] a secure DR based messaging protocol between parties A and B in the presence of an attacker $\mathcal{A}$ should have the following properties (see details in [4]):

- Correctness. If $\mathcal{A}$ is a passive attacker then A (B) receives all the messages sent by B (A) in the correct order.
- Immediate Decryption and Message-Loss Resilience. A message is decrypted upon arrival. In addition, the protocol execution continues even if a message is lost.

© Springer Nature Switzerland AG 2019
S. Dolev et al. (Eds.): CSCML 2019, LNCS 11527, pp. 33–46, 2019.
https://doi.org/10.1007/978-3-030-20951-3_3

- Authenticity. $\mathcal{A}$ cannot modify messages or inject new ones (unless one of the parties' state is compromised).
- Privacy. $\mathcal{A}$ does not learn anything about the contents of the messages (unless one of the parties state is compromised).
- Forward Secrecy (FS). If one of the parties' state is compromised, the previous messages remain confidential.
- Post-Compromise Security (PCS). The parties can recover from a state compromise. Here, we assume that the parties have access to a randomness source and that $\mathcal{A}$ remains passive.
- Randomness leakage/failures. Fresh randomness is required only for achieving Post-Compromise Security (PCS) and is not used to achieve other property.

A DR protocol achieves these properties by: (a) encrypting and authenticating every message with a fresh symmetric key; b) using fresh randomness (that is often used by some Public Key Encryption (PKE) scheme to achieve PCS).

In [4] the DR protocol uses a CKA (public-key ratchets), an AEAD with new keys for every message (symmetric-key ratchets), FS-AEAD hereafter, and a hash function. The CKA can be constructed from any PKE scheme, in particular, any IND-CPA KEM. The use of KEMs is also mentioned in [17] (although the construction in [4] is simpler). The DR scheme can be made quantum-safe[1] by using a quantum-safe KEM, FS-AEAD, and hash function.

To construct a CKA from a KEM, party A (wlog) uses a public key (received from B) to encapsulate a shared secret ss into a ciphertext ct, generates a new pair of secret/public keys (sk, pk) and sends ct and pk to B, at every round. This protocol doubles the communication bandwidth compared to DH CKA where only one public key is sent (assuming the DH and the KEM public keys of the same size). To reduce the bandwidth overhead, [4] mentions that deploying ElGamal KEM allows using the ciphertext as the subsequent public key. Note that ElGamal KEM is not quantum-safe.

Our Contribution:

- We define a new primitive that we call MKEM. An MKEM is derived from a KEM by merging the key generation and the encapsulation procedures. Using it can achieve 50% bandwidth reduction compared to the original CKA protocol with the same KEM. It also may save some of the operations executed during encapsulation. We point out that converting a KEM to an MKEM is not always possible (e. g., BIKE2).
- We present an instantiation of MKEM with BIKE1 [5].
- Following Bindel et al. [8] (who introduced compilers for quantum-safe hybrid Authenticated Key Exchange) we propose two compilers for a hybrid CKA. We believe that this is the first hybrid quantum-safe CKA compiler.

---

[1] We use the terminology quantum-safe to cryptographic algorithms that rely on problems that are believed to be hard even in the presence of quantum computers. For example, cryptographic algorithms that rely on factorization (e. g., RSA) are not considered quantum-safe due to Shor's algorithm [18]. On the other hand for some parameters cryptographic algorithms that rely on the Shortest Vector Problem over lattices are commonly considered quantum-safe.

The Organization of the Paper. Section 2 introduces some notation and background. In Sect. 3 we describe the MKEM scheme and its properties. We present an MKEM instantiation that is based on BIKE1 in Sect. 4, and two hybrid CKA constructions in Sect. 5. Section 6 is the conclusion.

2   Notation and Background

We denote null values and protocol failures by $\perp$. Uniform random sampling from a set W is denoted by $w \xleftarrow{\$} W$. For an algorithm A, we denote its output by $out = A()$ if A is deterministic, and by $out \leftarrow A()$ otherwise. The (Hamming) weight of a vector of bits x is denoted by $wt(x)$. The finite field of 2 elements is denoted by $\mathbb{F}_2$. The xor operation is denoted by $\oplus$. An attacker $\mathcal{A}$ is parameterized by its running time t. Let the term epoch denote the period between two consecutive messages sent by the same party in a DR protocol. During an epoch, the other party can send as many messages as it wishes.

2.1   Continuous Key Agreement (CKA)

A CKA (roughly) models the public-key ratchets in a DR protocol. It can use a PKE of choice and in particular a KEM. This synchronous protocol between parties A and B sends a message msg_i in round i: from A to B if i is even and from B to A otherwise. A fresh shared secret ss_i is agreed by both parties in round i. The state of the parties is denoted by $\gamma^{(A)}$ and $\gamma^{(B)}$, respectively.

Definition 1. *A CKA scheme consists of four algorithms CKA =* (CKA-Init-A, CKA-Init-B, CKA-S, CKA-R)*, where*

- CKA-Init-A *(*CKA-Init-B*) gets an input key k and outputs an initial state. The notation is $\gamma^{(A)} \leftarrow$* CKA-Init-A(k) $(\gamma^{(B)} \leftarrow$ CKA-Init-B$(k))$*, respectively.*
- CKA-S *updates the party's state $\gamma^{(\cdot)}$, generates a message msg_i, and a key ss_i. The notation is: $(\gamma^{(\cdot)'}, msg_i, ss_i) \leftarrow$* CKA-S $(\gamma^{(\cdot)})$*.*
- CKA-R *for an input message msg_i and a state $\gamma^{(\cdot)}$ generates a new state $\gamma^{(\cdot)'}$ and calculates the shared secret. The notation is $(\gamma^{(\cdot)'}, ss_i) \leftarrow$* CKA-R$(\gamma^{(\cdot)}, msg_i)$*.*

CKA-S$(\gamma^{(\cdot)})$ *is a randomized algorithm. For adversarial cases where the source of randomness is controlled by an adversary, we denote the algorithm by* CKA-S$(\gamma^{(\cdot)}, r)$*. Here r denotes the adversary controlled randomness. We use $\mathcal{K}$ to denote the set of initial keys and $\mathcal{SS}$ to denote the set of possible shared secrets ss_i, $i = 1, 2, \ldots$.*

We briefly describe the CKA correctness property and its security game (a full description is found in [4]).

Correctness. A CKA scheme is correct if for every $i = 1, 2, \ldots$, A and B agree (with high probability) on the same (shared) secret ss_i.

Security. A challenger Chal sets the epoch counters $t_A = t_B = 0$, samples a bit $b \xleftarrow{\$} \{0,1\}$, an initial key $k \xleftarrow{\$} \mathcal{K}$, and invokes $\gamma^{(A)} \leftarrow$ CKA-Init-A(k) and $\gamma^{(B)} \leftarrow$ CKA-Init-B(k). Chal receives an input t^* that defines the round on which the challenge oracle may be called.

Let U denote one of the users A or B. An adversary $\mathcal{A}$ interacts with Chal by making oracle calls to one of the following five oracles (in a ping-pong order $A \rightarrow B \rightarrow A \rightarrow \ldots$):

1. Send-U(): increment t_U by 1, perform $(\gamma^U, msg_{t_U}, ss_{t_U}) \leftarrow$ CKA-S(γ^U), and return (msg_{t_U}, ss_{t_U}).
2. Send-U'(r): increment t_U by 1, perform $(\gamma^U, msg_{t_U}, ss_{t_U}) \leftarrow$ CKA-S(γ^U, r), and return (msg_{t_U}, ss_{t_U}). This oracle can be called only if $\max(t_A, t_B) \leq t^* - 2$.
3. Receive-U(): increment t_U by 1 and perform $(\gamma^U, \cdot) =$ CKA-R(γ^U, msg_{t_U}).
4. Corr-U(): return γ^U. A call to this oracle is allowed only when $\max(t_A, t_B) \leq t^* - 2$ or $t_U \geq t^* + \Delta_{CKA}$. ($\Delta_{CKA}$ is defined below).
5. Chall-U(): increment t_U by 1, and perform $(\gamma^U, msg_{t_U}, ss_{t_U}) \leftarrow$ CKA-S(γ^U). If $b = 0$ return (msg_{t_U}, ss_{t_U}), and otherwise set $ss' \xleftarrow{\$} SS$ and return (msg_{t_U}, ss). This oracle can be invoked only when $t_U = t^*$ and if no Corr() or Send-U'() calls were performed less than two epochs before the call.

The game is parameterized by Δ_{CKA}: the minimum number of epochs between t^* and a state that do not contain secrets. When a party reaches epoch $t^* + \Delta_{CKA}$, its state may be revealed to $\mathcal{A}$ (by a Corr-U() call). The game is endless but we consider it terminated if $\gamma^{(A)}$ and $\gamma^{(B)}$ are revealed or when $\mathcal{A}$ outputs a bit b'. $\mathcal{A}$ wins if $b' = b$. The advantage of $\mathcal{A}$ against a CKA with $\Delta_{CKA} = \Delta$ is denoted by $Adv_{ror,\Delta}^{CKA}(\mathcal{A})$.

Definition 2. *A CKA scheme is (t, Δ, ϵ)-secure if for all t-attackers $\mathcal{A}$,*

$$Adv_{ror,\Delta}^{CKA}(\mathcal{A}) \leq \epsilon \tag{1}$$

2.2 Key Encapsulation Mechanism (KEM)

A KEM is a public key primitive. We denote the secret key and public key domains by SK and PK, respectively. A KEM consists of three functions: keygen, encaps, decaps. It is played between parties A and B through three messages (sent over an un-trusted channel). First, A invokes $(sk, pk) \leftarrow$ keygen(1^κ) generating a secret key $sk \in SK$ and a public key $pk \in PK$, and sends pk to B. B uses the received pk and invokes $(ss, ct) \leftarrow$ encaps$(1^\kappa, pk)$ to produce a ciphertext ct and a shared secret $ss \in SS$. B sends ct to A. A uses the received ct and invokes $ss =$ decaps(sk, ct) (in some KEM protocols decaps may occasionally fail. In such cases we say that the output is $\perp$).

3 Merged KEM (MKEM)

We propose MKEM as a primitive for CKA.

Definition 3. *An MKEM is a public-key primitive with two algorithms* $MKEM = (\mathsf{kgc}, \mathsf{decaps})$ *that have the following syntax:*

- kgc. *Take an (implicit) security parameter and a public key pk_0 and output* (sk_1, pk_1, ct_1, ss_1). *Here, (sk_1, pk_1) is a newly generated key pair. If $pk_0 = \perp$ then $ct_1 = ss_1 = \perp$ (i. e., output $(sk_1, pk_1, \perp, \perp) \leftarrow \mathsf{kgc}(\perp)$). Otherwise, use pk_0 to generate a ciphertext ct_1, in a way that pk_1 and a shared secret ss_1 can be retrieved from ct_1 by invoking* decaps.
- decaps: *receive a secret key sk_0 and a ciphertext ct_1 and retrieve the shared secret ss_1 and pk_1, i. e., $(ss_1, pk_1) = \mathsf{decaps}(sk_0, ct_1)$.*

Remark 1. In MKEM, only the initial public key pk_0 is non-secret. For $i \geq 1$, pk_{i-1} and pk_i have no use after calling $(\cdot, pk_i, \cdot, \cdot) \leftarrow \mathsf{kgc}(pk_{i-1})$, and can be deleted immediately after this invocation.

Correctness. Consider the (continuous) iterative sequences: A executes $(sk_0, pk_0, \perp, \perp) \leftarrow \mathsf{kgc}(\perp)$ and sends pk_0 to B; B executes $(sk_1, pk_1^B, ct_1, ss_1^B) \leftarrow \mathsf{kgc}(pk_0)$ and sends ct_1 to A; A repeat the process by executing $(ss_1^A, pk_1^A) = \mathsf{decaps}(sk_0, ct_1)$ and $(sk_2, pk_2^B, ct_2, ss_2^B) \leftarrow \mathsf{kgc}(pk_1)$ and sending ct_2 to B and so on. We say that an MKEM is correct if for each $i \geq 1$, $ss_i^A = ss_i^B$ and $pk_i^A = pk_i^B$.

Security. The security of an MKEM is defined similarly to the IND-CPA and IND-CCA security of a KEM. Let Chal be the game challenger and let $\mathcal{A}$ be an adversary.

- IND-CPA: Chal generates $(sk_1, pk_1, ct_1 = \perp, ss_1 = \perp) \leftarrow \mathsf{kgc}(\perp)$ or $(sk_1, pk_1, ct_1, ss_1) \leftarrow \mathsf{kgc}(pk_0)$, $pk_0 \in \mathcal{PK}$, computes $(\cdot, \cdot, ct_2, ss_2^0) \leftarrow \mathsf{kgc}(pk_1)$, and samples $ss_2^1 \xleftarrow{\$} \mathcal{SS}$, $b \xleftarrow{\$} \{0,1\}$. It hands (ct_1, ct_2, ss_2^b) to $\mathcal{A}$ that outputs a bit b' (indicating whether it believes it received ss_2^0 or ss_2^1). $\mathcal{A}$ wins if $b' = b$.
- IND-CCA - Here, $\mathcal{A}$ also has access to a decaps oracle. This oracle returns $(\hat{ss}, \hat{pk})$ for every input $\hat{ct} \neq ct_1, ct_2$.

Definition 4. *An MKEM scheme is (t, ϵ)-cpa-secure if for all t-attacker $\mathcal{A}$,*

$$Adv_{cpa}^{MKEM}(\mathcal{A}) \leq \epsilon \qquad (2)$$

Figure 1 shows the flow of a CKA that uses an MKEM (Panel (a)) and also compares (Panel (b)) to a CKA based on a KEM. We require that the MKEM is IND-CPA (similarly to KEM, IND-CCA is not required).

Constructing an MKEM scheme is not necessarily simple. Indeed, in Sect. 4 we show how to transform BIKE1 KEM into BIKE1-MKEM and explain why the same technique cannot be applied to BIKE2/3. Consequently, we work on each case separately, without stating a general security relation between an MKEM and its related KEM (although we believe that equivalence exists).

Lemma 1. *Let* MK *be a* (t', ϵ)-*cpa-secure MKEM. Then, the corresponding CKA scheme (denoted* CKA*) is* $(t, \Delta = 0, \epsilon)$-*secure for* $t \approx t'$.

Proof (outline). According to [4] (see Theorem 2 therein): for every KEM K that is (t'', ϵ)-cpa-secure $(t'' \approx t)$, there is an adversary $\mathcal{B}$ for which

$$Adv_{ror,0}^{CKA}(\mathcal{A}) \leq Adv_{cpa}^{KEM}(\mathcal{B}) \tag{3}$$

Replacing the KEM with the analogous MKEM does not change the confidentiality of the messages that $\mathcal{A}$ can see (it sees a ciphertext in both cases).

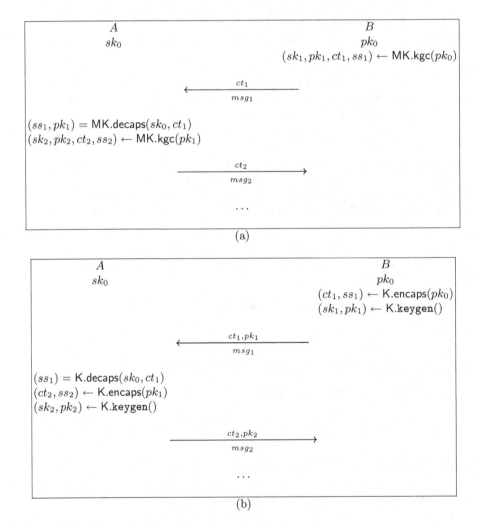

Fig. 1. Panel a: A CKA protocol that uses an MKEM (MK). Panel B: A CKA protocol that uses KEM (K). The initialization $sk_0 \leftarrow$ CKA-Init-A(k), $pk_0 \leftarrow$ CKA-Init-A(k) (not shown in the figures) starts A with sk_0 and B with pk_0. At each subsequent round (i) the new shared secret (ss_i) is generated.

Epoch t_A starts when A sends msg_{2t_A-1} and ends when it sends msg_{2t_A+1}. If in this epoch, $\mathcal{A}$ performs Corr-A(), it gets to see $\gamma^A = sk_{2t_A-1}$ (or $\gamma^A = (sk_{2t_A+1})$ if msg_{2t_A} was already received). This allows $\mathcal{A}$ to decapsulate ct_{2t_A} (resp. ct_{2t_A+2}) and extract (ss_{2t_A}, pk_{2t_A}) (resp. $(ss_{2t_A+2}, pk_{2t_A+2})$). It provides no information on sk_{2t_A} $(resp.ss_{2t_A+2})$ to $\mathcal{A}$, by the properties of the underlying KEM. Consequently, $\Delta = 0$ also when using MKEM.   □

Remark 2. In the proof of Lemma 1 if $\mathcal{A}$ gets to see some pk_i, $i \geq 1$ value it may be able to decrypt/decapsulate ct_i (that was derived from pk_i) and obtain ss_i. However by the properties of the underlying KEM, $\mathcal{A}$ cannot obtain sk_i.

4   BIKE-MKEM

BIKE [5] is a suite of 3 KEMs (BIKE1, BIKE2, BIKE3) submitted to the NIST Post-Quantum Cryptography (PQC) project ([2]). They are IND-CPA secure KEMs. BIKE1/2/3 use Quasi Cyclic - Moderate Density Parity Check (MDPC) codes, to enjoy shorter keys than McEliece KEM [7]. Figure 2 outlines BIKE1/2/3, and full details are available in [5].

The computations of BIKE are executed over $\mathcal{R} := \mathbb{F}_2[X]/\langle X^r - 1\rangle$, for the parameter r. Denote the (Hamming) weights of the secret key $sk = (sk_0, sk_1)$ and the errors vector e by w and t, respectively. Concrete BIKE1 parameters for NIST Level-1 are $|pk| = |ct| = 20,326$, $|ss| = 256$ $r = 10,163$, $w = 142$, and $t = 134$. BIKE1/2/3 are IND-CPA KEM because decoding failures may occur, at some low rate, estimated to be at most 10^{-8}. Therefore, and also to achieve forward secrecy, BIKE1/2/3 use ephemeral keys.

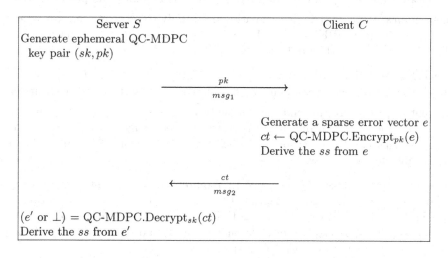

Fig. 2. A general description of BIKE1/2/3 protocol.

4.1 BIKE1-MKEM Transformation

Figure 3 shows the proposed BIKE1-MKEM. For every $X \in \{pk, sk, ct, e\}, i = \{0, 1\}$ X consists of two equal length halves $(X[0], X[1])$ (e. g., $pk = (pk[0], pk[1])$). We explain the elements of the protocol below.

- kgc(pk_0). Receive $pk_0 \in \mathcal{PK}$ as input. Generate a secret key sk_1 with odd weights of $\approx w/2$ (for $sk_1[0]$ and for $sk_1[1]$). Generate $g \xleftarrow{\$} \mathcal{R}$ and calculate the public key $pk_1 = (g \cdot sk_1[1], \ g \cdot sk_1[0])$. Sample $b_0, b_1 \xleftarrow{\$} \{0, 1\}$ and set $pk_1' = (pk_1[0] \oplus b_0, pk_1[1] \oplus b_1)$ (see Remark 4 for the requirement on pk_1'). Subsequently, generate an error vector $e \xleftarrow{\$} \mathcal{R}$ with weight t and use pk_1' and pk_0 to encrypt it to a ciphertext $ct = (pk_0[0] \cdot pk_1'[0] + e_0, \ pk_0[1] \cdot pk_1'[1] + e_1)$. Hash the error vector e to generate the value ss (which is the shared secret). Output sk, pk_1, ct, and ss.
- decaps(sk_0, ct). Receive $sk_0 \in \mathcal{SK}$ as input. Compute the syndrome $synd = ct[0] \cdot sk_0[0] + ct[1] \cdot sk_0[0]$ and decode $synd$ (with a QC-MDPC decoder) to extract the error vector e'. If the decoding succeeds and also $wt(e') = t$, calculate

$$pk_1' = (pk_1'[0], pk_1'[1])$$
$$= \left(pk_0^{-1}[0] \left(ct[0] - e'[0] \right), \ pk_0^{-1}[1] \left(ct[1] - e'[1] \right) \right)$$

(see Remark 5 for how to calculate $pk_0^{-1}[0]$ and $pk_0^{-1}[1]$). If $pk_1'[i]$, $i = 0, 1$ is even set $pk_1'[i] = pk_1'[i] \oplus 1$. Set $pk_1 = (pk_1'[0], pk_1'[1])$ and derive the shared secret ss by hashing e'.

Remark 3. The encapsulation in BIKE1 (which is a KEM) samples a random message $m \xleftarrow{\$} \{0, 1\}^n$. The decapsulation needs only to retrieve the error vector but not m itself. In BIKE1-MKEM the decapsulation needs to extract both the shared secret ss and the public key pk_1.

Remark 4. In BIKE1 MKEM we replace m with $pk_1 = (pk_1[0], pk_1[1]) \in \mathcal{PK} = \{0, 1\}^n$-with-even-weight. Thus, we need to convert it to be a uniform random element in $\{0, 1\}^n$. To this end, we sample two bits $b_i \xleftarrow{\$} \{0, 1\}$, $i = 0, 1$, and xor them to the least significant bit of $pk_1[i]$. During decapsulation (after extracting pk_1'), decaps checks if one of its halves has even weight, and flips its least significant bit accordingly.

Remark 5. The values $pk_0^{-1}[0], pk_0^{-1}[1]$, required to retrieve pk_1, can be calculated during either kgc or decaps (they are invertible by the definition of BIKE1). In the first case we extend the "structure" of the secret key to $sk_1 = (sk_1[0], sk_1[1], pk_0^{-1}[0], pk_0^{-1}[1])$ and in the second case we change it into $sk_1 = (sk_1[0], sk_1[1], pk_0[0], pk_0[1])$, respectively.

Correctness. The correctness of BIKE1-MKEM follows by inspecting the flows, up to possible decoding failures that, for BIKE1-MKEM occur at a Decoding Failure Rate (DFR) $\leq 10^{-8}$.

$(\mathbf{sk_1}, \mathbf{pk_1}, \mathbf{ct}, \mathbf{ss}) \leftarrow \mathsf{kgc}(\mathbf{pk_0})$	$(\mathbf{ss}, \mathbf{pk}) = \mathsf{decaps}(\mathbf{sk_0}, \mathbf{ct})$
$sk_1 \xleftarrow{\$} \mathcal{R},$ $\quad wt(sk_1[0]), \, wt(sk_1[1])$ is odd and $\approx w/2$ $g \xleftarrow{\$} \mathcal{R}$ of odd weight $pk = (g \cdot sk_1[1], g \cdot sk_1[0])$ $b_0, b_1 \xleftarrow{\$} \{0, 1\}$ $pk_1' = (pk_1[0] \oplus b_0, pk_1[1] \oplus b_1)$ $e \xleftarrow{\$} \mathcal{R}^2$ such that $wt(e[0]) + wt(e[1]) = t$ $ct = (pk_0[0] \cdot pk_1'[0] + e[0],$ $\quad pk_0[1] \cdot pk_1'[1] + e[1])$ $ss = \mathtt{Parallel\_SHA}^{384}(e)$	$synd = ct[0] \cdot sk_0[0] + ct[1] \cdot sk_0[1]$ $e' = \mathrm{BIKE.decode}(synd, sk')$ Abort if $(e' = \bot)$ Abort if $wt(e') \neq t$ $pk_1' = (pk_0^{-1}[0](ct[0] - e'[0]),$ $\quad pk_0^{-1}[1](ct[1] - e'[1]))$ If $wt(pk_1'[0])$ is even $pk_1'[0] = pk_1'[0] \oplus 1$ If $wt(pk_1'[1])$ is even $pk_1'[1] = pk_1'[1] \oplus 1$ $pk_1 = (pk_1'[0], pk_1'[1])$ $ss = \mathtt{Parallel\_SHA}^{384}(e')$

Fig. 3. BIKE1 MKEM. Here, note that for every $X \in \{pk_0, sk_0, pk_1, sk_1, e, ct\}$, X consists of two equal length halves $(X[0], X[1])$ (e.g., $ct = (ct[0], ct[1])$). $\mathtt{Parallel\_SHA}^{384}$ is the hash function (that was optimized for performance) used by BIKE [5].

Lemma 2. *Let BIKE1-KEM be a (t, ϵ)-cpa-secure KEM. Then, BIKE1-MKEM is a (t, ϵ)-cpa-secure MKEM.*

Proof. Let $\mathcal{A}$ be an adversary against BIKE1-MKEM. We construct an adversary $\mathcal{B}$ against the IND-CPA property of BIKE1. $\mathcal{B}$ receives a triple (pk, ct, ss_b) and attempts to guess $b = \{0, 1\}$ as described before. It hands (pk, ct, ss_b) to $\mathcal{A}$ and outputs the same bit that $\mathcal{A}$ outputs. $\mathcal{A}$ cannot distinguish a ciphertext that was generated by BIKE1-KEM from a ciphertext generated by BIKE1-MKEM, because the generation is equivalent. Therefore,

$$Adv_{cpa}^{BIKE1-MKEM}(\mathcal{A}) \leq Adv_{cpa}^{BIKE1-KEM}(\mathcal{B}) \leq \epsilon \qquad (4)$$

(we consider the same t for both $\mathcal{A}$ and $\mathcal{B}$). $\qquad\square$

4.2 CKA, MKEM and DFR

This section discusses the difficulties that arise from using a KEM/MKEM that has non-negligible DFR (e.g., BIKE1) for constructing a CKA[2]. Consider, the case in the DR protocol of [4], where (wlog) A sends a $msg_i = (ct, pk)$ to B, and B cannot decapsulate it (due to a decapsulation error). In this case the DR protocol stalls: B ignores msg_i and leaves its epoch counter t_B unchanged. A that does not expect an acknowledgement, continues to use the "bad" ciphertext

---

[2] CKA uses ephemeral keys for both KEM and MKEM. This protects the scheme from attacks that may exploit decapsulation failures, such as [12] in the context of QC-MDPC codes. We note that CKA is aborted (and subsequently re-initialized) upon encountering a decapsulation failure.

ct for its subsequent messages, during the epoch that has "no reason" to change. The motivation for not sending an acknowledgement in response to msg_i is: (a) the DR protocol is asynchronous; (b) avoid a Denial of Service (DoS) situation that occurs when $\mathcal{A}$ deliberately sends "bad" messages to B that cannot be decapsulated. Here, sending (a failure) "acknowledgement" would overload the network.

The DFR of BIKE1-MKEM is at most 10^{-8}. We argue that this can be tolerated from the practical viewpoint. Consider a user that performs $10,000$ conversations, using $10,000$ epochs. Every epoch includes at least one message. Even in this extreme scenario, the user is expected to experience a decoding failure at most once. From the practical viewpoint, it means that BIKE1-MKEM is correct 99.999999% of the time.

A general treatment for DFRs in DR protocols is left as a future work, but we provide here, some practical remedies.

1. A messaging application can offer "refresh"/"restart" functionality as commonly done in many applications. When a user expects messages but notices that none arrive for a "long" period of time he can invoke a "restart"/"refresh" for the conversation. This alleviates inconvenience inflicted by decoding errors. Stalls due to DoS attacks are captured in [4].
2. A messaging application can use a timer. If no response arrives after a long period of time the application can automatically restart the connection.
3. A receiver who fails to decapsulate a message can alert the sender. This approach is not ideal because it can lead to a DoS attack. Unless, the receiver can distinguish between benign decapsulation errors and maliciously-sent "bad" messages. An example for such case is the Public Key Secure-Messaging (PKSM) of [4].

5   A Hybrid CKA Constructions

Currently, new standards for quantum-safe key exchange, encryption and signatures are developed, but no finalize vetted schemes are available for immediate deployment (the NIST process [2] is expected to last a few more years). However, threats (at least theoretical) to current CKAs exist: recorded sessions that are secure in the classical world may be broken in a Post-Quantum (PQ) setting. A hybrid approach that combines a classical and a quantum-safe scheme seems to be a prudent approach, hoping to achieve post-quantum security without taking the risk of a premature transition to an un-vetted scheme. To this end, some hybrid Key Exchange (KEX) protocols and combiners have been recently suggested (constructions and useful survey are given in [8]).

We extend the list of hybrid KEX/AKE/SSH with a new notion, of a Hybrid CKA (H-CKA). Concretely, we propose two constructions. Parallel H-CKA and Interleaved H-CKA, both using the hybrid KEM of [8].

Parallel H-CKA. This is a combination of two CKA protocols: classical CKA^c and quantum-safe CKA^q (as illustrated in Fig. 4). Here, $\gamma_1^A = (sk^c, sk^q)$ ←CKA-Init-A(k^c, k^q) and $\gamma_2^B = (pk^c, pk^q)$ ←CKA-Init-B(k^c, k^q), where $k^c, k^q \in \mathcal{K}$, $pk^c \in \mathcal{PK}^c$, $pk^q \in \mathcal{PK}^q$ and sk^c, sk^q are the associated secret keys.

– The procedure $\big(\gamma', msg_i = (ct_i^c, ct_i^q), ss_i\big)$ ←CKA-S(γ): (1) calculate (in parallel)

$$(sk_i^c, pk_i^c, ct_i^c, ss_i^c) \leftarrow \mathsf{MK}^c.\mathsf{kgc}(pk_{i-1}^c)$$
$$(sk_i^q, pk_i^q, ct_i^q, ss_i^q) \leftarrow \mathsf{MK}^q.\mathsf{kgc}(pk_{i-1}^q)$$

(2) apply a combiner (e. g., as in [8]) $ss_i = \mathsf{combine}(ss_i^c, ss_i^q, msg_i)$ and generate the shared secret ss_i; (3) set $\gamma' = (sk_i^c, sk_i^q)$.
– The procedure (γ', ss_i) ←CKA-R(γ, msg_i): (1) decapsulate (ct_i^c, ct_i^q) to extract $(ss_i^c, ss_i^q, pk_i^c, pk_i^q)$; (2) set $\gamma = (pk_i^c, pk_i^q)$ and apply the same combiner as above.

There are no additional (sub)rounds in the Parallel H-CKA compared to CKA. However, the communication bandwidth is the sum of the bandwidths of the two involved schemes. We note that the H-CKA construction uses MKEMs, but it also possible to use KEMs instead.

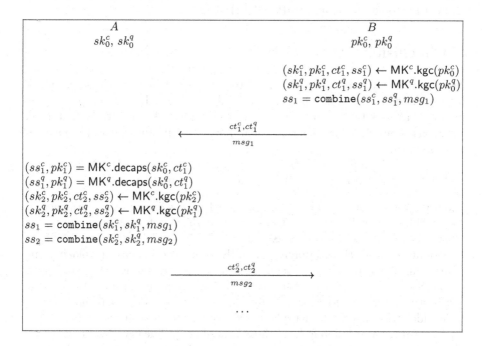

Fig. 4. Parallel Hybrid CKA (H-CKA) combining a classicical security and quantum-safe MKEMs (MK^c and MK^q, respectively). The combiner `combine` is one of the options of [8].

Interleaved CKA. An Interleaved CKA uses a CKA that is $(t, 2\Delta, \epsilon)$-secure instead of (t, Δ, ϵ)-secure. This means that recovering from a state compromise takes 2Δ rounds rather than only Δ. By [4], when a CKA uses KEM, we have $\Delta = 0$ (for comparison note that using DH has $\Delta = 2$). Therefore, our interleaved schemes are at least $(t, 1, \epsilon)$-secure. Instantiating an interleaved H-CKA can be done in two ways (deploying a "third ratchet").

1. Option 1. We break Parallel H-CKA into two interleaved flows: (1) $B \to A$: ct_1^c; (2) $A \to B : ct_1^q$ (3) $B \to A : ct_2^c$; (4) $A \to B : ct_2^q$. The sequence is repeated. The associated shared secrets of each round are ss_1^c, ss_1^q, ss_2^c, ss_2^q, ... In an odd round number i, $ss_i = \texttt{combine}(ss_{i/2}^c, ss_{i/2}^q)$. In an even round i, $ss_i = \texttt{combine}(ss_{i/2-1}^q, ss_{i/2}^c)$.
2. Option 2. We send the same messages msg_i as in Parallel H-CKA, but adding a Boolean toggle flag f to γ, where: if f = true CKA-S and CKA-R operate as before but $ss_i = \texttt{combine}(ct_{i-1}^c, ct_i^q)$; if f = false no message will be sent/received and $ss_i = \texttt{combine}(ct_i^c, ct_i^q)$.

The bandwidth in Option 1 is reduced (hopefully, by 50%) compared to Parallel H-CKA. The bandwidth in Option 2 is the same as in Parallel H-CKA but the number of rounds is halved. The tradeoff implied by using Interleaved H-CKA is that Δ is increased by at least 1. This can be tolerated for achieving better bandwidth/latency compared to Parallel H-CKA.

6   Conclusion

The new primitive MKEM is designed to reduce the bandwidth of the CKA protocol used by the DR scheme. It can also be used by any cryptographic protocol that uses two (or more) back to back KEMs. A concrete instantiation that is based on BIKE1, shows that it can have a significant impact (of 50%) on the bandwidth.

We are not sure if every KEM can be converted into an MKEM and if the bandwidth reduction is necessarily significant. Here are two examples.

– Many KEMs are based on a PKE scheme where the encryption is designed to operate on "short" messages. Consider Kyber512 [9] for instance. Its public key has 736 bytes, its ciphertext has 800 bytes, and it encrypts a 32-byte random message. Here, applying our MKEM method is easy (replacing one randomized value with another). However, this will reduce the bandwidth from $800 + 736 = 1,536$ to $800 + 704 = 1,504$ bytes i. e., save $32/1536 \approx 2\%$. It is still worth doing (at practically no cost), but the impact is modest.
– Consider BIKE2/3 that encrypt an error vector. This error vector has a specific weight that is different from the weight of the public key. Here, encrypting the public key (instead of the error vector) requires some transformation from different sets of bit strings (that have different cardinalities).

We suggest that H-CKA (Parallel H-CKA and Interleaved H-CKA) can be used by messaging applications to hopefully achieve quantum-safe security but without giving up the classical security.

We raised the difficulty of designing a general CKA primitive and DR scheme (beyond the practical proposed remedies) that can use KEMs that have a non-negligible DFR. This is left as an open problem.

Acknowledgments. This research was supported by: The Israel Science Foundation (grant No. 1018/16); The BIU Center for Research in Applied Cryptography and Cyber Security, in conjunction with the Israel National Cyber Bureau in the Prime Minister's Office; the Center for Cyber Law & Policy at the University of Haifa in conjunction with the Israel National Cyber Directorate in the Prime Minister's Office.

References

1. Messenger secret conversations: Technical whitepaper (2013). https://fbnewsroomus.files.wordpress.com/2016/07/secret_conversations_whitepaper-1.pdf
2. Nist:post-quantum cryptography - call for proposals, September 2017. https://csrc.nist.gov/Projects/Post-Quantum-Cryptography
3. Whatsapp encryption overview: Technical white paper, December 2017. https://www.whatsapp.com/security/WhatsApp-Security-Whitepaper.pdf
4. Alwen, J., Coretti, S., Dodis, Y.: The double ratchet: security notions, proofs, and modularization for the signal protocol. Cryptology ePrint Archive, Report 2018/1037 (2018). https://eprint.iacr.org/2018/1037
5. Aragon, N., et al.: BIKE: bit flipping key encapsulation (2017)
6. Bellare, M., Singh, A.C., Jaeger, J., Nyayapati, M., Stepanovs, I.: Ratcheted encryption and key exchange: the security of messaging. In: Katz, J., Shacham, H. (eds.) CRYPTO 2017. LNCS, vol. 10403, pp. 619–650. Springer, Cham (2017). https://doi.org/10.1007/978-3-319-63697-9_21
7. Bernstein, D.J., et al.: Classic McEliece: conservative code-based cryptography (2017)
8. Bindel, N., Brendel, J., Fischlin, M., Goncalves, B., Stebila, D.: Hybrid key encapsulation mechanisms and authenticated key exchange. Cryptology ePrint Archive, Report 2018/903, September 2018. http://eprint.iacr.org/
9. Bos, J., et al.: CRYSTALS - Kyber: a CCA-secure module-lattice-based KEM. Cryptology ePrint Archive, Report 2017/634 (2017). https://eprint.iacr.org/2017/634
10. Cohn-Gordon, K., Cremers, C., Dowling, B., Garratt, L., Stebila, D.: A formal security analysis of the signal messaging protocol. In: 2017 IEEE European Symposium on Security and Privacy (EuroS P), pp. 451–466, April 2017. https://doi.org/10.1109/EuroSP.2017.27
11. Durak, F.B., Vaudenay, S.: Bidirectional asynchronous ratcheted key agreement without key-update primitives. Cryptology ePrint Archive, Report 2018/889 (2018). https://eprint.iacr.org/2018/889
12. Guo, Q., Johansson, T., Stankovski, P.: A key recovery attack on MDPC with CCA security using decoding errors. In: Cheon, J.H., Takagi, T. (eds.) ASIACRYPT 2016. LNCS, vol. 10031, pp. 789–815. Springer, Heidelberg (2016). https://doi.org/10.1007/978-3-662-53887-6_29

13. Jaeger, J., Stepanovs, I.: Optimal channel security against fine-grained state compromise: the safety of messaging. In: Shacham, H., Boldyreva, A. (eds.) CRYPTO 2018. LNCS, vol. 10991, pp. 33–62. Springer, Cham (2018). https://doi.org/10.1007/978-3-319-96884-1_2

14. Lund, J.: Signal partners with microsoft to bring end-to-end encryption to skype, October 2018. https://signal.org/blog/skype-partnership

15. Marlinspike, M.: Open whisper systems partners with Google on end-to-end encryption for allo (2013). https://signal.org/blog/allo/

16. Perrin, T., Marlinspike, M.: The double ratchet algorithm. GitHub wiki (2016)

17. Poettering, B., Rösler, P.: Asynchronous ratcheted key exchange. Cryptology ePrint Archive, Report 2018/296 (2018). https://eprint.iacr.org/2018/296

18. Shor, P.W.: Algorithms for quantum computation: discrete logarithms and factoring. In: Proceedings 35th Annual Symposium on Foundations of Computer Science, pp. 124–134, November 1994. https://doi.org/10.1109/SFCS.1994.365700

Covert Channel Cyber-Attack over Video Stream DCT Payload

(Copyright Protection Algorithm for Video and Audio Streams)

Yoram Segal$^{(\boxtimes)}$ and Ofer Hadar

Communication Systems Engineering Department,
Ben Gurion University of the Negev (BGU), 84105 Beer-Sheva, Israel
yoramse@post.bgu.ac.il

Abstract. The two main cyber-attack techniques via video packets are based on using the packet header or the payload. Most of the standard software protection tools easily detect anomalies in headers since there are fewer places to embed the malicious content. Moreover, due to the relatively small header size, such attacks are limited by the data volumes that can transfer. On the other hand, a cyber-attack that uses video packets' payload can effectively conceal much more information and produce covert channels. Multimedia covert channels provide reasonable bandwidth and long-lasting transmission streams, suitable for planting malicious information and therefore used as an exploit alternative. The primary focus of this article is a proof of concept of cyber-attack that conceals malicious data in a video payload in the compressed domain, using steganography (in real time). This malicious data is extracted using a covert channel and a malware (that had previously planted at the end user side), on the other side. Additionally, after the implementation of the attack, it is necessary to review its parameters and conclude what the optimal parameters to use in different video scenarios.

In this paper, we will demonstrate attacks that take advantage of compressed domain video payload.

It is important to note that this method can be used as a method of copyright protection.

Keywords: Exploit · Invisible covert channel · Steganography · Watermarking · Cyber · Steno objects · Intra prediction · Inter prediction · Discrete Cosine Transform · DCT · Motion vectors

1 Introduction and Motivation

New multimedia platforms are introduced to our lives frequently (e.g., Spotify, CellcomTV, Netflix) and the relative part of digital media in internet traffic is increasing. Current studies [1] show that video traffic reached up to 73% of consumer internet traffic in 2016 and predicted to reach 82% by the year 2021.

This work was supported by the Israel National Cyber Bureau.

H.264, also known as MPEG-4 AVC (Advanced Video Coding) and H.265, are widely used in the new multimedia platforms. H.264\H.265 is suitable for a wide range of applications such as video conferencing, TV, storage, video streaming, surveillance and others. Video steganography over H264 is the process of secretly inserting and concealing data within videos. Steganography has been helpful in protecting media copyrights (via digital watermarks). On end, sophisticated users have used steganography as means of communication, transmitting hidden messages without anyone, but the intended recipient/s, being aware of it. Lately, newspaper reports have indicated that some users are using malicious software to break into smartphones, computers and even internet-connected televisions.

Multiple techniques have been reported for steganography and watermarking. An overview of digital image steganography is presented in [2]. In [3] basic building blocks for steganography in the compressed video were examined: the embedding operation and the choice of embedding alternatives.

It is shown in [4] that Facebook Cover Photos can effectively hide information using Discrete Cosine Transform (DCT) coefficient embedding algorithms [5]. Watermarking solves the challenge of illegal video distribution and manipulation. Watermark's robustness is critical for avoiding attackers' watermark disruption [6, 7]. Some methodologies developed in [5] for compressing the robustness of different watermarking techniques. The watermarking algorithm presented in [9] is embedding the watermark into the video by adjusting intermediate frequency coefficients.

An innovative approach for cyber-attack applying a Smart threshold and Anomaly Correction to compressed domain DCT coefficients described in [9]. In this paper, we focus on manipulations of compressed domain Error estimation of DCT coefficients.

Video compression protocols, such as H.264, for example, divide video frames to Macro Blocks (MB), perform pixel predictions, calculate errors between predicted values and original values, perform DCT transform on the error results and then quantization of the obtained DCT coefficients. We conceal malicious data in a video payload using steganography [11] algorithm that operates in the frequency domain and embeds binary codewords into a selected set of DCT coefficients.

The Cyber-attack algorithm takes advantage of lack of sensitivity of movie viewers to small deviations of Macro-Block (object) values from their original ones. Viewers are not likely to notice the minor noise of MBs. Moreover, since the viewer does not know the accurate real value of MBs in the original video movie, they are not likely to notice minor changes that affect MBs values accuracy.

2 Glossary

To complement the needed background, fundamental glossaries are presented in the following section.

Steganography: The art of data hiding within data. Steganography is an encryption technique that means to conceal the very existence of a message in oppose to cryptography that means to protect the content of a message.

Watermarking: The method of embedding data into digital multimedia content, not necessarily in a hidden manner. This is used to verify the credibility of the content or to recognize the identity of the content's owner. Watermarking has an additional requirement of robustness to possible attacks.

Covert channel: Communication paths that were neither designed nor intended to transfer information at all. These channels are typically used by untrustworthy programs to leak information to their owner while performing a service for another Program.

Compression: The conversion of information to a representation or form that requires fewer bits than the original. This is useful for transmitting across network as well as for storing. Two types of compression: Lossless compression: decompressed image is the same as the original. Lossy compression: decompressed image is not the same as the original but looks similar.

Intra Prediction: Prediction of a current video data block (e.g. macroblock) is created from previously coded block in the same frame. Exploiting the similarity to neighboring blocks, spatial redundancies.

Inter Prediction: Prediction of a current video data block (e.g. macroblock) is created from one or more past or future frames (i.e. reference frames). The accuracy of the prediction can usually be improved by compensating for motion between the reference frame(s) and the current frame. Exploiting the temporal redundancies.

DCT (Discrete Cosine Transform): A Fourier related transform which expresses a finite sequence of data points in terms of a sum of cosine functions oscillating at different frequencies. DCT is highly useful for lossy compression most of the signal information tends to be concentrated in a few low-frequency components of the DCT, and small high-frequency components can be discarded. The transform is calculated using a scaling matrix (S_f), combined with the quantization process into (M_f) where:

$$M_f \approx \frac{S_f \times 2^{15}}{Q_{step}} \qquad (1)$$

Quantization: Mapping of a signal with a range of values X to a quantized signal with a reduced range of values Y. Using fewer bits to represent the same signal in a lossy manner. Usually preformed after DCT conversion and described as division by a quantization step size, Q step, then rounding the result:

$$Q = round\left(\frac{1}{Q_{step}}\right) \qquad (2)$$

Entropy Coding: Removes statistical redundancy in the data by representing commonly occurring code words by short binary codes in a lossless manner. Huffman coding is a type of entropy coding that use prefix code for each symbol in an efficient way.

Motion Vectors: A two-dimensional vector used for inter-prediction that provides an offset from the coordinates in the decoded picture to the coordinates in a reference picture.

Median Vector: A two-dimensional vector (2D) that represents the estimated motion vector of a macroblock. It calculated from its neighbors. In video compression, instead of transmitting the macroblock motion vector, we are carrying the difference between the original motion vector and its median vector (predicted motion vector). A 2D motion vector has two components - the X component and the Y component. The median vector calculated per component. All X components from all neighbors motion vectors grouped into one sorted array. The value in the array that separates the higher half from the lower half is determinate as the X component value of the median vector. The Y component will be calculating in the same way.

YUV: YUV is a color encoding system that takes human perception into account in the encoding process, allowing reduced bandwidth for chrominance components and enabling transmission errors and compression artifacts to be more efficiently masked by the human perception than using a RGB representation. The YUV model defines a color space in terms of one luma component (Y) which represents the brightness, and two chrominance components (UV) which represent color. YUV is computed from linear RGB as follows:

$$Y = 0.299R + 0.587G + 0.114B \tag{3}$$

$$U \approx 0.492(B - Y) \tag{4}$$

$$V \approx 0.877(R - Y) \tag{5}$$

DES Encryption: The Data Encryption Standard (DES) uses a block cipher algorithm that takes a fixed length string of plaintext bits and transforms it through a series of complicated operations into another cipher text bit string of the same length. A key is used to customize the transformations, so decryption is only possible with the knowledge of the key used in the encryption process.

Reed–Solomon Code: Reed-Solomon codes are group of error correcting codes commonly used in commercial and consumer technologies and communications. The codes operate on a block of data treated as a set of finite field elements called symbols. The codes can detect and correct multiple symbol errors, depending on the number of symbols used in the code for checking: By adding t check symbols to the data, a Reed–Solomon code can detect any combination of up to and including t erroneous symbols, or correct up to and including t/2 symbols.

Data Packet Structure: A Typical data packet contains a header, payload and trailer. A header usually contains instructions about the data carried in the packet (such as length, numbering information and source/destination address). The payload represents the body of the packet and contains the actual data the packet is delivering to the destination. A trailer usually contains bits marking the end of the data in the payload and error checking bits.

ARP Spoofing: ARP spoofing, ARP cache poisoning, or ARP poison routing, is a technique by which an attacker sends (spoofed) Address Resolution Protocol (ARP) messages onto a local area network. Generally, the aim is to associate the attacker's MAC address with the IP address of another host, such as the default gateway, causing any traffic meant for that IP address to be sent to the attacker instead. ARP spoofing may allow an attacker to intercept data frames on a network, modify the traffic, or stop all traffic. Often the attack is used as an opening for other attacks, such as denial of service, man in the middle, or session hijacking attacks. The attack can only be used on networks that use ARP, and requires attacker have direct access to the local network segment to be attacked (Wikipedia).

MSE (Mean Square Error): The mean squared error (MSE) measures the average of the squares of the errors—that is, the average squared difference between the estimated values $\hat{Y}_i$ and the real value Y_i. The MSE is a measure of the quality of an estimator—it is always non-negative, and values closer to zero are better. If a vector of n predictions generated from a sample of n data points on all variables, Y is the vector of observed values of the variable being predicted $\hat{Y}$, then the within-sample MSE of the predictor is computed as:

$$MSE = \frac{1}{n}\sum_{i-1}^{n}\left(Y_i - \hat{Y}_i\right)^2 \qquad (6)$$

PSNR (Peak Signal-to-Noise Ratio): Peak signal-to-noise ratio describes the ratio between the maximum possible power of a signal and the power of corrupting noise that affects the fidelity of its representation and is usually expressed in terms of the logarithmic decibel scale. PSNR is most easily defined via the mean squared error (MSE). If Here, MAXI is the maximum possible pixel value of the image then the PSNR (in dB) is defined as:

$$PSNR = 10\,log_{10}\left(\frac{MAXI^2}{MSE}\right) \qquad (7)$$

SSIM (Structural Similarity Index): The structural similarity (SSIM) index is a method for predicting the perceived quality of digital images and videos and is used for measuring the similarity between two images. The measurement is based on a comparison to an unaltered image that is used as a reference. SSIM is designed to improve on traditional methods such as PSNR and MSE. The measure between two windows x and y of common size N × N is (Wikipedia):

$$s(x,y) = \frac{\left(2\mu_x\mu_y + C_1\right) + \left(2\sigma_{xy} + C_2\right)}{\left(\mu_x^2 + \mu_y^2 + C_1\right)\left(\sigma_x^2 + \sigma_y^2 + C_2\right)} \tag{8}$$

With: μ_x, μ_y the average and σ_x^2, σ_y^2 the variance, σ_{xy} the covariance of x and y. C_1, C_2 two variables to stabilize the division with weak denominator (see Wikipedia for more details).

3 Objective

The primary objective of this article is to supply proof of concept to a covert channel that is based on H264 DCT coefficients manipulations. We demonstrate a cyber-attack that conceals malicious data in a video payload, in the compressed domain, using steganography (in real time). It will be used as a remote-control tool of malicious code that already exist at the victim side. The video stream allows as communicate with the malicious code via our covert channel. This new method let us take advantage on the user device without any operating system constrains or firewall restrictions.

After the implementation of the attack, it is necessary to review its parameters and conclude what are the optimal parameters to be used in different scenarios contexts.

The suggested attack will be implemented in the H.264 standard since it is widely used and offer flexibility in the compression process. The H.264 standard defines a syntax for compressed video and a method for decoding this syntax to produce a displayable video sequence. The covert channel that connects the malware and the adversary will be the positions of DCT coefficients in the block, a known dictionary and the malicious data concealed within the coefficients' values.

The attack was implemented in MATLAB environment with an H.264 open source codec.

To measure the quality of the attack, we performed several tests to ensure high accuracy in detection of the malicious data upon receiving the infected H.264 bit-stream. Other quality metrics used are the well-known MSE (mean square error) and PSNR (peak sound to noise ratio) metrics to ensure that the additive infected data do not increase bitrate to a noticeable level.

Since this work deals with concealment of malicious data within DCT coefficients, our primary focus is on the I-macroblocks, in which the residual DCT coefficients are coded and transmitted rather than the motion vectors. P and B-frames consist of I-macroblocks as well as predicted macroblocks, while I-frames merely consist of I-macroblock.

Cyber protection algorithms have two basic models: Detection and Prevention. Detection is an alerting algorithm that typically uses signature analysis or statistical anomaly detection methods. It has the advantage of being attack specific but may not be able to generalize. The generalization gap is overcome by incorporating some automatic adaptation in the detection processor implementing some learning cycles, which might consider an attack as standard data. Prevention is a process that prevents malicious data from penetrating the site or the system. The Prevention process operates on a regular basis regardless of the existence or non-existence of attack, therefore, providing more general protection compared to the Detection process.

In this research work, we are exploring a real-time Prevention algorithm for H.264 video streams. It is part of a more General Prevention Research (GPR) against attacks that use the video or audio stream payload as a malicious data container.

Payload manipulations produce some artifacts that can be described as noise addition to original video stream images. Modern video coding techniques employ lossy coding schemes, which often create compression artifacts that may lead to degradation of perceived video quality. Payload attack takes advantage of naturally introduced compression artifacts and assumes that the user will not be able to distinguish between compression artifacts and malicious data of covert channel artifacts.

3.1 Attack Perspective

To be able to prevent attack via video, it is necessary to analyze and understand the attacker point of view. Video-based Cyber-attacks are divided into two stages: first, the planting of hostile malware which will perform offensive actions such as: taking control of the device, deleting information, denial of service and so on. The second stage is establishing of a hidden communication channel (covert channel), capable of communicating with the malicious software that was preinstalled and sending to it remote operation commands, such as timing the attack and determining the type of attack. In advanced attacks, the covert channel can be used to manage a rolling event, whereas the attack develops according to the victim's responses. The paper is focused on offensive prevention of the second cyber-attack stage (the covert channel), assuming that the hostile software already exists on the victim system. The first cyber-attack stage is out of the scope of this paper.

Attackers objective is maximizing covert channel bandwidth, thus maximize the amount of malicious data delivered in the stream payload, while minimizing the noise level. There are two types of such video attacks – Online and Offline. Offline attacks based on recorded movies. The attackers have access to or have some movies that they promote. This situation provides attackers with all the time that they need to plant malicious data in the video. Online attacks are much more complicated because of attacks based on intervening between the content streaming server and the user (man-in-the-middle attack) [11]. The online interference needs to guarantee very low latency. Brute-force payload manipulation requires online video transcoding process (decoding and encoding). The transcoding process consumes processing time and increases the latency. Therefore, online attacks will usually be done in the compressed domain and accomplished by manipulating the DCT and the MV components. Unlike the transcoding process, extracting DCT and MV consumes only 10% of the resources that required for full stream transcoding.

Our research to prevent such attacks focused on preventing MV and DCT manipulation. The fundamental concept is based on a random selection of MV and DCT coefficients and performing minor random changes of their values.

The prevention concept is mostly a self-immunization process by which an immune system becomes fortified against some types of malicious data (known as the immunogen). This process described as self-attacking with random parameters such that any attack will be impacted and destroyed by those random changes.

3.2   Infrastructure Implementation Method

In general, the attack method is to establish a covert channel between the attacker and a VLC media player malware that located at the end user PC - a VLC that implement the attack code that created with Matlab and converted to C code (see Fig. 1). The VLC had been planted on the victims' host using social engineering or other known vulnerabilities exploitations. The second step is to partially decompress a bitstream (which addressed to the malware) and conceal malicious data in a video payload using steganography algorithm that operates in the frequency domain and embeds a binary codeword into a selected set of DCT coefficients. Finally, upon receiving the incoming bitstream, the malware must successfully extract the malicious data while decoding the video.

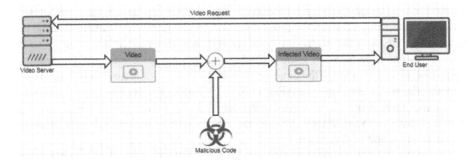

Fig. 1.   Real time man in the middle attack

H.264 provides a clearly defined syntax for representing compressed video and related information (see Fig. 2). Upon receiving a bitstream, a decoder parses the syntax, extracts the parameters and data elements and can then proceed to decode and display video. The syntax is organized hierarchically, from a complete video sequence at the highest level, down to coded macroblocks and blocks.

At the top level, an H.264 sequence consists of a series of 'packets' or Network Adaptation Layer Units (NAL). These can include parameter sets containing key parameters that are used by the decoder to correctly decode the video data and slices, which are coded video frames or parts of video frames. At the next level, a slice represents all or part of a coded video frame and consists of several coded macroblocks, each containing compressed data corresponding to a 16×16 block of displayed pixels in a video frame. At the lowest level, a macroblock contains type information describing the choice of methods used to code the macroblock, prediction information such as coded motion vectors or intra prediction mode information and coded residual data. Understanding the syntax is crucial for accessing the desired location while working in real time and analyzing a bitstream.

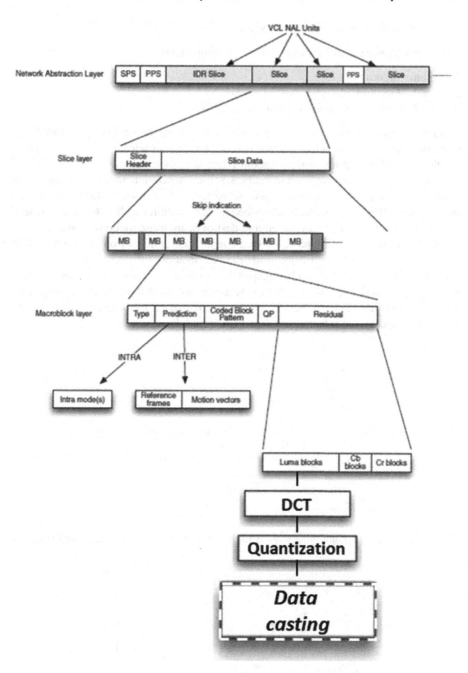

Fig. 2. H.264 protocol hierarchy syntax and data casting location

3.3   Research Structure and Lab Setup

The research program includes the following components:

1. Defense algorithm
2. Attack algorithm
3. Attack envelope (computers, smartphones, IoT)

Our research to prevent such attacks is focused on preventing MV and DCT manipulation. The fundamental concept is based on random selection of MV and DCT coefficients and performing minor random changes of their values.

The prevention concept is essentially a self-immunization process by which an immune system becomes fortified against some types of malicious data (known as the immunogen). This process can be described as self-attacking with random parameters such that any attack will be impacted and destroyed by those random changes.

As part of this research phase, we focus on attacks, initiated from within the LAN environment, thus performed from inside the organization. In order to evaluate covert channel available bandwidth and corresponding video quality degradation and in order to measure video delivery delays due to the attack, we created an attack envelope that uses ARP spoofing [11] for "hijacking" the user requested live channel video stream and replacing it by the infected one (see Figs. 3 and 4).

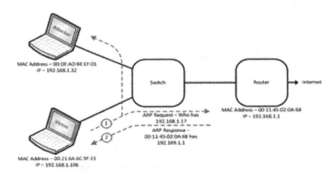

Fig. 3. Attack lab setup indicating stage A of the ARP spoofing used for hijacking the stream

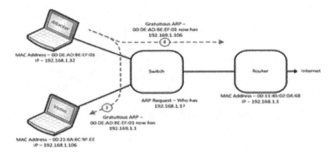

Fig. 4. Attack lab setup indicating stage B of the ARP spoofing used for hijacking the stream

Our measurement results indicate that the delay introduced to the requested live video stream, due to stream hijacking, ranges between 10's to 100's m_{sec}, which is unnoticeable and may be attributed to regular network delays.

Using this method, some of the ARP updates will still arrive from the original real live streaming content server. Therefore, we can expect some temporary disruptions in covert channel transmission (when the user client switches back to the original server). The switch is transparent to the user and only means that covert channel will deliver its malicious content only part of the time when it is the selected streaming server choice.

We use this attack to route the victim's HTTP request through the attacker who manipulates the data. The HTTP video requests are filtered with IPTABLES (Linux networking tool) and changed to a different destination port (and/or address).

As it can see from Fig. 3 and from Fig. 4, In our lab, we performed the following Proof of Concept measurements, to understand the effect of a MITM (Man-in-The-Middle) on the innocent viewer.

Switch the traffic routing through another computer between the Client and Video Server (Layer 3 re-routing only); Perform of simple proxying with SOCAT (TCP listening and forwarding tool). (Layer 4 proxying only); Repacking the video (from one type of stream to another) via FFMPEG, and full transcoding via FFMPEG.

3.4 Attack Algorithm and Related Work

The attack method in the article is based on [6, 7, 10]. In this section we will point out the similarities and differences between the approaches and how they were managed.

The papers mentioned above discuss embedding a watermark in single JPEG picture, therefore use different approach in embedding the watermark. The transition from handling pictures to handling videos required several adjustments such as:

- Work locally (macroblock by macroblock and frame by frame) rather than globally over an entire picture [6, 7]. This was done to comply with the MATLAB based H.264 codec.
- The basic unit on which the algorithm operates is 4×4 macroblock rather than 8×8 as in [9] to comply with the MATLAB based H.264 codec.
- The algorithm mentioned in [6, 7] embedded the watermark to the 1000 largest DCT coefficients (DC excluded). Since our algorithm operates macroblock by macroblock we decided to select DCT coefficients in the medium range frequencies as the algorithm mentioned in [10].
- By embedding the watermark to the medium frequencies, we achieve: robustness to noisy channel – if a noise is added to the video it will not affect the correlation results. Robustness to operations such as high and low pass filter.

To keep a robust attack while adjusting a picture algorithm to videos we have made few assumptions:

- A great advantage for this attack is the lack of need of reference video to determine if a watermark is present in a video or to determine which watermark was embedded [6].

- There is a symmetric secret key that must share between the adversary and the users' decoder. The symmetric secret key contains the location of the DCT coefficients in which we embedded the watermark, the length of a word and many times it duplicated.
- To extract and detect the watermark the decoder must have a copy of the dictionary [7]. The dictionary must be known to both sides but not necessary be secretive.

3.5   Implementation

The malicious data is concealed in the bitstream by embedding a single codeword to luma macroblocks. Although the term 'watermark' is usually used to describe a verification or an authenticity measure, in this subsection, we will refer to the malicious codeword to concealed in a macroblock as a watermark for simplicity.

The DCT watermarking technique in this project has two main characteristics: it operates in the transform domain instead of the spatial domain, and it can extract the watermark from a frame without comparison to an original un-marked image. The implemented technique is suitable for luminance samples of a source frame, or more precisely, for the luminance residual samples.

The H.264 codec used in the MATLAB environment operates on different macroblocks sizes according to the standard [12–14]. However, the residual macroblock which goes through the encoding process has a size of 4×4 (See Table 1).

Table 1. 4×4 macroblock DCT coefficients

DC	2	6	7
3	5	8	13
4	9	12	14
10	11	15	16

The watermark consists of a codeword sequence, which superimposed to some of the coefficients of the full-frame DCT transform. The mark always superimposed to the same set of coefficients in each block. The set of coefficients, which the watermark superimposed to can be in every frequency; however, due to the tradeoff between perceptual invisibility and robustness to compression and other conventional image processing techniques, it is essential to choose the coefficients carefully.

To regain some robustness properly choosing the set of DCT values the mark is superimposed to, and by perceptually hiding it in image areas characterized by high luminance variance is essential. For that reason, the set of coefficients belongs to the medium range frequencies.

There is a tradeoff between the size of the dictionary too and the length of a codeword versus the perceptual quality of a video, long codeword cause greater degradation and use higher bitrate to transmit a single symbol. A part of the research was to examine and construct a codebook with unique codewords. Each codeword is composed of M integers, and in our case since the code is binary, M bits. There are many ways to construct such dictionary, yet after extensive trial and error period the optimal dictionary included 16 codewords, each has 8 bits length. 14 of the codewords used as symbols and two more are signaling words for beginning or ending a transmission between the adversary and the malware.

The dictionary that used in this work is presented in Table 2, the first and last codewords used as signaling symbols:

Table 2. Dictionary

1. 0 0 0 0 1 1 1 1	9. 1 1 0 0 1 1 0 0
2. 0 0 1 1 0 0 1 1	10. 1 1 0 0 0 0 1 1
3. 0 0 1 1 1 1 0 0	11. 1 0 1 0 1 0 1 0
4. 0 1 0 1 0 1 0 1	12. 1 0 1 0 0 1 0 1
5. 0 1 0 1 1 0 1 0	13. 1 0 0 1 1 0 0 1
6. 0 1 1 0 0 1 1 0	14. 1 0 0 1 0 1 1 0
7. 0 1 1 0 1 0 0 1	15. 0 0 0 0 0 0 0 0
8. 1 1 1 1 0 0 0 0	16. 1 1 1 1 1 1 1 1

The primary objective in creating the dictionary was to achieve a highly successful detection rate by the malware. Although a dictionary that is formed by 8 bits codeword can consist of 256 unique codewords, the difference (bitwise) between any two codewords is a single bit. By creating greater Hamming distance (the number of bit differences between two codewords) between any two codewords, the detection, which uses correlation method, produce a significant difference in the correlation result when extracting the suspected codeword and correlating it with all the words in the dictionary. Another means to regain robustness and overcome false detections was to use redundant bits by duplicating a single codeword multiple times and referring to it as a single codeword. Denote the rule in which the adversary embeds the watermark as an embedding rule, and it goes as follows:

Let I be the luma Macro Block (MB) on which the embedding process will perform, T to be the coefficient set in the original bitstream (after integer transform & quantization) and X to be the codeword to embed in the MB.

$$X = \{x_i\}, i \in \text{coefficient set} \tag{9}$$

$$T = \{t_i\}, i \in \text{coefficient set} \tag{10}$$

The data T is added by modifying the selected DCT coefficients according to one of the following formulas:

$$t'_i = t_i + x_i \tag{11}$$

$$ti' = t_i(1 + x_i) \tag{12}$$

$$t_i' = t_i + |t_i| x_i \tag{13}$$

Let T' be the selected manipulated coefficient set to reinsert to the MB, and Y to be the codewords dictionary table.

$$z = \frac{Y \cdot T^*}{M} = \frac{1}{M} \sum_{i \in \text{coefficiant set}} y_i t_i^* \tag{14}$$

The above formula will allow us to determine which codeword was embedded. The Y codeword that yields the most significant z correlation is assumed to be the present in the MB. To find the exact location of the coefficients set we want to mark in a bitstream, a partial decompression is required. The bitstream is composed from NAL (Network Abstraction Layer) unit in the highest syntax layer which is composed of Slices and other control parameter units for the decoder. One layer under is the Slice layer in which a coded unit (frame) is made up of one or more slices. Each slice consists of a Slice Header and Slice Data. The Slice Data is a series of coded macroblocks and skip macroblock that contains no data. In the lowest layer, the Macroblock layer, each coded macroblock contains the following parameters:

- MB type: I, B or P type.
- Prediction information: prediction mode for I MB or reference frames for B/P MB.
- Coded Block Pattern (CBP): indicates which luma and chroma blocks contain non-zero residual elements.
- Quantization parameter: quantization step size.
- Residual data.

Denote the rule in which the malware identifies and extracts the codeword as extracting rule, and it goes as follows: Let I* be the infected luma MB from which we need to extract the codeword and let T* be the corrupted coefficient set. To identify the correct codeword, we will measure the correlation, between the corrupted coefficient set and every possible codeword, Y, from the dictionary (codebook).

4 Results

The video database was formed by movies with different characteristic such as: magnitude of motion between frames, amount of details or changes in a frame in the spatial domain (detailed frames tend to hold in the medium and high frequencies range more data than frames with greater smooth areas), natural and artificial objects in the video, etc.

All videos are of the same frame size of 144×176 pixels per frame (i.e., QCIF) and frame rate of 30 fps. The videos were initially loaded to the codec in raw (YUV) representation and then encoded to H.264 format to match the MATLAB based codec. The GOP (group of pictures) size set to 4 without B frames.

The codeword that embedded in the videos is of index 2 in the dictionary (i.e., 0 0 1 1 0 0 1 1). The same word was embedded 742 times in each video to examine the probability of detection and false alarm when given a fixed code word within a wide range of video scenes. Figure 5 demonstrates the mean correlation over all the word received versus all the words in the dictionary, while each plotline is a different video. The peak of all lines is in the codeword of index two that yields the highest mean correlation. The codeword of index 9 has the lowest correlation to codeword since it is the one's complement to the embedded codeword. All other codewords have mean correlation values around zero.

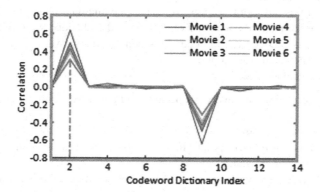

Fig. 5. Mean correlation values vs. dictionary codewords

Figure 6 demonstrates the hit (successful extraction and identification of the embedded codeword) and miss (false detection of the embedded codeword) rate for different videos.

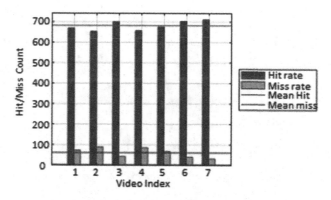

Fig. 6. Successful detection rate for several videos

The mean successful detection is 92%. That result improved by adding residual data, but it would cause higher MSE (if more DCT coefficients will change per macroblock) or creating a smaller dictionary with fewer symbols that would make us use more symbols to embed the same data in a video. The lowest successful detection is 88%, and the highest successful detection is 96%. This result means that even the lowest successful detection it is quite an excellent method to conceal and detect embedded data.

To avoid false detection, in addition to maximal computing correlation of the suspected manipulated DCT coefficients with the dictionary words it is necessary to establish a correlation threshold. If all correlation results are less than the threshold, we will assume no codeword sent.

To establish this threshold, we looked for the maximum correlation result with the minimum value over all codewords. Every codeword embedded with uniform distribution and a total of over 12000 codewords concealed in a variety of videos. The threshold that calculated was 0.0606.

Threshold calculation method:

1. Compute correlation for every suspected coefficient set with all words in the dictionary.
2. Find maximal correlation.
3. If the maximal correlation points the codeword that was embedded (successful identification) save its value.
4. Among all correlation values that saved find the minimal and this is the threshold.

For the watermark casting simulation, we used formula 11 that produced the highest successful identification rate as well as the lowest MSE. In the following graph - Fig. 7, we can see the effect of the MSE differences between the embedded frames (that contain malicious data) and clear frames with no additional information. As we can see the effect of the embedded data is to increase MSE (~ 350 or PSNR 22 db) in videos which includes minor motions and lower MSE (~ 65 or PSNR 30 db) in videos

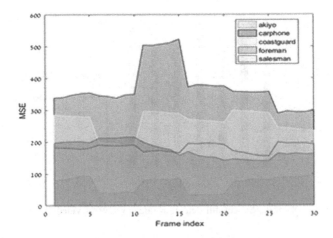

Fig. 7. MSE vs. frame index per video

with enough motion. It happens since as the motion in a video increase, the residual macroblocks contain more information and more DCT coefficients have non-zero values. So, when adding to the coefficients the binary word, it would effect on the MSE only half of the time (only when we add 1 and no effect by adding 0).

At the initial design of the algorithm the manner in which the attack operates relied mostly on the methods described in [6, 7, 9]. After the changes and additional code to embed and extract malicious codewords to the codec, the success ratio and correlation results did not fully comply with the results in the papers above. The results of these experiments are presented in Fig. 8. The extraction of a suspected codeword from an incoming bitstream first step is to produce a corrupted set of DCT coefficients with an added codeword with the same size. The second step is to calculate the correlation of the corrupted coefficients with the codewords in the dictionary. With the use of these results, we created a false-positive and true-positive graph that describe number of hits versus the correlation value (see Fig. 8). The cut point between the two graphs is our selected threshold. The first version of the dictionary was composed of binary code-words with 8 bits, and the total size of the dictionary was 256. That means the minimal Hamming distance between the words was 1 bit. However, with the use of this method, the success rate was around 62%.

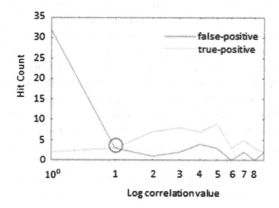

Fig. 8. Distribution of correlation vs. hit count

Changes in the implementation were needed to adjust the gap between the papers and the work with H.264 codec. Therefore, we made changes at the dictionary and extended the Hamming distance in the expense of dictionary size that led to lower bitrate but increased the mean successful detection rate to 92%.

5   Comparative Analysis DCT Steganography Techniques

In paper [16] various video steganography techniques in compressed domain are discussed. Researchers used videos for steganography, which are compressed in MPEG-2, MPEG-4 or H.264/AVC format, although H.265 format is also available but still not utilized for steganography. In video compressed domain, the commonly used methods for steganography are categorized according to the literature and for embedding secret data researchers utilized motion vector, macroblocks, variable length code etc. based techniques. These video steganography techniques are discussed by highlighting various quality parameters.

Yang et al. [17] proposed an algorithm to hide data in videos using 4×4 DCT coefficients. They used vector quantization for hiding 1 bit of secret data in each 4×4 DCT block and the hiding was done in the low frequency components of the subblocks. After hiding data, the stego video was compressed using different quantization parameters using H.264/AVC coding standard. Experimental results showed that this technique was highly robust against compression. Shao-dao et al. [18] proposed an approach for video steganography based on high bitrate hiding algorithm to hide video as a secret message. They embedded 1 bit of secret message in each 4×4 macroblocks of DCT using vector quantization. The utilized 8 low frequency coefficients for embedding the information and the extraction was a blind retrieval for this scheme. By analyzing the result, it can be concluded that the scheme was highly robust against compression and PSNR was degraded by only 0.22 dB on average and BER at receiver's end was only 0.015%. But in terms of capacity, this scheme was able to hide only 2 frames of QCIF format in 96 frames of CIF format. Ma et al. [19] presented a technique based on intra-frame distortion drift introduced after embedding in H.264/AVC videos. In this technique the intra-frame distortion was introduced after embedding but not propagated to the neighboring blocks. They deployed the I-frame DCT quantized coefficients to hide data in the 4×4 luminance blocks and there was no intra-frame distortion drift to the covert video. They used block coefficient pairs for embedding with one used for embedding the secret data and the other one was used to fix the level of distortion. The obtained results demonstrated that the embedding capacity of the scheme was high and average PSNR was above 40 db. Esen et al. [20] proposed an adaptive block-based technique by utilizing forbidden zone hiding and selective embedding. The de-synchronization occurred because of adaptive block selection was handled by Repeat Accumulate (RA) codes. For embedding Y component of the frame was utilized and middle-frequency. A comparative summary of the various methods can be seen in Table 3.

Table 3. Comparative analysis of steganography techniques

	Hiding scheme	Quality parameters	PSNR
[17]	4×4 DCT macroblock coefficients	PSNR, Bit Error Rate	–
[18]	4×4 DCT macroblocks	PSNR, Bit Error Rate	42 db
[19]	4×4 DCT block paired coefficients	Capacity, PSNR	40 db
[20]	Y components of middle frequency band of DCT	Capacity, PSNR	37 db
Our	**DCT block correlation coefficients**	**PSNR**	**30 db @ 150 Kbps** **45 db @ 80 Kbps**

6   Conclusion and Future Research Directions

In this paper we suggested a covert channel technic, that is based on video stream. Such method can be used for remote-control cyber-attack without any operating system dependency. The new idea based on manipulating DCT of compressed H.264 standard video streams. The paper offers to prevent such attack by generate random data within the potential DCT. Future work in this area can consider a hybrid technique in which the watermark added in the frequency domain, but spatial information is also exploited by marking only a subset of the image blocks in which there is a lot of changes and details. This hybrid technique can increase the robustness of the watermark, as well as better perceptual quality. Future work in this area can consider a hybrid technique in which the watermark or stego information added in the frequency domain, but spatial information is also exploited by marking only a subset of the image blocks in which there is a lot of changes and details. This hybrid technique can increase the robustness of the watermark, as well as better perceptual quality. Another future work can be to consider CDR (Content Disarm & Reconstruction) techniques that may cope with such watermarks.

Acknowledgment. This work was supported by the Israel National Cyber Bureau. The authors gratefully thank Mr. Lior Yahav for implementing the attack algorithm.

References

1. Cisco: Cisco Visual Networking Index: Forecast and Methodology, 2016–2021 (2017)
2. Neufeld, A., Ker, A.D.: A study of embedding operations and locations for steganography in H.264 video. In: SPIE, Multimedia Watermarking, Security, and Forensics, vol. 8665 (2013)
3. Morkel, T., Eloff, J.H., Olivier, M.S.: An overview of image steganography. In: Proceedings of the Fifth Annual Information Security South Africa Conference, ISSA 2005 (2005)
4. Amsden, N.D., Chen, L., Yuan, X.: Transmitting hidden information using steganography via Facebook. In: International Conference on Computing, Communication and Networking Technologies (ICCCNT) (2014)
5. Lampson, B.: A note on the confinement problem. Commun. ACM, 613–615 (1973)
6. Cox, I.J., Kilian, J., Leighton, T., Shamoon, T.: Secure spread spectrum watermarking for image, audio and video. In: IEEE International Conference on Image Processing, vol. 3, pp. 243–246 (1996)
7. Barni, M.: A DCT-domain system for robust image watermarking. Signal Process. **66**, 357–372 (1998)
8. Verma, H.K., Singh, A.N., Kumar, R.: Robustness of the digital image watermarking techniques against brightness and rotation attack. Int. J. Comput. Sci. Inf. Secur. IJCSIS, **5** (2009)
9. Jianfeng, L., Zhenhua, Y., Fan, Y., Li, L.: A MPEG2 video watermarking algorithm based on DCT domain. In: Digital Media and Digital Content Management (DMDCM) (2011)
10. Amsalem, Y., Hadar, O., Puzanov, A., Bedinerman, A., Kutcher, M.: DCT-based cyber defense techniques. In: Applications of Digital Image Processing XXXVIII (2015)
11. Katzenbeisser, S.: Information Hiding Techniques for Steganography and Digital. Artech House (2000)

12. Fouant, S.: Man in the Middle (MITM) Attacks Explained: ARP Poisoning. ShortestPathFirs (2010)
13. Richardson, I.E.G.: The H.264 Advanced Video Compression Standard. Wiley (2011)
14. "H.264 encoder decoder scheme"
15. Sullivan, G.: Overview of the H.264/AVC video coding standard. IEEE Trans. Circuits Syst. Video Technol. **13**, 560–576 (2003)
16. Juneja, M., Mukesh, D.: Overview of video steganography in compressed domain. Int. J. Control. Theory Appl. 1–11 (2018)
17. Yang, M., Bourbakis, N.: A high bitrate information hiding algorithm for digital video content under H.264/AVC compression. In: Midwest Symposium on Circuits and Systems, vol. 2005, pp. 935–938 (2005)
18. Shou-Dao, W., Chuang-Bai, X., Yu, L.: A high bitrate information hiding algorithm for video in video. Eng. Technol. 413–418 (2009)
19. Ma, X., Li, Z., Tu, H., Zhang, B.: A data hiding algorithm for H.264/AVC video streams without intra-frame distortion drift. IEEE Trans. Circuits Syst. Video Technol. **20**(10), 1320–1330 (2010)
20. Esen, E., Alatan, A.A.: Robust video data hiding using forbidden zone data hiding and selective embedding. IEEE Trans. Circuits Syst. Video Technol. **21**, 1130–1138 (2011)

Effects of Weather on Drone to IoT QKD

Shlomi Arnon[(✉)] and Judy Kupferman

Ben-Gurion University of the Negev, Beer Sheva, Israel
shlomi@bgu.ac.il

Abstract. The Internet of Things (IoT) is playing a growing role in society, and includes control over a range from household appliances to municipal power grids and nationwide assets. As a result, hackers from a national level down to low level criminals are looking to take advantage of important IoT infrastructures. These present an immediate target for cyber-terrorists as well as more mundane attacks by thieves and personal enemies, and it is imperative to devise defensive measures. In this work, we describe potential possible attacks on several IoT systems. As a result, vendors of the IoT infrastructure employ conventional encryption which is based on complexity to fight against hackers. However the emerging technology of quantum computing will make deciphering of the conventional encryption an easy task. This leads us to propose a scheme for use of QKD (quantum key distribution) which could be effective as a countermeasure. In this paper we will describe the feasibility study of weather effect design guidelines for a small, short range, mobile QKD system from drone to IoT on the ground.

Keywords: Internet of Things · Quantum Key Distribution · Free Space Optics

1 Introduction

The Internet of Things (IoT) is found in critical applications of everyday life today. These range from the home, including appliances, lighting and wearables, to a much larger scale that affects thousands of people. IoT is used in transportation, vehicles and smart road infrastructures, in architecture using smart building design, in hospitals and medical devices, and on a municipal and even larger scale: pollution monitoring, smart traffic systems, water supply, gas supply, and power plants with a smart grid. As the scale of use increases, the danger of hacking is growing exponentially. If a mobile phone or computer is hacked, this can cause financial loss. But if a medical device is hacked, the life of the patient can be affected. If there is a power outage, millions of lives could be at risk. If street lights all turn green at the same time multiple deaths will result. And when sensors that serve to detect pollution in a water supply are disrupted or disabled, large scale slaughter can ensure.

Examples of this are numerous. In 2015, hackers broke into dozens of energy firms in the US, Turkey and Switzerland, and in some cases gained operational access to vital equipment [1]. In 2015 hackers shut off power for 225,000 Ukrainians. In 2017, North Korean hackers breached an American energy utility using malware emails [2]. In 2018, probably Russian hackers hit three energy and transport companies in the

© Springer Nature Switzerland AG 2019
S. Dolev et al. (Eds.): CSCML 2019, LNCS 11527, pp. 67–74, 2019.
https://doi.org/10.1007/978-3-030-20951-3_5

Ukraine and Poland [3]. In 2017, in California, St. Jude Medical's implantable cardiac devices were declared by the FDA to be vulnerable to hackers. These contained transmitters that read data and sent it remotely to physicians [4]. As for transport, vehicles are connected by internet to other vehicles, to infrastructure and to internet and radio supporting communications, where by 2021 connected automobiles will account for over 82% of cars sold [5]. Vehicle hacking has already been demonstrated, beginning with the Jeep Cherokee hack of 2015 where security researchers gained control of steering wheel brakes and engine, causing Fiat Chrysler to recall 1.4 million vehicles, and most recently at the Black Hat security conference where Keen Security Labs presented details of how they remotely hacked a Tesla Model S [6, 7].

Today such systems are protected by classical cryptography. However, quantum computers will be able to hack classical cryptography [8, 9]. According to Arvind Krishna, head of IBM Research, in 2026 quantum computers will be able to hack any classical cryptographic system. It has been known since the 1980s that quantum computers could factor large numbers, which is one of the mainstays of public key cryptography. At that time construction of large quantum computers was not possible, but due to advances in novel materials and in low temperature physics, large commercial quantum computer systems will be viable and available within five years, and anyone wanting to ensure their data is protected for over 10 years should move immediately to alternate forms of encryption.

An effective solution to this is quantum cryptography. Classical cryptography is based on computational hardness, e.g. factoring of large numbers. Conversely, quantum cryptography is based on the underlying physics, and thus is not vulnerable to more powerful computers. The basis of quantum cryptography is Quantum Key Distribution (QKD), which involves sharing of a secret key between two partners that in theory cannot be hacked by an outside source. QKD networks have been in commercial use for several years, and working QKD networks have been installed in the US, Europe, Japan and China, where in January 2019, the Chinese Micius satellite passed encrypted data between China and Austria over a distance of 7600 km [10]. These have been proven theoretically to be completely secure. Another solution being explored is post quantum cryptography [11], with algorithms that would be secure against quantum hacking. We focus on QKD because it has already been successfully implemented.

QKD has two basic technologies: discrete variable (DV-QKD) where each bit of private information is encoded onto the discrete degrees of freedom of an optical signal, and continuous variable (CV-QKD) which employs coherent communication techniques. Implementation has been done over fiber and through free space, but an interesting development is that of mobile transmitters, namely drone based [12] and hand-held devices [13]. Since IoT is implemented in a broad range of situations, flexible and mobile defenses against hacking may prove of prime importance. In this work we present a free space optics (FSO) scheme for mobile quantum key distribution to systems that are controlled using IoT, and analyze the effect of weather conditions on transmission. The scheme is aimed at infrastructure components that would be particularly vulnerable to cyber-terror, such as power stations, controllers of water supply, street lighting, etc. but it could be effective for any system linked to IoT. This paper is organized as follows. First we give a description of the proposed system. We calculate the probability for the quantum key to be received, as a function of transmitter height. We perform a numerical simulation, and end with a discussion.

2   Scenario Under Consideration

The quantum key QKD concept under consideration employs polarization of single photons to transmit the key. These photons are called qubits – quantum bits – which is a generic name for any quantum two level system. The qubits encode bits, so that such a qubit could carry bit 0 or bit 1. This technique is used in many DV- QKD protocols. These protocols are divided into two general types: "prepare and measure", where the first and most representative example is BB84 [14] and "entanglement based" such as E91 [15]. In this work the system could be BB84 for example. This is well tested, and proven secure in theory and practice, and used by banks and government [16]. In BB84 (developed by Bennett and Brassard in 1984, of course), Alice sends a string of random bits in one of two bases at random. Bob chooses a basis for measurement. After measuring they disclose over a public channel which basis was used for each measurement. They throw out the measurements where a different basis was used, and half the bits remain as a shared key. The bits could be encoded in photon polarization, where one basis could have polarization angle 0° for bit 0 and 90° for bit 1, while the other basis would be 45° for 0, −45° for 1. Thus the shared key is distributed. This is secure against eavesdropping because quantum mechanics prohibits cloning; the eavesdropper, Eve, cannot make an exact copy of a qubit. She can intercept it, measure it, and send it on, but she doesn't know which basis to measure it in, and with probability of ½ she will use the wrong basis. Afterwards Alice and Bob compare small portions of the key to determine error rate, and if it's more than 0, they know Eve has been there and take action accordingly. Of course errors could result from hardware problems, but they assume it's all eavesdropping.

We now describe the proposed scenario. As usual in quantum information systems, we denote the sender as Alice and the receiver as Bob. The infrastructure consists of several Bobs on the ground, each controlled over the internet. Alice wishes to send each Bob a quantum key for signal encryption/decryption. This key cannot be broken by hackers, and Alice can send a different key at regular intervals. We place Alice in a drone, moving in the air from one Bob to another. The drone hovers directly above the receiver, Bob, and moves from one Bob to the next like bees that go from one flower to the next. It repeats the pattern at regular intervals, so that the key is replaced regularly for each Bob. We treat the case of one Bob, and for simplicity, we assume he is located on a static platform on the ground. Extension to mobile platforms is straightforward. Figure 1 illustrates the scheme in question.

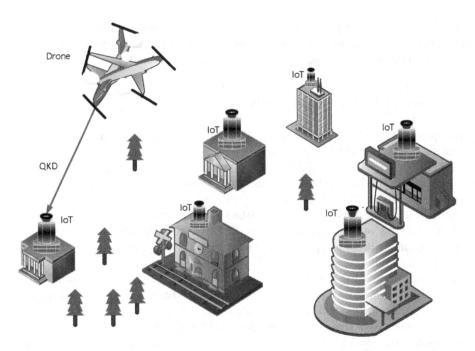

Fig. 1. QKD. Alice sends a signal containing a quantum key to IoT stations on the ground.

Alice sends the message to Bob through free space over a distance Z. The probability for Bob to receive a photon transmitted by Alice, as a function of Z, the distance between them, is given [17–19] by

$$P_{Bob}(Z) = P_{Alice}K_1(Z). \tag{1}$$

where K_1 is a constant and G_{Bob} is the gain of Bob's telescope. G_{Bob} is equal to $(\pi d_{Bob}/\lambda)^2$ [16] where d_{Bob} is the unobscured circular aperture diameter of Bob's telescope, and λ is the wavelength.

The probability to transmit one photon, assuming the source is Poisson distributed, is given as

$$P_{Alice} = (rT)^n \frac{e^{-rT}}{n!}. \tag{2}$$

where T is the pulse duration, r is rate and in our case we assume that n = 1

K_1 is given by

$$K_1(Z) = \eta_q \, G_{Bob}G_{Alice}\eta_{Alice} \, \eta_{Bob} \, \frac{L_A(Z)}{Z^2} \left(\frac{\lambda}{4\pi}\right)^2 \tag{3}$$

where, η_q is quantum efficiency, η_{Alice}, η_{Bob} are optical efficiencies, G_{Alice} is Alice's telescope gain, and G_{Alice} is equal to $(\pi\, d_{Alice}/\lambda)^2$ [20] where d_{Alice} is the unobscured circular aperture diameter of Alice's telescope. $L_A(Z)$ is atmospheric loss. Since Alice will be directly above Bob, atmospheric loss should be minimal, but factors such as weather, fog etc. must also be taken into account. The atmospheric loss as a function of distance is give as

$$L_A(Z) = 10^{\frac{-\gamma_a Z}{10}} \qquad (4)$$

where γ_a is the attenuation. Here we will take several samples of average atmospheric loss, for various weather conditions. We performed a numerical simulation of the probability for Bob to receive a photon, using typical values shown in Table 1. Table 2 shows the atmospheric attenuation due to weather for a wavelength of 780 nm [21]. The range chosen was up to 100 m between the drone Bob and the ground station Alice. Figure 2 shows the decrease in Bob's probability with increased height of Alice.

Table 1. Values for simulation

Definition	Symbol	Value
Gain of Alice's telescope	G_{Alice}	$5 10^5$
Gain of Bob's telescope	G_{Bob}	$5 10^6$
Alice's optical efficiency	η_{Alice}	0.9
Bob's optical efficiency	η_{Bob}	0.9
Bob's receiver quantum efficiency	η_q	0.1
Optical wave length	λ	780 nm
Pulse duration	T	1 ns
Photon rate	r	10^9 photon/s
Number of photon	n	1

Table 2. Weather attenuation [21]

Aerosols	Visibility [m]	γ_a Attenuation [dB/km] (at 780 nm)
Clear	∞	0
Haze	5200	3
Fog	830	20
Cloud	170	100

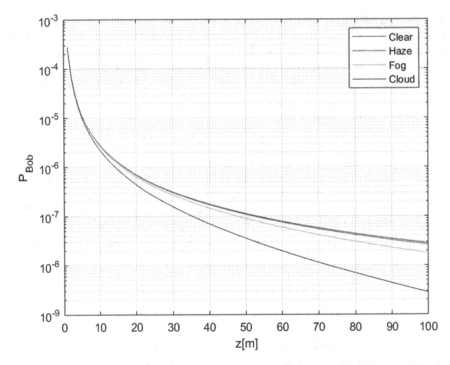

Fig. 2. Bob's detection probability as a function of the distance separation between Alice and Bob (IoT), for four different values of atmospheric loss.

From Fig. 2 we see that the probability for Bob drops sharply as the distance goes from 0 to about 100 m, but after that the decrease is slower. There is almost no difference between clear visibility and for haze, and only a slight difference for fog, while for cloudy weather the difference becomes significant after a distance of about 30 m.

3 Discussion

We have proposed a system where a quantum key is repeatedly distributed by a mobile transmitter to ground based receivers. QKD in the proposed scheme uses single photon transmission and reception. As seen from Fig. 2 the probability for Bob to receive a photon drops steeply with the increased distance from Alice. Clearly the height of the transmitter should be as low as possible. Atmospheric loss affects the probability for reception, where clouds have a greater effect than fog or haze and the disparity between them is greater for distances of over 30 m. This suggests that varying weather conditions would not be a serious obstacle to operation of such a system if the drone height can be kept relatively low. If atmospheric loss were significant such a system would be impractical for a mobile system, since one could not guarantee consistent and identical weather in the different locations. Thus it appears that drone borne transmission may be a preferable and efficient method of transmitting QKD to the ground system. The mobility of the system enables flexibility in the ground system as well, so the proposal may be adapted to forms of IoT that are mobile such as medical appliances worn by patients, who could receive instructions to stop at "charging stations" at prescribed intervals where the device could receive a new cryptographic key, or vehicle QKD. With the increase in mobile internet applications, flexibility of the QKD system seems to be a natural development.

References

1. http://fortune.com/2017/09/06/hack-energy-grid-symantec/
2. https://www.nbcnews.com/news/north-korea/experts-northkorea-targeted-u-s-electric-power-copanies-n808996
3. https://www.euractiv.com/section/cybersecurity/news/hackers-accused-of-ties-to-russia-hit-3-east-european-companies-cybersecurity-firm/
4. https://money.cnn.com/2017/01/09/technology/fda-st-jude-cardiac-hack/
5. https://info.entrustdatacard.com/iot-tesla?_ga=2.95926104.559287255.1513006603-14616 2010.1496333764
6. https://www.kaspersky.com/blog/blackhat-jeep-cherokee-hack-explained/9493/
7. https://hackernoon.com/smart-car-hacking-a-major-problem-for-iot-a66c14562419
8. https://www.zdnet.com/article/ibm-warns-of-instant-breaking-of-encryption-by-quantum-computers-move-your-data-today/
9. https://it.slashdot.org/story/18/05/19/200225/ibm-warns-quantum-computing-will-break-encryption
10. Liao, S.-K., et al.: Satellite-relayed intercontinental quantum network. Phys. Rev. Lett. **120**(3), 030501 (2018)
11. Bernstein, D.J.: Introduction to post-quantum cryptography. In: Bernstein, D.J., Buchmann, J., Dahmen, E. (eds.) Post-Quantum Cryptography, pp. 1–14. Springer, Berlin (2009). https://doi.org/10.1007/978-3-540-88702-7_1
12. Hill, A.D., Chapman, J., Herndon, K., Chopp, C., Gauthier, D.J., Kwiat, P.: Drone-based quantum key distribution. Urbana **51**, 61801–63003 (2017)
13. Chun, H., et al.: Handheld free space quantum key distribution with dynamic motion compensation. Optics Express **25**(6), 6784–6795 (2017)
14. Bennett, C.H., Brassard, G.: Quantum cryptography: public key distribution and coin tossing. In: Proceedings of IEEE International Conference on Computers, Systems and Signal Processing, vol. 175, p. 8, New York (1984)
15. Ekert, A.K.: Quantum cryptography based on Bell's theorem. Phys. Rev. Lett. **67**(6), 661 (1991)
16. Tentrup, T.B.H., et al.: Large-alphabet Quantum Key Distribution using spatially encoded light. arXiv preprint arXiv:1808.02823 (2018)
17. Arnon, S., Kopeika, N.S.: Laser satellite communication network-vibration effect and possible solutions. Proc. IEEE **85**(10), 1646–1661 (1997)
18. Arnon, S.: Effects of atmospheric turbulence and building sway on optical wireless-communication systems. Opt. Lett. **28**(2), 129–131 (2003)
19. Yang, F., Cheng, J., Tsiftsis, T.A.: Free-space optical communication with nonzero boresight pointing errors. IEEE Trans. Commun. **62**(2), 713–725 (2014)

20. Chen, C.-C., Gardner, C.S.: Impact of random pointing and tracking errors on the design of coherent and incoherent optical intersatellite communication links. IEEE Trans. Commun. **37**(3), 252–260 (1989)
21. Kopeika, N.: A System Engineering Approach to Imaging, 700 p. SPIE Press (1998). (2nd printing. April 2000)

Malware Classification Using Image Representation

Ajay Singh, Anand Handa$^{(\boxtimes)}$, Nitesh Kumar, and Sandeep Kumar Shukla

C3I Center, Department of CSE,
Indian Institute of Technology, Kanpur, India
ajay199109@gmail.com, {ahanda,niteskr,sandeeps}@cse.iitk.ac.in

Abstract. In the recent years, there has been a rapid rise in the number of files submitted to anti-virus companies for analysis. It has become very difficult to analyse the functionality of each file manually. Malware developers have been highly successful in evading signature-based detection techniques. Most of the prevailing static analysis techniques involve a tool to parse the executable, and extract features or signatures. Most of the dynamic analysis techniques involve the binary file to be run in a sand-boxed environment to examine its behaviour. This can be easily thwarted by hiding the malicious activities of the file if it is being run inside a virtual environment. Hence, there has been a need to explore new approaches to overcome the limitations of static or dynamic analysis such as time intensity, resource consumption, scalability. In this paper, we have explored a new technique to represent malware as images. We have used 37, 374 samples belonging to 22 families and then applied deep neural network architectures such as ResNet-50 architecture including a dense Convolutional Neural Network (CNN) for classifying images. By converting the executable into an image representation, we have made our analysis process free from the problems faced by standard static and dynamic analyses. With our models, we have been able to get an accuracy of 98.98%, and 99.40% in classifying malware samples by using deep CNN, and ResNet-50 respectively on our dataset. In this paper, we have also compared the results of our proposed model on our collected dataset with the results obtained on publically available datasets like Malimg having 9,339 samples belonging to 25 families. We also present our findings on the limitation of this method through experimentation on packed and previously unseen classes of malware.

Keywords: Malware classification · Convolutional neural network · Machine learning · Deep neural network · Image processing

1 Introduction

The Internet has become an integral part of our daily life. Almost 57% of the world's population as of 2017 is connected over the Internet [8]. We use it for

S. Dolev et al. (Eds.): CSCML 2019, LNCS 11527, pp. 75–92, 2019.
https://doi.org/10.1007/978-3-030-20951-3_6

banking, communicating, entertainment, shopping, and various other commercial and non-commercial activities. Albeit making our life convenient, the Internet has exposed us to the risk of getting attacked. Illegitimate users use malware programs to commit financial frauds or steal private/sensitive information from legitimate users. The number of reported attacks are increasing every year. Pandalabs has reported identifying 227,000 malware samples every day in 2016 [9]. What started as a hobby of tech-enthusiast and researchers, has now evolved into an international community of highly trained programmers motivated by easy profits [32]. It has now grown to be a multi-million dollar industry [6] where hacking tools are sold and bought, just like the legal software industry. Even technical support and customer services are available to allure pillagers.

The proliferation of malware at an ever-increasing rate poses a serious threat in the post-internet world. Malware detection and classification has become one of the most crucial problems in the field of cyber security. With the ever increasing risk of attack, the onus lies on the security researchers for devising new techniques for detecting malware and developing new security mechanisms against them.

Traditional malware identification tool, anti-virus software, use signature matching to identify malware. The analyst at security companies analyse a sample received by them and develop unique signatures related to that sample. The anti-virus database is then updated with these signatures, which then compares the signature of every file on the machine with its database. If the signature of a particular file matches with any of the signatures in the anti-virus database then that file is labelled as malware. Due to their high matching speed and high accuracy in finding known threats signature-based techniques are effective, but these techniques fail to cope with code obfuscation and fail to effectively identify newly arrived threats. More than 800,000 files are submitted every day to VirusTotal [11] for analysis. Since the volume of samples obtained by Antivirus companies for analysing is very large, so doing the analysis manually is not possible. So the process of analysis needs to be automated, which will help in reducing the number of files which requires manual analysis.

Cohen has shown that detecting whether a given program is malware is an undecidable problem [1]. Automated detection and analysis techniques are limited by this theoretical result and might fail in some cases. So for such cases, manual intervention is required to understand new attacks and analyses evasion techniques. The new techniques learned from such manual analysis is then incorporated into the automated software improving its efficacy.

The famous quote by Fred R. Barnard, "A picture is worth a thousand words" motivated us. In this paper, we will examine whether it holds for malware also. Visualizations have always proven to be beneficial in getting a comprehensive view of any system or data. We are intuitively more capable of making more sense out of images than any other representation. So this paper explores how we can generate a visual representation for representing a binary file and examine whether there are any patterns visible in those visual representations. Then it leverages those representations for classifying malware samples into their respective classes/families. Classification of malware is helpful for the analyst as it helps them to get a better insight into the functioning of the malware. Malware samples which have similar code structure are grouped into one class. This is very helpful for analysts because just by knowing the class/family of the malware they can have an idea about how to devise sanitation and detection techniques for that malware. Also by knowing the family to which a malware belong we have a general idea about its behaviour. This helps in sharing of knowledge between malware analysts.

Specifically, this paper contributes a new method for visually representing malware. Using this new representation technique we have been successful in effectively classifying malware to their respective families/classes. Also, our technique can be used for real-time classification because the pre-processing time is almost negligible and the image can be directly given as input to the classifier. We have used RGB representation over grey-scale for malware images because the accuracy of our model is not very much promising for the grey-scale image representation. With the new representation, we have been able to achieve an improvement in the results as shown in the previous work. We have discussed the results in the Sect. 5.

Also, we have successfully applied state of the art neural network technique for malware analysis, which was found missing in the work we surveyed.

Rest of the paper is organised as follows: Sect. 2 gives a general overview of some of the popular and common malware analysis from literature and their advantages and disadvantages. Section 3 discusses our methodology. Section 4 includes the configuration details of the models used in the present work. Section 5 discusses the experimental results and their comparison with previous work, and Sect. 6 concludes the paper.

2   Related Work

Malware are being used to attack critical infrastructures, for espionage against a nation, for stealing private information or for conducting financial frauds. All the attacks use the network as a medium. Almost all the malware detection system in the industry use either a signature based approach or anomaly-based approach. A signature is a unique sequence of bytes that is present in the malicious binary and in the files that have been damaged by that malware [34]. Signature-based methods use the unique signatures developed by the anti-virus companies using the known malware to capture the threat. This approach is fast and has high accuracy, but it fails in detecting previously unseen malware. So generally, after a new malware has infected numerous systems, an analyst may be able to generate its signature. Also, the signature database has to be prepared manually which is a time-consuming process [24]. In the anomaly-based approach, the anti-virus companies form a database of actions that are considered safe. If a process breaks any of these predefined rules, it is labelled as malicious [37]. Although with anomaly-based method we are able to identify new unseen malware samples, but the false alarm rate is very high.

Bazrafshan et al. presented a heuristic based method [18]. In a heuristic based approach analysts use machine learning techniques to train a malware classifier. Static, dynamic, visual feature representations or a combination are used for training a classifier on a dataset composed of both malign and benign binaries. Various machine learning techniques such as Support Vector Machines, Random Forests, Decision Trees, Naive Bayes, K-means Clustering and Gradient Boost and Ada-boost have been suggested for classifying and detecting malware samples into either their respective classes or to filter out the malware that requires further exhaustive analysis by an analyst. A few of these techniques, used in the literature, are discussed in this section.

Static analysis includes extraction of static features from the binary file using binary analysis tools. The static analysis have certain limitations as they can be easily evaded if the malware is obfuscated or packed, we require some robust behavioural features for our analysis. This brings us to various Dynamic Analysis Approaches. Common to all dynamic analysis based approaches is that the execution of the binary sample is done in a controlled environment for extracting behavioural features inside a virtual machine.

Similar to static analysis dynamic analysis also have certain limitations as it cannot explore all the execution paths of an executable and it tries to detect the virtual environment during the execution process. So another field of study forked out in the area of malware analysis, *visualization approach* which improves detection and classification accuracy for malware. Some of the visualization approaches are discussed in the next subsection of the paper.

2.1 Visualization Approaches

Several Hex viewer tools were already available to visualize and edit a binary file, but they just display the file in hexadecimal and ASCII formats and fails to convey any structural information to the analyst. First, we will discuss how various researchers tried to visualize binaries.

Nataraj et al. [31] were the first to explore the use of byte plot visualization for automatic malware classification. They converted all the malware sample to grey-scale byte plot representations and extracted texture based features from the malware image. They used an abstract representation technique, GIST, for computing texture features from images. Their dataset consists of 9,458 malware samples belonging to 25 different classes, collected from Anubis [3] system. They used the global image-based features to train a K-Nearest Neighbour model, with Euclidean distance as the distance measure, to classify malware samples into their respective classes and accuracy of 97.18% was obtained. The results obtained showed that image processing based malware classifying techniques can classify malware more quickly than existing dynamic approaches. Inspite of that, their approach has a huge computational overhead of calculating texture-based features.

Han et al. [21] proposed a new way of visualizing malware using op-code sequences to detect and classify malware samples. They used image matrices to visually represent malware which assisted in detecting features of malware and also in finding similarities between different samples swiftly. First, the binary file is disassembled using IDAPro [7] or OllyDbg [15], and the op-code sequence is divided into blocks. Then they used two hash functions and for each block of op-code sequence, computed a coordinate and the RGB value using the two hash functions. Then they plotted all the RGB values to their corresponding coordinates in a matrix of dimension 8 by 8 to get an image matrix. They used "*selective area matching*" for calculating similarities between image matrices and evaluated their model on malware samples from 10 different families. Their results showed that image matrices of malware from the same family had a higher similarity score than with malware from different families. This shows that image matrices can effectively classify malware families.

Makandar et al. [27] converted malware into a 2-dimension grey-scale image and classified the samples using texture-based features. They extracted texture based global features using Gabor wavelet transform and GIST and used Mahenhur dataset [27] for experiments, which comprises of 3131 binaries samples from 24 unique malware families. They used the Artificial Neural Networks (ANN) for classifying malware and reported an accuracy of 96.35%.

Liu et al. [26] proposed an incremental approach to automatically assign malware to their respective families and detect new malware. They used a combination of grey-scale byte plot, Op-code n-grams, and import functions. The decision-making module uses these features to classify malware samples to their respective families and to identify new unknown malware. They used Shared Nearest Neighbour (SNN) as the clustering algorithm to detect new malware families. Their model is evaluated on a dataset consisting of 21,740 malware samples from 9 different families and reported classification accuracy of 98.9% and the detection accuracy of 86.7%.

Aziz et al. [29] proposed a malware class recognition and classification using supervised learning classifier. The proposed model has three-stages. In the first stage, pre-processing is done by applying wavelet transforms. In the second stage, feature extraction is performed using Discrete Wavelet Transform (DWT) which decompose the image into four levels. Lastly, in the third stage classification is performed using Support Vector Machine (SVM) classifiers. They achieved a classification accuracy on two datasets (Malimg [31] and Mahenhur [27]) as 91.05% and 92.53% respectively.

In 2016, Seonhee et al. [35] proposed a malware classification model using a deep neural network. Firstly, the model converts the malware code to malware image and then it is trained using a convolutional neural network. They have performed two sets of experiments. In the first set, they have classified 9-families with an accuracy of 96.2%, 98.4% of top-I, and top-II error rates respectively and in the second set of experiments, the model classified 27 malware families with an accuracy of 82.9% and 89% of top-I, and top-II error rate.

Barath et al. [30] proposed a malware classification method that visualizes the malware as an image without changing its global structure. Principal Component Analysis (PCA) is used for feature extraction. The authors used Artificial Neural Network (ANN), k- Nearest Neighbors (k-NN) and Support Vector Machine

(SVM) for classifying the malware into their respective classes. The highest accuracy reported is 96.6% for k-NN on the dataset BIG 2015 provided by Kaggle for Microsoft malware classification challenge.

In another paper, Aziz et al. [28] recognized malware classes with image processing techniques using SVM. Texture-based features like Gabor wavelet, GIST and Discrete Wavelet Transform (DWT) were extracted. The proposed model outputs an accuracy of 98.84% and 98.88% using k-NN(k = 3) and SVM respectively on Malimg dataset having 12,470 samples.

Kalash et al. [23] recently proposed a deep learning framework for malware classification. They have introduced a CNN- based architecture to classify malware samples by converting malware binaries to grey-scale images. They have then trained a CNN for classification. The experiments were conducted on two datasets namely Malimg and Microsoft malware dataset. Authors achieved 95.52% and 99.97% accuracy on Malimg and Microsoft respectively.

Yakura et al. [38] proposed a method to reduce the overhead in the investigation of samples by extracting the essential byte sequences in malware samples. Along with CNN, they have applied an attention mechanism [17,25] to an image. Attention mechanism is a technique to dynamically select important features which improves the performance. The approach is based on region distinction which extracts the characteristic byte sequences mainly related to a malware family. The treated information proves to be very useful in case the malware samples were packed. The authors have used 147803 samples belonging to 542 families from VX Heaven [10] as the dataset. The 2D- CNN achieves an accuracy of 50.97%.

Although a lot of work has been already done in this area using visualization approaches, still there is a scope of improvement in accuracy for classifying malware into their respective families. Image-based detection and classification prove to be effective because it leverages the structural similarity between the known and new malware binaries. Moreover, visual analytic helps analysts to recognize patterns in malware's code and behaviour, thus helping them to come up with better results. We used a novel way of representing a binary file as a coloured image matrix to analyse and classify malware. Our approach requires no code extraction or decompilation or execution. We converted the malware samples into images and used a machine learning algorithm to classify them into their respective classes.

3   Our Methodology

A large number of malware samples are created using polymorphic and metamorphic techniques, so different malware will possess some structural similarity, share some attributes and behaviours. Despite most of the new malware being very similar to the known malware samples, signature-based anti-virus programs still fail to detect them because they do not take into account structural and behavioural properties for detection.

3.1   Dataset Collection and Pre-processing

Collection: We collected more than sixty thousand malware samples from various malware repositories such as Malshare [5], VirusShare [4], VirusTotal [2]. These portals collect malware using Honeypots and also users around the world submit to them for analysis and sharing malware samples. Then we removed the duplicates from the malware collection by comparing MD5 hash of each file. To assert that all of those samples were valid malware samples, we analysed them using VirusTotal and selected only those which were labelled as malicious by more than 50% of the anti-virus engines in the VirusTotal report.

Labelling: Since we are using supervised learning for classification, therefore we require labelled samples. So for labelling these samples we used the label provided by Microsoft anti-virus engine in the VirusTotal report. For this we had to provide the MD5 hash of the binary file to VirusTotal. If that file had already been analysed by their engine then it would return a report otherwise we had to upload the file to get the report. There were a few samples in our dataset that Microsoft anti-virus engine failed to classify, we decided to drop such samples to maintain consistency of labels. After this we were left with $37,374$ valid malware samples as shown in Table 1.

Table 1. Our dataset details

Malware type	Malware family	Number of samples
Virus	Krepper	1127
	Luder.B	1291
	Sality	1342
	Expiro	2097
	Virut	728
Worm	Yuner.A	3906
	Allaple.A	6126
	VB.AT	3748
Backdoor	Agent	1024
	Rbot	856
TrojanDownloader	Tugspay.A	3652
	Renos	1880
	Small	447
TrojanDropper	Sventore.C	1654
	Sventore.A	1503
Trojan	Comame!gmb	1874
	Bulta!rfn	608
	startpage	1327
	Skintrim.N	228
Virtool	Vbinject	1247
Rogue	FakeRean	128
	Winwebsec	581
Total		37,374

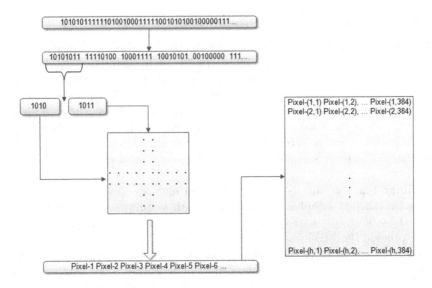

Fig. 1. Conversion of binary file to coloured image. (Color figure online)

Conversion of Binary File to Image: Generally, all binary files can be considered as a sequence of ones and zeros. So first we converted each binary file into a string of ones and zeros. Then we divide the content of the string into units of 8 bits each, that is, 8 characters for every unit. Now considering each unit as a byte, we took their upper and lower nibbles as indices of a 2-dimensional colour map that stores RGB values corresponding to that Byte. Repeating this for every unit we got a sequence of RGB values (pixel values) corresponding to each Byte in the binary file.

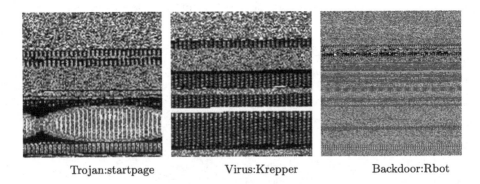

Trojan:startpage   Virus:Krepper   Backdoor:Rbot

Fig. 2. Sample images of malware belonging to different families

Now we converted this sequence of pixel values into a 2-dimensional matrix, thus getting an image representation for a binary file. For this work we have fixed the width of the matrix to 384 Bytes or units. So the height of image is variable and depends on the size of the binary file. Figure 1 shows the method for conversion of binary file to coloured image.

Figure 2 shows image representations of malware from three different families. From the images we can easily discern that there is some textural differences among malware from different classes. This is possibly due to the recycling of old malware code, as most of the new malware created reuse the preexisting code and to evade detection by signature matching they use techniques such as obfuscation, packing or encryption. The question is how can we leverage these similarities to classify malware samples to their respective families.

Proposed Model: Neural networks have been very successful in finding meaning or recognising patterns from a set of images. We used a Residual Neural Network (ResNet-50) for training a classifier to group malware into their classes [33]. Residual learning means that every layer is responsible for fine tuning the outputs from its previous layer. Figure 3 shows the flow of the proposed model.

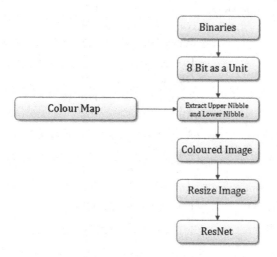

Fig. 3. Flow of proposed model.

The images are re-sized to a common size of 32 rows and 32 columns. The dataset comprising of samples from 22 classes is divided and 26,149 samples are used for training and 11,225 samples are used for validation. The training set samples are fed to Residual Neural Network (ResNet-50). The ResNet-50 architecture and the experimental results are explained in Sect. 4.2.

We initially used deep convolutional neural network for classification and it gave about 98.98% accuracy. The results were comparable with those in some of the previous work but upon using ResNet-50 we got accuracy of 99.40%, which is a significant improvement both on CNN based approach and previous work.

Table 2. Malimg dataset from Natraj et al. [31]

Malware type	Malware family	Number of samples
Worm	Allaple.L	1591
	Allaple.A	2949
	Yuner.A	800
	VB.A T	408
PWS	Lolyda.AA1	213
	Lolyda.AA2	184
	Lolyda.AA3	123
	Lolyda.AT	159
Trojan	C2Lop.P	146
	C2Lop.gen!g	200
	Skintrim.N	80
	Alueron.gen!J	198
	Malex.gen!J	136
TDownloader	Swizzot.gen!I	132
	Swizzor.gen!E	128
	Wintrim.BX	97
	Dontovo.A	162
	Obfuscator.AD	142
Backdoor	Agent.FYI	116
	Rbot!gen	158
Dialer	Adialer.C	122
	Dialplatform.B	177
	Instantaccess	431
Worm: AutoIT	Autorun.K	106
Rogue	Fakerean	381
Total		9339

We also compared our model with that proposed by Natraj et al. [31] who used byte plot representation and classified malware using GIST [36] features extracted from the images. GIST are a set of global features which tends to capture textural similarity between images. They used a K-Nearest Neighbour model to classify a malware dataset of 9339 samples belonging to 25 classes. They got classification accuracy of 97.18% for the following dataset as shown in Table 2.

For implementing the proposed system we used Python programming language and a plethora of different Python libraries. The entire code for dataset preparation and labelling using VirusTotal API service is implemented in Python. PIL library of python was used for image generation and resizing. For learning models we used Keras with Tensorflow as background. Scikit-learn was used for performance evaluation and matplotlib along with seaborn was used for plotting.

4   Model Configuration

4.1   Dense CNN Configuration

Initially we tried to classify the malware images using CNN. We used a 15 layer CNN with 5 convolutional layers and 2 dense layers and the architecture is discussed in the Table 3. This gave us an accuracy of 98.98%.

Table 3. CNN architecture configuration details

#	Layer (type)	Output shape	Param#	#	Layer (type)	Output shape	Param#
1	Conv2D	(None, 32, 32, 32)	832	9	Conv2D	(None, 1, 1, 120)	300120
2	MaxPooling	(None, 7, 7, 32)	0	10	MaxPooling	(None, 1, 1, 120)	0
3	Conv2D	(None, 7, 7, 50)	40050	11	Dropout	(None, 1, 1, 120)	0
4	MaxPooling	(None, 2, 2, 50)	0	12	Flatten	(None, 120)	0
5	Conv2D	(None, 2, 2, 80)	200100	13	Dense	(None, 512)	61952
6	MaxPooling	(None, 1, 1, 80)	0	14	Dropout	(None, 512)	0
7	Conv2D	(None, 1, 1, 100)	300120	15	Dense	(None, 22)	11286
8	MaxPooling	(None, 1, 1, 100)	0	16	N/A	N/A	N/A

The total no. of parameters are: 714, 420; Trainable parameters are: 714, 420.
Non-trainable parameters are: 0

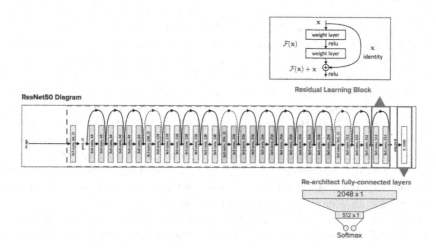

Fig. 4. A building block of ResNet-50 and complete architecture. The number of MLP layers might differ. Many such blocks are stacked with varying MLP layers [12,22].

4.2   ResNet-50 Architectural Details

Weizmann Institute of Science has recently published a mathematical proof that establishes the utility of having deeper network as compared to wider. In the future, deep nets are going to be deeper. As standard fully connected Multi Layer Perceptron (MLP) get deeper, problems such as exploding/vanishing of gradients [19] start appearing, thus disturbing the convergence. Degradation problem also starts to appear with increasing depths as accuracy gets saturated and then degrades rapidly. In residual networks, this is tackled by feeding inputs of a layer to other layers ahead which help the stack of layers in between to learn a particular mapping.

So instead of just hoping that the deep networks will divide the stack of the layers and will learn desired mappings better on their own as we increase the depth, we explicitly make a stack of layers to learn the mapping. Figure 4 shows a unit of such network. As shown, the input is shorted to later layers.

In our experiments, we have used ResNet-50 architecture which is shown in the Fig. 4 because deeper network give better results whereas CNN suffers from vanishing gradient problem. Therefore we moved to ResNet (residual networks). ResNet has been able to handle the vanishing gradient problem and gives better results than CNN on image classification [20].

5   Experimental Results and Comparison with Previous Work

We have performed experiments on two different datasets. One is our dataset that we have generated as discussed in Sect. 3.1 and the second is the Malimg dataset used by Natraj et al. [31]. Malimg dataset consists of only grey-scale images of malware samples whose details are shown in Table 2.

To validate that our model gives at par results with the past work, we compared it with the model presented by Natraj et al. We have separately trained and tested the models on our dataset and Malimg dataset. The Tables 4 and 6 lists the precision and recall score for each class using deep CNN and ResNet-50 models. These comparisons show that our proposed CNN and ResNet-50 models perform better for both the datasets. Table 7 shows that the dense CNN model proposed in our work gives classification accuracy of 96.08% and 98.98% on Malimg dataset and our dataset respectively and ResNet-50 gives classification accuracy of 98.10% and 99.40% on Malimg dataset and our dataset respectively. These facts are comparable to the accuracy with the model proposed by Natraj et al. who got an accuracy of 97.18% on Malimg dataset.

One of the reason for using the RGB representation over grey-scale representation of malware images is that grey-scale images have very small differences between individual pixels and CNN and ResNet further averages out the adjacent pixels so the amount of pattern information we are trying to capture by representing the malware as image is somewhat higher in coloured representation. Another reason for using the RGB representation of malware images is

Table 4. Comparison of results using deep CNN model.

| Result of deep CNN model on our dataset | | | | | Result of deep CNN model on malimg dataset | | | | |
Classes	Precision	Recall	F1-score	Support	Classes	Precision	Recall	F1-score	Support
0	1.00	0.98	0.99	257	0	1.00	1.00	1.00	37
1	1.00	1.00	1.00	308	1	1.00	1.00	1.00	35
2	1.00	1.00	1.00	39	2	0.98	1.00	0.99	885
3	0.99	0.96	0.97	135	3	1.00	0.99	1.00	478
4	1.00	1.00	1.00	497	4	0.98	1.00	0.99	60
5	0.99	0.97	0.98	175	5	0.97	1.00	0.98	32
6	1.00	0.98	0.99	403	6	0.77	0.73	0.75	60
7	1.00	1.00	1.00	1096	7	0.64	0.61	0.63	44
8	1.00	1.00	1.00	339	8	1.00	1.00	1.00	54
9	0.99	1.00	1.00	388	9	1.00	1.00	1.00	49
10	1.00	1.00	1.00	563	10	0.98	0.98	0.98	115
11	1.00	1.00	1.00	1172	11	1.00	1.00	1.00	130
12	1.00	1.00	1.00	69	12	0.97	0.91	0.94	64
13	0.99	0.97	0.98	219	13	0.98	0.96	0.97	56
14	1.00	0.98	0.99	630	14	1.00	1.00	1.00	37
15	0.99	0.98	0.98	375	15	0.98	1.00	0.99	48
16	1.00	0.98	0.99	183	16	0.85	0.68	0.76	41
17	1.00	0.99	1.00	399	17	1.00	1.00	1.00	43
18	1.00	1.00	1.00	564	18	0.96	0.98	0.97	48
19	1.00	1.00	1.00	1838	19	1.00	1.00	1.00	24
20	1.00	1.00	1.00	451	20	0.39	0.49	0.43	39
21	0.96	1.00	0.98	1125	21	0.48	0.38	0.42	40
-	-	-	-	-	22	1.00	1.00	1.00	123
-	-	-	-	-	23	1.00	1.00	1.00	30
-	-	-	-	-	24	1.00	1.00	1.00	240
Avg	0.99	0.99	0.99	-	**Avg**	0.96	0.96	0.96	-
Total	-	-	-	11225	**Total**	-	-	-	2812

Table 5. Experimental results for packed and unknown malware

Classification model	Packed malware Test samples	Accuracy	Unknown malware Test samples	Accuracy
CNN	714	60.50%	10961	76.97%
ResNet-50	714	53.22%	10961	72.50%

that the accuracy of the model is relatively less for grey-scale representation as compared to colour map representation. The accuracy of our model came out to be 73% and 75% for CNN and ResNet-50 architecture respectively for grey-scale images on our dataset. The results are comparatively less as compared to the results achieved by using RGB or colour map representation on our dataset.

We have also performed experiments on our trained model using 714 test samples of packed malware and 10961 test samples of previously unseen malware

Table 6. Comparison of results using ResNet-50 model.

Result of ResNet-50 model on our dataset					Result of ResNet-50 model on malimg dataset				
Classes	Precision	Recall	F1-score	Support	Classes	Precision	Recall	F1-score	Support
0	1.00	0.99	0.99	257	0	1.00	1.00	1.00	37
1	1.00	1.00	1.00	308	1	1.00	1.00	1.00	35
2	1.00	1.00	1.00	39	2	0.98	1.00	0.99	885
3	0.99	0.97	0.98	135	3	0.99	0.98	0.98	478
4	1.00	1.00	1.00	497	4	1.00	0.98	0.99	60
5	0.99	0.98	0.99	175	5	1.00	1.00	1.00	32
6	1.00	0.98	0.99	403	6	0.98	0.99	0.97	60
7	1.00	1.00	1.00	1096	7	0.98	0.99	0.99	44
8	1.00	1.00	1.00	339	8	1.00	0.96	0.98	54
9	1.00	1.00	1.00	388	9	1.00	1.00	1.00	49
10	1.00	1.00	1.00	563	10	0.98	0.98	0.98	115
11	1.00	1.00	1.00	1172	11	1.00	0.99	1.00	130
12	1.00	1.00	1.00	69	12	1.00	0.99	0.98	64
13	0.99	0.98	0.99	219	13	1.00	0.98	0.99	56
14	1.00	0.98	0.99	630	14	1.00	1.00	1.00	37
15	0.99	0.99	0.99	375	15	0.96	1.00	0.98	48
16	1.00	0.99	0.99	183	16	1.00	0.99	0.99	41
17	1.00	0.99	1.00	399	17	1.00	1.00	1.00	43
18	1.00	1.00	1.00	564	18	1.00	0.98	0.95	48
19	1.00	1.00	1.00	1838	19	1.00	1.00	1.00	24
20	1.00	1.00	1.00	451	20	0.98	0.99	0.96	39
21	0.99	1.00	0.98	1125	21	0.98	0.99	0.97	40
-	-	-	-	-	22	0.98	0.98	0.99	123
-	-	-	-	-	23	1.00	0.97	0.98	30
-	-	-	-	-	24	1.00	1.00	1.00	240
Avg	0.99	0.99	0.99	-	**Avg**	0.98	0.98	0.98	-
Total	-	-	-	11225	**Total**	-	-	-	2812

Table 7. Experimental results

Classification model	Malware dataset			Accuracy	Malimg dataset			Accuracy
	Samples	Train set	Test set		Samples	Train set	Test set	
CNN	37374	26149	11225	98.98%	9339	6527	2812	96.08%
ResNet-50	37374	26149	11225	99.40%	9339	6527	2812	98.10%

which are not the part of our dataset. The trained model is not trained on these previously unseen and packed malware.

The results discussed in the Table 5 shows that the accuracy % values are 60.50% and 53.22% for CNN and ResNet-50 respectively when tested on packed malware and 76.97% (CNN) and 72.50%(ResNet-50) for previously unseen malware samples. To obtain our packed malware samples we have used a packer [14] which packs the malware executable and then they are being tested on the trained model. The previously unseen samples are gathered from sources

VXHeaven [10], Virustotal [2], Contagio [13]. Finally, in this section, we have compared our model results with the results from other visualization approaches in the literature. Table 8 shows that our model outperforms in terms of accuracy as compared to the other state-of-the-art models.

Table 8. Accuracy (%) comparison with other visualization approaches as reported in the literature.

Authors	Dataset	Approach	Classifiers (%)	Accuracy
Nataraj et al. 2011 [31]	9458 malware 25 families	Visualization using a grey scale byte plot representation	K-NN	97.18%
Han et al. 2013 [21]	Samples from 10 families	Visualization using op-code sequences	Selective area matching	
Makandar et al. 2015 [27]	Mahenhur (3131 malware and 24 families)	Visualization	ANN	96.35%
Seonhee et al. 2016 [35]	9 Families (I-stage) 27 Families (II-stage)	Two stage visualization	Deep neural network	98.4% 89%
Barath et al. 2016 [30]	BIG 2015 by Kaggle	Visualization	K-NN	96.6%
Liu et al. 2017 [26]	Kingsoft, ESNET NOD 32, and Anubis (20,000 samples)	Visualization	SNN	86.7%
Aziz et al. 2017 [28]	Malimg (12,470 samples)	Visualization	K-NN SVM	98.84% 98.88%
Aziz et al. 2017 [29]	Malimg Mahenhur	Three stage visualization	SVM	91.05% 92.53%
Kalash et al. 2018 [23]	Malimg Microsoft	Visualization	CNN	95.52% 99.97%
Yakura et al. 2018 [38]	VX Heaven (147803 samples and 542 families)	Visualization by extracting byte sequences	2D-CNN	50.97%
Our approach	37,374 samples 22 families	Visualization	CNN ResNet-50	98.98% 99.40%

6   Limitations and Future Work

In this paper, we have presented an approach based on image processing but there can be some adversarial effects to this approach. One of them is that if packed or previously unseen malware are used then our model detects it with a low accuracy as discussed in Sect. 5. This is due to the reason that packers use various cryptographic algorithms to encrypt the malware and it becomes hard for the model to detect the byte sequences for classification.

To remain undetected from this visualization approach of detecting malware, the malware authors can use obfuscation techniques such as adding jump instructions, redundant code fragments and applying permutations to the executable. This can be another area for future work where implementation can also be done for obfuscated malware.

Another dimension for future work can be the detection of evasive malware. The evasive malware are the one which remain undetected even by dynamic analysis as they are able to fool the controlled environment or sandbox and hide their original behaviour. Like, Cerber ransomware [16] is "sandbox aware" and refuse to detonate if it finds any virtual environment.

7   Conclusion

This work proposed a visualization based approach to classify malware using image representation. For image representation we have used RGB colour map representation over grey-scale. We have prepared our dataset by converting executable to images and trained our model using our dataset and one of the publicly available Malimg dataset. The model proposed in this work gives an improvement on the previous works as reported in the literature and also shows that applying state of the art neural network techniques in malware analysis is useful. Deep CNN and ResNet-50 models are used for training and testing both the datasets. The experiments are also performed on packed and previously unseen malware samples which lays down the foundation for future work.

Acknowledgement. This work was partially funded by Science and Engineering Research Board, Government of India.

References

1. Cohen, F.: Computer Viruses: Theory and experiments (1987). http://web.eecs.umich.edu/~aprakash/eecs588/handouts/cohen-viruses.html
2. Online malware report generator (2004). https://www.virustotal.com/
3. Kolbitsch, C., Anubis (2011). https://seclab.cs.ucsb.edu/academic/projects/projects/anubis/
4. Virusshare - malware repository (2011). https://virusshare.com/
5. Malshare- malware repository (2012). http://malshare.com/
6. Kaspersky Cybercrime, Inc.: How profitable is the business? (2014). https://blog.kaspersky.com/cybercrime-inc-how-profitable-is-the-business/15034/

7. Ida: About (2015). https://www.hex-rays.com/products/ida/
8. Ict: Facts and figures (2016). http://www.itu.int/en/ITU-D/Statistics/Documents/facts/ICTFactsFigures2016.pdf
9. Pandalabs-quaterly report (2016). http://www.pandasecurity.com/mediacenter/src/uploads/2016/05/Pandalabs-2016-T1-EN-LR.pdf
10. Vx heaven dataset (2016). https://archive.org/download/vxheaven-windows-virus-collection
11. Virustotal- daily statistics (2017). https://www.virustotal.com/en/statistics/
12. Airbnb engineering & data science - image classification (2018). https://medium.com/airbnb-engineering/categorizing-listing-photos-at-airbnb-f9483f3ab7e3
13. Contagio-malware dump (2018). http://contagiodump.blogspot.com/
14. Packer-tool upx 3.95, 26 August 2018. https://github.com/upx/upx/releases/tag/v3.95
15. Ollydbg v1.10, 27 September 2013. http://www.ollydbg.de/
16. Cerbr ransomware, 29 March 2017. https://www.securityweek.com/cerber-ransomware-tries-evade-machine-learning-security
17. Bahdanau, D., Cho, K., Bengio, Y.: Neural machine translation by jointly learning to align and translate. arXiv preprint arXiv:1409.0473 (2014)
18. Bazrafshan, Z., Hashemi, H., Fard, S.M.H., Hamzeh, A.: A survey on heuristic malware detection techniques. In: The 5th Conference on Information and Knowledge Technology, pp. 113–120. IEEE (2013)
19. Bengio, Y., Simard, P., Frasconi, P., et al.: Learning long-term dependencies with gradient descent is difficult. IEEE Trans. Neural Netw. 5(2), 157–166 (1994)
20. Glorot, X., Bengio, Y.: Understanding the difficulty of training deep feedforward neural networks. In: Proceedings of the Thirteenth International Conference on Artificial Intelligence and Statistics, pp. 249–256 (2010)
21. Han, K., Lim, J.H., Im, E.G.: Malware analysis method using visualization of binary files. In: Proceedings of the 2013 Research in Adaptive and Convergent Systems, pp. 317–321. ACM (2013)
22. He, K., Zhang, X., Ren, S., Sun, J.: Deep residual learning for image recognition. In: Proceedings of the IEEE Conference on Computer Vision and Pattern Recognition, pp. 770–778 (2016)
23. Kalash, M., Rochan, M., Mohammed, N., Bruce, N.D., Wang, Y., Iqbal, F.: Malware classification with deep convolutional neural networks. In: 2018 9th IFIP International Conference on New Technologies, Mobility and Security (NTMS), pp. 1–5. IEEE (2018)
24. Kong, D., Yan, G.: Discriminant malware distance learning on structural information for automated malware classification. In: Proceedings of the 19th ACM SIGKDD International Conference on Knowledge Discovery and Data Mining, pp. 1357–1365. ACM (2013)
25. Lin, Z., Feng, M., Santos, C.N.D., Yu, M., Xiang, B., Zhou, B., Bengio, Y.: A structured self-attentive sentence embedding. arXiv preprint arXiv:1703.03130 (2017)
26. Liu, L., Wang, B.S., Yu, B., Zhong, Q.X.: Automatic malware classification and new malware detection using machine learning. Front. Inf. Technol. Electron. Eng. 18(9), 1336–1347 (2017)
27. Makandar, A., Patrot, A.: Malware analysis and classification using artificial neural network. In: 2015 International Conference on Trends in Automation, Communications and Computing Technology (I-TACT-15), pp. 1–6. IEEE (2015)
28. Makandar, A., Patrot, A.: Malware class recognition using image processing techniques. In: 2017 International Conference on Data Management, Analytics and Innovation (ICDMAI), pp. 76–80. IEEE (2017)

29. Makandar, A., Patrot, A.: Wavelet statistical feature based malware class recognition and classification using supervised learning classifier. Orient. J. Comput. Sci. Technol. **10**(2), 400–406 (2017)
30. Narayanan, B.N., Djaneye-Boundjou, O., Kebede, T.M.: Performance analysis of machine learning and pattern recognition algorithms for malware classification. In: 2016 IEEE National Aerospace and Electronics Conference (NAECON) and Ohio Innovation Summit (OIS), pp. 338–342. IEEE (2016)
31. Nataraj, L., Karthikeyan, S., Jacob, G., Manjunath, B.: Malware images: visualization and automatic classification. In: Proceedings of the 8th International Symposium on Visualization for Cyber Security, p. 4. ACM (2011)
32. Ollmann, G.: The evolution of commercial malware development kits and colour-by-numbers custom malware. Comput. Fraud Secur. **2008**(9), 4–7 (2008)
33. Raghakot.: Resnet (2015). https://github.com/raghakot/keras-resnet
34. Santos, I., Nieves, J., Bringas, P.G.: Semi-supervised learning for unknown malware detection. In: Abraham, A., Corchado, J.M., González, S.R., De Paz Santana, J.F. (eds.) International Symposium on Distributed Computing and Artificial Intelligence. Advances in Intelligent and Soft Computing, vol. 91, pp. 415–422. Springer, Heidelberg (2011). https://doi.org/10.1007/978-3-642-19934-9_53
35. Seok, S., Kim, H.: Visualized malware classification based-on convolutional neural network. J. Korea Inst. Inf. Secur. Cryptology **26**(1), 197–208 (2016)
36. Torralba, A., Murphy, K.P., Freeman, W.T., Rubin, M.A.: Context-based vision system for place and object recognition (2003)
37. Vinod, P., Jaipur, R., Laxmi, V., Gaur, M.: Survey on malware detection methods. In: Proceedings of the 3rd Hackers Workshop on Computer and Internet Security (IITKHACK 2009), pp. 74–79 (2009)
38. Yakura, H., Shinozaki, S., Nishimura, R., Oyama, Y., Sakuma, J.: Malware analysis of imaged binary samples by convolutional neural network with attention mechanism. In: Proceedings of the Eighth ACM Conference on Data and Application Security and Privacy, pp. 127–134. ACM (2018)

MLDStore
DNNs as Similitude Models for Sharing Big Data
(Brief Announcement)

Philip Derbeko[(✉)], Shlomi Dolev, and Ehud Gudes

Ben-Gurion University of the Negev, Beer-Sheva, Israel
philip.derbeko@gmail.com, {dolev,ehud}@cs.bgu.ac.il

Abstract. The amount of data grows exponentially with time and the growth shows no signs of stopping. However, the data in itself is not useful until it can be processed, mined for information and queried. Thus, data sharing is a crucial component of modern computations. On the other hand, exposing the data might lead to serious privacy implications.

In our past research we suggested the use of similitude models, as compact models of data representation instead of the data itself. In this paper we suggest the use of deep neural networks (DNN) as data models to answer different types of queries. In addition, we discuss ownership of the DNN models and how to retain the ownership of the model after sharing it.

Keywords: Similitude model · Big data · Deep neural networks

1 Introduction

The conflict of data usage is that the data has to be shared with different parties to calculate correlations and infer insights. However, the sharing of the data leads to a significant risk to privacy, as shown by many recent data leaks.

To solve this conflict we suggest the use of a representative data model instead of the data itself [4,5]. We call such a model Similitude Model, i.e. a smaller model that is design to answer future unknown queries as if they were performed over the entire dataset. Similitude models are in common use in architecture and mechanical engineering [9]. In this research we suggest to use generative deep neural network models for data sharing instead of the data itself.

2 Motivation and Related Work

In our model, the data provider generates and maintains one or two types of the model and shares it with the cloud providers. Those cloud providers use the

We thank the Lynne and William Frankel Center for Computer Science and the Rita Altura Trust Chair in Computer Science.

© Springer Nature Switzerland AG 2019
S. Dolev et al. (Eds.): CSCML 2019, LNCS 11527, pp. 93–96, 2019.
https://doi.org/10.1007/978-3-030-20951-3_7

models to answer clients queries. Our goal is to allow data providers to share their data in succinct and computation efficient way without worrying about privacy leakage and also to allow clients to use the shared data for queries.

While the idea of building an accurate and probabilistic model of data is not a new one, in recent years as deep neural networks techniques are developed, there have been new advances in this area [1–3,6,14,16]. Using deep neural networks (DNN) as a basis for probabilistic models has few advantages. DNNs are able to capture complex structures in the data, able to generate a synthetic dataset without a high computational load and, they are scalable and can be adapted to high-dimensional data.

Once the data provider has trained the models, they are sent to the cloud to future use. In fact, new service, Machine Learning Data Store (MLDStore), just like the "AppStore" or "GooglePlay", in the domain of data can be created. MLDStore may support uploading and maintaining similitude models for others to be used, free of charge or per payment. The similitude models may not be copied to the clients but be kept in the cloud for the sake of sampling up to certain number of samples, allowing good enough answers to statistical queries. With time, the observed data changes, which requires updates to the model, that are then kept in the cloud. The continuous learning with changing data often leads to forgetting of the previously learnt data [8,12].

A simple, but expensive solution is to generate a dataset from the old model and mix it with the new data. This solution has the advantage of not increasing the size of the DNN model. Another solution with a constant size of the model was suggested in [15] where a set of pre-trained models are kept but they are connected laterally with learning connections. A slightly less expensive solution is to record the responses of the previous layers and mix them with a training data [10] or changing the objective function to include previous weights [16]. The choice of a specific algorithm is important but does not impact the rest of the paper.

3   Data Sharing Protocol

To answer different types of queries we use two types of networks. One is based on Generative Stochastic Networks (GSN) [1] whose accuracy can be improved by adversarial networks [3,6,11,16]. This type of networks is useful for the task of generating a synthetic sample and then running a statistical query on the generated data.

The second type of network is an auto-encoder based networks (see [2,20] for an overview). In this research, we use the encoder network for answering a point membership queries by adding an output layer to the encoder network. If the fit is good, then corresponding hidden units are activated and the output value will rise, otherwise the output value will be low.

The data sharing protocol is as follow.

1. The data provider builds (using well-known methods) two models: generative and encoder. The models are shared with a cloud provider.

2. Given the query from the user, if the query is a statistical query, the cloud uses the model to generate a synthetic dataset that is used to answer statistical queries. The size of the synthetic dataset is dictated by the required accuracy according to concentration inequalities [7,17].
3. If the user query is a point membership query, the cloud queries the kept encoder model. The output of the model indicates a fit of the data point for the model.
4. As the data provider receives more data, it continues to train the model [16] or adds a new model to the previous one [15]. A comparison of the techniques will be done in the full paper.
5. When the model is sufficiently changed, the updates or the entire model is then sent to the cloud to replace the previous one.

4   Ownership of the Model

We have described a mechanism that allows the data providers to share the data without really sharing the data. However, once the data provider shares the data model with the cloud, the cloud provider can use the model as it wishes to and can run as many queries as it wants. We want to prevent that and leave the ownership of the model in the hands of the data providers.

The way to do that is to use Secure Multi-Party Computations (MPC), see [18,19]. MPC were applied to DNN learning in [13] which used MPC to privately train models on shared data. In our case, it is enough to use Garbled Circuit for two parties, as described originally in [19]. The algorithm allows two parties to calculate a function f without exposing its own calculations.

To use MPC calculations the DNN has to be divided between two cloud providers, such that they can calculate network inference collaboratively. A simple way to do that is to replicate the network while the weights of the networks are split between the two providers. The split is done randomly as long as the combination of the weights equals to the original weight. The cloud providers will calculate the activation function for each of the unit using Garbled Circuit between them, at the end of the process both cloud providers will have a result of the networks inference. The client can send the query to any cloud provider. When the query is received an MPC protocol is initiated that performs the inference step of the model. The client does not have to be part of the MPC protocol, however, by being a part of the protocol the client can ensure that the clouds do not cooperate. The protocol, first agrees on the network unit that is has been calculated and performs unit calculations similarly to [13]. The calculated result is then returned to the client.

5   Conclusion

We briefly discuss a way to enable data providers to share their data without worrying that private information will leak. In addition, we discuss the notion of data ownership and suggest a solution. The full paper includes more details and experimental results.

References

1. Bengio, Y., Laufer, E., Alain, G., Yosinski, J.: Deep generative stochastic networks trainable by backprop. In: ICML (2014)
2. Bengio, Y., Yao, L., Alain, G., Vincent, P.: Generalized denoising auto-encoders as generative models. In: NIPS (2013)
3. Creswell, A., Bharath, A.A.: Denoising adversarial autoencoders. IEEE Trans. Neural Netw. Learn. Syst. (2018)
4. Derbeko, P., Dolev, S., Gudes, E.: Privacy via maintaining small similitude data for big data statistical representation. In: Dinur, I., Dolev, S., Lodha, S. (eds.) CSCML 2018. LNCS, vol. 10879, pp. 105–119. Springer, Cham (2018). https://doi.org/10.1007/978-3-319-94147-9_9
5. Derbeko, P., Dolev, S., Gudes, E., Ullman, J.D.: Efficient and private approximations of distributed databases calculations. In: 2017 IEEE International Conference on Big Data, BigData 2017, Boston, MA, USA, 11–14 December 2017, pp. 4487–4496 (2017)
6. Goodfellow, I.J., et al.: Generative adversarial nets. In: NIPS (2014)
7. Hoeffding, W.: Probability inequalities for sums of bounded random variables. In: Fisher, N.I., Sen, P.K. (eds.) The Collected Works of Wassily Hoeffding. Springer Series in Statistics (Perspectives in Statistics). Springer, New York (1962). https://doi.org/10.1007/978-1-4612-0865-5_26
8. Kirkpatrick, J., et al.: Overcoming catastrophic forgetting in neural networks. Proc. Natl. Acad. Sci. **114**(13), 3521–3526 (2017)
9. Kline, S.: Similitude and Approximation Theory. Springer, Heidelberg (1986). https://doi.org/10.1007/978-3-642-61638-9
10. Li, Z., Hoiem, D.: Learning without forgetting. IEEE Trans. Pattern Anal. Mach. Intell. **40**(12), 2935–2947 (2018)
11. Makhzani, A., Shlens, J., Jaitly, N., Goodfellow, I., Frey, B.: Adversarial autoencoders. CoRR, abs/1511.05644 (2015)
12. McCloskey, M., Cohen, N.J.: Catastrophic interference in connectionist networks: the sequential learning problem. In: Psychology of Learning and Motivation, vol. 24, pp. 109–165. Academic Press (1989)
13. Mohassel, P., Zhang, Y.: SecureML: a system for scalable privacy-preserving machine learning. In: 2017 IEEE Symposium on Security and Privacy (SP), pp. 19–38, May 2017
14. Rezende, D.J., Mohamed, S., Wierstra, D.: Stochastic backpropagation and approximate inference in deep generative models. arXiv preprint arXiv:1401.4082 (2014)
15. Rusu, A.A., et al.: Progressive neural networks. CoRR, abs/1606.04671 (2016)
16. Seff, A., Beatson, A., Suo, D., Liu, H.: Continual learning in generative adversarial nets. CoRR, abs/1705.08395 (2017)
17. Serfling, R.J.: Probability inequalities for the sum in sampling without replacement. Ann. Statist. **2**(1), 39–48 (1974)
18. Tassa, T., Gudes, E.: Secure distributed computation of anonymized views of shared databases. ACM Trans. Database Syst. **37**(2), 11:1–11:43 (2012)
19. Yao, A.C.: Protocols for secure computations. In: 2013 IEEE 54th Annual Symposium on Foundations of Computer Science, pp. 160–164 (1982)
20. Yoshua, B.: Learning deep architectures for AI. Foundations **2**, 1–55 (2009)

Cyber Attack Localization in Smart Grids by Graph Modulation (Brief Announcement)

Elisabeth Drayer$^{(\boxtimes)}$ and Tirza Routtenberg

Department of Electrical and Computer Engineering,
Ben-Gurion University of the Negev, Beer Sheva, Israel
drayer@post.bgu.ac.il, tirzar@bgu.ac.il

Abstract. In this brief announcement we present our ongoing work to localize "false data injection" (FDI) attacks on the system state of modern power systems, better known as smart grids. Because of their exceptional importance for our society and together with the increasing presence of information and telecommunication (ICT) components, these power systems are a vulnerable target for cyber attacks. In our method, we represent the power system as a graph and use a generalized modulation operator that is applied on the states of the system. Our preliminary results indicate that attacked grid states exhibit specific modulation patterns that facilitate the localization of the attacks on the particular buses of the grid. This approach is demonstrated by several case study simulations.

Keywords: False data injection (FDI) attacks · Anomaly detection · Graph signal processing · Laplacian matrix · Smart grid

1 Introduction and Motivation

With the shift from the classical, hardware dominated power system towards the "smart grid", that includes extensive use of information and communication technology (ICT), cyber security becomes a serious concern. Smart grids are considered to be a vulnerable target, as continuous electricity supply is essential for our society [6,7]. In particular, the false data injection (FDI) attack is an especially considered type of attack, which is not limited to smart grids, but can appear in all industrial control systems [3]. In these attacks, the attacker is able to compromise a portion of the measurement sensors of the power system. As a result, the state of the system is miscalculated, which affects the system operation status and may lead to serious physical consequences, including systematic problems and failures [3]. Thus, the ability to detect this type of attack on the power system is crucial.

Supported by the Kreitman School of Advanced Graduate Studies and the BGU Cyber Security Research Center.

S. Dolev et al. (Eds.): CSCML 2019, LNCS 11527, pp. 97–100, 2019.
https://doi.org/10.1007/978-3-030-20951-3_8

In our previous work we focused on methods to detect the presence of FDI attacks [1,2]. These methods are able to alert the grid operator about the presence of FDI attacks. In this brief announcement we present preliminary results from our ongoing research on an extension of these works that enables us to identify and localize FDI attacks within a certain geographic area of the grid. We represent the power system as an undirected weighted graph and use the concept of *generalized modulation* [5] on graph signals to localize FDI attacks.

2   Methodology

In this work we model the power system as an undirected graph, $G = (\mathcal{V}, E)$, where $\mathcal{V} = \{v_1, \ldots, v_M\}$ is a set of M nodes representing the buses where loads or generators are connected, and $E = \{(e_{i,j})\}$ is a set of transmission lines connecting bus i with bus j. Under the linear power flow model, the state of the power system is defined by the voltage angles at every bus of the system, $\varphi = [\varphi_1, \ldots, \varphi_M]^T$. The electric behavior of the lines, i.e. the line admittance, is represented by the weight of the edge $w_{i,j} : E \to \mathbb{R}$. This facilitates the modeling of the power system topology by a weighted Laplacian matrix $\mathbf{Y} \in \mathbb{R}^{M \times M}$. This matrix admits the eigenvalue decomposition

$$\mathbf{Y} = \mathbf{U\Lambda U}^T, \tag{1}$$

where $\mathbf{U}$ is the matrix of the orthonormal eigenvectors $\mathbf{U} = [u_1, \ldots, u_M]$ and $\mathbf{\Lambda}$ the diagonal matrix containing the real eigenvalues $\lambda_1, \ldots, \lambda_M$, respectively.

In [5], the generalized modulation operator for signals related to graphs is defined for the k-th eigenvector of $\mathbf{Y}$ as

$$\mathbf{H}_{k,i} = (M_k\varphi)_i \stackrel{\triangle}{=} \varphi_i \mathbf{u}_{i,k}, \tag{2}$$

where i is the bus number. This definition of modulation is a generalization of the classic modulation operator known in signal processing [5]. The modulation operator, M_k, can be applied on all buses and eigenvectors, leading to a matrix of modulations, $\mathbf{H} \in \mathbb{R}^{M \times M}$.

In an FDI attack measurements of the power system are compromised, leading to the attacked grid state

$$\varphi_{\text{FDI}} = \varphi + \mathbf{c}, \tag{3}$$

where $\mathbf{c}$ is the impact of the attack on the state vector. As the unattacked grid state, φ, is not known, the attack can not be detected or localized offhandedly.

The method we propose for the localization of such attacks is based on a comparison between the modulation matrices of different states of the system. In particular, if we have $\mathbf{H}^1$ and $\mathbf{H}^2$ for two different states of the grid, e.g. for two different time steps, we can calculate the matrix of the absolute difference between each element of these two matrices as

$$\Delta\mathbf{H}_{k,i} = \left| \mathbf{H}_{k,i}^1 - \mathbf{H}_{k,i}^2 \right|. \tag{4}$$

The main assumption that we use to localize FDI attacks is that, for two unattacked states, $\Delta\mathbf{H}$ from (4) will be a matrix with a random pattern and small values. This is related to the "smoothness" of the unattacked state with regard to the underlying graph structure [4,5]. FDI attacks destroy this smoothness and thus it is expected that the matrix $\Delta\mathbf{H}$ will contain a peak in the column related to the bus that is attacked.

3   Case Study

We have validated the assumptions and our proposed method on the IEEE 14-bus test system, a classic test system in the power system domain [8]. In the first step we generated a reference matrix, $\mathbf{H}_{\text{norm}}$, against which we have compared every new grid state. In a real world application, $\mathbf{H}_{\text{norm}}$ would be derived based on building the average over historic grid states. In our case, we used Monte Carlo simulations and (2) to generate $\mathbf{H}_{\text{norm}}$ as an average of undisturbed grid states.

In the second step, we simulated attacks on the buses of the system by modifying the grid state, φ, by arbitrary values, c: $\varphi_{i,\text{FDI}} = \varphi_i + c$. Then, according to (2), we calculate the modulation matrix $\mathbf{H}_{\text{attacked}}$. To localize a potential attack, the difference between $\mathbf{H}_{\text{norm}}$ and $\mathbf{H}_{\text{attacked}}$ is calculated as

$$\Delta\mathbf{H} = |\mathbf{H}_{\text{norm}} - \mathbf{H}_{\text{attacked}}| . \qquad (5)$$

Figure 1 illustrates the matrix $\Delta\mathbf{H}$ in the form of a heatmap for an unattacked grid state. The pattern is random with small values. On the other hand, Fig. 2a

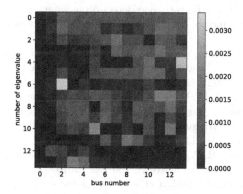

Fig. 1. $\Delta\mathbf{H}$ between $\mathbf{H}_{\text{norm}}$ and an unattacked grid state.

illustrates $\Delta\mathbf{H}$ for an attack on bus 7. The peak values in the corresponding column are clearly visible. Further simulations showed that our method not only works if one node is attacked, but also for multiple attacked nodes, see Fig. 2b. Currently we are extending our work to be able to use it to localize general bad

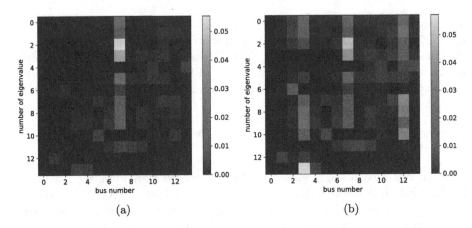

Fig. 2. $\Delta\mathbf{H}$ of a grid state: (a) with an attack on bus 7 (b) with an attack on the buses 3, 7, and 12.

data in the power system, as well as to detect topology changes. We will also formalize and statically analyze the localization method and will derive closed-form tests based on the here presented modulation matrices.

References

1. Drayer, E., Routtenberg, T.: Detection of false data injection attacks in smart grids based on graph signal processing. ArXiv e-prints https://arxiv.org/abs/1810.04894, December 2018
2. Drayer, E., Routtenberg, T.: Intrusion detection in smart grid measurement infrastructures based on principal component analysis. In: Accepted for IEEE PowerTech (2019)
3. Liang, G., Zhao, J., Luo, F., Weller, S.R., Dong, Z.Y.: A review of false data injection attacks against modern power systems. IEEE Trans. Smart Grid **8**(4), 1630–1638 (2017). https://doi.org/10.1109/TSG.2015.2495133
4. Shuman, D.I., Narang, S.K., Frossard, P., Ortega, A., Vandergheynst, P.: The emerging field of signal processing on graphs: extending high-dimensional data analysis to networks and other irregular domains. IEEE Signal Process. Mag. **30**(3), 83–98 (2013). https://doi.org/10.1109/MSP.2012.2235192
5. Shuman, D.I., Ricaud, B., Vandergheynst, P.: Vertex-frequency analysis on graphs. Appl. Comput. Harmonic Anal. **40**(2), 260–291 (2016)
6. Sridhar, S., Hahn, A., Govindarasu, M.: Cyber-physical system security for the electric power grid. Proc. IEEE **100**(1), 210–224 (2012). https://doi.org/10.1109/JPROC.2011.2165269
7. Ten, C., Manimaran, G., Liu, C.: Cybersecurity for critical infrastructures: attack and defense modeling. IEEE Trans. Syst. Man Cybern. - Part A: Syst. Hum. **40**(4), 853–865 (2010). https://doi.org/10.1109/TSMCA.2010.2048028
8. Thurner, L., et al.: Pandapower - an open source python tool for convenient modeling, analysis and optimization of electric power systems. IEEE Trans. Power Syst. **33**(6), 6510–6521 (2018). https://doi.org/10.1109/TPWRS.2018.2829021

Beyond Replications in Blockchain

On/Off-Blockchain IDA for Storage Efficiency and Confidentiality (Brief Announcement)

Shlomi Dolev$^{(\boxtimes)}$ and Yuval Poleg

Department of Computer Science, Ben-Gurion University of the Negev,
Beersheba, Israel
dolev@cs.bgu.ac.il, p.yuval@gmail.com

1 Introduction

We present on/off-Blockchain schemes for storing private data within the framework of public Blockchains that conceal its content and origin, spreading the data using information dispersal algorithm (IDA) [5] for preserving storage efficiency. The *on-chain* scheme encrypts the data and distributively store IDA shards over different blocks. Linkage of shards is also avoided by associating each shard with a different public key. The *off-chain* solution is based on storing Merkle tree root over the Blockchain while the actual shards are stored off the chain in the storage of the participants, and therefore is not replicated, achieving the Blockchain distributed trust without the drawback of replicating the entire data with every participant.

Our method presented in this paper is focused on the client's data, and storing hers sensitive information, even *off-chain*, while gaining availability and authenticity for the data, this achieved by using Blockchain technology as a proven mechanism for storing data that need to be immutable, and the use of IDA core capabilities. As our goal is to store client's data, we do not focus in improving the performance of the IDA as suggested in [1] or the Blockchain consensus infrastructure as suggested in [8].

Next we elaborate on Blockchain, then we describe our *on-Blockchain solution* and our *off-Blockchain solution*.

Blockchain. Blockchain's concept and the various applications that use Blockchain have rapidly evolved in the last years. Blockchain enables the usage of distributed ledgers across the Internet, storing immutable records on business actions and transactions. The trust for storing and maintaining the records is distributed rather than trust in a central entity.

We thank the Lynne and William Frankel Center for Computer Science, the Rita Altura Trust Chair in Computer Science. This research was also partially supported by a grant from the Ministry of Science and Technology, Israel & the Japan Science and Technology Agency (JST), and the German Research Funding Organization (DFG, Grant#8767581199).

S. Dolev et al. (Eds.): CSCML 2019, LNCS 11527, pp. 101–105, 2019.
https://doi.org/10.1007/978-3-030-20951-3_9

The most notable application that uses Blockchain is the crypto-currency Bitcoin [4], a distributed currency that was launched at the beginning of 2009. Besides crypto-currency, there are variety applications for Blockchain, in the domain of contracts, copyrights, intellectual property, supply chain tracking, and many more.

Transactions with Bitcoin are saved inside a block of the Blockchain. Each block contains several transactions. A block and the content of the block are designed to be immutable, by using (linked) signatures in the forms of hash functions. The blocks are replicated across many computers and servers participants. Prior to adding a new block, each such participant verifies the block validity (e.g., link-ability to previous block) and the validity of the transactions within the block (e.g., the balance of the entity with a certain public key allows the payment so there is no double spending).

Blockchain is based on the (trust-able) assumption that the majority of the participants are honest and will add only consistent blocks. Thus, any attempt to add an inconsistent block (that will imply a fork of the chain) will eventually be overcame by the consistent chain extension, where shorter chains are abandoned.

2   On-Blockchain Scheme

We propose to apply the IDA to each record that we want to store in the Blockchain, and store each shard with its index (matrix row number) in a different block. Whenever we would like to read back our record or data, we will need to read enough shards that are stored in multiple blocks and reconstruct them back using IDA.

We note that shards maybe stored in different Blockchains. Each of these Blockchain maybe implemented by different participants or (partially) the same participants and be based on the same technology or different technologies (e.g., Ethereum, Hyperledger).

IDA allows us to produce m shards from the data, such that unauthorized party that does not have enough shards i.e., at least n, and the random matrix, cannot reconstruct the data back. To ensure data confidentiality we do encrypt the data with a secret private key (different from the wallet's private key, possibly hash of the wallet's private key) prior to applying IDA. Since each shard is stored in a block, and each block is immutable and distributed across the system, we obtain all three aspects of information security: *Data Confidentiality*: with IDA no one can read and correlate the shard of our data among all other shard and even correlated needs to decrypt the data. *Data Integrity*: each block is immutable and cannot be tampered. *Data Availability*: here we benefit twice, each IDA product has a redundancy of $m - n$, and each shard is replicate and distributed across the web.

Shards Access Information. In Cryptocurrency like Bitcoin there is a utility named wallet [2] that stores private and public keys which identify a specific owner (e.g., person, organization). The wallet uses the associated private and public keys to perform operations such as a payment transfer or receive. The wallet stores and aggregates all the operations that are related to the owner's account, so she can see her balance. A way to manage our data is to use the same mechanism of Bitcoin's Deterministic wallet [7] that generates a new public key for each transaction. By generating a new public key for every transaction, an adversary cannot track down the owner's account operations i.e., to know what the balance of her wallet is. Using this capability in the scale of data shards can prevent linkage among shards of the same transaction. When we index the shards, we also store for each shard, it's index i.e., the row of the matrix that produced the shard.

IDA and Encryption. To achieve provable confidentiality of the data stored in the Blockchain, we also use encryption to encrypt the record before apply IDA, while IDA itself can gain us some degree of security with computational complexity for reconstructing the data under brute force attack, encryption adds another layer of security that can help us in case that an adversary obtains all the necessary shards. Because we encrypt the data, we do not need to regard the matrix value as an encryption key keeping the matrix value private. On the contrary, we can assume that the matrix is public; Since an adversary has to try many combination to try to trace back the shard, and even if the adversary manages to, the data is encrypted, knowing the matrix does not contribute much to the security.

3   Off-Blockchain Scheme

The mechanism of Blockchain to replicate every block is responsible for the security of the method, but also consumes storage. In general, while Information dispersal is an efficient storage solution for high availability the data, Blockchain is not. Our *On-Blockchain scheme* is particularly useful when we do not care about efficient storage, or when the data needed to be stored is small (e.g., passwords, keys) our *Off-Blockchain scheme* becomes handy when we want to store larger data e.g., contracts, photos, documents.

We propose to apply the IDA on the data that we want to store, as before, but now, each shard is stored locally by a different participant, at her own storage solution like on-premise storage, or cloud storage (e.g., Object storage), stored with an on-blockchain authentication using a Merkle tree data structure, and to store the root of the Merkle tree and the tree depth in the Blockchain. Therefore, we are using the Blockchain distributed trust capability without the necessity to replicate the entire data.

One benefit of Blockchain is the possibility to cope with dynamic set of participants, namely, to withstand reasonable churn. We suggest to employ *off-chain* memory of participants, thus, we have to consider erasures of off-Blockchain shards. One way to handle churn, is to periodically, prior to the erasure of too many shards, to read and rewrite any (distributed) *off-chain* stored data. Another possibility, is to store the *off-chain* data in third parties storage. Where the third parties are not necessarily a storage of the participants, but still most of which are trusted. In this case, in order to reconstruct the data, links to the location of the shared are needed. Such links may require storage on the chain. One can use a random number (e.g., the Merkle tree root) as a seed for producing a pseudorandom sequence that defines the links to the shared, the first link is associated with the first row of the matrix, the second link is associated to the second row of the matrix, and so on. The mapping between random numbers and a valid link maybe based on hamming distance to the closest valid link, or any analogous mapping.

As before, we assume that the IDA matrix is public as we encrypt the data prior to applying the IDA. Once a Merkle tree is constructed, we send each participant a pair $\langle T, P \rangle$, where P is a proof used to verify that $T = \langle i, v_i \rangle$ is indeed the i'th leaf in our Merkle tree. When we want to reconstruct our data, we ask from sufficient number of participants (depends on our initial setup for the IDA) the pair $\langle T, P \rangle$. Using P and T we can verify the integrity of the shard, and using the matrix rows we can apply reverse IDA to get back the data.

With this list, we can recalculate the entire path to the root without knowing the other leaves original values. Note that we need to verify that the length of P corresponds to the depth stored in the Blockchain for the tree. Once we recalculated the tree root, if the root value is identical to the one stored in the Blockchain, and the number of calculations we have made is equal to the depth of the tree stored in the Blockchain, then the leaf value we have is authenticated.

Encryption of the Data. As we discussed in the previous scheme, our IDA matrix is public, and we encrypt the data to achieve provable confidentiality, if we do not need the level of security implied by the encryption, we can reduce the calculation's complexity and have the matrix values being the secret.

We further suggest distributing the encryption key using secret sharing [6]. Each participant maintains not only the IDA shard but also a share of encryption key [3]. Shamir's secret sharing is a method to distribute a secret S into m unique parts, where each participant receives one part. There is a minimum number n, called threshold, that represents the number of parts needed to reconstruct the secret, any $n - 1$ parts cannot reconstruct (in fact has no information on) the secret. In our case we use secret sharing where we distribute the encryption key into the same size of the IDA key matrix, where m is the number of participants, and n is the minimum number of shards needed to reconstruct the data with IDA. Therefore, each participant besides its own shard, also receives a share of the secret so, when we reconstruct the data, we can reconstruct the secret and decrypt the data. To do so we add a third value to the verifier T tuple, $T = \langle i, v_i, D_i \rangle$ where D_i is the secret share for the i'th participant.

The steps to reconstruct the data now include also calculating the secret, using Lagrange interpolation over a finite field, to obtain the encryption key, and to decrypt the data.

References

1. Alon, N., Kaplan, H., Krivelevich, M., Malkhi, D., Stern, J.P.: Addendum to "scalable secure storage when half the system is faulty". Inf. Comput. **205**(7), 1114–1116 (2007)
2. CoinDesk: How to store your bitcoin (2017)
3. Krawczyk, H.: Secret sharing made short. In: Stinson, D.R. (ed.) CRYPTO 1993. LNCS, vol. 773, pp. 136–146. Springer, Heidelberg (1994). https://doi.org/10.1007/3-540-48329-2_12
4. Nakamoto, S.: Bitcoin: a peer-to-peer electronic cash system. Cryptography Mailing list, March 2009. https://metzdowd.com
5. Rabin, M.O.: Efficient dispersal of information for security, load balancing, and fault tolerance. J. ACM **36**(2), 335–348 (1989)
6. Shamir, A.: How to share a secret. Commun. ACM **22**(11), 612–613 (1979)
7. Wuille, P.: Hierarchical deterministic wallets (2012)
8. Zamani, M., Movahedi, M., Raykova, M.: RapidChain: scaling blockchain via full sharding. In: Proceedings of the 2018 ACM SIGSAC Conference on Computer and Communications Security, CCS 2018, pp. 931–948. ACM, New York (2018)

Self-stabilizing Byzantine Consensus for Blockchain
(Brief Announcement)

Alexander Binun, Shlomi Dolev$^{(\boxtimes)}$, and Tal Hadad

Department of Computer Science, Ben-Gurion University of the Negev,
Beersheba, Israel
dolev@cs.bgu.ac.il

1 Introduction

Blockchain is designed to cope with Byzantine participants using proof of work or proof of stake, see [2,14–16,19]. It is also designed to converge following potential disagreements that lead to the creation of forks; in some sense such a convergence causes the eventual stabilization of the Blockchain. The self-stabilization property of long lived systems is very important [6,10,11], ensuring for automatic recovery without human intervention.

Coping with unexpected faults (e.g., the executable code of each participant is altered), the system may lose consistency for a while. Then, when the recovery precondition are met (e.g., a majority of the participants execute their code, after a periodic refresh) the system automatically regains its consistency regardless of the state it starts from. The Blocks added to the Blockchain before and during recovery may be totally corrupted. Once recovered the participants can scan the history recorded in the Blockchain and add a block that corrects misconducted operations within the execution history.

Several Blockchain systems employ Byzantine agreement to decide on the next block (e.g., [5]), others (e.g., [13]) use Byzantine agreement for ordering the transactions within a block. Byzantine agreement is designed to cope with a given threshold on the number of Byzantine participants. See e.g., [3,7,8], and the references therein, on the way to address the cases in which this number of Byzantine threshold as well as other assumptions are temporally violated.

In this paper we demonstrate the effect of the temporary threshold violation on Hyperledger [13]. We demonstrate a specific case in which Hyperledger never recovers from a transient violation of the system state. We show that when the timestamp variables used by the Byzantine faults tolerant consensus algorithm

We thank the Lynne and William Frankel Center for Computer Science, the Rita Altura Trust Chair in Computer Science. This research was also partially supported by a grant from the Ministry of Science and Technology, Israel & the Japan Science and Technology Agency (JST), and the German Research Funding Organization (DFG, Grant#8767581199). We thank Chryssis Georgiou, Ioannis Marcoullis, Elad Michael Schiller for helpful discussions.

S. Dolev et al. (Eds.): CSCML 2019, LNCS 11527, pp. 106–110, 2019.
https://doi.org/10.1007/978-3-030-20951-3_10

are set to their maximal values the BFT-SMaRT used by the Hyperledger hangs forever. Then we propose to use the self-stabilizing Byzantine agreement (e.g., [3,7]) in order to facilitate recovery of BFT-SMaRT.

2 Terminology

In most Blockchain platforms (e.g., [1,12]) the life-cycle of a transaction is twofold:

- **Order:** Transactions are added to the ledger in some order and disseminated to all peers.
- **Execute:** Transactions are sequentially executed on all peers.

In Hyperledger Fabric (HLF) the transaction is three-fold:

- **Execute:** Transactions can be executed in any order.
- **Order:** When a sufficient number of peers responsible for ordering, called *orderers*, agree on the results of a transaction, the transaction is added to the ledger and disseminated to all nodes. This is the phase where the transactions are ordered. Before this happens there is no concept of one transaction happening before or after another.
- **Validate:** Each orderer validates and applies the transactions in a sequence defined by the ordering cluster.

For example, the orderers can check whether a later transaction was invalidated by an earlier transaction.

The transactions are ordered according to their timestamps. The content is not examined, e.g., to reveal Byzantine parties. So HLF (in its current distribution) is designed to tolerate only crashes. The case of Byzantine fault tolerance is considered in [4] that adds Byzantine Fault-Tolerant (BFT) functionality to the ordering phase. It is implemented as a HLF plugin and will be incorporated into the upcoming HLF distributions.

The BFT module [4] still suffers from the following drawback: A transient error might cause the BFT layer to be stuck forever. Unless an external party forcibly resets the entire system, the Hyperledger remains incapacitated. We suggest implementing the Byzantine fault-tolerant self-stabilization algorithm as in [3,8] to let the HLF ordering layer recover from such transient errors.

3 Transient Error that Incapacitates BFT

The transient faults used to demonstrate the missing stabilization property of Hyperledger that uses BFT-SMaRT is the modification of the timestamp variable *Epoch.timestamp* to hold the maximum possible value (e.g., [10,11] for analogous event). This can be done at runtime (using Java reflection) as in [22].

The code looks as follows:

```
Class<?> epoch = Class.forName("bftsmart.consensus.Epoch");
Field ftstamp = epoch.getDeclaredField("timestamp");
ftstamp.setAccessible(true);
ftstamp.set(cc, Integer.MAX_VALUE);
```

We reproduce the transient error as follows:

1. Set timestamps to the maximal possible value.
2. Reassemble BFT-SMaRT and Hyperledger following the instructions in [21].
3. Relaunch BFT-Smart and Hyperledger following the instructions in [20].

The resulting output is as follows:

```
Invocation 0-- ###################TIMEOUT######################
-- Reply timeout for reqId=0, Replies received: 0
, ERROR!

Orderer:
    Exception in thread "Server" java.lang.StackOverflowError
        at java.util.concurrent.locks.ReentrantLock.lock(ReentrantLock.java:285)
        at bftsmart.consensus.Consensus.getEpoch(Consensus.java:118)
        at bftsmart.consensus.Consensus.getEpoch(Consensus.java:107)
        at bftsmart.consensus.Epoch.<init>(Epoch.java:105)
```

Note that the executables of the Hyperledger and BFT-SMaRT were not changed. Only values of the variables were altered, just as a transient fault, e.g., soft error, single event upset, or insufficient redundancy in the used error detection code, may yield the change of variables values (e.g., [9]).

Many blockchains, e.g., RedBelly [18] and Tendermint [17] support the BFT consensus feature. At the heart of the BFT module lies the notion of "message timestamp counter" similar to the one of Hyperledger. Once corrupted due to a transient error, the message counter may be too large. By setting the counter to the maximal possible infinite value we can incapacitate any such Blockchain in the same way we did for Hyperledger.

4   Byzantine Self-stabilization for Orderers

We demonstrate that we are capable of adding self-stabilization to the Hyperledger and BFT-SMaRT by adding the Byzantine fault-tolerant synchronized clock from [3] to the prototype. Technically, we perform the following steps:

1. Compile the BFT clock module into the executable **clock.jar**
2. Update the entrypoint script of the Docker script **Dockerfile-orderingnode** that forms image of an ordering node as follows: (a) save the node IP for the future use by the self-stabilization BFT clock and (b) launch the BFT clock module.

The entrypoint script **startBFT.sh** will be as follows:

```
hostname -I >> hosts.txt
java -jar clock.jar &
./startReplica.sh
```

The self-stabilizing Byzantine clock synchronization will return indication on a too late response of the BFT-SMaRT and invoke a new instance of BFT-SMaRT for the next attempt of the Hyperledger to add a Block.

References

1. Androulaki, E., et al.: Hyperledger fabric: a distributed operating system for permissioned blockchains. In: Proceedings of the Thirteenth EuroSys Conference (EuroSys 2018), Article no. 30, 15 p. ACM, New York (2018). https://doi.org/10.1145/3190508.3190538
2. Amelchenko, M., Dolev, S.: Blockchain abbreviation: implemented by message passing and shared memory (extended abstract). In: NCA, pp. 385–391 (2017)
3. Binun, A., et al.: Self-stabilizing Byzantine-tolerant distributed replicated state machine. In: Bonakdarpour, B., Petit, F. (eds.) SSS 2016. LNCS, vol. 10083, pp. 36–53. Springer, Cham (2016). https://doi.org/10.1007/978-3-319-49259-9_4
4. Bessani, A., Sousa, J., Alchieri, E.: State machine replication for the masses with BFT-SMaRt. In: The IEEE/IFIP International Conference on Dependable Systems and Networks, DSN 2014, Atlanta, USA, June 2014
5. Chen, J., Gorbunov, S., Micali, S., Vlachos, G.: ALGORAND AGREEMENT: super fast and partition resilient Byzantine agreement. IACR Cryptology ePrint Archive 2018, 377 (2018)
6. Dolev, S.: Self-Stabilization. MIT Press, Cambridge (2000)
7. Dolev, S., Eldefrawy, K., Garay, J.A., Kumaramangalam, M.V., Ostrovsky, R., Yung, M.: Brief announcement: secure self-stabilizing computation. In: PODC, pp. 415–417 (2017)
8. Dolev, S., Georgiou, C., Marcoullis, I., Schiller, E.M.: Self-stabilizing Byzantine tolerant replicated state machine based on failure detectors. In: Dinur, I., Dolev, S., Lodha, S. (eds.) CSCML 2018. LNCS, vol. 10879, pp. 84–100. Springer, Cham (2018). https://doi.org/10.1007/978-3-319-94147-9_7
9. Dolev, S., Haviv, Y.A.: Self-stabilizing microprocessor: analyzing and overcoming soft errors. IEEE Trans. Comput. **55**(4), 385–399 (2006)
10. Perlman, R.: Fault-tolerant broadcast of routing information. Comput. Netw. **7**, 395–405 (1983)
11. Rosen, E.: Vulnerabilities of network control protocols: an example, RFC 789, July 1981
12. Sousa, J., Bessani, A., Vukolic, M.: A Byzantine fault-tolerant ordering service for the hyperledger fabric blockchain platform. In: The IEEE/IFIP International Conference on Dependable Systems and Networks, DSN 2018, June 2018
13. The hyperledger fabric ledger description. https://hyperledger-fabric.readthedocs.io/en/release-1.4/ledger/ledger.html
14. BFT-SMaRt in hyperledger fabric. https://github.com/bft-smart/fabric-ordering service
15. Hyperledger fabric: a distributed operating system for permissioned blockchains. https://arxiv.org/pdf/1801.10228v2.pdf

16. BFT-SMaRt. https://github.com/bft-smart/library
17. Tendermint. https://github.com/tendermint/tendermint
18. Redbelly. http://redbellyblockchain.io/
19. Proof of work vs. proof of stake. https://medium.com/@hydrominer/proof-of-work-vs-proof-of-stake-7b3afe24f0cc
20. Byzantine fault-tolerant ordering service for hyperledger fabric. https://github.com/bft-smart/fabric-orderingservice
21. Compiling the Byzantine fault-tolerant ordering service for hyperledger fabric. https://github.com/bft-smart/fabric-orderingservice/wiki/Compiling
22. Java reflection. https://docs.oracle.com/javase/tutorial/reflect/member/fieldValues.html

The Advantage of Truncated Permutations

Shoni Gilboa[1] and Shay Gueron[2,3(✉)]

[1] The Open University of Israel, Ra'anana, Israel
[2] University of Haifa, Haifa, Israel
shay.gueron@gmail.com
[3] Amazon, Seattle, USA

Abstract. Constructing a Pseudo Random Function (PRF) from a pseudorandom permutation is a fundamental problem in cryptology. Such a construction, implemented by truncating the last m bits of permutations of $\{0,1\}^n$ was suggested by Hall et al. (1998). They conjectured that the distinguishing advantage of an adversary with q quesires, $\mathbf{Adv}_{n,m}(q)$, is small if $q = o(2^{(m+n)/2})$, established an upper bound on $\mathbf{Adv}_{n,m}(q)$ that confirms the conjecture for $m < n/7$, and also declared a general lower bound $\mathbf{Adv}_{n,m}(q) = \Omega(q^2/2^{n+m})$. The conjecture was essentially confirmed by Bellare and Impagliazzo in 1999. Nevertheless, the problem of *estimating* $\mathbf{Adv}_{n,m}(q)$ remained open. Combining the trivial bound 1, the birthday bound, and a result by Stam (1978) leads to the following upper bound:

$$\mathbf{Adv}_{n,m}(q) \leq O\left(\min\left\{\frac{q^2}{2^n}, \frac{q}{2^{\frac{n+m}{2}}}, 1\right\}\right)$$

This upper bound shows that the number of times that a truncated permutation can be used as a PRF can exceed the birthday bound by at least a factor of $2^{m/2}$. In this paper we show that this upper bound is tight for every $m < n$ and $q > 1$. This, in turn, verifies that the converse to the conjecture of Hall et al. is also correct, i.e., that $\mathbf{Adv}_{n,m}(q)$ is negligible only for $q = o(2^{(m+n)/2})$.

Keywords: Pseudo random permutations ·
Pseudo random functions · Advantage

1 Introduction

The (in)distinguishablity of a random permutation from a random function is a combinatorial problem which has a fundamental role in cryptology. Indeed, various cryptographic primitives (block ciphers, hash and MAC schemes) are analyzed by starting from an idealization as a random permutation. This paper discusses a generalization of this problem.

Let ℓ, n be positive integers and let $\mathcal{F}_{n,\ell}$ be the set of functions from $\{0,1\}^n$ to $\{0,1\}^\ell$. A Pseudo Random Function (PRF) $\Phi : \{0,1\}^n \to \{0,1\}^\ell$ is a selection

© Springer Nature Switzerland AG 2019
S. Dolev et al. (Eds.): CSCML 2019, LNCS 11527, pp. 111–120, 2019.
https://doi.org/10.1007/978-3-030-20951-3_11

of a function from $\mathcal{F}_{n,\ell}$, according to some probability distribution. The quality of a PRF Φ is determined by the ability of an "adversary" to distinguish an instance of Φ from a function chosen uniformly at random from $\mathcal{F}_{n,\ell}$, in the following setting. It is assumed that the adversary has only query access to a function $\varphi : \{0,1\}^n \to \{0,1\}^\ell$, which is either selected uniformly at random from $\mathcal{F}_{n,\ell}$, or is an instance of the PRF Φ. The adversary may use any algorithm $\mathcal{A}$ that first selects (possibly adaptively) a sequence of queries to the function, i.e., strings in $\{0,1\}^n$, and then outputs a bit. We may interpret this bit as the guess of $\mathcal{A}$. For $b \in \{0,1\}$, let $P_\Phi^{\mathcal{A}}(b)$ be the probability that the output is b when φ is the PRF, and let $P_U^{\mathcal{A}}(b)$ be the probability that the output is b when φ is selected from $\mathcal{F}_{n,\ell}$ uniformly at random. The advantage of the algorithm $\mathcal{A}$ against the PRF Φ is defined as $\left| P_\Phi^{\mathcal{A}}(1) - P_U^{\mathcal{A}}(1) \right|$ (which also equals $\left| P_\Phi^{\mathcal{A}}(0) - P_U^{\mathcal{A}}(0) \right|$). The advantage, $\mathbf{Adv}_\Phi$, of the adversary against the PRF Φ is the maximal advantage of $\mathcal{A}$ against Φ over all the algorithms it may use, as a function of the number of queries (when the PRF Φ is clear from the context, we omit it and simply write $\mathbf{Adv}$). Hereafter, we consider adversaries with no computational limitations where the advantage has an explicit expression (see Sect. 2).

PRF Based on a Permutation. The classical example of a PRF from $\{0,1\}^n$ to $\{0,1\}^n$ is a permutation of $\{0,1\}^n$, chosen uniformly at random. In this case, the advantage of the PRF (i.e., the maximal advantage over all possible adversaries) is

$$\mathbf{Adv}(q) = 1 - \left(1 - \frac{1}{2^n}\right)\left(1 - \frac{2}{2^n}\right) \cdots \left(1 - \frac{\min\{q, 2^n\} - 1}{2^n}\right),$$

achieved by an adversary that executes the "collision test" (i.e., submits $\tilde{q} := \min\{q, 2^n\}$ distinct queries and outputs 1 if no two replies are equal, and 0 otherwise). An approximation for $\mathbf{Adv}(q)$ can be obtained by the following inequalities. For every $1 \le k \le \tilde{q} - 1$ we have

$$\left(1 - \frac{k}{2^n}\right)\left(1 - \frac{\tilde{q} - k}{2^n}\right) \ge 1 - \frac{\tilde{q}}{2^n},$$

and hence

$$\mathbf{Adv}(q) \le 1 - \left(1 - \frac{\tilde{q}}{2^n}\right)^{\frac{\tilde{q}-1}{2}} \le \min\left\{\frac{\tilde{q}(\tilde{q}-1)}{2^{n+1}}, 1\right\} = \min\left\{\frac{q(q-1)}{2^{n+1}}, 1\right\}.$$

On the other hand,

$$\left(1 - \frac{1}{2^n}\right)\left(1 - \frac{2}{2^n}\right) \cdots \left(1 - \frac{\tilde{q}-1}{2^n}\right) \le \frac{1}{\left(1 + \frac{1}{2^n}\right)\left(1 + \frac{2}{2^n}\right) \cdots \left(1 + \frac{\tilde{q}-1}{2^n}\right)}$$

$$\le \frac{1}{1 + \frac{1+2+\ldots+(\tilde{q}-1)}{2^n}} = \frac{1}{1 + \frac{\tilde{q}(\tilde{q}-1)}{2^{n+1}}},$$

and hence

$$\mathbf{Adv}(q) \geq 1 - \frac{1}{1 + \frac{\tilde{q}(\tilde{q}-1)}{2^{n+1}}} = \frac{\frac{\tilde{q}(\tilde{q}-1)}{2^{n+1}}}{1 + \frac{\tilde{q}(\tilde{q}-1)}{2^{n+1}}} \geq \frac{\frac{\tilde{q}(\tilde{q}-1)}{2^{n+1}}}{2 \max\left\{1, \frac{\tilde{q}(\tilde{q}-1)}{2^{n+1}}\right\}}$$

$$= \frac{1}{2} \min\left\{\frac{\tilde{q}(\tilde{q}-1)}{2^{n+1}}, 1\right\} = \frac{1}{2} \min\left\{\frac{q(q-1)}{2^{n+1}}, 1\right\}.$$

Therefore,

$$\mathbf{Adv}(q) = \Theta\left(\min\left\{q^2/2^n, 1\right\}\right). \tag{1}$$

This implies that the number of queries required to distinguish a random permutation from a random function, with success probability significantly larger than, say, $1/2$, is $\Theta(2^{n/2})$. In other words, a permutation can be used safely (e.g., as a one-time-pad) as long as the number of outputs (q) that it produces is sufficiently lower than $2^{n/2}$.

A generalization of the above PRF is the following.

Definition 1.1 (Truncated Permutation PRF). *Let* $TRUNC_{n,m} : \{0,1\}^n \to \{0,1\}^{n-m}$ *be defined by the mapping* $(x_1, x_2, \ldots x_n) \mapsto (x_1, x_2, \ldots x_{n-m})$. *The "Truncated permutation" PRF is the PRF defined by the composition* $TRUNC_{n,m} \circ \pi$, *where* π *is a permutation of* $\{0,1\}^n$, *chosen uniformly at random.*

Notation 1. *The advantage of an (computationally unbounded) adversary against the Truncated Permutation PRF is denoted by* $\mathbf{Adv}_{n,m}$.

The following problem arises naturally.

Problem 1. *For every* $0 \leq m < n$ *and* q, *find (the order of magnitude of)* $\mathbf{Adv}_{n,m}(q)$.

A different, related, problem is the following.

Problem 2. *For every* $0 \leq m < n$, *how many queries does the adversary need in order to gain non-negligible advantage against the Truncated Permutation PRF? Specifically, what is (the order of magnitude) of* $q_{1/2}(n,m) = \min\{q \mid \mathbf{Adv}_{n,m}(q) \geq 1/2\}$?

We proceed to describe a short history of these problems.

The Birthday Bound. We start by remarking that the classical 'birthday bounds'

$$\mathbf{Adv}_{n,m}(q) \leq \min\left\{\frac{q(q-1)}{2^{n+1}}, 1\right\}, \tag{2}$$

and $q_{1/2}(n,m) = \Omega(2^{n/2})$ are obviously valid. Every algorithm that the adversary can use with the truncated replies of $(n-m)$ bits from $\pi(w)$ ($w \in \{0,1\}^n$) can also be used by the adversary who sees the full $\pi(w)$ (it can simply ignore m bits and apply the same algorithm). Of course, we expect 'better' bounds that would reflect the fact that the adversary receives less information when $f(w)$ is truncated, and would allow for using the outputs of a (truncated) permutation for significantly more than $2^{n/2}$ times.

Hall et al. (1998). Problems 1 and 2 were studied by Hall et al. [6] in 1998, where the truncated (random) permutation were proposed as a PRF construction. The authors of [6] declared[1] the lower bound

$$\mathbf{Adv}_{n,m}(q) = \Omega(q^2/2^{n+m}), \tag{3}$$

for every $0 \le m < n$ and $q \le 2^{(n+m)/2}$. This bound implies that $q_{1/2}(n,m) = O(2^{(n+m)/2})$ for every $0 \le m < n$. Hall et al. [6] also proved the following upper bound:

$$\mathbf{Adv}_{n,m}(q) \le 5\left(\frac{q}{2^{\frac{n+m}{2}}}\right)^{\frac{2}{3}} + \frac{1}{2}\left(\frac{q}{2^{\frac{n+m}{2}}}\right)^{3}\frac{1}{2^{\frac{n-7m}{2}}} \tag{4}$$

For $m \le n/7$ this implies that $q_{1/2}(n,m) = \Omega(2^{(m+n)/2})$. However, for larger values of m, the bound on $q_{1/2}(n,m)$ that is offered by (4) deteriorates, and becomes (already for $m > n/4$) worse than the trivial birthday bound $q_{1/2}(n,m) = \Omega(2^{n/2})$. Hall et al. [6] conjectured that an adversary needs $\Omega(2^{(n+m)/2})$ queries in order to get non-negligible advantage, in the general case.

Bellare and Impagliazzo (1999). Bellare and Impagliazzo derived the following result in 1999 [1, Theorem 4.2].

$$\mathbf{Adv}_{n,m}(q) = O(n)\frac{q}{2^{\frac{n+m}{2}}} \tag{5}$$

whenever $2^{n-m} < q < 2^{\frac{n+m}{2}}$. This implies that $q_{\frac{1}{2}} = \Omega(\frac{1}{n}2^{\frac{m+n}{2}})$ for $m > \frac{1}{3}n + \frac{2}{3}\log_2 n + \Omega(1)$.

Gilboa and Gueron (2015). The method used to show (4) can be pushed to prove the conjecture made in [6], thus settling Problem 2, for almost every m. In particular, [2] showed that

$$\mathbf{Adv}_{n,m}(q) \le 2\sqrt[3]{2}\left(\frac{q}{2^{\frac{n+m}{2}}}\right)^{\frac{2}{3}} + \frac{2\sqrt{2}}{\sqrt{3}}\left(\frac{q}{2^{\frac{n+m}{2}}}\right)^{\frac{3}{2}} + \left(\frac{q}{2^{\frac{n+m}{2}}}\right)^{2} \tag{6}$$

for $m \le \frac{n}{3}$ and that

$$\mathbf{Adv}_{n,m}(q) \le 3\left(\frac{q}{2^{\frac{n+m}{2}}}\right)^{\frac{2}{3}} + 2\left(\frac{q}{2^{\frac{n+m}{2}}}\right) + 5\left(\frac{q}{2^{\frac{n+m}{2}}}\right)^{2} + \frac{1}{2}\left(\frac{2q}{2^{\frac{n+m}{2}}}\right)^{\frac{n}{n-m}} \tag{7}$$

for $\frac{n}{3} < m \le n - \log_2(16n)$. This implies that $q_{1/2}(n,m) = \Omega(2^{\frac{m+n}{2}})$ for every $0 \le m \le n - \log_2(16n)$.

---

[1] The paper [6] only provide a sketch of proof of (3) and claims that the computation may be completed by using techniques presented in the paper. We could not see how this is the case. We therefore refer to (3) only as a 'declared' result.

Stam (1978). Surprisingly, it turns out that Problem 2 was solved 20 years before Hall et al. [6], in a different context. The bound

$$\mathbf{Adv}_{n,m}(q) \leq \frac{1}{2}\sqrt{\frac{(2^{n-m}-1)q(q-1)}{(2^n-1)(2^n-(q-1))}} \leq \frac{1}{2\sqrt{1-\frac{q-1}{2^n}}} \cdot \frac{q}{2^{\frac{n+m}{2}}}, \tag{8}$$

which is valid for every $0 \leq m < n$ and $q \leq 2^n$, follows directly from a result of Stam [7, Theorem 2.3]. This implies that $q_{1/2}(n,m) = \Omega(2^{(m+n)/2})$ for every $0 \leq m < n$, confirming the conjecture of [6] in all generality (20 years before the conjecture was raised). We point out that the bound in [7] can be simplified to the more amenable form

$$\mathbf{Adv}_{n,m}(q) \leq \frac{q}{2^{\frac{m+n}{2}}}, \quad q \leq \frac{3}{4}2^n \tag{9}$$

This settles Problem 2, but note that Problem 1 still remains quite open.

The Best Known Bounds for Problem 1. Note that the bound (8) is tighter than the bounds (4), (5), (6) and (7). Therefore, summarizing the above results, the best known upper bound for the advantage in Problem 1, is the one obtained by combining (2) and (8), namely

$$\mathbf{Adv}_{n,m}(q) \leq \min\left\{\frac{q(q-1)}{2^{n+1}}, \frac{1}{2}\sqrt{\frac{(2^{n-m}-1)q(q-1)}{(2^n-1)(2^n-(q-1))}}, 1\right\}$$
$$= \Theta\left(\min\left\{\frac{q^2}{2^n}, \frac{q}{2^{\frac{n+m}{2}}}, 1\right\}\right), \tag{10}$$

whereas the only general lower bound that we are aware of is the bound (3), declared in [6]. By (1), we know that the bound (10) is tight if $m = 0$, and it was shown in [3] that it is tight also in the case $m = n - 1$.

Our Contribution. In this paper we answer Problem 1 by showing that (10) is tight for every $q > 1$, as formulated in the following theorem.

Theorem 1.1. *Assume $m < n$, $q > 1$. Then*

$$\mathbf{Adv}_{n,m}(q) = \Theta\left(\min\left\{\frac{q^2}{2^n}, \frac{q}{2^{\frac{n+m}{2}}}, 1\right\}\right).$$

In particular, note that this implies that the bound (3) is, in general, not tight.

2 Notation and Preliminaries

We fix $0 \leq m < n$ and $q \geq 1$. Let:

$$\Omega := \left(\{0,1\}^{n-m}\right)^q.$$

We view Ω as the set of all possible sequences of replies that the adversary gets for his q queries. We remark here that in our problem, we may assume that all the queries are fixed and distinct (and hence $q \leq 2^n$). For every $\omega \in \Omega$, $\alpha \in \{0,1\}^{n-m}$ let

$$d_\alpha(\omega) := \#\{1 \leq i \leq q \mid \omega_i = \alpha\}.$$

For every positive t, let $W(0,t) := 1$ and for every positive integer k,

$$W(k,t) := \prod_{j=0}^{k-1} \left(1 - \frac{j}{t}\right).$$

For $\omega \in \Omega$, let

$$R(\omega) := \frac{\prod_{\alpha \in \{0,1\}^{n-m}} W(d_\alpha(\omega), 2^m)}{W(q, 2^n)} = \frac{\prod_{\alpha \in \{0,1\}^{n-m}, d_\alpha(\omega) \geq 2} W(d_\alpha(\omega), 2^m)}{W(q, 2^n)}.$$

As in Sect. 1, consider an adversary that has only query access to a function $\varphi : \{0,1\}^n \rightarrow \{0,1\}^{n-m}$, which is either selected uniformly at random from $\mathcal{F}_{n,n-m}$, or is $\text{TRUNC}_{n,m} \circ \pi$, where π is a permutation of $\{0,1\}^n$, chosen uniformly at random. For every $\omega \in \Omega$, it is easy to verify the following: the probability that ω is the actual sequence of replies that the adversary gets for his queries is $1/|\Omega|$ in the former case, and $R(\omega)/|\Omega|$ in the latter. Suppose that the adversary uses an algorithm $\mathcal{A}$. Let $S \subseteq \Omega$ be the set of sequences of replies for which $\mathcal{A}$ outputs 1. Then

$$P_U^{\mathcal{A}}(1) = \sum_{\omega \in S} \frac{1}{|\Omega|}, \quad P_{\text{TRUNC}_{n,m} \circ \pi}^{\mathcal{A}}(1) = \sum_{\omega \in S} \frac{R(\omega)}{|\Omega|},$$

and the advantage of $\mathcal{A}$ against the PRF $\text{TRUNC}_{n,m} \circ \pi$ is therefore

$$\left| P_{\text{TRUNC}_{n,m} \circ \pi}^{\mathcal{A}}(1) - P_U^{\mathcal{A}}(1) \right| = \left| \sum_{\omega \in S} \frac{R(\omega) - 1}{|\Omega|} \right|.$$

Assuming the adversary has no computational limitations, we may conclude that

$$\mathbf{Adv}_{n,m}(q) = \mathbf{Adv}_{\text{TRUNC}_{n,m} \circ \pi}(q) = \max_{S \subseteq \Omega} \left| \sum_{\omega \in S} \frac{R(\omega) - 1}{|\Omega|} \right|.$$

Since

$$\left| \sum_{\omega \in S} \frac{R(\omega) - 1}{|\Omega|} \right| = \left| \sum_{\substack{\omega \in S \\ R(\omega) > 1}} \frac{R(\omega) - 1}{|\Omega|} - \sum_{\substack{\omega \in S \\ R(\omega) < 1}} \frac{1 - R(\omega)}{|\Omega|} \right|$$

$$\leq \max \left\{ \sum_{\substack{\omega \in S \\ R(\omega) > 1}} \frac{R(\omega) - 1}{|\Omega|}, \sum_{\substack{\omega \in S \\ R(\omega) < 1}} \frac{1 - R(\omega)}{|\Omega|} \right\},$$

with equality if $S = \{\omega \in \Omega \mid R(\omega) > 1\}$ or $S = \{\omega \in \Omega \mid R(\omega) < 1\}$, we conclude that[2]

$$\mathbf{Adv}_{n,m}(q) = \sum_{\substack{\omega \in \Omega \\ R(\omega) > 1}} \frac{R(\omega) - 1}{|\Omega|} = \mathrm{E}\max\{R - 1, 0\}, \tag{11}$$

and

$$\mathbf{Adv}_{n,m}(q) = \sum_{\substack{\omega \in \Omega \\ R(\omega) < 1}} \frac{1 - R(\omega)}{|\Omega|} = \mathrm{E}\max\{1 - R, 0\}, \tag{12}$$

where all expectations, here and below, are with respect to the uniform distribution on Ω.

3 Proof of Theorem 1.1

In this section we prove our main result. We first address the regime $1 < q \leq 2^{\frac{n-m}{2}+8}$, in which

$$\min\left\{\frac{q^2}{2^n}, \frac{q}{2^{\frac{n+m}{2}}}, 1\right\} = \Theta\left(\frac{q^2}{2^n}\right).$$

Proposition 3.1. *If* $1 < q \leq 2^{\frac{n-m}{2}+8}$ *then*

$$\mathbf{Adv}_{n,m}(q) = \Omega\left(\frac{q^2}{2^n}\right).$$

In the proof of Proposition 3.1 we will use the following technical lemma. We omit the proof.

Lemma 3.1. *For every positive t and positive integer $k \leq t/2$,*

$$\ln W(k,t) \geq -\frac{2k^2}{3t}. \tag{13}$$

Proof of Proposition 3.1. Assume first, in addition, that $q \leq 2^{n-m-1}$. Let

$$S := \{\omega \in \Omega \mid \forall \alpha \in \{0,1\}^{n-m} : d_\alpha(\omega) \leq 1\}.$$

For every $\omega \in S$,

$$R(\omega) = \frac{1}{W(q, 2^n)} = \prod_{j=0}^{q-1} \frac{1}{1 - \frac{j}{2^n}} \geq \prod_{j=0}^{q-1}\left(1 + \frac{j}{2^n}\right)$$

---

[2] Here is an adversary algorithm (attack) realizing this advantage: make a sequence of q arbitrary distinct queries and apply the function R on the sequence of replies. Output 0 if the result is smaller than 1 and 1 otherwise.

and hence

$$R(\omega) - 1 \geq \sum_{j=0}^{q-1} \frac{j}{2^n} = \frac{q(q-1)/2}{2^n}.$$

By (13),

$$\Pr(S) = W(q, 2^{n-m}) = \Omega(1).$$

Therefore, by (11),

$$\mathbf{Adv}_{n,m}(q) = \mathrm{E}\max\{R-1, 0\} \geq \Pr(S)\frac{q(q-1)/2}{2^n} = \Omega\left(\frac{q^2}{2^n}\right).$$

Now, if $2^{n-m-1} < q \leq 2^{\frac{n-m}{2}+8}$, then by what we already proved

$$\mathbf{Adv}_{n,m}(q) \geq \mathbf{Adv}_{n,m}(2^{n-m-1}) = \Omega\left(\frac{\left(2^{n-m-1}\right)^2}{2^n}\right) = \Omega\left(\frac{q^2}{2^n}\right).$$

We now address the regime $2^{\frac{n-m}{2}+8} < q \leq 2^{\frac{n+m}{2}-3}$, in which

$$\min\left\{\frac{q^2}{2^n}, \frac{q}{2^{\frac{n+m}{2}}}, 1\right\} = \Theta\left(\frac{q}{2^{\frac{n+m}{2}}}\right).$$

Proposition 3.2. *Assume that* $2^{\frac{n-m}{2}+8} < q \leq 2^{\frac{n+m}{2}-3}$. *Then*

$$\mathbf{Adv}_{n,m}(q) = \Omega\left(\frac{q}{2^{\frac{n+m}{2}}}\right).$$

Proposition 3.2 will follow easily from the following technical lemmas. We omit the proofs. For $\omega \in \Omega$, let $C(\omega)$ be the number of 'collisions' in ω, i.e.,

$$C(\omega) = \#\{1 \leq i < j \leq q \mid \omega_i = \omega_j\} = \sum_{\alpha \in \{0,1\}^{n-m}} \binom{d_\alpha(\omega)}{2}.$$

Lemma 3.2. *Suppose q is a power of 2. Then*

$$R \leq e^{\frac{1}{2}\cdot\frac{q(q-1)}{2^{n+m}} - \frac{1}{2^m}(C-EC)}.$$

Lemma 3.3. *If $q > 2^{\frac{n-m}{2}+8}$ then*

$$\Pr\left(C - EC > \frac{1}{10}\sqrt{\frac{q(q-1)}{2^{n-m}}}\right) > \frac{1}{400}$$

We will now proceed to prove Proposition 3.2.

Proof of Proposition 3.2. With no loss of generality we may assume that q is a power of 2. If $C(\omega) - \text{EC} > \frac{1}{10}\sqrt{\frac{q(q-1)}{2^{n-m}}}$ then

$$\frac{1}{2} \cdot \frac{q(q-1)}{2^{n+m}} - \frac{1}{2^m}(C(\omega) - \text{EC}) < \frac{1}{2} \cdot \frac{q(q-1)}{2^{n+m}} - \frac{1}{2^m} \cdot \frac{1}{10}\sqrt{\frac{q(q-1)}{2^{n-m}}}$$

$$= -\frac{1}{10}\left(1 - 5\sqrt{\frac{q(q-1)}{2^{n+m}}}\right)\sqrt{\frac{q(q-1)}{2^{n+m}}} < -\frac{3}{80}\sqrt{\frac{q(q-1)}{2^{n+m}}},$$

hence, by Lemma 3.2,

$$1 - R(\omega) > 1 - e^{-\frac{3}{80}\sqrt{\frac{q(q-1)}{2^{n+m}}}}.$$

Therefore, by (12) and Lemma 3.3,

$$\mathbf{Adv}_{n,m}(q) = \text{E}\max\{1 - R, 0\} > \frac{1}{400}\left(1 - e^{-\frac{3}{80}\sqrt{\frac{q(q-1)}{2^{n+m}}}}\right) = \Omega\left(\frac{q}{2^{\frac{n+m}{2}}}\right).$$

Now we can prove Theorem 1.1.

Proof of Theorem 1.1. The upper bound was already demonstrated in the introduction, so we only need to show that

$$\mathbf{Adv}_{n,m}(q) = \Omega\left(\min\left\{\frac{q^2}{2^n}, \frac{q}{2^{\frac{n+m}{2}}}, 1\right\}\right).$$

If $1 < q \le 2^{\frac{n-m}{2}+8}$ then by Proposition 3.1

$$\mathbf{Adv}_{n,m}(q) = \Omega\left(\frac{q^2}{2^n}\right).$$

If $2^{\frac{n-m}{2}+8} < q \le 2^{\frac{n+m}{2}-3}$ then by Proposition 3.2

$$\mathbf{Adv}_{n,m}(q) = \Omega\left(\frac{q}{2^{\frac{n+m}{2}}}\right).$$

Finally, if $q > 2^{\frac{n+m}{2}-3}$ then by Proposition 3.2

$$\mathbf{Adv}_{n,m}(q) \ge \mathbf{Adv}_{n,m}\left(2^{\frac{n+m}{2}-3}\right) = \Omega\left(\frac{2^{\frac{n+m}{2}-3}}{2^{\frac{n+m}{2}}}\right) = \Omega(1).$$

4   Conclusions

Theorem 1.1 settled Problem 1 by showing that the upper bound (10) is tight for every $q > 1$.

Note that truncated permutations are used in practice, due to the simplicity of this construction, as a Beyond-Birthday-Bound PRF. Examples (specifically with $m = n/2$) for the use of truncated permutations for key derivation can be seen in [5] and also in the AES-GCM-SIV emerging standard [4].

An extended version, containing detailed proofs of all statements, is available at https://arxiv.org/abs/1610.02518.

Acknowledgments. We thank Ron Peled for fruitful discussion.

This research was partially supported by: The Israel Science Foundation (grant No. 1018/16); The BIU Center for Research in Applied Cryptography and Cyber Security, in conjunction with the Israel National Cyber Bureau in the Prime Minister's Office; The Center for Cyber Law and Policy at the University of Haifa in conjunction with the Israel National Cyber Directorate in the Prime Minister's Office.

References

1. Bellare, M., Impagliazzo, R.: A tool for obtaining tighter security analyses of pseudorandom function based constructions, with applications to PRP to PRF conversion. ePrint 1999/024. http://eprint.iacr.org/1999/024
2. Gilboa, S., Gueron, S.: Distinguishing a truncated random permutation from a random function, manuscript (2015). https://arxiv.org/abs/1508.00462
3. Gilboa, S., Gueron, S., Morris, B.: How many queries are needed to distinguish a truncated random permutation from a random function? J. Cryptol. **31**(1), 162–171 (2018)
4. Gueron, S., Langley, A., Lindell, Y.: AES-GCM-SIV: nonce misuse-resistant authenticated encryption. https://datatracker.ietf.org/doc/draft-irtf-cfrg-gcmsiv/
5. Gueron, S., Lindell, Y.: Better bounds for block cipher modes of operation via nonce-based key derivation. In: Proceedings of the 2017 ACM SIGSAC Conference on Computer and Communications Security, CCS 2017, pp. 1019–1036 (2017)
6. Hall, C., Wagner, D., Kelsey, J., Schneier, B.: Building PRFs from PRPs. In: Krawczyk, H. (ed.) CRYPTO 1998. LNCS, vol. 1462, pp. 370–389. Springer, Heidelberg (1998). https://doi.org/10.1007/BFb0055742
7. Stam, A.J.: Distance between sampling with and without replacement. Stat. Neerl. **32**(2), 81–91 (1978)

Reconstructing C2 Servers for Remote Access Trojans with Symbolic Execution

Luca Borzacchiello, Emilio Coppa[✉], Daniele Cono D'Elia,
and Camil Demetrescu

Sapienza University of Rome, Rome, Italy
{borzacchiello,coppa,delia,demetres}@diag.uniroma1.it

Abstract. The analysis of a malicious piece of software that involves a remote counterpart that instructs it can be troublesome for security professionals, as they may have to unravel the communication protocol in use to figure out what actions can be carried out on the victim's machine. The possibility to recur to dynamic analysis hinges on the availability of an active remote counterpart, a requirement that may be difficult to meet in several scenarios. In this paper we explore how symbolic execution techniques can be used to synthesize a command-and-control server for a remote access trojan, enabling in-vivo analysis by malware analysts. We evaluate our ideas against two real-world malware instances.

Keywords: Malware analysis · Symbolic execution · Protocol reversing

1 Introduction

Remote Access Trojan (RAT) is a term used to identify a cyber menace that can steal information and carry out malicious behaviors on a victim machine at the command of a remote counterpart. RATs provide attackers with capabilities like file upload, key logging, and remote code execution, communicating with a counterpart commonly dubbed C2 (Command & Control) server. Communication protocols are specific to RAT families and can become richer as families evolve over time: although packets are carried out using standard means like HTTP or IRC, their format is proprietary and the contents possibly encrypted.

Unlike other malware categories, analyzing a RAT typically requires active ongoing communications for the results of the analysis to be rich. This is the case not only with an initial assessment in a sandbox, but also with an in-depth analysis by malware analysts on its code. Unfortunately this may not be possible for a variety of reasons. For instance, a company that discovers and promptly contains an infection [14] may not allow communications for the sake of analysis, especially where there is a suspicion of a targeted attack—as such communications would reveal that the target has been reached. A server counterpart may also decline connection attempts when the analysis takes place

S. Dolev et al. (Eds.): CSCML 2019, LNCS 11527, pp. 121–140, 2019.
https://doi.org/10.1007/978-3-030-20951-3_12

from an unexpected network origin or time frame. Another common scenario is when the server disappears from the network—either at the attacker's will or because of an intervention by the authorities—but the analysis of the RAT could still be valuable (e.g., to unveil its infection spreading mechanisms).

Automatic analysis systems may be of little use in the absence of an active counterpart, leaving manual dissection as the only avenue to analysis. RATs can accept dozens distinct commands as part of the communications with the C2 server: while commands are usually not hard to analyze when taken individually, their number and interplay can make the analysis quite complex and time consuming. Authentication schemes can make the work of human analysts even more tedious as they have to mimic them when carrying out the analysis. Finally, even in the presence of an active counterpart the server may not be sending all the supported commands within a reasonable timeframe, leaving to the analyst the task of unveiling the characteristics of the remaining ones.

Protocol reverse engineering techniques may reveal details of the communication scheme, producing automata and grammars that capture facts inferred by analyzing packets. Their applicability to RAT analysis may however be limited by constraints, e.g., on having to communicate with the server for validating messages, or on having access to its binary. Although the output of such techniques can bring valuable insights to analysts, they could not be used readily in the setting where malware dissection normally takes place, which would instead benefit from having a synthesized counterpart to interact with in order to reveal indicators and features of the sample other than its communication protocol.

Previous research has explored static analysis techniques to ease RAT dissection: in particular, [2] proposes symbolic execution to reveal and analyze the commands supported by a RAT without requiring the presence of the server counterpart. The output is a collection of execution traces enriched with symbolic constraints on the data buffers exchanged throughout communications. Unfortunately, such traces typically encompass at most one command due to scalability issues, and may come in numbers often much greater than the supported commands due to the nature of the symbolic exploration: for instance, multiple paths can be generated for the same command when its handler contains loops or when memory is dereferenced using a symbolic pointer [3,11]. Another problem is that such reports cannot be merged to form longer paths descriptive of communication patterns with the C2 server, as protocol rules may shape subsequent packets differently than in a naive concatenation of recorded communications (consider for instance the use of sequence numbers).

Contributions. We propose a technique to reconstruct the C2 server counterpart for a RAT by having access only to the sample meant to run on the victim's machine. Our goal is to synthesize a program so that the analyst can make the client connect to it, enabling in-vivo analysis of the RAT. To this end:

- we produce execution traces for a sample using symbolic execution, exploring the full software stack to avoid writing API models required by [2];
- we assemble traces into a compact automata representation inspired by previous protocol reverse engineering research;

- we augment the automaton with speculative edges not seen in recorded traces to build paths that span multiple commands in a C2 communication session, and validate them with symbolic execution to generate server instances.

We implement the technique in the context of the S2E platform [7], and perform a preliminary assessment against two well-known RAT samples.

2   Approach

In the present section we provide the reader with an overview of our approach. We then describe in detail every step of the proposed technique, using a simple C2 communication protocol implemented in an artificial RAT as running example to highlights challenges and key points in our strategy. Finally, we discuss open problems and limitations of our solution.

2.1   Overview

Figure 1 visually summarizes the main steps behind our approach:

1. *Trace Generation.* Given a RAT sample, we use symbolic execution [3] as in [2] to reveal different executions paths, trying to maximize code coverage during the exploration. For each path we record traces of taken branches and relevant APIs that get executed. The presence of input-dependent loops and the uncertainty on other portions of the input may lead to a high number of alternative states in the symbolic executor, but we expect a significant fraction of the recorded traces to reveal at least one command of the RAT (i.e., the associated paths are deep enough to perform authentication and carry out one of the supported functionalities). Traces where no interesting APIs have been executed are discarded.
2. *Trace Analysis.* To reason over the possibly large number of reports generated during the previous step we build an Augmented Prefix Tree Acceptor (APTA) [6], a tree-shaped DFA used in previous research on protocol reverse engineering [10]. This representation allows us to compactly represent traces into a single data structure, capturing which APIs and branches have been observed along different paths.
3. *Speculation.* While an APTA can capture information about distinct (symbolically executed) paths, our goal is to generate a small number of paths— ideally one—that can cover all the commands. We use information from past executions to speculate over richer paths that could be possible in the RAT but were not observed possibly due to the limited scalability of the symbolic analysis. To this end, we add speculative edges to the APTA—turning it into a graph—and compute path(s) that can cover all its nodes, describing an execution where multiple commands are taken in by the RAT.
4. *Validation.* We validate the feasibility of a speculatively generated path with symbolic execution, using knowledge on the branches from initially recorded traces to drive the exploration. We rely on the symbolic engine to fill the

blanks for the actions that take place between two commands linked by a speculative edge, as the latter is not backed by a trace. When the symbolic exploration succeeds, we record a sequence of API calls and results that in a native execution would lead the client to follow the path. When we cannot produce a valid sequence, we go back and try a different speculation.

5. *C2 Server Generation.* For each validated path spanning multiple commands, we synthesize a C2 server counterpart for executing the client natively. At each step the server executes APIs that symmetrically interact with the ones invoked by the client (e.g., they send data when a client is expecting to receive some), using inputs that were instantiated in the symbolic exploration.

2.2   Steps

To illustrate the different steps of our approach we will use the artificial RAT instance of Fig. 2 as running example: as we mentioned, its code is meant to capture common traits of several real-world RATs. The client instantiates a connection to the C2 server and waits from the attacker for the commands to be executed on the victim's machine. Its dispatcher takes the form of an infinite loop for processing incoming packets: our RAT supports only two commands, namely the first allows the attacker to execute a program using the WinExec Windows API, while the second can remove a file using DeleteFile. A simple authentication scheme is implemented at branches B2 and B3 in the code, while sequence numbers are used for packet validation at branch B4.

Trace Generation. Similarly as in [2] we use symbolic execution techniques to reveal interesting control-flow paths that the execution may follow within a RAT. A symbolic engine supplies symbolic expressions in place of concrete inputs to a program, where an input may represent data coming from the network or other interactions with the OS. When symbolically executing instructions in the program, the engine maintains a collection of constraints on the program state, forking the execution when a branch involving symbolic expressions is met and both outcomes are feasible. An SMT solver is used to evaluate symbolic expressions as well as to obtain valid concrete assignments for them.

Symbolic execution can be very valuable in our setting, as the analysis can be carried out by modeling the communications with the C2 server using symbolic buffers in network-related APIs. Unfortunately though symbolic techniques incur scalability issues (especially the path explosion problem [2,3]) that make it hard to analyze long program paths. Fully automatic approaches to the exploration of a RAT are unlikely to reveal the commands without heuristics tailored to the structure of the sample under analysis; also, the presence of code for its initial activities (e.g., environmental checks, achieving persistence) may prevent the exploration from reaching the command dispatching loop at all. For this reason we ask the analyst to provide hints in the form of the location of the dispatcher loop and relevant details for reaching it (such as the thread on which the analysis should focus or branches that were possibly forced in the debugger).

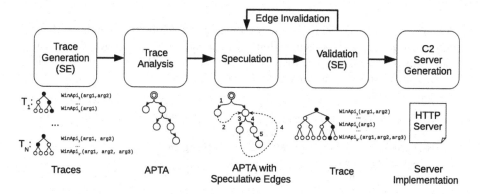

Fig. 1. Overview of the steps for the proposed approach.

```
unsigned char seqNum = 0;
unsigned char data[N];
int socket = connectWithServer(); // socket + connect
while (1) { // B1
    clearBuffer(data, N);
    read(socket, data, N);
    if (seqNum == 0) { // B2
        if (strncmp("MAGIC_STR", data, N) == 0) // B3
            seqNum += 1; // authentication success
    } else if (seqNum == data[0]) { // B4
        switch (data[1]) {
            case 1: // B5
                WinExec(data + 2, 0); break;
            case 2: // B6
                DeleteFile(data + 2); break;
        }
        seqNum += 1;
    }
}
```

Fig. 2. Artificial RAT instance. For the sake of presentation, conditional branches and case statements in the C code are annotated with labels B_K.

Once the symbolic exploration reaches the loop for the first time, we adopt an iterative deepening search strategy as in [2] to combine the benefits of BFS and DFS in this specific setting: each alternative path originating from the uncertainty on received inputs is explored for a given number of instructions before the exploration switches to another path in the queue. Optionally the analyst can provide further hints on the location of the handler for individual commands, which may be simple to spot in a debugger unless the code is heavily obfuscated. For each path we record the sequence of taken branches and Windows API calls for communications or anyhow relevant in malicious code analysis (we will refer to such APIs as *interesting*). Branches are split in groups across invocations of APIs that produce new symbolic inputs. The exploration is terminated upon exhaustion of the memory and time budget for the analysis.

When symbolically executing our artificial RAT using the search strategy described above, and assuming that we exhaust the time budget after completing two iterations of the dispatcher loop (branch B1) along each possible path, our approach generates the following traces:

- *Trace 1*
  (a) API: socket(...), connect(..., SERVER_ADDR, ...), read(..., D_1, 64), read(..., D_2, 64), WinExec(D_3, 0)
  (b) buffers: *D_1 := "MAGIC_STR", *D_2 := "11Program.exe", *D_3 := "Program.exe"
  (c) taken branches: [B1], [B2, B3], [B4, B5]
- *Trace 2*
  (a) API: socket(...), connect(..., SERVER_ADDR, ...), read(..., D_1, 64), read(..., D_2, 64), DeleteFile(D_3)
  (b) buffers: *D_1 = "MAGIC_STR", *D_2 = "12File.doc", *D_3 = "File.doc"
  (c) taken branches: [B1], [B2, B3], [B4, B6]
- *Other traces*
  Traces that failed to authenticate (i.e., branch B3 not taken) or received invalid commands (i.e., sequence number not validated at B4 or unimplemented switch). Discarded as they do not contain any interesting Windows APIs.

For each trace we maintain three records: (a) a list of executed APIs and their call sites (omitted for brevity, we use them to distinguish different calls to the same API), (b) a concrete assignment for each symbolic buffer D_i manipulated by one or more API in the trace, and (c) a list of branches taken along the explored path. For instance, the first trace reports that the client instantiates a connection to a C2 server identified by the sockaddr structure SERVER_ADDR, performs two consecutive read operations, and executes the WinExec API. The trace provides concrete assignments for buffers D_1, D_2, and D_3, obtained by querying the solver before terminating the exploration. When buffers used as arguments for known APIs contain unconstrained or loosely constrained symbolic values, we add constraints to make the solver produce an answer meaningful for a human agent. For instance, we ask the solver whether symbolic buffer D_3 can hold a path to some executable. Taken branches are split across the two invocations of read. In our traces read yields symbolic buffers D_1 and D_2, while D_3 is a substring of D_2.

Observe that the two traces cannot directly be merged to form a longer one involving both commands: the sequence numbering scheme would drop replayed packets for commands issued in different communication sessions.

Trace Analysis. To compactly represent the generated traces we use an APTA representation inspired by prior protocol reversing research [10]. An APTA is a tree-shaped, incompletely specified DFA (deterministic finite state automaton) [6]: its root represents the common initial state for the explored traces,

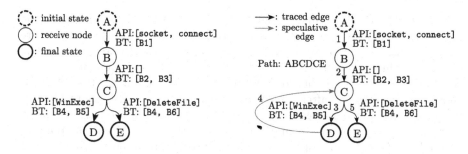

Fig. 3. APTA for the artificial RAT.   **Fig. 4.** Speculation step.

while each path in the tree denotes a communication session (in other words, a trace). Each path ends with a final state that marks the end of a trace: such a state does not necessarily correspond to the end of communications with the C2 server, but may be part of a session that we explored only partially under the given resource budget. In our setting, internal nodes of the APTA other than the root represent *receive* operations, i.e., APIs such as the **read** function that generate new symbolic inputs and thus identify incoming data buffers from the C2 server. Edges are characterized by two records extracted from traces: the interesting APIs invoked (API) and the branches taken (BT) between the two actions encoded by the two nodes of the APTA. Paths with the same prefix of nodes and edges get merged by the tree representation.

Previous research [10] uses inferred message types for edge labels, while we do not assume to know such information. Instead, we choose labels according to the relevant effects from receiving a message, that is, the interesting APIs executed in the trace. Our goal is clearly different than the one pursued in [10]: we are not interested in building a specification of the communication protocol, but rather in generating a synthetic C2 server for in-vivo RAT dissection.

Figure 3 shows the APTA built for our artificial RAT. Given the two traces generated in the initial step, we construct a tree characterized by two distinct paths with a common prefix. Node A is the initial state. Nodes B and C represent the two invocations of the **read** function executed in the body of the dispatcher loop across two loop iterations. Nodes D and E denote the final states for the first trace and the second trace, respectively. Edge AB is characterized by the invocation of **socket** and **connect** and by the taken branch B1. Edge BC reports only the taken branches B2 and B3 since no interesting API appeared in the traces between the two **read** invocations. Edges CD and CE represent what has been recorded in two traces from the last invocation of the **read** function (node C) and the end of each trace.

Speculation. We would like to identify a theoretical path that could drive symbolic execution into generating a single trace that exposes all the commands implemented by the RAT under analysis. As the list of such commands is not know a priori, we can try and learn from traces generated in the first step, leveraging the practical observation that several real-world RATs are implemented through an infinite dispatcher loop: although we expect a few commands to sink the communication (e.g., shutdown command), a significant fraction of them could be executable one after the other. Instead of using heuristics to identify commands, we limit our reasoning to the APIs observed in the initial step. In other words, we characterize commands based on the set of APIs that could be executed by the RAT in response to some network data received from the C2 server. Hence, the aim of this step is to speculate over the feasibility of an execution path in the RAT able to execute the entire set of APIs observed across several traces during the first step of our approach.

We start by choosing the order by which we would like to visit interesting edges in the APTA. This order could be arbitrary or based on hints provided by an analyst[1]. To make exploration easier, we require that subsequent edges within alternative paths inside the APTA appear consecutively (i.e., edges are not interleaved). To build a path we start from the root node of the APTA and visit edges according to the chosen order until a leaf node is met. We then add a speculative edge from the leaf node to the source node of the next edge that we would like to visit. We continue to visit edges according to the order until another leaf is reached. We repeat the process of adding speculative edges as long as needed, until all the interesting edges are covered by the generated path.

For the APTA of Fig. 3 we choose to visit edges in the following order: AB, BC, CD, CE. Edge AB has to come before BC and CD due to their ordering in the first trace. Similarly, BC comes before CD. The ordering between CD and CE is arbitrary. To build a valid path covering all edges, we start from the root node A and follow edges in order until the leaf D is met. To hit the remaining edge CE we add a speculative edge between nodes D and C, and eventually we visit E to cover CE. Hence, the trace that we would like to generate in the next phase should follow the path: ABCDCE. Figure 4 shows the path on the APTA after adding the speculative edge.

Validation. To validate the feasibility of the speculatively generated path we resort to symbolic execution. Differently from the first step, we can now exploit knowledge from past executions. Any non-speculative edge in the path is found in the APTA too, so it represents a portion of a trace recorded in the initial step: the taken branches associated with non-speculative edges can thus be used to guide symbolic execution when attempting to cover them.

We carry out the symbolic execution following three different exploration strategies: *strictly-branch-guided*, *target-guided*, and *loosely-branch-guided*.

---

[1] An analyst may desire to test whether the RAT can execute a speculated sequence of APIs that they build by combining insights from previous observations.

The first strategy is only used at the beginning when starting the symbolic execution from the same point used in the first step. Since the speculative path begins with a prefix that *strictly* coincides with one of the traces generated during that step, the exploration is guided along the branches that were taken in each edge along that prefix. Assuming the execution is deterministic, the control flow should reach the first node in the speculative path that corresponds to a leaf in the APTA following exactly the same branches as in the original trace, i.e., the symbolic engine does not yield alternative execution paths.

Upon reaching the first leaf, we switch to the *target-guided* exploration strategy switches. Since the execution should now aim at covering a speculative edge, there is no record of taken branches to reach it from past executions. However, the exploration has a well-defined target location: the node reached by the speculative edge. Hence, we now allow for a strategy where multiple alternative paths can be explored by the engine, and see whether within a given time and memory budget at least one such path reaches the target location. When one is found, the exploration continues along it and we switch to the third strategy.

In the *loosely-branch-guided* strategy we are trying to cover a non-speculative edge from the current execution path. Although this edge is present in the APTA and thus a list of taken branches is available, we cannot expect execution to strictly follow it: as the internal program state may have changed along the path, there is no guarantee that the RAT can now take branch decisions observed in the exact same manner as in the original trace behind that edge. We thus try to drive execution towards such list of branches using a *loose* enforcement: the strategy is designed to tolerate up to k divergences (i.e., different branch decisions) with respect to the original branches. If at least one execution path reaches the next leaf in the speculative path, we discard any other alternative paths and switch back to the *target-guided* strategy, aiming at covering the next speculative edge in the path. We repeat this process as long as needed to validate the entire path.

During this process the *target-guided* and *loosely-branch-guided* strategies may possibly fail. In this case, our technique goes back to the speculation phase, marks as invalid the speculative edge that led to the failure and tries a different speculation. In particular, for such an invalid edge (s, t) we replace it with a new edge between node s and the nearest ancestor of node t, i.e., its parent. We then recompute the speculative path using the new edge in place of the old one and we attempt validation. Observe that another failure would lead us to consider the second nearest ancestor for t and so on. In case of repeated failures when considering other of its ancestors, we update the speculative path by dropping any edge along the sub-path from t to the next leaf. After completing the validation phase, if any edge present in the APTA has been dropped in the process we go back to the speculation phase and compute an alternative additional path covering the dropped edges. As every edge in the APTA gets covered by at least one speculative path, a pathological exploration sequence may lead to a number of speculative paths equal to the number of traces obtained in the first step.

Given the speculative path ABCDCE for our artificial RAT, we start the symbolic exploration from node A using the strictly-branch-guided strategy. The execution path follows branches B1, B2, B3, B4 and B5 (just as expected as we are replaying the first recorded trace) and reaches node D, which is a leaf in the APTA. From now on, the exploration switches to the target-guided strategy in order to reach node C. Assuming a time budget sufficient to cover a few instructions, the symbolic engine can lead the execution path to successfully reach C. Then, the engine switches to the loosely-branch-guided strategy, trying to drive the exploration towards branches B4 and B5. At least one symbolic execution path can reach node E (leaf) at the end of our speculative path, thus terminating the validation step. No APTA edge was dropped from the initial speculative path, thus no extra speculative paths are required. The trace generated for the speculative path is:

(a) API: `socket(...)`, `connect(..., SERVER_ADDR, ...)`, `read( ..., $D_1$, 64)`, `read(..., $D_2$, 64)`, `WinExec($D_3$, 0)`, `read(..., $D_4$, 64)`, `DeleteFile($D_5$)`
(b) buffers: `*$D_1$ = "MAGIC_STR"`, `*$D_2$ = "12Program.exe"`, `*$D_3$ = "Program.exe"`, `*$D_4$ = "22File.doc"`, `*$D_5$ = "File.doc"`
(c) branch taken: `[B1]`, `[B2, B3]`, `[B4, B5]`, `[B4, B6]`

C2 Server Generation. We synthesize a distinct C2 server for each trace generated from a speculative path. Each server sends back to the RAT the network buffers reported in the trace. To this end, we use network APIs that carry out symmetric functionalities for those that get executed in the RAT client.

Given the network APIs and the buffers listed in the trace generated during the previous step for our RAT, the C2 server implementation is characterized by the following flow of actions:

```
s1 = socket(...); bind(s1, ...); // symmetric to socket()
s2 = accept(s1, ...);            // symmetric to connect()
write(s2, D₁, 64);               // symmetric to read(..., D₁, ...)
write(s2, D₂, 64);               // symmetric to read(..., D₂, ...)
write(s2, D₄, 64);               // symmetric to read(..., D₄, ...)
```

The analyst sets up redirection for connections from the RAT to the server instance, then in-vivo analysis can take place in a debugger or other tools.

2.3 Discussion

A number of issues may hinder the applicability of our approach when considering real-world RATs. In the following we discuss relevant challenges we identified.

Encryption. Communications with C2 servers may be protected by crypto schemes. Although this may seem a showstopper at first—as SMT solvers used in symbolic execution cannot defeat robust encryption—we may still be able to analyze several real-world such instances. RATs often use symmetric crypto functions with keys embedded in the binary or sent by the server: since symbolic execution can handle both scenarios, our approach may sustain C2 server reconstruction for such RATs. Asymmetric crypto schemes are instead likely to make symbolic execution fail at reasoning over exchanged data. However, if the sample is using standard crypto APIs we could extend our approach to perform function call interposition, rewriting API arguments to use custom private and public keys. For instance, a symbolic engine may model the Windows `CryptDecrypt` API internally in order to return a valid content for an encrypted network buffer. To make the synthesized server work, similar hooks should be applied also when running the RAT within the analyst's environment.

Nondeterminism and Other Input Types. Another challenge is represented by nondeterministic factors in the execution. Recorded traces during phase one could not be directly *repeatable* [18] due to nondeterminism in OS interactions, the network or other external factors such as time sources. Since we implemented our approach on top of S2E [7], a framework for whole-system analysis, some of these issues could be mitigated in practice. However, the problem of limiting nondeterminism in the RAT execution when running it in the analyst's analysis environment remains an open problem.

A crucial assumption behind our approach is that the execution of interesting APIs causally depends on the receival of specific commands from the C2 server. This assumption may be not always be true and several factors can thus undermine our reasoning. In general, network may not be the only source of input: as we will see in Sect. 3, real-world RATs may use other data coming from the environment (e.g., obtained through a system call) as an input. Our approach builds on top of the assumption that any input source can be identified and marked as symbolic. In practice, this may require additional effort from the analyst. RATs using multiple channels for communicating with the attacker, e.g., samples relying on bifurcated or covert signaling channels, are not currently handled by our approach. Also, our model should be extended to account for concurrent communications with the C2 server carried out by using, e.g., multiple threads.

Obfuscation. Our approach relies on symbolic execution to reveal interesting behaviors in RATs. Code obfuscation techniques, such the ones described in [4, 24], could be used by malware writers to render symbolic execution ineffective. Nonetheless, to the best of our knowledge, these kinds of code obfuscations are not currently widespread in the malware realm. This situation may change in the future and thus symbolic execution frameworks may require enhancements in order to better cope with these techniques.

Number of Paths in the APTA. When constructing an APTA using the approach presented in Sect. 2.2, we may get an extremely large number of paths inside the APTA. Unlike our toy example, a command handler of a real-world RAT may embed a logic made of several conditional branches: unfortunately, each such branch can make the exploration fork, yielding several traces for the

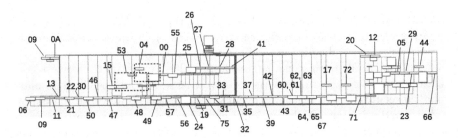

Fig. 5. NetWire – Control flow graph of the RAT's dispatcher loop.

same command and increasing the number of paths in the APTA. To mitigate this problem, we merge APTA edges that refer to the same source and target receive nodes and report the same list of interesting APIs. In other words, we merge edges that differ only for the taken branches. To avoid losing useful information when merging, we define the BT record as a set of lists, where each list identifies the branches taken in some trace. Besides reducing the size of the APTA, this allows our approach to consider multiple—alternative—ways of guiding a path over an edge during the validation step, possibly increasing the chances of covering a command.

Speculation. Finally, we point out that the order by which during the speculation phase we pick edges of the APTA to be visited plays a crucial role. The interplay between commands may make a chosen speculative path unfeasible, yielding in the worst case to traces just as short as those we were able to record during the first step of our approach. Nonetheless, testing and validating any possible speculation decision for path construction is not feasible as we would be dealing with a combinatorial choice problem.

3 Experimental Evaluation

In the following we discuss a preliminary experimental evaluation of our approach considering two real-world RATs. We prototyped our technique in S2E [7] to perform symbolic execution on the entire software stack (including kernel and libraries), and extended it with more than 70 hooks for Windows APIs—used to inject symbolic data in case of network communications and to track interesting APIs—and the three exploration strategies discussed in Sect. 2.2.

We run the experiments on a server equipped with two Intel Xeon E5-2630 v3 CPUs (16 cores in total, @2.40 GHz) and 256 GB of RAM, running Debian Linux 9. We use a budget of 6 h and 32 GB of RAM for the trace generation step, and one of 12 h and 64 GB of RAM for the validation step. To validate the results of our experiments, we manually reviewed the synthesized C2 servers by running them alongside the RAT samples, checking their functionalities and verifying that commands described in public reports on the two RATs were actually handled by the generated servers.

3.1   NetWire

NetWire is a RAT with keylogging capabilities sold on the black market. It exists in several variants and has been used by criminals since 2012. In 2016 this RAT received particular attention from security vendors after taking part in a large campaign for stealing payment card data [17]. The variant we considered [16] allows an attacker to perform 51 commands on the infected machine, e.g., sending a file, stealing browser credentials, or taking a screenshot of the victim's desktop. Figure 5 provides an annotated CFG for its dispatcher.

Trace Generation. Starting the exploration from the executable's entry point would likely lead to the generation of a large number of paths in the symbolic executor, exhausting the resource budget well before reaching the dispatcher loop. For this reason, as in [2] we assume that the analyst can identify the thread executing the loop and provide hints for steering the exploration toward this component. Since in NetWire it is implemented as a `switch` statement with a large number of cases, detecting it in an initial inspection was straightforward. Our prototype generated over 2000 traces, covering 41 commands while 10 led to internal crashes. An excerpt[2] from a valid trace is the following:

(a) API: ..., `socket(...)`, `connect(...)`, ..., `time(T)`, ..., `send(...,`D_1`, ...)`, ...,
   `recv(...,` D_2 `, ...)`, `recv(...,` D_3 `, ...)`, `fopen(`D_4`, ...)`, `send(...,`D_5`, ...)`, ...
(b) buffers: `*`D_1`= f(T)`, `*`D_2`= SEED_IV`, `*`D_3`= {0x3e, ...}`,
   `*`D_4`= "C:\Users\...\Opera\profile\wand.dat"`, `*`D_5`= {...}`

When analyzing the entire trace, we can learn several interesting facts about NetWire. First, it uses a raw TCP socket for communicating with the C2 server. Second, it sends to the server a buffer that contains some data `f(T)` derived from a timestamp `T` obtained using the function `time`. The server sends back a buffer that likely contains a seed and an initialization vector, internally used by NetWire in combination with a statically embedded password to generate a symmetric key. This key is then used during communications to encrypt data using a custom implementation of AES. As discussed in Sect. 2.3, symmetric encryption can be handled by our approach when the key is embedded in the binary or is dynamically generated with a computation. NetWire derives the symmetric key from a buffer received from the server, falling in the latter case. Since we generate the server and thus can control the buffer's content, our approach is able to successfully deal with the symmetric encryption scheme of NetWire. However, to make the trace *replayable* outside our environment the `time` function should be hooked in order to produce the same value used in the symbolic exploration. Another interesting element from this trace is that NetWire implements a command (`0x3e`) that sends to the server the content of profile files for the Opera browser.

---

[2] Addresses of taken branches seem of little interest and are thus omitted.

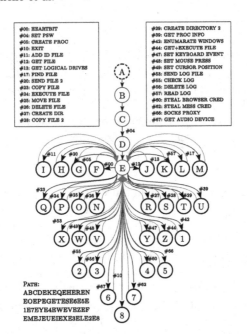

Fig. 6. NetWire – APTA with speculative edges after completing the validation step.

Trace Analysis, Speculation, and Validation. The APTA built from analyzing the traces is depicted in Fig. 6. To make the representation compact, we merged paths related to the same command (see Sect. 2.3) and discarded traces where no interesting APIs were observed. The resulting APTA contains 29 distinct paths, covering 30 commands (since command 0x4 is a prefix for all the paths). We discarded traces related to 11 commands for which no interesting APIs were recorded. Figure 6 shows the path chosen in the speculation step: the path was successfully validated during the fourth step, generating a single execution trace able to cover all 30 commands.

C2 Server Generation. To synthesize a C2 server instance for NetWire, our prototype programmatically generated a Python program template using wrappers for network APIs such as socket, bind, accept, read, and write. When generating the server, our prototype reports that the analyst should hook (e.g., using debugger scripting or by rewriting API results in a sandbox) the invocation of the time function that takes place at a specific call site inside the sample.

3.2   GoldSun

The first specimen of the GoldSun RAT dates back to 2004: over the years, the RAT has infected machines in over 60 countries [23]. We considered a variant [2] that injects code in Windows Explorer to remain stealthy and lets the attacker

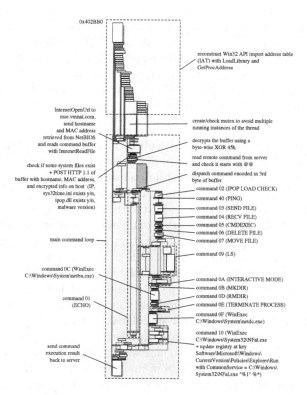

Fig. 7. GoldSun – Control flow graph of the RAT's command processing thread [2].

perform 16 types of commands on the victim's machine, such as executing a file or stealing one. Figure 7 provides an annotated version of the control flow graph (CFG) for the dispatcher loop of the variant we analyzed.

Trace Generation. Similarly as for NetWire, we rely on the initial guidance of the analyst to reach the dispatcher loop: our prototype could generate more than 300 traces originating in it, exposing all the 16 commands implemented by the RAT. An excerpt from one of the traces is the following:

(a) API: ..., `InternetOpenA(...)`, `InternetConnectA(..., D_1, 80,...)`,
    ..., `InternetReadFile(..., D_2, 4096, ...)`, ..., `WinExec(D_3, 0)`, ...
(b) buffers: `*D_1= "mse.vmnat.com"`, `*D_2= XOR(0x45, "@@5File.exe")`,
    `*D_3= "File.exe"`

where $*D_1$ is the server domain used by the C2 server (listening on port 80) and $*D_2$ is the buffer for requesting the RAT to execute the program `File.exe` on the victim's machine using `WinExec`. Notice that $*D_2$ is encrypted with a single-byte XOR scheme (key 0x45) while buffer $*D_3$ is just a substring of decrypted $*D_2$.

Although such encryption scheme is rather weak, it is sufficient to hinder reuse of messages across different communication sessions: the C2 server can instruct the sample to change the key, making messages from one session possibly invalid for another. In addition to message format and encryption factors, classic network simulators like FireEye FakeNet-NG would be defeated by the authentication scheme using by this RAT, which requires the C2 server to execute the first command two times before allowing the execution of any other command.

Trace Analysis, Speculation, and Validation. The APTA built after analyzing the recorded traces is depicted in Fig. 8. As for NetWire, we merged paths for the same commands and discarded uninteresting traces, yielding a tree with 15 paths (as the first command appears twice in each path).

To build the speculative path, we added to the approach presented in Sect. 2.2 the requirement for the path to cover the command 0x10 after the last speculative edge. This choice results from the observation that this command makes the dispatcher loop terminate, thus acting as a shutdown action. This reasoning could be easily integrated into the approach by devising a heuristic for detecting traces that terminate the execution, e.g., by using exit-like APIs.

Interestingly, we experienced several edge invalidations when performing the speculation step. While our original speculative path had all the speculative edges reaching the deepest receive node in the APTA (node K in Fig. 8), the final validated path shows several speculative edges reaching other receive nodes (i.e., ancestors of K). This resulted from multiple failures during the symbolic exploration. Nonetheless, no interesting edge was dropped during the validation phase, resulting in a single speculative path (reported in Fig. 8) able to execute all the 16 commands implemented by GoldSun.

C2 Server Generation. The sample communicates with the C2 server using the HTTP protocol (see, e.g., the InternetConnectA API in the trace excerpt above). Our prototype can synthesize C2 server instances for this protocol in the form of Python Flask applications. For GoldSun, the C2 server is mainly implemented by handling request on the route /httpdocs/mm/ <victim_id>/Cmwhite, where victim_id is a unique identifier for the victim computed in the sample by concatenating the hostname and the MAC address of the victim's machine. When generating the server, our prototype reports that the analyst should set the host name and the MAC address in the analysis environment to same values used in the symbolic exploration to prevent path divergences in the execution.

4   Related Work

Symbolic execution and protocol reverse engineering techniques constitute the backbone of our approach. We briefly review works targeting such research.

Symbolic Execution. Symbolic execution is a program analysis technique pioneered in the '70s. The technique is used to explore multiple paths of a program

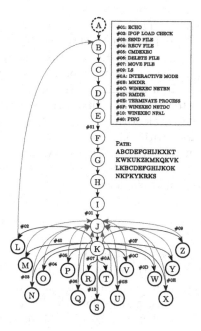

Fig. 8. GoldSun – APTA with speculative edges after completing the validation step.

by using symbolic instead of concrete inputs and it is widely used by the cyber-security community [19–22]. Due to space limitation, we refer the reader to the work by *Baldoni et al.* [3] for a complete treatment of the subject.

Protocol Reverse Engineering. In the last two decades, protocol reverse engineering has received large attention from the research community. A recent survey [13] divides works on this topic in two fields:

Message Format Inference. The goal is to classify the messages exchanged between client and server and, for each identified class, to deduce the fields which compose a message from the class and the relations (if any) among these fields. The ultimate goal is to reconstruct the grammar that defines the structure of messages. Automatic approaches can be further categorized based on the type of inference applied. Techniques based on *network inference* analyze the packets exchanged between client and server. For instance, [5] uses sequence alignment algorithms to find similarities among the exchanged messages and exploits this knowledge to identify recurring patterns and field boundaries. [12] assumes that fields delimiters are known and uses a set of heuristics to classify the messages and to identify hierarchical relations between fields. Techniques based on *application inference* monitor not only packets, but also the code. [15] leverages the idea that an application manipulates logically-related fields in code portions that are close to each other. [10] uses instead a combination of system-call monitoring and taint analysis to deduce the field boundaries and possibly the semantics of the fields (e.g., if a field encodes a length).

Protocol Grammar Inference. The aim of such works is to reconstruct valid sequences of messages accepted by client and server. Message format inference is typically a prerequisite for this phase. *Active* inference approaches start from an inaccurate model and iteratively refine it by probing an application that implements the protocol; automaton learning algorithms are typically involved. For instance, [8] infers the protocol state machine of the MegaD C2 server by probing an active server using the L* algorithm [1]. [9] performs active protocol grammar inference in combination with concolic execution. *Passive* approaches deduce instead the protocol grammar by examining network traces. [10] constructs an automaton that models the protocol by processing sequences of captured messages that have been previously classified.

5   Conclusion

In this paper we have proposed new ideas for synthesizing a server counterpart for a RAT malware when only the client is available for inspection. As directions for future work, we plan to extend our automata representation to account for concurrent communications, and explore the limits of our implementation when dealing with more complex protocols with respect to packet format and interactions with the OS other than network-related ones.

Acknowledgments. This work is supported in part by a grant of the Italian Presidency of the Council of Ministers.

References

1. Angluin, D.: Learning regular sets from queries and counterexamples. Inf. Comput. **75**(2), 87–106 (1987). https://doi.org/10.1016/0890-5401(87)90052-6
2. Baldoni, R., Coppa, E., D'Elia, D.C., Demetrescu, C.: Assisting malware analysis with symbolic execution: a case study. In: Dolev, S., Lodha, S. (eds.) CSCML 2017. LNCS, vol. 10332, pp. 171–188. Springer, Cham (2017). https://doi.org/10.1007/978-3-319-60080-2_12
3. Baldoni, R., Coppa, E., D'Elia, D.C., Demetrescu, C., Finocchi, I.: A survey of symbolic execution techniques. ACM Comput. Surv. **51**(3), 50:1–50:39 (2018). https://doi.org/10.1145/3182657
4. Banescu, S., Collberg, C., Ganesh, V., Newsham, Z., Pretschner, A.: Code obfuscation against symbolic execution attacks. In: Proceedings of the 32nd Annual Conference on Computer Security Applications, ACSAC 2016, pp. 189–200 (2016). https://doi.org/10.1145/2991079.2991114
5. Beddoe, M.A.: Network protocol analysis using bioinformatics algorithms. Toorcon (2004)
6. Bugalho, M., Oliveira, A.L.: Inference of regular languages using state merging algorithms with search. Pattern Recogn. **38**(9), 1457–1467 (2005). https://doi.org/10.1016/j.patcog.2004.03.027
7. Chipounov, V., Kuznetsov, V., Candea, G.: The S2E platform: design, implementation, and applications. ACM Trans. Comput. Syst. (TOCS) **30**(1), 2:1–2:49 (2012). https://doi.org/10.1145/2110356.2110358

8. Cho, C.Y., Babić, D., Shin, E.C.R., Song, D.: Inference and analysis of formal models of botnet command and control protocols. In: Proceedings of the 17th ACM Conference on Computer and Communications Security, CCS 2010, pp. 426–439. ACM (2010). https://doi.org/10.1145/1866307.1866355
9. Cho, C.Y., Babić, D., Poosankam, P., Chen, K.Z., Wu, E.X., Song, D.: MACE: model-inference-assisted concolic exploration for protocol and vulnerability discovery. In: Proceedings of the 20th USENIX Conference on Security, pp. 10–10 (2011)
10. Comparetti, P.M., Wondracek, G., Kruegel, C., Kirda, E.: Prospex: protocol specification extraction. In: Proceedings of the 2009 30th IEEE Symposium on Security and Privacy, SP 2009 (2009). https://doi.org/10.1109/SP.2009.14
11. Coppa, E., D'Elia, D.C., Demetrescu, C.: Rethinking pointer reasoning in symbolic execution. In: Proceedings of the 32nd IEEE/ACM International Conference on Automated Software Engineering, ASE 2017 (2017). https://doi.org/10.1109/ASE.2017.8115671
12. Cui, W., Kannan, J., Wang, H.J.: Discoverer: automatic protocol reverse engineering from network traces. In: Proceedings of 16th USENIX Security Symposium on USENIX Security Symposium (2007). http://dl.acm.org/citation.cfm?id=1362903.1362917
13. Duchêne, J., Le Guernic, C., Alata, E., Nicomette, V., Kaaniche, M.: Stateof the art of network protocol reverse engineering tools. J. Comput. Virol. Hacking Tech. **14**, 53–68 (2017). https://doi.org/10.1007/s11416-016-0289-8
14. Jiang, D., Omote, K.: An approach to detect remote access trojan in the early stage of communication. In: 2015 IEEE 29th International Conference on Advanced Information Networking and Applications, pp. 706–713, March 2015. https://doi.org/10.1109/AINA.2015.257
15. Lin, Z., Jiang, X., Xu, D., Zhang, X.: Automatic protocol format reverse engineering through context-aware monitored execution. In: 15th Symposium on Network And Distributed System Sexurity (NDSS) (2008)
16. Computer Incident Response Center Luxembourg: TR-23 Analysis - NetWiredRC malware (2014). https://www.circl.lu/pub/tr-23/
17. SecureWorks: NetWire RAT Steals Payment Card Data (2016). https://www.secureworks.com/blog/netwire-rat-steals-payment-card-data
18. Severi, G., Leek, T., Dolan-Gavitt, B.: MALREC: compact full-trace malware recording for retrospective deep analysis. In: Giuffrida, C., Bardin, S., Blanc, G. (eds.) DIMVA 2018. LNCS, vol. 10885, pp. 3–23. Springer, Cham (2018). https://doi.org/10.1007/978-3-319-93411-2_1
19. Shoshitaishvili, Y., Wang, R., Hauser, C., Kruegel, C., Vigna, G.: Firmalice - automatic detection of authentication bypass vulnerabilities in binary firmware. In: Proceedings of the 2015 Network and Distributed System Security Symposium, NDSS 2015 (2015). https://doi.org/10.14722/ndss.2015.23294
20. Shoshitaishvili, Y., et al.: SoK: (state of) the art of war: offensive techniques in binary analysis. In: IEEE Symposium on Security and Privacy, SP 2016, pp. 138–157 (2016). https://doi.org/10.1109/SP.2016.17
21. Song, D., et al.: BitBlaze: a new approach to computer security via binary analysis. In: Sekar, R., Pujari, A.K. (eds.) ICISS 2008. LNCS, vol. 5352, pp. 1–25. Springer, Heidelberg (2008). https://doi.org/10.1007/978-3-540-89862-7_1
22. Stephens, N., et al.: Driller: augmenting fuzzing through selective symbolic execution. In: Proceedings of the 2016 Network and Distributed System Security Symposium, NDSS 2016 (2016). https://doi.org/10.14722/ndss.2016.23368

23. Villeneuve, N., Sancho, D.: The "Lurid" Downloader. Trend Micro Incorporated (2011). http://la.trendmicro.com/media/misc/lurid-downloader-enfal-report-en.pdf
24. Yadegari, B., Debray, S.: Symbolic execution of obfuscated code. In: Proceedings of the 22nd ACM SIGSAC Conference on Computer and Communications Security, CCS 2015 (2015). https://doi.org/10.1145/2810103.2813663

Generating a Random String with a Fixed Weight

Nir Drucker[1,2($\boxtimes$)] and Shay Gueron[1,2]

[1] University of Haifa, Haifa, Israel
[2] Amazon, Seattle, USA
drucker.nir@gmail.com, shay@math.haifa.ac.il

Abstract. Generating, uniformly at random, a binary or a ternary string with a fixed length L and a prescribed weight W, is a step in several quantum safe cryptosystems (e. g., BIKE, NTRUEncrypt, NTRU LPrime, Lizard, McEliece).

This *fixed weight vector selection* generation is often implemented via a shuffling method or a rejection method, but not always in "constant time" side channel protected flow. A recently suggested constant time algorithm for this problem, uses Network Sorting and turns out to be quite efficient. This paper proposes a new method for this computation, with a side channel protected implementation. We compare it to the other methods for different combinations of L and W values. Our method turns out to be the fastest approach for the cases where L is (relatively) short and $0.1 < W/L \leq 0.5$. For example, this range falls within the parameters of NTRU LPrime, where our method achieves a 3× speedup in the string generation. This leads to an overall 1.14× speedup for the NTRU LPrime key generation.

Keywords: Software optimization · Combinatorics ·
Post Quantum Cryptography · Coding

1 Introduction

This paper deals with efficient methods for what we call the Fixed Weight Vector Selection (FWVS) problem, defined as follows.

Definition 1. *Let L, W, q, m be integers such that $0 < W \leq L$ and let $q \geq 2$ be a prime. Denote the set of all vectors with L symbols from $\mathbb{F}_{q^m}$ having weight W by S_L^W (the weight of a vector is defined to be the number of its nonzero symbols).*

Problem 1 (Fixed Weight Vector Selection (FWVS)). Select, uniformly at random, a vector from S_L^W (here, uniformly at random means that every vector from S_L^W has equal probability to be selected in the process).

To illustrate, we give a simple example.

© Springer Nature Switzerland AG 2019
S. Dolev et al. (Eds.): CSCML 2019, LNCS 11527, pp. 141–155, 2019.
https://doi.org/10.1007/978-3-030-20951-3_13

Example 1. $L = 5, W = 4, q = 2, m = 1$. Here $(q = 2)$, the elements of the vectors are bits. With these parameters, $S_L^W = \{11110, 11101, 11011, 10111, 01111\}$. The FWVS problem is to select X from S_L^W such that $Pr(X = s) = \frac{1}{5}$ for every $s \in S_L^W$.

Problem 1 is one of the steps in several cryptosystems that have been proposed to the first round [2] of NIST Post-Quantum Cryptography (PQC) project. Five such schemes (BIKE, HQC, McEliece, NTRUEncrypt, and NTRU LPrime) were recently selected for the second round of the project [3]. A selection of the relevant parameters that shows the different range of interest for L and W, is shown in Table 1. Note that these algorithms use symbols from $\mathbb{F}_2$ (binary strings) or $\mathbb{F}_3$ (ternary strings). These correspond to $m = 1$ and $q = 2$ or $q = 3$.

Table 1. Some of the proposals submitted to the first round of NIST PQC project [2] for which the FWVS problem is a step in their key generation/encapsulation/decapsulation. The schemes BIKE, HQC, McEliece, NTRUEncrypt, and NTRU LPrime were recently selected for the second round of the project [3]. The cryptosystems are sorted in alphabetic order. Note the different ranges of L and W values.

Cryptosystem	NIST security category	L	W
BIG QUAKE	1	3,600	78
BIG QUAKE	5	9,000	135
BIKE1 (keygen)	1	10,163	71
BIKE1 (encaps)	1	20,326	134
BIKE1 (keygen)	5	32,749	137
BIKE1 (encaps)	5	65,498	261
HQC	1	22,229	67
HQC	5	59,011	133
Lizard	1	536	140
Lizard	5	1024	200
McElice6960119	5	6960	119
McElice8192128	5	8192	128
NTRUEncrypt	1	443	143
NTRUEncrypt	5	743	247
NTRU LPrime	5	761	250

We point out that a construction for the case $q = 3$ can be implemented by means of post processing the results of a construction for the case $q = 2$ (see Sect. 5). Therefore, we hereafter deal only with $q = 2$. We seek fast implementations of the FWVS problem with the following constraint: the execution should be in "constant time"[1]. By constant time we mean that the algorithm: (a) does

---

[1] "Constant time" is the standard term for algorithms/implementations that are secure against (some) side channel attacks. Other terms that are used are "side channel protected" and "Isochronous".

not involve access to elements of the vectors in a way that depends on the values of the symbols; (b) does not involve branches that depend on the values of the symbols.

Proper software implementations of such algorithms are considered to be secure against the known micro-architectural side channel analyses (side channel attacks hereafter)[2]. To illustrate the term "constant time" we give two examples:

Example 2. Assume an implementation that sets one bit in an array of bits by accessing only the relevant location in the array. A spy process that monitors the CPU caches can infer the memory address that was accessed, and therefore can learn the bit location.

Example 3. Assume an implementation that sets a bit only if it equals zero by performing the "read" operation but performing a "write" operation only when needed. A spy process that can measure the implementation's execution time can distinguish between the two cases (read or read+write) and learn if the relevant bit was set before the operation. A constant time implementation should always write a value.

Remark 1. The *overall execution time* does not have to be fixed (constant) in order to satisfy these requirements, but since "constant time" is the common term used for describing such software implementations, we adopt it.

Remark 2. It is straightforward to write side channel protected software for an inherently constant time algorithm. For other algorithms, the software implementations need to use special techniques in order to become side channels safe.

Our Contributions. we proposed a new method (RepeatedAND) to address the FWVS problem and compare it to the alternative methods for different L and W combinations that are relevant to the Post-Quantum (PQ) proposals mentioned above. Our method(s) speedup the vectors' generation significantly for some size combinations. They lead to a noticeable speedup in the overall performance of e. g., NTRU LPrime [6].

The paper is organized as follows. Section 2 starts with preliminaries and notation. Section 3 describes the "RepeatedAND" method. Conversions (from binary to ternary) are described in Sect. 5. Our results are reported in Sect. 6 and a conclusion is brought in Sect. 7.

2 Preliminaries, Notation, and Conventions

We use $\mathbb{F}_{q^m}$ to denote a finite field with q^m symbols $\{0, 1, \ldots, q^m\}$, where in this paper we set $m = 1$ and $q \in \{2, 3\}$. Polynomials $a(x) = a_{L-1}x^{L-1} + \ldots a_1x + a_0 \in \mathbb{F}_2[x]$ are represented, interchangeably, as strings of L bits. If A is such a string, then $A[i] = a(i)$, $0 \le i < L$. Polynomials $b(x) = b_{L-1}x^{L-1} + \ldots b_1x + b_0 \in \mathbb{F}_3[x]$ are represented as strings of 2-bit symbols $(2 \cdot L$ bits). If B is such a string, then $B[2i + 1 : 2i] = b(i)$, $0 \le i < L$.

---

[2] Differential power attacks and fault injection attacks are outside the scope of this paper.

Example 4. The polynomial $x^9 + x^6 + x^2 + x + 1 \in \mathbb{F}_2[x]$ corresponds to the bits string 1001000111 of length $L = 10$. The polynomial $2x^9 + x^6 + x^2 + x + 2 \in \mathbb{F}_3[x]$ corresponds to the bits string 10000001000000010110 of length $L = 2 \cdot 10$.

Let A be an array of bits. The weight of A is denoted by $wt(A)$ and is the number of set bits in A. We denote by 1^ℓ (resp. 0^ℓ) the ℓ-bit string of all ones (resp. zeros). Bit-wise "and", "or" and "not" are denoted by $\wedge$ and $\vee$ and $\neg$, respectively. In the algorithms below, unless otherwise stated, uninitialized variables equal 0.

A Pseudorandom Function (PRF) for Generating Uniform Random Samples. We assume access to a PRF that consists of two functions. It is initialized by calling $st = \mathsf{InitPRF}(seed)$, where $seed$ is some input seed (256-bit in our case) and the output is a PRF state st. Subsequently, the function $r = \mathsf{GetRand}(st, \ell)$ is called in order to obtain a pseudorandom integer r in the range $0 \le r < \ell$.

Remark 3. In general generating a long sequence of true random bits is slow (e. g., using RDRAND and RDSEED on x86 platforms), therefore we use some PRF to efficiently collect pseudorandom numbers.

2.1 The Shuffling Method

The classical approach to the FWVS problem is the Fisher-Yates Shuffle algorithm [11] (a.k.a known as Knuth shuffle). One of its variants [10] is described in Algorithm 1. It performs an in-place shuffle on a pre-initialized array. Steps 6–8 depend on the values in the array A. Thus, their (software) implementation is not inherently "constant time" unless the implementation takes the performance penalty for sweeping over the whole array in every iteration.

Algorithm 1. "inside-out", Fisher-Yates Shuffle algorithm [10, 11]

    Input: $seed$, L, W
    Output: A (an L bits string with weight W)
1: **procedure** GENSTRING($seed$, L, W)
2:      $A = 0^{L-W}1^W$
3:      $st = \mathsf{InitPRF}(seed)$
4:      **for** i $= 0$ to L **do**
5:          $j = \mathsf{GetRand}(st, L)$
6:          $t = A[j]$
7:          $A[j] = A[i]$
8:          $A[i] = t$
9:      **return** A

2.2 Rejection Method

Algorithm 2 is commonly known as the Rejection method (e. g., used in NTRU-Encrypt [12,13] and BIKE [4,8]). Here, Step 6 is a branch that depends on the value of A. Thus, its software implementation is not inherently "constant time" unless the implementation takes the performance penalty for sweeping over the whole array in every iteration.

Algorithm 2. Rejection method

    Input: *seed*, L, W
    Output: A (an L bits string with weight W)
1: **procedure** GENSTRING(*seed*, L, W)
2:     $A = 0^L$
3:     st = InitPRF(seed)
4:     **while** $wt(A) \neq W$ **do**
5:         $j = $ GetRand(st, L)
6:         **if** A[j]=0 **then**
7:             $A[j] = 1$
8:     **return** A

2.3 Sorting Method

Algorithm 3 shows another approach to Problem 1 that we call here Sorting method. This method has been recently proposed for NTRU LPrime [6]. It is based on constant time sorting algorithms (details and review are provided in [5]), and enjoys an efficient software implementation (using AVX2) demonstrated in [5]. Note that the code in NTRU LPrime generates strings with $q = 3$, but as explained above, we describe Algorithm 3 for the case $q = 2$. This algorithm is inherently constant time.

Algorithm 3. Sorting method (based on [5])

    Input: *seed*, L, W
    Output: A (an L bits string with weight W)
    Comment: B is a $32L$ bits string. Sort operates on a 32-bit integers array.
1: **procedure** GENSTRING(*seed*, L, W)
2:     st = InitPRF(seed)
3:     $B[32L - 1 : 0] = $ GetRand($st, 2^{32L} - 1$)
4:     **for** i in 0 to $W - 1$ **do**
5:         $B[32i] = 1$
6:     **for** i in W to $L - 1$ **do**
7:         $B[32i] = 0$
8:     Sort(B, L)
9:     **for** i in 0 to $L - 1$ **do**
10:         $A[i] = B[32i]$
11:     **return** A

---

3   RepeatedAND method

We propose an alternative method to tackle Problem 1, as illustrated in Algorithm 4. The main idea is that if X and Y are two (pseudo)random independent strings of length L then: (a) the expected weight of X and of Y is $\mathbb{E}\left[wt(X)\right] = \mathbb{E}\left[wt(Y)\right] = \frac{L}{2}$; (b) $\mathbb{E}\left[wt(X \wedge Y)\right] = \frac{L}{4}$.

Steps 10–14 in Algorithm 4 generate a string $\bar{A}$ of length L with $wt(\bar{A}) \leq W$. The algorithm takes a sequence A_i, $i = 1, 2, , \ldots, J$ of (pseudo)random independent strings of length L, where $J \approx \lfloor log_2(L/W) \rfloor$, and sets

$$\bar{A} = \bigwedge_{j=0}^{J} A_j \tag{1}$$

The value of J is not pre-determined, but its expected value is $\mathbb{E}\left[J\right] = \lfloor log_2(L/W) \rfloor$. To illustrate, we give an example.

Example 5. Let $L = 1,024$, $W = 128$. Then

$$\mathbb{E}\left[wt(A_0)\right] = 512$$
$$\mathbb{E}\left[wt(A_0 \wedge A_1)\right] = 256$$
$$\mathbb{E}\left[wt(A_0 \wedge A_1 \wedge A_2)\right] = 128$$

The expected number of iterations required for generating $\bar{A}$ as in (1) is $J = 3$. In practice, J is typically 3 or 4.

Steps 6–17 use $\bar{A}$ in order to generate a new vector A with $wt(A) = W$ (exactly). Starting from $A = \bar{A}$ (with $wt(\bar{A}) \leq W$), we set $w = W - wt(\bar{A}) \geq 0$. Next, another string $\bar{A}'$ of length L with $wt(\bar{A}') \leq w$ is generated (Steps 10–14). The value $A = A \vee \bar{A}'$ satisfies $wt(\bar{A}) \leq wt(A) \leq W$. Steps 6–17 are repeated while $w > 0$. The expected number of rounds is at most $\lceil log_2 W \rceil$.

Remark 4. Algorithm 4 requires independent (pseudo)random values A_j. Sampling A_j from GetRand($\cdot$) is (performance wise) costly, so reusing sampled strings may seem like a tempting shortcut. However, this approach violates the independence property. For example, circular rotation of $\bar{A}$ on Step 12, generates correlation between the bits of A. In practice, some bit manipulation techniques could possibly lead to sufficiently uncorrelated vectors, and perhaps make the selection acceptable. We do not adopt this approach here.

Lemma 1. *Algorithm 4 generates every string in S_L^W with equal probability.*

Proof. Algorithm 4 outputs only strings from S_L^W. For every round of Algorithm 4, we have, Step 15,

$$wt(A) + wt(\bar{A}) < wt(A) + w$$
$$= wt(A) + W - wt(A) = W$$

Algorithm 4. RepeatedAND method

Input: *seed, L, W*
Output: *A* (an *L* bits string with weight *W*)
1: **procedure** GENSTRING(*seed, L, W*)
2:     $st = \mathsf{InitPRF}(seed)$
3:     $ctr = 0$
4:     $w = W$
5:     $A[L-1:0] = 0^L$
6:     **do**
7:         $j = 0$
8:         $A_j = \mathsf{GetRand}(st, L)$
9:         $\bar{A} = A_j \wedge \neg A$ ▷ Optimization
10:        **do**
11:            $j = j + 1$
12:            $A_j = \mathsf{GetRand}(st, L)$
13:            $\bar{A} = \bar{A} \wedge A_j$
14:        **while** $(wt(\bar{A}) > w)$
15:        $A = A \vee \bar{A}$
16:        $w = W - wt(A)$
17:    **while** $(w \neq 0)$
18:    **return** A

Therefore, in Step 18, we have $wt(A) \leq W$. Since $Pr(wt(\bar{A}) = 0) < 1$, we can conclude that $\mathbb{E}\left[wt(A)\right] \leq \mathbb{E}\left[wt(A) + wt(\bar{A})\right]$. This implies that the algorithm stops after some number of rounds, and when it does, we have $wt(A) = W$. Clearly, Algorithm 4 outputs every string in S_L^W with equal probability because $Pr(A[i] = 1) = \frac{W}{L}$ for every bit $0 \leq i < L$, independently of the other bits.   □

4   Different Representations of Strings

In general, algorithms use the sparse polynomials (in $\mathbb{F}_2[x]$ or $\mathbb{F}_3[x]$) in different ways that may use different representations of the data. As a result, Algorithm 4 that generates binary strings, may be less efficient than its alternatives, due to the performance cost of moving across the different representations used in a specific scheme (especially in constant time implementations). We give two examples. The additional implementation of BIKE [4] uses three representations for $a(x) \in \mathbb{F}_2[x]$: (a) an L-bit string A; (b) an $8L$-bit string (B) where each byte holds one bit $(B[8i] = A[i], 0 \leq i < L)$; (c) a list of indexes $\{i : A[i] = 1, 0 \leq i < L\}$. The implementations of NTRU LPrime [6] represent a polynomial $b(x) \in \mathbb{F}_3[x]$ in three ways: (a) a 32-bit integers array C, where $C[32i + 1 : 32i] = b_i + 1 \pmod 3$, $0 \leq i < L$ (used for sorting); (b) a $2L$-bit array D, where $D[2i + 1 : 2i] = b_i + 1 \pmod 3$, $0 \leq i < L$; (c) An $8L$-bit array E, where $E[8i + 7 : 8i] = D[2i + 1 : 2i] - 1$ (the values are 00000000, 00000001, and 11111111).

Indeed, converting a binary string into a list of indexes in constant time is expensive and therefore the Rejection method is first used for generating the list of indexes, which is later converted into a binary string. By contrast, moving across the representation in NTRU LPrime is sufficiently fast, thus using the RepeatedAND method is preferred (see Sect. 6).

5   Handling the Case $q = 3$

An algorithm for converting a binary string into a ternary string is described in Algorithm 5. The algorithm gets a binary string S with a fixed weight W and an auxiliary (pseudo)random L-bit string B with $wt(B \wedge S) < W$ as its inputs ($B = B' \wedge S$, where B' is a (pseudo)random L bit vector). It outputs a $2L$ bits ternary string D where the "zero" symbol is 01 and the other two symbols are 10 and 00 (as in NTRU LPrime [6]). Step 1 of Algorithm 5 maps $0 \rightarrow 01$ and $1 \rightarrow 10$. Step 2 uses B to decide which 10 symbol will be converted into a 00 symbol. To this end, it squares B (adds a 0 bit next to each bit) and multiplies the result by x. This ensures that only bits in even positions can equal 1. Finally, we achieve the results by XORing the two strings. Note that for cases like NTRUEncrypt that use a ternary vector with a fixed number of 1 symbols (d) and -1 symbols (e), we require that $wt(B \wedge S) = d$. To generate B, we use a modified version of Algorithm 4, where we replace Step 9 with $\bar{A} = A_j \wedge (\neg A) \wedge S$ and set $W = d$.

A fast implementation on modern x86 platforms can use the carry less multiplication (PCLMUL) instruction for squaring a polynomial in $\mathbb{F}_2[x]$, bit-wise XOR for addition and shift left for multiplication by x.

Algorithm 5. Converting a binary string into a ternary string

---

Input: S (an L bits string with weight W), B (an L bits string with $wt(B \wedge S)$)
Output: $C \in \mathbb{F}_3[x]$ (a $2L$ bits string with weight W)
Comment: The operations are in $\mathbb{F}_2[x]$

1: **procedure** CONVBINARY2TERNARY
2:     $tmp = S^2 + \sum_{i=0, i-even}^{l} x^i$
3:     $D = (x \cdot B^2) + tmp$
4:     **return** D

---

6   Results

To compare the RepeatedAND method to the studied alternatives, we prepared optimized software implementations (specifically, in C using AVX/AVX2 intrinsics). For the Rejection method, we used our Additional implementation of BIKE [4] (written in C and x86 assembly). For the Sorting method, we used the implementation given in [5] (written in C and uses AVX2 intrinsics). We did not implement the Shuffling method because arguably, its constant time implementation would have roughly the same performance as the Rejection methods.

For all these methods we used the same PRF. Specifically, an efficient implementation (using AES-NI) of AES256 streaming mode, with a 256-bit seed (key) over a 32-bit counter. For computing the weight of an array in constant time we divided the array to 64-bit sub-arrays, and used the POPCNT instruction. This instruction receives a 64-bit value and returns its hamming weight (in 3 cycles). The algorithms were compiled with gcc (version 5.4.0) in 64-bit mode, using the "O3" Optimization level, and run on a Linux (Ubuntu 16.04.3 LTS) OS. We carried out the experiments on an Intel® desktop of the 7th Intel® Core^{TM} Generation (Micro-architecture Codename "Kaby Lake" [KBL]) 3.60 GHz Core^{TM} i7 − 7700. This platform had 16 GB RAM, 32K L1d and L1i cache, 256K L2 cache, and $8,192$K L3 cache. The Intel® Turbo Boost, Intel® Hyper-Threading Technology, and the Enhanced Intel Speedstep® Technology were disabled.

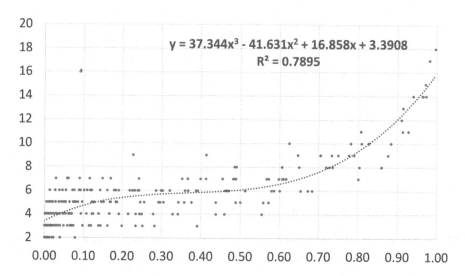

Fig. 1. The average number of rounds (vertical axis) in the RepeatedAND method (lower is better). The points in the graph represent (L, W) pairs and displayed according to the ratio $\frac{W}{L}$.

We performed several experiments. In the first experiment we tested 18 arbitrary values[3] of L, and 32 arbitrary values[4] of W. Altogether, there were 290 legitimate cases (i.e., $W < L$). For every legitimate pair, we ran the RepeatedAND method $30,000$ times and recorded the average number of rounds. Figure 1 shows the results. We encountered a small number of rounds $(2 − 4)$ only when $\frac{W}{L} < 0.5$ with more occurrences when $\frac{W}{L} < 0.2$. For $\frac{W}{L} > 0.6$, we

---

[3] $L = 128, 251, 437, 512, 761, 1,024, 1,493, 2,048, 4,096, 5,312, 8,192, 6,451, 10,163, 16,384, 24,567, 32,749, 32,768, 65,536.$

[4] $W = 10, 30, 50, 71, 110, 250, 286, 350, 512, 897, 1,200, 1,900, 2,500, 3,012, 3,981, 4,196, 4,691, 5,890, 7,891, 9,801, 12,010, 14,909, 15,901, 19,876, 23,090, 27,090, 32,123, 40,954, 51,209, 52,908, 59,908, 65,536.$

encountered a relatively large number of rounds (10+). Note that the FWVS problem is symmetric, i.e., solving it for some L and W is the same as solving it for the same L but with $\bar{W} = L - W$ and then negate the results. Thus, it is possible to ignore the cases where $\frac{W}{L} > 0.5$.

The second experiment is the same as above where we disabled the optimization of Algorithm 4, Step 9. Figure 2 shows the difference between the average number of rounds for the same (L, W) pairs in both experiments. Algorithm 4 (with the optimization) is significantly more efficient when $\frac{W}{L} \geq 0.2$ (the difference is usually more than 5 rounds).

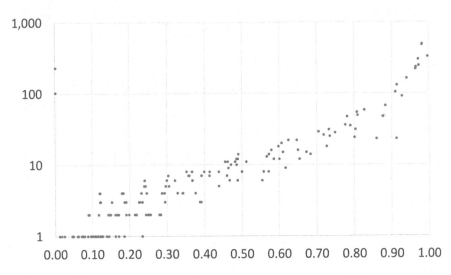

Fig. 2. Number of additional rounds per pair (L, W) (See pairs values in the text) aggregated according to the ratio $\frac{W}{L}$, when the optimization of Algorithm 4, Step 9 is disabled.

Table 2 compares the constant time implementations of the RepeatedAND, to the Rejection, and Sorting methods over the parameters of BIKE1, Lizard, NTRUEncrypt, and NTRU LPrime. Note that the final measurements for NTRUEncrypt should take into account the generation time of vector B in Algorithm 5.

For easy reproducibility of the results, we used the benchmarking system SUPERCOP [7] in order to measure the impact of Algorithm 4 on the overall performance of NTRU LPrime (ntrulpr4591761)[5]. We modified the function small_seeded_weightw in the NTRU LPrime implementation so that it calls Algorithms 4 and 5. Subsequently, we used the function small_decode (of the original code) to convert the resulting string into the required format.

---

[5] Note that SUPERCOP uses checksums that were generated by running NTRU LPrime with its original Sorting method. Thus, to use SUPERCOP for measuring the performance with our (different) method, we removed the checksums.

Table 2. Method comparison over some of the parameters of BIKE1, Lizard, NTRU-Encrypt (NTRUEn), and NTRU LPrime (NTRULPr). The reported cycles include the (pseudo)random data generation. Fastest result for each parameter choice is marked with bold. The RepeatedAND and the Sorting implementations generate ternary strings while the Rejection implementation generate binary strings

Alg.	Cat.	L (bits)	W (bits)	$\frac{W}{L}$	RepeatedAND method (cycles)	Rejection method (cycles)	Sorting method (cycles)
BIKE1	1	10,163	71	0.007	57,086	**17,460**	160,313
BIKE1	1	20,326	134	0.006	137,130	**45,301**	390,546
BIKE1	5	32,749	137	0.004	189,791	**43,699**	643,000
BIKE1	5	65,498	261	0.004	426,333	**141,499**	1,502,388
Lizard	1	536	140	0.261	**2,377**	41,510	7,589
Lizard	5	1,024	200	0.195	**5,072**	81,251	13,811
NTRUEn	1	443	143	0.322	**2,006**	33,871	6,710
NTRUEn	5	743	247	0.332	**3,414**	82,928	10,722
NTRULPr	5	761	250	0.328	**3,086**	81,674	9,000

Figure 3 compares the 32 measurements taken by SUPERCOP for the key generation/encapsulation/decapsulation steps of the original implementation and of our optimization. The original implementations run them in constant time, unlike our optimized implementation, where Algorithm 4 has a variable number of rounds (but no secret information is leaked). Our optimization outperforms the baseline in $27/32 = 84\%$ (point A - key generation), $25/32 = 78\%$ (point B - encapsulation), and $21/32 = 65\%$ (point C - decapsulation), achieving a speedup of around $1.07\times$, $1.12\times$, $1.21\times$, respectively.

7   Conclusion

We presented a new algorithm for speeding up the FWVS problem. The implementation of Algorithm 4 achieves speedup of $3\times$ over the equivalent latest implementation in NTRU LPrime one of the schemes that were selected for the NIST PQC project round 2 [3].

In addition, our experiments show that the RepeatedAND method can speed-up other cryptosystems (e. g., Lizard) when L is small. If the value of L is high (as in BIKE1) it is preferable to use the Rejection method (or the Shuffling method). In addition, our experiments show that the RepeatedAND method is usually faster than the Sorting method (on the measured sizes). We point out that in cases where constant-time implementation is not required, the Shuffling or the Rejection methods are probably the fastest.

The performance of the RepeatedAND method depends on the performance of the underlying PRF. In our experiments, we used AES256 as an efficient choice. However, if a 128 bits key is sufficient (e. g., for NIST Category 1 algorithms), using AES128 will speed-up the algorithm. In addition, our experiments target x86 platforms with AES-NI enabled. On these platforms, using AES in

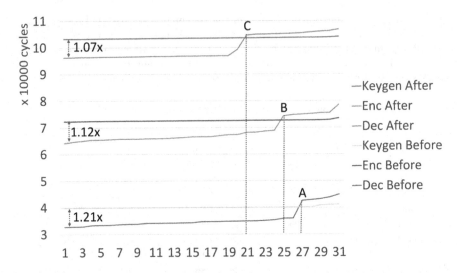

Fig. 3. Cycles count comparison for 32 NTRU LPrime (ntrulpr4591761) keygen/encapsulate/decapsulate measurements taken by SUPERCOP. Lower number of cycles is better. Here, "Before" refers to the original implementation and "After" refers to the optimization through Algorithm 4.

counter mode leads to a very fast PRF. Implementations that target other platforms (without AES-NI) may choose to use a different PRF (e. g., based on hash functions).

Better News Are Coming Soon: Vector AES and POPCNT New Instructions Intel has recently announced [1] that its future architecture, microarchitecture codename "Ice Lake", will add vectorized capabilities to the existing AES-NI instructions. These instructions are intended to push the performance of AES software further down, to a new (theoretically achievable) throughput of 0.16 C/B [9]. In addition, CPUs with AVX512 capabilities arrive with a new vectorized POPCNT instruction that performs eight 64-bit POPCNT in one instruction. Judicious use of these new instructions will significantly accelerate the RepeatedAND algorithm.

Acknowledgments. We thank an anonymous reviewer for the comment that led to Algorithm 6. This research was supported by: The Israel Science Foundation (grant No. 1018/ 16); The BIU Center for Research in Applied Cryptography and Cyber Security, in conjunction with the Israel National Cyber Bureau in the Prime Minister's Office; the Center for Cyber Law & Policy at the University of Haifa in conjunction with the Israel National Cyber Directorate in the Prime Minister's Office.

A   A variant of the RepeatedAND method

Step 13 of Algorithm 4 ($\bar{A} = \bar{A} \wedge A_j$) can be replaced with $\bar{A} = \bar{A} \wedge \neg A_j$ without affecting the correctness or the performance characteristics of the algorithm.

This is because

$$wt(\bar{A} \wedge A_j) \approx wt(\bar{A} \wedge \neg A_j) \approx \frac{wt(\bar{A})}{2} \qquad (2)$$

and

$$\mathbb{E}\left[wt(\bar{A} \wedge A_j)\right] = \mathbb{E}\left[wt(\bar{A} \wedge \neg A_j\right] = \mathbb{E}\left[wt(\bar{A})/2\right] \qquad (3)$$

Algorithm 6 is a variant of Algorithm 4 that leverages this fact. It replaces Step 13 in Algorithm 4 with Steps 13–19. The following example illustrates this optimization.

Algorithm 6. A variant of the RepeatedAND method

    Input: *seed, L, W*
    Output: A (an L bits string with weight W)
1: **procedure** GENSTRING(*seed, L, W*)
2:     $st = \mathsf{InitPRF}(seed)$
3:     $ctr = 0$
4:     $w = W$
5:     $A[L - 1 : 0] = 0^L$
6:     **do**
7:       $j = 0$
8:       $A_j = \mathsf{GetRand}(st, L)$
9:       $\bar{A} = A_j \wedge \neg A$ ▷ Optimization
10:       **do**
11:         $j = j + 1$
12:         $A_j = \mathsf{GetRand}(st, L)$
13:         **if** $wt(\bar{A} \wedge A_j) \le w$ **and** $wt(\bar{A} \wedge \neg A_j) \le w$ **then**
14:           $\bar{A} = max(\bar{A} \wedge A_j, \bar{A} \wedge \neg A_j)$
15:         **else**
16:           **if** $wt(\bar{A} \wedge A_j) \le w$ **then**
17:             $\bar{A} = \bar{A} \wedge A_j$
18:           **else**
19:             $\bar{A} = \bar{A} \wedge \neg A_j$
20:       **while** $(wt(\bar{A}) > w)$
21:     $A = A \vee \bar{A}$
22:     $w = W - wt(A)$
23:     **while** $(w \ne 0)$
24:     **return** A

Example 6. Let $L = 2,048$, $W = 500$, and assume that $wt(A_0) = 1,024$ and $wt(A_0) \wedge wt(A_1) = 524$. Then $wt(A_0) \wedge \neg wt(A_1) = 1,024 - 524 = 500 = W$. Therefore, Algorithm 6 ends after one round, while Algorithm 4 will ends after at least two rounds.

    Algorithm 6 is only one example of a greedy algorithm that uses (2) to optimize Algorithm 4. Other optimizations may apply for specific choices of L and W. For example, when $L = 2,048$ and $W = 200$ a sequence $\bar{A}_{i \ge 0} = \{\ldots, 800, 400, 200\}$ will probably lead to a smaller number of rounds compared to the expected sequence $\bar{A}_{i \ge 0} = \{\ldots, 512, 256, 128\}$.

B   Bounding the probability that the RepeatedAND algorithm does not stop

In theory, Algorithm 4 can enter an infinite loop if $wt(A)$ does not change for an infinite number of times at (a) Step 13 ; (b) Step 15.

We first explain (heuristically) the claim in Lemma 1 that Algorithm 4 stops almost surely (i. e., the probability that it does not stops is negligible). We start by calculating the probability that the loop in Steps 10–14 ends after $L - w$ iterations. Suppose that the vector A with weight $x = wt(A)$ is converted to the vector A' with $y = wt(A')$ at the end of a single iteration. If $y \leq w$ the loop ends. We consider the Markov chain that corresponds to transition from x to y, where we label the $L+1$ weights (states) by $0, \ldots, L$. The transition matrix $P_{x,y}$ is:

$$P_{x,y} = \begin{cases} \frac{1}{2^x} \cdot \binom{x}{y} & w < x \leq L,\ 0 \leq y \leq x, \\ 1 & 0 \leq x = y \leq w \\ 0 & \text{otherwise} \end{cases}$$

In particular, $P_{x,x} = \frac{1}{2^x} < \frac{1}{2^w}$ for $x > w$. Denote by $X \sim Geo(1 - P_{x,x})$ the geometric random variable that counts the number of iterations until a state change occurs ($y \neq x$). Then for some k

$$P\left(X \leq k\right) = 1 - \left(1 - (1 - P_{x,x})\right)^k = 1 - P_{x,x}^k = 1 - \frac{1}{2^{kx}} > 1 - \frac{1}{2^{kw}}$$

If $x > y$ in at least $L - w$ iterations we get $y < w$ (because every iteration reduces the weight by at least 1). Since the loop iterations are independent, after at most $k(L - w)$ iterations we get (if $2^{kw} \geq 5$)

$$P\left(wt(A) \leq w\right) > \left(1 - \frac{1}{2^{kw}}\right)^{L-w}$$

$$= \left(\left(1 - \frac{1}{2^{kw}}\right)^{2^{kw}}\right)^{\frac{L-w}{2^{kw}}}$$

$$> \left(\frac{1}{e} - 0.05\right)^{\frac{L-w}{2^{kw}}} > \left(\frac{1}{2}\right)^{\frac{L-w}{2^{(kw-1)}}} = \left(\frac{1}{2}\right)^{\delta_{L,w,k}}$$

where $\delta_{L,w,k} = \frac{L-w}{2^{(kw-1)}}$. For example, in the first round of NTRU LPrime, $L = 761$, $w = 250$, we get $\delta_{761,250,1} = \frac{511}{2^{250-1}} \approx \frac{1}{2^{239}}$. Consequently, the probability that the loop ends after at most $k(L - w) = 511$ iterations is almost 1. To bound the number of iterations when $\delta_{L,w,k} > 1$, we first choose some $1 < w_1 < w$ such that $\delta_{L,w_1,1} < 1$ then continue recursively. For example, if $L = 761$, $w = 1$, we choose $w_1 = 21$, and get $\delta_{761,21,1} = \frac{740}{2^{20}} < \frac{1}{2^{10}}$. Thus, after $L - w_1$ iterations $P(wt(A) \leq 20) > \sqrt[2^{10}]{0.5} \approx 0.999$. Subsequently, we set $k_2 = 16$ such that with

$k_2(w_1 - w) = k_2(21-1) = 20k_2$ additional iterations we get $\delta_{w_1,w,k_2} = \dfrac{20}{2^{k_2-1}} <$
$\dfrac{1}{2^{10}}$ and the probability $P(wt(A) \leq w) > \sqrt[2^{10}]{0.5} \approx 0.999$. Consequently, the loop
ends with $(L - w_1) + 20k_2$ iterations with probability at least 0.999. Obviously,
a different choice of parameters can lead to a probability that is closer to 1.

Case (b) is the case where $y = 0$ for an infinite number of rounds of the
external loop (Steps 6–17), i. e., the Markov chain hits the absorbing state with
weight 0 an infinite number of times. The probability to hit this absorbing state
is $0 < h_{n,0} < \frac{1}{2^w}$ (for every $x < w$, $P_{x,0} = \frac{1}{2^x} < \frac{1}{2^w}$) and by the same reasoning
as above, the probability to avoid it in a bounded number of rounds/attempts
is close to 1.

References

1. Intel architecture instruction set extensions programming reference October 2017. https://software.intel.com/sites/default/files/managed/c5/15/architecture-instruction-set-extensions-programming-reference.pdf
2. NIST Post Quantum Cryptography - Round 1 Submissions (2018). https://csrc.nist.gov/projects/post-quantum-cryptography/round-1-submissions
3. Alagic, G., et al.: Status report on the first round of the NIST post-quantum cryptography standardization process. Technical report (2019). https://doi.org/10.6028/NIST.IR.8240
4. Aragon, N., et al.: BIKE: bit flipping key encapsulation (2017), https://bikesuite.org/files/BIKE.pdf
5. Bernstein, D.J.: djbsort (2018). https://sorting.cr.yp.to/index.html
6. Bernstein, D.J., Chuengsatiansup, C., Lange, T., van Vredendaal, C.: NTRU prime: reducing attack surface at low cost. In: Adams, C., Camenisch, J. (eds.) SAC 2017. LNCS, vol. 10719, pp. 235–260. Springer, Cham (2018). https://doi.org/10.1007/978-3-319-72565-9_12
7. Bernstein, D.J., Lange, T.: eBACS: ECRYPT Benchmarking of Cryptographic Systems, December 2018. https://bench.cr.yp.to/
8. Drucker, N., Gueron, S.: A toolbox for software optimization of QC-MDPC code-based cryptosystems. Cryptology ePrint Archive, Report 2017/1251 (2017). https://eprint.iacr.org/2017/1251
9. Drucker, N., Gueron, S., Krasnov, V.: Making AES great again: the forthcoming vectorized AES instruction. Cryptology ePrint Archive, Report 2018/392 (2018). https://eprint.iacr.org/2018/392
10. Durstenfeld, R.: Algorithm 235: random permutation. Commun. ACM 7(7), 420 (1964)
11. Fisher, R.A., Yates, F., et al.: Statistical tables for biological, agricultural and medical research. In: Statistical Tables for Biological, Agricultural and Medical Research, 3 edn. (1949)
12. Hoffstein, J., Howgrave-Graham, N., Pipher, J., Whyte, W.: Practical lattice-based cryptography: NTRUEncrypt and NTRUSign. In: Nguyen, P., Vallée, B. (eds.) The LLL Algorithm. Information Security and Cryptography, pp. 349–390. Springer, Heidelberg (2009). https://doi.org/10.1007/978-3-642-02295-1_11
13. Hoffstein, J., Pipher, J., Silverman, J.H.: NTRU: a ring-based public key cryptosystem. In: Buhler, J.P. (ed.) Algorithmic Number Theory, pp. 267–288. Springer, Berlin Heidelberg, Berlin, Heidelberg (1998). https://doi.org/10.1007/BFb0054868

An Access Control Model for Data Security in Online Social Networks Based on Role and User Credibility

Nadav Voloch[(✉)], Priel Levy, Mor Elmakies, and Ehud Gudes

Ben-Gurion University of the Negev, P.O.B. 653, 8410501 Beer-Sheva, Israel
voloch@post.bgu.ac.il

Abstract. During the past decade Online Social Networks (OSN) privacy has been thoroughly studied in many aspects. Some of these privacy related aspects are trust and credibility involving the OSN user-data conveyed by different relationships in the network. One of OSN major problems is that users expose their information in a manner thought to be relatively private, or even partially public, to unknown and possibly unwanted entities, such as adversaries, social bots, fake users, spammers or data-harvesters. That is one of the reasons OSN have become a major source of information for companies, different organizations and personal users, possibly misusing it for personal or business gain. Preventing this information leakage is the target of many OSN privacy models, such as Access Control, Relationship based models, Trust based models and many others. In this paper we suggest a new Role and Trust based Access Control model, denoted here as RTBAC, in which roles, that manifest different permissions, are assigned to the users connected to the Ego-node (the user sharing the information), and in addition, every user is evaluated trust wise by several criteria, such as total number of friends, age of user account, and friendship duration. These role and trust assessments provide more precise and viable information sharing decisions and enable better privacy control in the social network.

Keywords: Online Social Networks Privacy · Access control ·
Trust-based privacy models

1 Introduction

Online Social Networks (OSN) privacy models have been a source of much research over the past few years. Some of which focused on handling the OSN information sharing instances as an Access Control system, in which there is a selective restriction of access to the network's resources. The permission to access resources is the main concern of the different models, and the decision of giving a certain user authorization to access a resource is usually made under several criteria, based on many different factors. Access Control models have different variations, some are more widely-used than others.

[1] gives a survey of most of the OSN Access Control models, elaborating the functionalities of the different types. [2] presents a new model for privacy control based

© Springer Nature Switzerland AG 2019
S. Dolev et al. (Eds.): CSCML 2019, LNCS 11527, pp. 156–168, 2019.
https://doi.org/10.1007/978-3-030-20951-3_14

on sharing habits, controlling the information flow by a graph algorithm that prevents potential data leakage. In [3] a relationship-based approach is being handled, giving priority to the users' relationships qualities, on which we have based our initial idea for the model.

This paper presents a new privacy model for access control in an OSN, in which the decisions of permission granting combines both pre-defined roles and trust-based factors derived from user-attributes, such as total number of friends, age of user account, and resembling attributes between the two users. Similar attributes have appeared in a previous work [4], which deals with information-flow control, and creates a model for adversary detection. However, in this paper we present specific parametric values for these attributes, which are experimentally based. Furthermore, the current paper focuses on Trust and Access Control, while [4] deals with information-flow control. The Access Control model presented here is dynamic, in a manner of permission assignments, changing by the modularity of the user entities and their attributes. The model relies on previous researches and models, which will be mentioned and discussed in the upcoming parts of this paper, and its parameters are evaluated by experimental results conducted on real OSN users. The combination of the use of Roles and the novel way for computing users' Trust provides a much finer level of privacy control than the one that currently exists in social networks (e.g. [5, 6]), and this is the main contribution of this paper.

The rest of this paper is structured as follows: Sect. 2 discusses the background for our work, with explanations for the related papers it relies on, Sect. 3 describes and defines our model thoroughly with several examples of its operation and presents its preliminary evaluation, Sect. 4 discusses the model's implementation and connection to the work done in previous models and approaches, and Sect. 5 is the conclusion of the paper, with future prospect on further research on this subject.

2 Background and Related Work

Access Control models, and specifically ones describing OSN privacy, have been studied extensively over the past decade. A major problem, that exists especially in OSN, is an information flow to unwanted entities, violating the privacy of individuals. Even with a proper Access Control model, one likes to prevent such flow, and this is a subject of recent research. In the sharing-habits research mentioned above a privacy control model is established by defining the other users into three closeness categories (close friend, acquaintance, and adversary), then it presents an algorithm that moves edges from the OSN graph, having the amount of information flowing to the adversaries minimized, while the information flow to friends and acquaintances remains intact. The access given to information instances is decided by a Min-Cut algorithm, dividing the community graph for the purpose of preventing data leakage to unwanted entities, such as spammers or other potential adversaries. In this model, the access granted to the user's information is based on user-to-user relationships, and we have based our Access Control method on this approach.

The main Access Control model used in OSN is Role-Based Access Control (RBAC) that has many versions, as presented in [7], and limits access by creating user-role assignments. The user must have a role that has permission to access that resource. The most prominent advantage of this method is that permissions are not assigned directly to users but to roles, making it much easier to manage the access control of a single user, since it must only be assigned the right role. To this model we add the Trust factor [8], and it is based on the network users' interactions history, which could be problematic in assessing relatively unknown new connections. In this paper we circumvent this problem by adding independent user attributes to this estimation. An example of using RBAC specifically in Facebook is done in [5], that describes the use of roles in it and the possible breaches that can occur due to the flexible privacy settings of the network. [9] gives an extensive and formal Access Control model for Facebook-like networks, based on incrementing policies obtained by dynamic relationships in the network. Another important model we rely on is Relationship-Based Access Control (ReBAC), presented in [10] that is based on user-relationships in OSN.

The model is topology-based and establishes relationships between users on the social network by a sequence of binary conditions. [11] presents a model that implements the contextual nature of relationships, in which a policy language for ReBAC is devised, based on modal logic, for composing trust-based access control policies with an applicative paradigm for it. In [12] the formal ReBAC was developed into a two-stage method for evaluating policies. These policies were defined by semantics for path conditions, similar to regular expressions, which were used to develop a policy evaluation method. A model based on relationship strength between friends – RSBAC (Relationship Strength Based Access Control) is presented in [13]. The model calculates the level of closeness between users according to their social activities and their profile similarities. The model's main idea is that OSN users that have profile similarity (in terms of attributes) and communicate frequently, necessarily have a high degree of closeness, and therefore should get broader permissions to each other's data instances. Using Trust in OSN is widely used in different models, and even in relatively early researches such as [14], the idea of involving trust in Access Control for OSN user data is handled, in creating Trust criteria for different subjects (users) and objects (data instances). A research that handles an OSN access control model based on Trust is [15]. The model presents a policy that refers to an access right that a subject can have on an object, based on relationship, trust, purpose and obligations in the network. [16] present a model named IMPROVE-Identifying Minimal Profile Vectors for similarity-based access control. It elaborates on this specific subject, and gives a 30-item list of attributes, some direct and some derived, that define the user information in an OSN. An important ranking is given to these attributes, based on information gaining from each attribute, assessing their importance in the closeness approximation between users and evaluating their information sharing willingness. This trust is used differently in various roles, depending on the model's policies.

We have based our Role and Trust Based Access Control (RTBAC) model on the above works, and it is presented in the following section. The novelty of our model is that the relationships and their strengths do not determine Access Control directly, but are used along with other characteristics to compute the trust of an OSN user in accordance with a specific Ego-user.

3   OSN Role and Trust Based Access Control (RTBAC)

3.1   The RTBAC Model

The basic idea of the model is that besides the general roles given to different users, each user will be given a certain level of trust, and permissions to access different data instances will be authorized only if the trust level passes a certain threshold. In this manner, the generalization disadvantage of RBAC can be solved, and better data distribution can be achieved. We should first emphasize the way, relative to a specific Ego-user, RBAC is generally used in an OSN. A user may belong to multiple hierarchic roles, but all of them are on a single path (as seen in [17]). Therefore, when a user, and an Access chosen for it, is the lowest in the hierarchy it has the maximal set of permissions per role. We denote this role as R (U, Ego), but we will use just R as a short notation. The main contribution of RTBAC is the way Trust is computed. Trust is computed by assigning values of credibility and connection strength to the different users, based on the criteria presented below.

A minimum trust value threshold is the core condition of accessing a specific permission. The purpose of combining trust is to provide an additional stage of screening besides the RBAC roles. Another advantage of the model is that the combination of trust elements allows dynamic assignments of permissions to users over time, meaning their trust level can be dropped, and vice versa.

The formal definition of the RTBAC model instance is as follows:

An RTBAC instance is a tuple $<u\_id, R, P(R), UTV, MTV, P(U)>$ where:

- u_id - *String*, the identification of a user connected to the Ego-node
- R - *String*, the assigned user role of u_id, same as in RBAC
- P - *String*, An access permission to an OSN data instance
- B (P, R) - *Boolean*, the preliminary access Permission P of the assigned role R
- UTV - *Float*, the User Trust Value for u_id, that will be explained in the following part, values range between 0 and 1
- MTV (P, R) - *Float*, the Minimal Trust Value of role R for permission P, that will be explained in the following part, values range between 0 and 1
- B (U, P) - *Boolean*, the final access decision for u_id U for permission P.

In Fig. 1 we can see the access granting decision made by the model, where the user must have a role and a minimal trust value to access the specific data instance.

In Fig. 2 we can see an example for the model's structure – The Ego-user is the user sharing the information. There are 7 other users in the system in this example, that obtain different roles.

In this example, we give a minimal trust value (MTV) of 0.745 for a family member role to access the permission of "Tagging". This value can be altered per role and per permission in other cases. An Example of the trust decision making can be clearly seen in User 6. Users 6 and 7 have a "Family" role, but only User 7 achieves a trust value >0.745 and gets the "Tagging" permission that User 6 does not obtain.

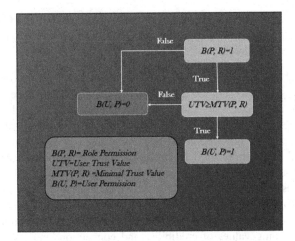

Fig. 1. Access decision in the RTBAC model

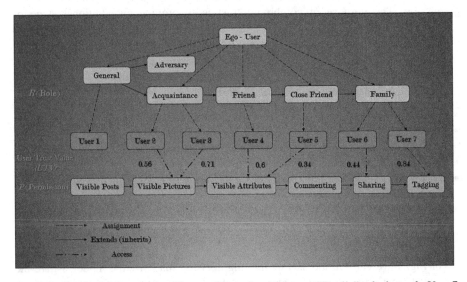

Fig. 2. RTBAC model example of 7 users. Users 6 and 7 have a "Family" role, but only User 7 achieves a trust value >0.745 and gets the "Tagging" permission.

3.2   Criteria Choice for Trust Estimation

The choice of the attributes, for determining the level of trust for the model, is based on the criteria mentioned in the above sections, and the two main categories of criteria for our model are:

- **Connection strength (c):** the connection strength of users is determined by characteristics that indicate their level of closeness such as Friendship Duration (FD), Mutual Friends (MF), etc. The full characteristics list and their notations are shown in Table 1. The notation given to these factors are by this c notation. For example, c_{MF} is the value for the Mutual Friends attribute.

- **User credibility (u):** the user credibly criterion assesses the user attributes that convey his OSN reputation and trustworthiness, such as Total number of Friends (TF) and Age of User Account (AUA), calculated from the time the user joined the OSN, etc. The full list and notations are also shown in Table 1. The resemblance attributes (RA) that are taken into consideration are: Gender, Age (range), Education, Workplace, and Relationship status (married, single, etc.). The notation given to these factors are by this u notation. For example, u_{AUA} is the value for the Age of User Account attribute.

Table 1. User-credibility and connection-strength characteristics variables for RTBAC

Variable	Attribute	User/Connection
TF	Total number of Friends	User
AUA	Age of User Account (OSN seniority)	User
FFR	Followers/Followees Ratio	User
MF	Mutual Friends	Connection
FD	Friendship Duration	Connection
OIR	Outflow/Inflow Ratio	Connection
RA	Resemblance Attributes	Connection

3.3   Calculating Trust Parameters' Values

All the parameters' values presented in this section are based on an experimental evaluation we have performed and is discussed in more detail in Sect. 3.5 of this paper. These values are as follows:

$$u_{TF} = \begin{cases} \frac{TF}{245} & (TF < 245), \\ 1 & (TF \geq 245). \end{cases} \tag{1}$$

u_{TF} value is based on the Total Friends attribute, and the average value shown in [18], having fake profiles, social-bots, etc., with an allotted number of friends. The questionnaire result for this attribute was the lower bound of 244.34.

$$u_{AUA} = \begin{cases} \frac{AUA}{24} & (AUA < 24), \\ 1 & (AUA \geq 24). \end{cases} \tag{2}$$

u_{AUA} value is calculated in months. It is based on the estimation of the AUA attribute of [19], that an active spammer profile will not remain active for a long term, due to OSN security updating policies.

$$u_{FFR} = \begin{cases} FFR & (FFR < 1), \\ 1 & (FFR \geq 1). \end{cases} \tag{3}$$

For the c_{RA} value we take into consideration 10 of the users' attributes, based on the researches presented above, that resemble the Ego-user's attributes that are gender, age (range), current educational institute, past educational institute, current workplace, past workplace, current town, home-town, current country, home-country.

Let us denote the following factors:

- TA_{ego} is the total number of non-null attributes (from the 10 attributes mentioned above) of the Ego-user.
- $TRA_{ego, other}$ is the total number of non-null resembling attributes (from the 10 attributes mentioned above) of the Ego-user and the other user.

Now we can define c_{RA}:

$$c_{RA} = \frac{TRAego, other}{TAego} \tag{4}$$

For these resemblance cases, the Pearson correlation coefficient [20] is often used for ratio calculation, but it defines a symmetric value for both ends of the connection, whilst our model describes an asymmetric one, since the other user is the one being checked for resemblance, in relevance to the Ego-user, and not vice versa.

$$c_{MF} = \begin{cases} \frac{MF}{37} & (MF < 37), \\ 1 & (MF \geq 37). \end{cases} \tag{5}$$

c_{MF} value is also taken from the Mutual Friends attribute having fake profiles, social-bots, or even adversaries, with a small number of mutual friends, if any.

$$c_{FD} = \begin{cases} \frac{FD}{18} & (FD < 18), \\ 1 & (FD \geq 18). \end{cases} \tag{6}$$

c_{FD} value is calculated in months. It is based on the Friendship Duration attribute, having a relatively unknown user, or even a fake profile or spammer, being friends with the Ego-user not for a substantial amount of time, is of an unwanted sharing willingness potential.

The attribute of c_{OIR}, that is the ratio of Outflow/Inflow created in [6].

$$c_{OIR} = \begin{cases} Outflow/Inflow & (Outflow < Inflow), \\ 1 & (Outflow \geq Inflow). \end{cases} \tag{7}$$

Now we can assess the access permission decisions by defining the total values of user credibility and connection strength in a manner of averaging the different factors noted above.

$$
\begin{aligned}
u = \langle WiUi \rangle &= \frac{\sum_{i=1}^{|u|} WiUi}{\langle W \rangle |u|} = \frac{WuTF + WuAUA + WuFFR}{5.24 \cdot 3} \\
&= \frac{5.37uTF + 5.2uAUA + 5.16uFFR}{15.72}
\end{aligned}
\tag{8}
$$

$$
\begin{aligned}
c = \langle WiCi \rangle &= \frac{\sum_{i=1}^{|c|} WiCi}{\langle W \rangle |c|} = \frac{WcMF + WcFD + WcOIR + WcRA}{5.52 \cdot 4} \\
&= \frac{5.93cMF + 5.1cFD + 5.7cOIR + 5.34cRA}{22.8}
\end{aligned}
\tag{9}
$$

These weights (W_i) were the survey results for the significance (weight) of every attribute-factor (U_i or C_i) in u and c. They could theoretically be altered by other user-preferences or future results. We can now conclude the definition of the model's User Trust Value (UTV), taking into consideration that there are 7 attributes: 4 connection attributes and 3 user attributes (marked as $|c|$ and $|u|$):

$$
UTV = \frac{c \cdot |c| + u \cdot |u|}{|c + u|} = \frac{4 \cdot c + 3 \cdot u}{7}
\tag{10}
$$

The Minimal Trust Value (MTV) set in this model is based on the Trust-based dynamic RBAC model presented above and is altered per role and per permission by the user-preferences if such exist, or by an OSN administration policy, if such exists for these specific cases.

In Table 2 we can see an example, portrayed in Fig. 2, where there is a difference between two users that have the same role, but not the same UTV, thus not getting the same permission. The MTV set for this specific role and permission (Family - Tagging) is 0.745, and User 6 achieves a UTV value of 0.44 and does not get the permission, whilst User 7 achieves a UTV of 0.84, thus gets the permission.

In the following parts we will see the model's algorithm, and the experimental evaluation done for determining its different parameters.

Table 2. Difference in UTV between same-role users

User	$WuTF$	$WuAUA$	$WuFFR$	$WcRA$	$WcFD$	$WcOIR$	$WcMF$	u	c	UTV	MTV
6	0.44	0.33	0.89	0.4	0.67	0.13	0.22	**0.55**	**0.36**	**0.44**	**0.745**
7	0.78	0.59	0.91	0.8	0.86	0.96	1	**0.76**	**0.91**	**0.84**	**0.745**

3.4   The Model's Algorithm

The decision algorithm, seen in Fig. 1 and described above, is as follows:

Algorithm 1. PermissionDecisionOfRTSBAC (User *U*, Role *R*, Permission *P*)

Input: Minimal Trust value: *MTV(P(R))*
Output: User Permission: *P(U)*
     if $P(R(U)) = 1$ // *permission belongs to role*
          if *UTV (U)* ≥ *MTV(P(R))* // *UTV: pre-calculated, set as attribute*
               P(U) ← 1 // *Access Granted*
        else
               P(U) ← 0 // *Access Denied*
    else
        P(U) ← 0

3.5   Experimental Assessment and Real OSN Data Estimation of Trust

As mentioned above, the experimental evaluation of the model's trust parameters consisted of two parts:

A. A validation of the parameters by a survey of 282 OSN users that were asked for the importance of various attributes in their decisions to grant various permissions to their private data.

The survey included the quantifiable attributes of user credibility and connection strength described in Table 1. For all these attributes, the request was for the needed threshold value of Trust of a certain user. For example, an average of 245 total friends (TF) and above was considered as a trustworthy user, which we can share information with. The results are the ones presented in the Trust values calculation section above: MF $\geq$ 37, TF $\geq$ 245, AUA $\geq$ 24 and FD $\geq$ 18. Two more aspects were examined in the survey: the importance (weight) of every one of the Resembling Attributes (RA) on a scale of 1 to 10, and the importance of every one of the model's Trust attributes (from Table 1). These two aspects' results are presented in Fig. 3.

B. In the second experimental evaluation we attempt to validate the trust computation in a real OSN dataset that included 162 user nodes and their attributes. These were checked, and the Friend role was being examined Trust wise in a real part of a Facebook network. This dataset of user nodes was checked for the model parameters' Trust quantifiable attribute values mentioned in the previous parts. The nodes' *UTV* was calculated by the formulas presented above, and the average *UTV* achieved by the 162 users was 0.745. For the median theoretical probabilistic *MTV* value of 0.5, only 3 out of the 162 users, were not granted access to the permission. In Fig. 4 we can see the results of the *UTV* calculations of the 162 user nodes.

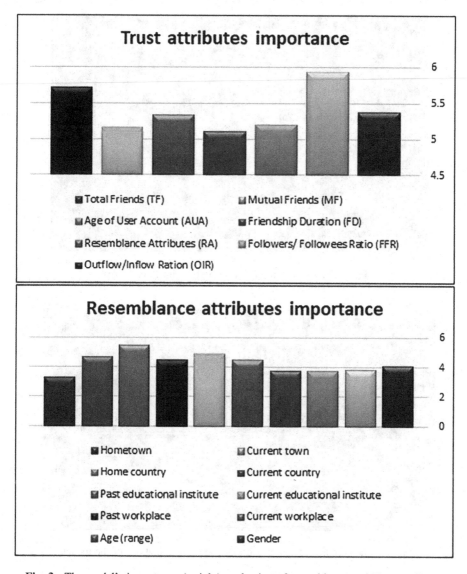

Fig. 3. The model's importance (weight) evaluation of resemblance and Trust attributes

In Fig. 5 we can see the compliance of the two experimental evaluations – the survey and the real OSN data. As we can see, there is a strong correlation between the values in the two experiments. Note that the TF attribute has a much higher value in the OSN real dataset since the OSN data presents definitive sharing probabilities (actual friends) whilst the survey presents a more general user-preference estimation.

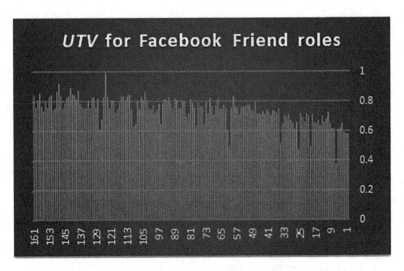

Fig. 4. *UTV* values for 162 user nodes with Friend roles

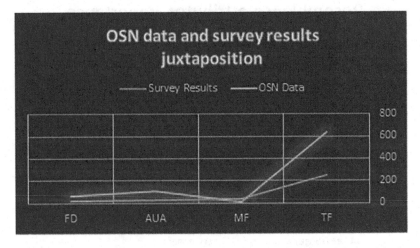

Fig. 5. The compliance of the two experimental evaluations of the model

4 Discussion

The RTBAC privacy model we have presented here helps to improve the current Role-based models, in which members of the same role (e.g. family or close friend) have the same set of permissions, disregarding their relationship with the Ego-user and other users, and not taking into consideration their dynamic behavior. Past Trust-based dynamic RBAC also used trust values for Access Control in non OSN environments (e.g. [5]), but its attributes are dependent on users' interactions history alone, making it difficult to determine if a permission can be given if this history is not available, and making it hard to evaluate the true nature of the user's network. Our privacy model solves this problem and improves this permission decision by the novel approach of taking into consideration both the user-roles and the user-attributes relevant to the specific permission decisions. The model also makes this permission's decision dynamic in time, since these attributes can change during time: The user gains or loses friends, its age of user account grows over time, etc. A certain weakness of this and any Trust related Access Control model is that new OSN users "fall through the cracks" since their Trust parameter values, such as AUA and TF, are very low, even though they could be legitimate users that will be mistaken for fake profiles or spammers. For these specific cases of new users, we can remedy the problem by giving extra weight to the OIR attribute, since spammers and bots have a very low value of OIR (they mainly Outflow data, and rarely Inflow), whilst genuine new user profiles have a high or moderate OIR value.

5   Conclusion and Future Work

In this paper we have presented an Access-Control model for privacy in OSN. The novelty of our RTBAC model is its combination of User-Trust attributes, based on real OSN characteristics, in an RBAC, that usually grants permissions solely to roles, and by that improving the privacy features of the network. The attributes of this model and their values were carefully picked and are based on previous research described in previous sections. These can improve information-sharing decisions done in an OSN.

Our experimental evaluation showed a strong indication of the validity of the Trust computation model and its attribute threshold parameters. Obviously, these parameters can be tuned further for different social networks and different size samples.

Current and future work on this model is further validation by experimental OSN user data, and the combination of the Information Flow model and this current Access Control model in the part of the role assessment. As seen in Fig. 2 a role that is "General" is the role of a user that is not directly connected to the Ego-user, and the decision of the acquaintance or adversary role can be done by an information-flow model [4].

References

1. Sayaf, R., Clarke, D.: Access control models for online social networks. Social Network Engineering for Secure Web Data and Services, pp. 32–65 (2012)
2. Levy, S., Gudes, E., Gal-Oz, N.: Sharing-habits based privacy control in social networks. In: Ranise, S., Swarup, V. (eds.) DBSec 2016. LNCS, vol. 9766, pp. 217–232. Springer, Cham (2016). https://doi.org/10.1007/978-3-319-41483-6_16
3. Cheng, Y., Park, J., Sandhu, R.: An access control model for online social networks using user-to-user relationships. IEEE Trans. Dependable Secure Comput. 13(4), 424–436 (2016)
4. Gudes, E., Voloch, N.: An information-flow control model for online social networks based on user-attribute credibility and connection-strength factors. In: Dinur, I., Dolev, S., Lodha, S. (eds.) CSCML 2018. LNCS, vol. 10879, pp. 55–67. Springer, Cham (2018). https://doi.org/10.1007/978-3-319-94147-9_5

5. Patil, V.T., Shyamasundar, R.K.: Undoing of privacy policies on Facebook. In: Livraga, G., Zhu, S. (eds.) DBSec 2017. LNCS, vol. 10359, pp. 239–255. Springer, Cham (2017). https://doi.org/10.1007/978-3-319-61176-1_13

6. Ranjbar, A., Maheswaran, M.: Using community structure to control information sharing in online social networks. Comput. Commun. **41**, 11–21 (2014)

7. Sandhu, R.S., Coyne, E.J., Feinstein, H.L., Youman, C.E.: Role-based access control models. Computer **29**(2), 38–47 (1996)

8. Lavi, T., Gudes, E.: Trust-based dynamic RBAC. In: Proceedings of the 2nd International Conference on Information Systems Security and Privacy (ICISSP) 2016, pp. 317–324 (2016)

9. Anwar, M., Zhao, Z., Fong, P.W.: An Access Control Model for Facebook-Style Social Network Systems. University of Calgary, Calgary (2010)

10. Cheng, Y., Park, J., Sandhu, R.: Relationship-based access control for online social networks: beyond user-to-user relationships. In: 2012 International Conference on Privacy, Security, Risk and Trust (PASSAT), and 2012 International Conference on Social Computing (SocialCom), pp. 646–655. IEEE (2012)

11. Fong, P.W.: Relationship-based access control: protection model and policy language. In: Proceedings of the first ACM Conference on Data and Application Security and Privacy, pp. 191–202. ACM (2011)

12. Crampton, J., Sellwood, J.: Path conditions and principal matching: a new approach to access control. In: Proceedings of the 19th ACM Symposium on Access Control Models and Technologies, pp. 187–198. ACM (2014)

13. Kumar, A., Rathore, N.C.: Relationship strength based access control in online social networks. In: Satapathy, S.C., Das, S. (eds.) Proceedings of First International Conference on Information and Communication Technology for Intelligent Systems: Volume 2. SIST, vol. 51, pp. 197–206. Springer, Cham (2016). https://doi.org/10.1007/978-3-319-30927-9_20

14. Ali, B., Villegas, W., Maheswaran, M.: A trust based approach for protecting user data in social networks. In: Proceedings of the 2007 Conference of the Center for Advanced Studies on Collaborative Research, pp. 288–293. IBM Corp. (2007)

15. Wang, H., Sun, L.: Trust-involved access control in collaborative open social networks. In: 2010 4th International Conference on Network and System Security (NSS), pp. 239–246. IEEE (2010)

16. Misra, G., Such, J.M., Balogun, H.: IMPROVE-identifying minimal PROfile VEctors for similarity-based access control. In: Trustcom/BigDataSE/ISPA, 2016 IEEE, pp. 868–875. IEEE (2016)

17. Facebook help: roles. https://www.facebook.com/help/323502271070625/

18. Dunbar, R.I.: Do online social media cut through the constraints that limit the size of offline social networks? Roy. Soc. Open Sci. **3**(1), 150292 (2016)

19. Zheng, X., Zeng, Z., Chen, Z., Yu, Y., Rong, C.: Detecting spammers on social networks. Neurocomputing **159**, 27–34 (2015)

20. Benesty, J., Chen, J., Huang, Y., Cohen, I.: Pearson correlation coefficient. In: Cohen, I., Huang, Y., Chen, J., Benesty, J. (eds.) Noise Reduction in Speech Processing, pp. 1–4. Springer, Heidelberg (2009). https://doi.org/10.1007/978-3-642-00296-0_5

Enhancing Image Steganalysis with Adversarially Generated Examples

Kevin Alex Zhang$^{(\boxtimes)}$ and Kalyan Veeramachaneni

MIT, Cambridge, MA 02139, USA
{kevz,kalyanv}@mit.edu

Abstract. The goal of image steganalysis is to counter steganography algorithms which attempt to hide a secret message within an image file. We focus specifically on blind image steganalysis in the spatial domain which involves detecting the presence of secret messages in image files without knowing the exact algorithm used to embed them. In this paper, we demonstrate that we can achieve better performance on the blind steganalysis task by training the YeNet architecture with adversarially generated examples provided by SteganoGAN.

Keywords: Steganalysis · Steganography · Deep learning

1 Introduction

Modern image steganography has found applications in everything from malware, where it can be used to transmit command-and-control instructions, to industrial espionage, where it can be used to hide or exfiltrate information. Unlike cryptography, which attempts to hide the content of the message, steganography attempts to hide the presence of the message itself by embedding it within otherwise benign content.

To combat image steganography, we can turn to image steganalysis algorithms which attempt to detect steganographic images. In general, these techniques work by analyzing the image file and identifying statistical anomalies in the pixel value distribution. Examples of steganalysis techniques include Primary Sets [4], RS analysis [7], Sample Pairs [5], and Spatial Rich Models [6]. Recently, new deep learning-based techniques have been developed for this task and have achieved state-of-the-art detection rates [11].

At the same time, new deep learning-based techniques have been developed for image steganography, yielding impressive results and achieving higher relative payloads as in [1,8,10,12,13]. Interestingly, since deep learning-based techniques are learned from data (and a random initial state), a new instance of a deep learning-based technique can be created simply by re-training the model, significantly reducing the cost of inventing a "new" steganography algorithm. This further complicates our analysis since an effective steganalysis algorithm now must not only defeat a specific instance of a steganography model but must, in

© Springer Nature Switzerland AG 2019
S. Dolev et al. (Eds.): CSCML 2019, LNCS 11527, pp. 169–177, 2019.
https://doi.org/10.1007/978-3-030-20951-3_15

fact, defeat all possible instances. In this paper, we will focus specifically on two techniques, HiDDeN [13] and SteganoGAN [12], which use generative adversarial networks to create hard-to-detect steganographic images.

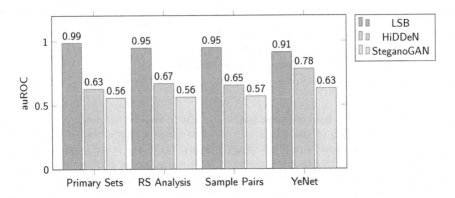

Fig. 1. This figure shows the performance of four different steganalysis techniques on steganographic images produced by the Least Significant Bits (LSB) algorithm, HiD-DeN [13], and SteganoGAN [12]. We examine three different static (e.g. non-trainable) spatial steganalysis tools as well as one deep learning-based method (YeNet) that was trained to detect LSB images. Based on these results, we see that none of these techniques are particularly effective at detecting steganographic images generated by HiD-DeN or SteganoGAN, suggesting that models trained on LSB steganography do not generalize well to deep learning-based steganography.

Due to the simultaneous development of both improved steganography methods and improved steganalysis algorithms, we start by running a simple experiment to determine the current state of steganography and steganalysis. We generated steganographic images using the least significant bits (LSB) algorithm, HiDDeN, and SteganoGAN; then, we used multiple steganalysis tools to try and detect these steganographic images. Figure 1 presents the performance of these steganalysis tools and we observe that although all the models are capable of detecting images generated using the simple least significant bits algorithm, none of them excel at detecting steganographic images generated by HiDDeN or SteganoGAN. The results from this experiment raise several questions:

1. Existing steganalysis algorithms are not effective at detecting steganographic images generated by methods not represented in the training set. Can we overcome this limitation and build steganalysis systems that generalize better?
2. We can easily create new instances of deep learning-based steganography algorithms by re-training the model with a different initial state. Can we take advantage of the fact to build more robust steganalysis systems?

To address these questions, we will borrow existing steganography and steganalysis architectures and use them to investigate the implications of being able to create new "instances" of steganography algorithms. In addition, we will examine the behavior of the YeNet architecture as we change the composition of the training dataset and evaluate its ability to generalize to previously unseen steganography algorithms.

The paper is organized as follows: Sect. 2 presents the different steganography methods used to generate our dataset, Sect. 3 presents the different steganalysis methods used in our experiments, Sect. 4 describes our experimental setup, and Sect. 5 presents our results.

2   Steganography

The standard image steganography task involves two operations: encoding and decoding. The encoding operation takes a cover image and a secret message and combines them to create a steganographic image which closely resembles the cover image but has the secret message hidden inside. Then, after the steganographic image is transmitted to the recipient, the decoding operation is applied to the steganographic image and the secret message is extracted.

In our experiments, we will be using three different techniques to generate steganographic images: least significant bits (LSB), HiDDeN [13], and SteganoGAN [12]. Examples of stenographic images generated by some of these techniques are shown in Fig. 2. Both HiDDeN and SteganoGAN use convolutional neural networks and adversarial training to learn to produce realistic steganographic images.

Fig. 2. Examples of cover images (top) and the corresponding steganographic images generated using LSB (middle) and SteganoGAN (bottom) with a relative payload of one bit per pixel. Both steganography techniques produce high quality images which, to the human eye, appear identical to the cover images.

2.1 Least Significant Bits

The simplest way to embed data in images is to simply swap the least significant bit of each pixel with the corresponding data bit. For example, given a standard RGB image and a sequence of data bits, we can simply loop from left-to-right, from top-to-bottom, and over the color channels and replace the lowest bit of each pixel value with the data bit. This naive approach is well-known by practitioners, easy to create paired datasets for, and simple to defend against. Examples of steganographic images generated by this technique are presented in the middle row of Fig. 2. We will use steganographic images generated by this technique to initialize our steganalysis models and provide a baseline.

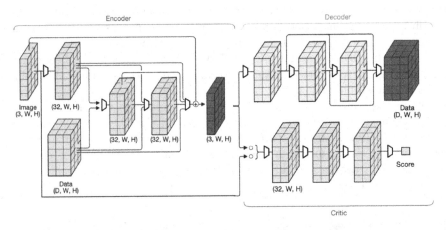

Fig. 3. The SteganoGAN architecture, reproduced with modifications from [12]. The encoder module maps a data tensor and a cover image to a steganographic image, the decoder module maps a steganographic image to a data tensor, and the critic module provides feedback on the quality of the steganographic image. The trapezoids represent convolutional blocks which consist of a convolutional layer, a leaky ReLU activation function, and a batch normalization operation. Two or more arrows merging represent concatenation operations and the curly bracket represents a batching operation.

2.2 HiDDeN

The first deep learning-based steganography algorithm we will examine is HiD-DeN [13]. This model is designed to take a fixed-length bit vector and an arbitrarily sized cover image and produce a steganographic image; note that a given model is only capable of embedding a fixed number of bits into an image, regardless of the size of the image. The HiDDeN architecture uses convolutional neural networks to represent (1) the encoder, which learns to take the image and bit vector and produces a steganographic image, (2) the decoder, which learns to take the steganographic image and decode the bit vector, and (3) the adversary, which learns to detect steganographic images and provides feedback to the encoder on how to avoid detection.

2.3 SteganoGAN

We will also use SteganoGAN, a competing deep learning-based steganography technique proposed in [12], to generate steganographic images. Examples of steganographic images generated by this technique are presented in the bottom row of Fig. 2. This model is conceptually similar to [13] and features a similar encoder-decoder-critic architecture, but is able to scale more effectively to larger images while maintaining a constant embedding rate. The SteganoGAN architecture, shown in Fig. 3, is designed to take in a data tensor and an arbitrarily sized cover image and create a steganographic image. Unlike the HiDDeN architecture where the data vector is of a fixed length, the size of the data tensor in SteganoGAN scales with the size of the cover image so that larger cover images will naturally be able to hold more data.

3 Steganalysis

Compared to the steganography task, the steganalysis task seems simple: given an image, the goal is to identify whether it is cover image or a steganographic image. We use two steganalysis tools, StegExpose [3] and YeNet [11], to evaluate our ability to detect steganographic images. The former is a collection of static steganalysis tools which does not need to be trained, whereas the latter is intended to be trained on datasets containing examples of cover and steganographic images.

3.1 StegExpose

To set a baseline for detecting steganographic images, we use StegExpose [3], a popular steganalysis tool which implements several different steganalysis algorithms including Primary Sets [4], RS analysis [7], and Sample Pairs [5]. We generate steganographic images using each of the techniques discussed in the previous section and report the detection performance as measured by the area under the receiver operating characteristic in Fig. 1. Based on these results, we see that the steganalysis algorithms all excel at detecting steganographic images generated using the least significant bit algorithm but fail to detect images generated by either HiDDeN or SteganoGAN.

3.2 YeNet

We also experiment with the YeNet architecture from [11], which can be trained on paired datasets containing examples of cover images and the corresponding steganographic images generated by various models. The YeNet architecture is similar to standard image classification architectures but the first set of convolutional layers are manually set to extract Spatial Rich Model [6] features. Spatial Rich Models are, in their own right, an effective technique for detecting steganographic images, but by embedding them into a convolutional neural network, [11] is able to achieve even better detection performance against a wide variety of steganography algorithms. We explore the performance of this model on various tasks in more detail in the following section (Fig. 4).

Table 1. This table shows the detection performance for YeNet models trained on various subsets of our base training datasets. We report the performance on the test sets which contain examples from LSB, HiDDeN, and SteganoGAN.

Base datasets	Test performance		
	LSB	HiDDeN	SteganoGAN
LSB	0.914 ± 0.130	0.783 ± 0.067	0.629 ± 0.050
LSB + 1 SteganoGAN	0.929 ± 0.007	0.834 ± 0.019	0.815 ± 0.028
LSB + 2 SteganoGAN	0.940 ± 0.002	0.868 ± 0.013	0.890 ± 0.015
LSB + 3 SteganoGAN	0.950 ± 0.003	0.893 ± 0.002	0.892 ± 0.009
LSB + 4 SteganoGAN	0.946 ± 0.003	0.868 ± 0.007	0.939 ± 0.003
LSB + 5 SteganoGAN	0.952 ± 0.013	0.894 ± 0.009	0.940 ± 0.002
LSB + 6 SteganoGAN	0.955 ± 0.005	0.891 ± 0.009	0.962 ± 0.003
LSB + 7 SteganoGAN	0.965 ± 0.002	0.930 ± 0.020	0.958 ± 0.003
LSB + 8 SteganoGAN	0.962 ± 0.006	0.891 ± 0.009	0.973 ± 0.005
LSB + 9 SteganoGAN	0.971 ± 0.003	0.925 ± 0.007	0.971 ± 0.008
LSB + 10 SteganoGAN	0.965 ± 0.006	0.911 ± 0.004	0.978 ± 0.003

4 Experiments

To support our experiments, we start by creating two sets of cover images: *base* and *large*. The *base* set is smaller and consists of 1,000 randomly selected images, common objects and scenes from the COCO dataset [9]. The size of this *base* set is on par with other steganalysis datasets such as the datasets used in the "break our steganographic system" challenge [2]. The *large* set is also randomly selected from the COCO dataset but contains 10,000 images. Both of these datasets are partitioned into a train and test partition which contain 70% and 30% of the images, respectively.

Train. To create our training datasets, we take the images in the *base* train partition and generate the corresponding steganographic images using the least significant bits algorithm as well as 10 different instances of SteganoGAN, giving us a total of 11 different *base* training datasets corresponding to different steganography algorithms. We use an identical procedure to generate the *large* training datasets.

Test. To create our test datasets, we take the images in the *base* test partition and generate the corresponding steganographic images using the least significant bit algorithm, a *secret* instance of SteganoGAN, and a *secret* instance of HiDDeN. Once again, we use an identical procedure to generate the *large* test

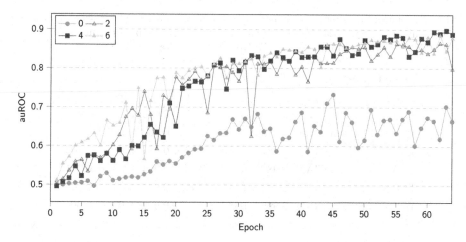

Fig. 4. This figure shows the area under the ROC curve on the SteganoGAN test set over time for models trained on different numbers of model instances. We see that models trained on more instances generally outperform models trained on fewer instances.

datasets. This procedure ensures that (1) the LSB test set contains images that the model has never seen before, (2) the SteganoGAN test set contains images generated by a *specific set of neural network weights* that the model has never seen before, and (3) the HiDDeN test set contains images generated by a *entire class of steganography algorithms* that the model has never seen before.

Optimization. To train the YeNet model, we use the Adam optimizer with a batch size of 32 and an initial learning rate of 0.001, and decay the learning rate when the loss plateaus for 10 epochs. We train the model for 64 epochs and report the average of the area under the receiver operating characteristic over three training runs for each of the test sets. By varying the number of SteganoGAN instances used to train the YeNet model, we can measure the resulting change in performance on each of the test datasets.

5   Analysis

The results on the *base* datasets are shown in Table 1. We immediately see that a model trained solely on LSB images is not effective at detecting HiDDeN or SteganoGAN images. However, we also observe that as we add examples of steganographic images generated by different instances of SteganoGAN, the test performance increases across the board. Not only does the model get better at detecting steganographic images generated by a secret *instance* of SteganoGAN that it has never seen before, but it also gets better at detecting steganographic images generated by HiDDeN, a secret *class* of steganography algorithms that it has never seen before (Table 2).

Table 2. This table shows the detection performance for YeNet models trained on various subsets of our *large* training datasets. We report the performance on the test sets, which contain examples from LSB, HiDDeN, and SteganoGAN.

Large Datasets	Test performance		
	LSB	HiDDeN	SteganoGAN
LSB	0.989 ± 0.002	0.895 ± 0.013	0.812 ± 0.009
LSB + 1 SteganoGAN	0.983 ± 0.004	0.952 ± 0.004	0.976 ± 0.003
LSB + 2 SteganoGAN	0.989 ± 0.001	0.967 ± 0.001	0.984 ± 0.003
LSB + 3 SteganoGAN	0.988 ± 0.001	0.964 ± 0.004	0.989 ± 0.001
LSB + 4 SteganoGAN	0.989 ± 0.002	0.970 ± 0.001	0.991 ± 0.001
LSB + 5 SteganoGAN	0.990 ± 0.002	0.962 ± 0.002	0.993 ± 0.001

To further establish the robustness of our results, we repeat these experiments with the *large* datasets. The models trained on this dataset achieve dramatically higher detection accuracy than the models trained on the *base* dataset. However, we still observe similar trends: as we add more instances of SteganoGAN, our model becomes better at detecting images generated by previously unseen steganography algorithms. We find that despite not providing a single example of a steganographic image generated by HiDDeN, we are able to detect them with an auROC of 0.971. These results suggests that using a diverse set of adversarially generated examples to train a steganalysis tool is a promising strategy for enabling steganalysis models to generalize well to steganography algorithms that it has never seen before.

6   Conclusion

In this paper, we explored the relationship between deep learning-based steganography algorithms and steganalysis techniques. We examined the impact of using multiple instances of the SteganoGAN steganography algorithm to train the YeNet steganalysis tool and found significant improvements on all of our test sets. Finally, we found evidence to suggest that by using a diverse set of adversarially generated examples as our test set, we can train steganalysis models which generalize well and are able to achieve high detection rates on steganography algorithms that the model has not seen before.

References

1. Baluja, S.: Hiding images in plain sight: deep steganography. In: Guyon, I., et al. (eds.) Advances in Neural Information Processing Systems 30, pp. 2069–2079. Curran Associates, Inc. (2017)
2. Bas, P., Filler, T., Pevný, T.: "Break our steganographic system": the ins and outs of organizing BOSS. In: Filler, T., Pevný, T., Craver, S., Ker, A. (eds.) IH 2011. LNCS, vol. 6958, pp. 59–70. Springer, Heidelberg (2011). https://doi.org/10.1007/978-3-642-24178-9_5
3. Boehm, B.: StegExpose - a tool for detecting LSB steganography. CoRR abs/1410.6656 (2014)
4. Dumitrescu, S., Wu, X., Memon, N.: On steganalysis of random LSB embedding in continuous-tone images 3, 641–644 (2002). https://doi.org/10.1109/ICIP.2002.1039052
5. Dumitrescu, S., Wu, X., Wang, Z.: Detection of LSB steganography via sample pair analysis. In: Petitcolas, F.A.P. (ed.) IH 2002. LNCS, vol. 2578, pp. 355–372. Springer, Heidelberg (2003). https://doi.org/10.1007/3-540-36415-3_23
6. Fridrich, J., Kodovsky, J.: Rich models for steganalysis of digital images. IEEE Trans. Inf. Forensics Secur. 7(3), 868–882 (2012). https://doi.org/10.1109/TIFS.2012.2190402
7. Fridrich, J., Goljan, M., Du, R.: Reliable detection of LSB steganography in color and grayscale images. In: Proceedings of the 2001 Workshop on Multimedia and Security: New Challenges, pp. 27–30. ACM (2001). https://doi.org/10.1145/1232454.1232466
8. Hayes, J., Danezis, G.: Generating steganographic images via adversarial training. In: NIPS (2017)
9. Lin, T., et al.: Microsoft COCO: common objects in context. CoRR abs/1405.0312 (2014)
10. Wu, P., Yang, Y., Li, X.: StegNet: mega image steganography capacity with deep convolutional network. Future Internet 10, 54 (2018). https://doi.org/10.3390/fi10060054
11. Ye, J., Ni, J., Yi, Y.: Deep learning hierarchical representations for image steganalysis. IEEE Trans. Inf. Forensics Secur. 12(11), 2545–2557 (2017). https://doi.org/10.1109/TIFS.2017.2710946
12. Zhang, K.A., Cuesta-Infante, A., Xu, L., Veeramachaneni, K.: SteganoGAN: high capacity image steganography with gans. CoRR abs/1901.03892 (2019). http://arxiv.org/abs/1901.03892
13. Zhu, J., Kaplan, R., Johnson, J., Fei-Fei, L.: HiDDeN: hiding data with deep networks. CoRR abs/1807.09937 (2018)

Controllable Privacy Preserving Blockchain
FiatChain: Distributed Privacy Preserving Cryptocurrency with Law Enforcement Capabilities

Rami Puzis[✉], Guy Barshap, Polina Zilberman, and Oded Leiba

Telekom Innovation Laboratories,
Department of Software and Information Systems Engineering,
Ben-Gurion University of the Negev, P.O.B. 653, Beer-Sheva, Israel
{puzis,barshag,polinaz,odedlei}@post.bgu.ac.il

Abstract. Central banks are reluctant to accept cryptocurrency, because current implementations of decentralized privacy preserving transactions make it impossible to apply know your customer (KYC) and anti-money laundering (AML) procedures. In this paper, we augment a distributed privacy preserving cyptocurrency known as Monero with KYC and AML procedures. The proposed solution relies on secretly sharing of the clients' private view keys and private transaction keys among a large number of permissioned signers (PSs). The resulting cryptocurrency maintains the notion of distributed trust while allowing a group of PSs to cooperate, collectively applying KYC and AML procedures.

Keywords: Cryptocurrency · Privacy · Anonymity · Blockchain · Anti-money laundering

1 Introduction

Blockchain is an innovative technology for which new applications are constantly emerging. Naturally, many of the applications are in the field of finance, and cryptocurrencies are one of the most popular trends. Blockchain provides fertile ground for cryptocurrency, because it provides distributed storage, transparency, auditability, low fees for international transfers, and of course, no double spending.

Current cryptocurrency approaches can be categorized as either permissionless or permissioned. The former approaches provide complete visibility of transaction content to anyone that has access to the blockchain. Such visibility ensures the integrity and nonrepudiation of all transactions, however this runs the risk of compromising the privacy (and in some cases the anonymity) of the transactions [8,27,31,38,39]. The latter approaches obscure transaction details (e.g., the sender, receiver and amount), making it easy for the parties to repudiate a transaction. Unfortunately, neither approach can be adopted for applications in which regulation is required, such as national cryptocurrency.

S. Dolev et al. (Eds.): CSCML 2019, LNCS 11527, pp. 178–197, 2019.
https://doi.org/10.1007/978-3-030-20951-3_16

National and central banks consider cryptocurrency because they reduce black market activity, encourage settlement and collaboration, and offer faster payments and auditability [4,5,10]. Yet, one of the greatest concerns of the banks are the risks associated with unregulated currency transactions, such as money laundering, scam operations, and terrorism funding [20] (see Table 1). However, removing the anonymity and decentralized nature of cryptocurrency defeats the point of cryptocurrency. This creates a gap that prevents the issuing of fiat cryptocurrency.

Table 1. Quotes from representatives of financial institutions.

"We predict that no reputable central bank would issue a decentralized virtual currency where users can remain anonymous. The reputational risk would simply be too high. Rather, central banks could issue central bank electronic money. This money would be tightly controlled by them, and users would be subject to standard KYC ("know your customer") and AML ("anti-money laundering") procedures." [5]

"Crypto exchanges in Malaysia are now required to identify traders after the government enacted AML legislation in February. Regulators emphasized the need to restrict the criminal use of the virtual marketplace" [20,43].

"The time has come to hold the crypto-asset ecosystem to the same standards as the rest of the financial system." [13]

In this paper, we present FiatChain, a novel, disclosable, privacy preserving cryptocurrency which is immutable and privacy maintaining, but can also be subject to regulations and lawful interception when necessary. To enable transaction disclosure we share the keys among n permissioned signers. More formally, the proposed cryptocurrency satisfies the following requirements:

1. Disclosure of a client's transactions upon the consortium of a size greater than or equal to k permissioned signers, where $k < n$.
2. Non-disclosure upon a consortium of fewer than k permissioned signers.
3. During investigation of some client (Alice), transactions that are not directly related to Alice will not be disclosed.
4. Only the receiver of money can spend it. In particular, no consortium of permissioned signers, miners or legal authorities can spend the money of the investigated client.
5. No entity can forge money, including double spending.

The proposed cryptocurrency is based on (1) Monero, a cryptocurrency which provides its clients with anonymity and privacy, and (2) Shamir's secret sharing and multi-party computation (MPC) which allow a client's disclosure by a consortium of authorities. Furthermore, our novel cryptocurrency is supported by four main protocols: client registration, generation of disclosable stealth address and transaction key, transaction issuance and validation, and a protocol for disclosing transaction details upon a consortium of k or more permissioned signers.

The rest of the paper is structured as follows. Section 2 outlines related work. Sections 3 and 4 briefly describe relevant background on cryptography and Monero, respectively. The terminology used and the requirements of the proposed FiatChain cryptocurrency are outlined in Sect. 5. FiatChain registration and transaction protocols are described in Sect. 6, while the disclosure protocols are discussed in Sect. 7. Section 8 presents the implementation details of the employed MPCs, and Sect. 9 concludes the paper.

2   Related Work

FiatChain, the cryptocurrency proposed in this paper, can be positioned according the following dimensions (see Fig. 1): decentralization (from a centralized trusted third party to a decentralized distributed trust); accountability and regulation compliance; and privacy and confidentiality.

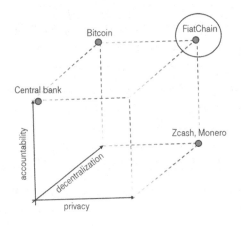

Fig. 1. FiatChain's positioning in the field of digital money

Centralized digital currencies, such as [11,12], have no distribution of trust or transparency for increased public trust; they also fail to provide sufficient privacy, since they leak the total amount received by the merchant to the bank once it has been deposited.

In order to remove the need for a trusted third party, Satoshi Nakamoto introduced Bitcoin [33], which provides a distribution of trust and transparency of its ledger which contains the growing list of transactions. However, the ledger layer of Bitcoin lacks full client privacy, as it is possible to track and analyze its transactions graph as demonstrated in [31,39]. Blockchain-based cryptocurrencies that preserve privacy can be roughly divided into two categorizes: privacy preserving extensions to Bitcoin (Coinjoin [2], CoinShuffle [40], Mixcoin [9],

TumbleBit [23]) and alternative currencies (known as altcoins) that are not compatible with Bitcoin (Monero [41], ZCash [24], ZeroCash [42]). Regardless, cryptocurrency that provides complete privacy and anonymity lack law enforcement capabilities, and thus, are unlikely to be accepted by banks.

In recent years, there have been many attempts to suggest a blockchain-based cryptocurrency that can be adopted by banks. Stablecoins like Tether [3] and MakerDAO [1] were designed to minimize price volatility, however they are not fully decentralized, since there must be a centralized custodian of the reserve assets.

A positioning report conducted for the Central Bank of Brazil [44] surveys the latest attempts to develop cryptocurrencies that can be issued by central banks. The most relevant studies are those that try to tackle the requirements for client's privacy and law enforcement capabilities.

RSCoin [16] is a centrally-issued cryptocurrency solution. The main technical contribution of this method is its scalability of consensus. Fedcoin [21] is a central bank cryptocurrency based on RSCoin. Fedcoin includes a system to maintain KYC rules and a plan to provide anonymity with zero-knowledge proofs. However like RSCoin, Fedcoin relies on a trusted central bank instead of distributed nodes to reach consensus on the blockchain. Moreover, the proposed identity verification protocol allows the central bank to link a user and all of his transactions.

Garman et al. [19] proposed a solution for regulation of Zerocash payments using zk-SNARK proofs. In their solution, zk-SNARK proofs are used to prove the validity of zk-SNARK transactions and demonstrate compliance with general predefined policies (such as tax payments, deposit limits, etc.), while protecting privacy.

PRcash [45] relies on MimbleWimble blockchain architecture's privacy design [26]. zk-SNARK proofs are used to prove that transaction amounts are below a certain threshold in order to not reveal its value to regulators. However, PRcash does not provide arbitrary disclosure of transactions upon lawful interception. Furthermore, the privacy of each transaction is based on the *active* participation of other clients.

3 Cryptographic Toolkit

In this section, we provide background on the cryptographic primitives and protocols used in FiatChain. We begin with commonly used notations.

First, let us denote $\mathbb{F}_q$ as a finite field of size q. A scalar mapping hash function $H_s : \{0,1\}^* \to \mathbb{F}_q$, and a point mapping hash function $H_p : E(\mathbb{F}_q) \to E(\mathbb{F}_q)$. Similar to Monero, we use Ed25519 elliptic curve [6] with a base point denoted as G and scalars in $\mathbb{F}_q$, where $q = 2^{255-19}$. Let $k \in [0, l)$ be a randomly selected scalar, where l is the order of G. Then $(k, K = kG)$ is a pair of private and public EC-keys respectively. Note that in Monero, private keys are scalars, while public keys are points on the elliptic curve.

3.1 Pedersen Commitment

A Pedersen commitment [37] is a cryptographic scheme that allows the commitment issuer to commit to a chosen value while keeping the value itself hidden until the issuer decides to reveal it. After the commitment is published, the issuer cannot change the value. The commitment to a value v, $C(v)$ is defined as: $C(v) = \alpha \cdot G + v \cdot H$, where G and H are the field generators (of the elliptic curve), and α is a random value that is called the *blinding factor* or *mask value*. Furthermore, a Pedersen commitment is additive homomorphic, i.e., for two commitment values $C(v_1) = \alpha_1 G + v_1 H$ and $C(v_2) = \alpha_2 G + v_2 H$, it holds that $C(v_1) + C(v_2) = C(v_1 + v_2)$.

3.2 Ring Signature

A ring signature provides the ability to sign a message m with a set of n unrelated public keys, without inferring the real signer with probability $1/n$. Ring signatures have the following properties:

1. Signer Ambiguity – given a list of n public keys of a ring signature, an outside observer would not be able to identify which member signed it.
2. Linkability – in cases in which the same private key x_j is reused, the corresponding public key $\tilde{P}_j$ supplied in the ring signature will reveal it. This property is essential to check for double-spending of transactions.
3. Unforgeability – with very high probability, no attacker can forge a signature without access to corresponding private keys. This property prevents money theft.

Multilayer Linkable Spontaneous Anonymous Group Signatures (MLSAG) allow combining confidential transactions with a ring signature in such a way that using multiple inputs and outputs is possible, anonymity is preserved, and double-spending is prevented [35]. An MLSAG signature is a ring signature on a set of n key-vectors. A key-vector is a collection $\bar{y} = (y_1, ..., y_r)$ of public keys with corresponding private keys $\bar{x} = (x_1, ..., x_r)$.

Suppose that each signer of a (generalized) ring containing n members has exactly m keys $\{P_i^j\}_{j=1,...,m}^{i=1,...,n}$. The intent of the MLSAG signature is the following:

- To prove that one of the n signers knows the secret keys of the entire key vector.
- To enforce the following: if the signer uses any of their m signing keys in another MLSAG signature, the two rings are linked, and the second MLSAG signature (ordered by the Monero blockchain) is discarded.

3.3   Multi-Party Computations

SPDZ [14,15] is a secure multi-party computation (sMPC) scheme that allows general arithmetic sMPC with active security against malicious participants in a dishonest majority scenario. While there are exist several improvements to the original protocol, all of these protocols consist of two phases, online and offline in which they are performed by n participants. The online phase computes a function represented as an arithmetic circuit (i.e., consist of addition and multiplication gates). Since linear operations (addition and scalar multiplication over a shared value) can be performed locally, the main focus of this protocol is how to compute multiplication gates of shared values.

The privacy of this protocol is maintained by performing the computations on additive secret sharing of the inputs and outputs of each gate. The correctness and resilience of this protocol against malicious participants is guaranteed by additive secret sharing of MACs on each gate of the arithmetic circuit.

Furthermore, the scheme is performed over a fixed finite field $\mathbb{F}_p$ which is suitable for conducting computation over the Ed25519 field that is used in Monero and our proposed scheme.

Private Membership Testing is a concrete problem of Private Set Intersection (PSI), which is a well-studied problem with many suggested solutions [17,18,32]. Herein, we describe a folklore solution that assumes a general sMPC primitive, such as SPDZ [14,15] or a Yao garbled circuit [46].[1] Let us assume that participant P_1 holds a list of n elements $A = \{a_1, \ldots, a_n\}_{a_i \in \mathbb{F}_q}$, and P_2 holds an element $b \in \mathbb{F}_q$. Both participants want to test whether $b \in A$ without exposing the exact value of b to P_1. To that end, both parties compute the following Boolean circuit $\bigvee_{i=1}^{n} (a_i \wedge b)$, with $a_{i \in [n]}$ and b as P_1 and P_2 inputs, respectively. The security and privacy of this scheme rely upon the MPC scheme that is used and the Boolean circuit's output value which does not reveal anything but whether $b \in A$.

3.4   Feldman's Verifiable Secret Sharing Scheme (VSS)

A general secret sharing scheme consists of two phases and involves the dealer, who wants to share the secret, and participants that receive shares of the secret. The first phase is called *sharing*, in which the dealer "breaks down" his secret and distributes the shares among the participants. In the second phase, which is called *reconstruction*, the participants reconstruct the secret by using Lagrange polynomial interpolation. In a VSS scheme, the participants can verify that the shares that they received can indeed construct the dealer's secret. In other words, the dealer has a secret $s \in \mathbb{F}_p$ and shares it among participants $P_1, \ldots, P_n$, such that any $t + 1 \leq n$ participants would be able to reconstruct it. To that end, the

---

[1] This scheme is implemented on the SPDZ arithmetic circuit because of implementation details.

dealer generates a random polynomial of degree t with coefficients in $\mathbb{F}_p$. Let us denote that polynomial $P(x) = \sum_{i=0}^{t} a_i x^i$, where $a_0 = s$. Then, the dealer sends the value $P(i) \mod p$ to each participant $P_{i,i\in[n]}$ and publicly publishes the commitments of the coefficients of $P(x)$, i.e., $C_0 = g^{a_0}, C_1 = g^{a_1}, \ldots, C_t = g^{a_t}$. By using the commitments, each participant can verify the share they received. Formally, participant P_i checks:

$$g^{P(i)} \stackrel{?}{=} \prod_{j=0}^{t} C_j^{i^j} = g^{\sum_{j=0}^{t} a_j \cdot i^j} \tag{1}$$

In the protocols described in this paper, we use a variant of Feldman's scheme that works on elliptic curves [25]. Using this scheme, we can ensure that the secret sharing of values is valid, in cases in which the client is the dealer.

4   Background on Monero

A blockchain is a distributed ledger that stores blocks of data. We consider a blockchain whose primary objective is to facilitate the issuing of money and performing transfer transactions, also known as cryptocurrency. Monero is a blockchain architecture that implements privacy preserving cryptocurrency, which involve the roles of miners, clients and nodes, like any classical blockchain. Monero offers its clients a high degree of privacy by using the following methods.

First, the sender's identity is hidden by using MLSAG (see Sect. 3) which does not require *active* participation from other clients. In addition, MLSAG helps in both providing ownership and preventing the double-spending of money by signing with the client's private keys.

Second, the identity of the receiver, which is defined by the receiver's pair of public keys (pubic view key A_{RC} and public spend key B_{RC}) is hidden by using an one-time public key called *stealth address*. Specifically, the sender generates a new random address, which is equal to $P = H_s(rA_{RC})G + B_{RC}$, where r is a random value from $E(\mathbb{F}_q)$.[2]

Third, with Monero the amount is not explicitly written on the blockchain, but rather the Pedersen commitment is written with a technique called RingCT [36]. This technique prevents the fabrication of money out of air by exploiting the homomorphic feature of a Pedersen commitment, in order to validate that the sum of all output values does not exceed the input values and by providing range proofs [30].

It is important to note the reasons why Monero, in its current form, is not (by design) compatible with law enforcement requirements. First, it was designed to be permission-less. Therefore, there are no controls regarding the clients that can

---

[2] According to the implementation the exact term is $P = H_s(8 \cdot rA||i)G + B$, where multiplying by eight forces the rA point to be in the group base point G and $||$ denotes byte concatenation with output index (oi). The output index prevents the generation of multiple identical stealth addresses for the same receiver (which will prevent the receiver from spending more than one output).

participate in the platform. Second, authorities that wish to investigate certain transactions are dependent on clients' consent and cooperation. Third, sharing a client view key does not permit viewing the transactions that where spent (only the transactions the client has received can be seen). We describe our modifications to Monero and the protocol developed to support law enforcement capabilities in Sect. 6.

5   Terminology and Requirements

In our setting, the stakeholders are:

- **Permissioned Signers (PSs)** – ensure that the transaction's encrypted data can be revealed by a consortium of the permissioned signers. Let us denote a permissioned signer as PS_j, where $1 \leq j \leq n$, and n is the number of PSs in the current setting.
- **Miners** – validate and aggregate the transactions into blocks and append them to the blockchain.
- **Clients** – send and receive amounts of money. The senders issue the transactions.
- **Legal Authority** – can check transaction details (with the cooperation of at least k PSs, but without consent of clients), in order to perform legal investigations.

Herein, we describe FiatChain's requirements.

Requirement 1 (Disclosure upon consortium). *Given a consortium of k (out of n) PSs and provided with the identity of a specific client, the consortium can (with a computational power polynomial of the size of the dataset):*

1. *Identify all transactions in which the client participated as either the receiver or sender.*
2. *Expose the following fields for each of these transactions: amount sent, the identity of the receiver, and the identity of the sender.*

Requirement 2 (Secrecy: no consortium → no disclosure). *No subset of PSs of a size less than k can expose any of the fields detailed in Requirement 1.*

Requirement 3 (Investigation scope). *Only if k PSs agree to perform an investigation of client's transactions, his transactions will be disclosed. During the investigation no private information of other clients will be disclosed, including private view keys and transaction keys.*

Requirement 4 (Obligations for the receiver). *In each transaction the receiver:*

1. *is aware of the amount sent,*
2. *can spend the money he received.*

No other entity can spend the money on his behalf.

Requirement 5 (Transaction validation). *Each transaction is considered as valid according to the transaction validation consensus rules if and only if:*

1. *The sender received enough funds to cover the amount declared in the transaction.*
2. *The sender did not already spend the inputs of the transaction in previous blocks of the blockcahin.*
3. *The sender and the receiver are registered clients of FiatChain.*
4. *The sender uses a disclosable stealth address and the transaction's public key which was computed by the sender and the PSs.*

Note that Requirements 4, 5.1 and 5.2 are inherently supported by Monero.

5.1 Security Model

The security model of FiatChain is based on the following assumptions, which are consistent with the cryptographic toolkit that was described in Sect. 3.

Assumption 1 (Semi-honest miners and PSs). *We assume that PSs and miners follow the protocol as specified and do not try to deviate from it. We also assume that, they try to learn as much as they can from the messages they receive from other parties during the protocol.*

Assumption 2 (Malicious clients). *The clients that participate in the protocol can act maliciously, meaning that they are not committed to follow the protocol, and are presumed to act according to their personal benefits.*

Assumption 3 (Adversaries in the protocol are computationally bound). *We assume that an adversary (i.e., any corrupt party) is computationally bound, or otherwise known as a probabilistic polynomial time attacker.*

Assumption 4 (Monero mixing). *No subset of clients that is not directly involved in the transaction can reveal details regarding the transaction (i.e., the receiver, sender, and transaction amount).*

Assumption 5 (Private secure channel between participants). *We assume that a secure channel between any two participants in the FiatChain exists or can be created ad hoc; a secure channel preserves the confidentiality of the transmitted data. Furthermore, no other participants in the protocol will be aware of the existence of such a communication channel besides the channel participants.*

6   FiatChain Protocols

The proposed cryptocurrency is supported by four main protocols:

1. Client registration – The identities of the registered clients are stored by n PSs.
2. Transaction keys and stealth address generation – The client participates with k PSs in MPC to compute the transaction's key and the stealth addresses for each transaction.
3. Transaction issuance and validation – The transaction is based on Monero's transaction with the addition of a field that contains the transaction's public key and the stealth addresses signed by a PS. During validation, the miner verifies the validity of the signature.
4. Authorities' disclosure – The system supports two disclosure processes for a transaction of a suspected client. In the first, the suspected client is the sender of a transaction, while in the second, the suspected client is one of the receivers in a transaction.

As stated in Requirement 1, the proposed blockchain, given a consortium of k PSs must facilitate the disclosure of a specific client's transactions. This means that every payment transaction must include elements that encapsulate the identity of the client in such a manner that the client cannot forge it. On the other hand, as stated in Requirement 2, without a consortium, no entity in the system can link the identity encapsulating elements to the client. To ensure that the sender of a transaction is disclosable, we suggest a practice in which the PSs use MPC to compute the transaction's public. To ensure that the receivers of transaction's outputs will be disclosable, we suggest using VSS to share the clients' private view keys among the PSs during the registration process.

6.1   Client's Registration

As in Monero, a client i generates two pairs of elliptic curve cryptography keys (EC-keys) as follows.

1. View keys pair: $(\alpha^i, A^i = \alpha^i G)$ which are private and public EC-keys, respectively.
2. Spend keys pair: $(\beta^i, B^i = \beta^i G)$ which are private and public EC-keys, respectively.

Then, the client registers with k PSs by sharing the private view key and revealing his public view and spend keys using Feldman's scheme which is described in Sect. 3.4.

6.2   Transaction Keys and Stealth Address Generation

To simplify the discussion, let us call the issuer of a transaction *Alice*. Alice wants to send a payment transaction to Bob (a registered client). In Monero, when constructing a transaction, Alice generates a random private transaction key r, resulting in the public transaction key $R = rG$. Furthermore, for each receiver with public keys (A, B), Alice generates a stealth address $P = H_s(rA)G + B$.

In FiatChain, Alice applies to k PSs, $PS_1, \ldots, PS_k$, and they engage in secure MPC to compute R and P. Let us assume for the sake of simplicity that the transaction only consists of outputs addressed to Bob. The input that Alice provides consists of Bob's public keys of Bob (A, B), while together, the PSs provide a random value r. Alice also applies, via an anonymous communication channel, to another PS, PS_{k+1}, whose task in the MPC is to sign elliptic curve digital signature on R and P. The first step that the PSs perform in the MPC is private membership testing (as described in Sect. 3.3) to verify that the public keys (A, B) belong to a registered client (without exposing to which client the keys belong).[3] The output of the MPC, revealed only to Alice, is P, r, and signed P and R.

Alice, as is usually done in Monero, inserts P and $rG = R$ into the transaction. In addition, Alice adds the signed R and P to the transaction, and a miner verifies that these elements were also signed by one of the PSs. The PSs receive a global unique identifier (GUID) which they store with Alice identity and the share of r that they used in the MPC.

See Figs. 2 and 3 and Algorithm 1 for a detailed description of the MPC that takes place for each transaction.

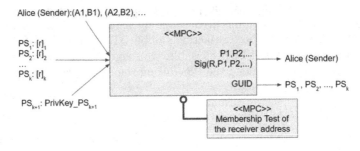

Fig. 2. MPC of the stealth addresses and transaction's public keys per transaction.

Note that in the MPC implementation used in this research, the PSs are not exposed to Alice's input. As a result, the PSs just know that Alice wants to issue a transaction without knowing the identity of the receivers. In addition, after receiving R and P, Alice can wait for an unbounded amount of time before issuing the transaction, in order to prevent the PSs from inferring and disclosing Alice by linking the time they were communication with her.

---

[3] The value (A, B) is translated into the x-term of that function.

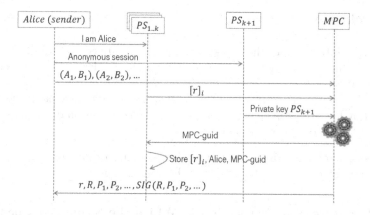

Fig. 3. Sequence diagram of the computation of the stealth addresses and transaction's public key per transaction

---

Algorithm 1. MPC of receiver's stealth address and transaction's keys

---

Input: Alice:$(A, B)_{Bob}$, $PS_{i \in [k]}$: $[r]_i$, PS_{k+1}: sk_σ, $L_{RegisteredUsers(RU)}$.
Output: Alice:$(r, P, \sigma(P, R))$, $PS_{i \in [k]}$: $GUID$, PS_{k+1} : $\perp$.

/* **Stage 1** : PSs generate together shared random r */
1 **for** $i \leftarrow 1$ **to** k **do**
2 | $PS_i \leftarrow [r]_i$ /* Without single dealer by using [23]. */
3 **end**

/* **Stage 2** : *Alice* and PSs test that the receiver has valid public key. */
4 **if** $(A, B)_{Bob} \notin L_{RU}$ **then**
5 | **return** $\perp$
6 **for** $i \leftarrow 1$ **to** k **do**
7 | $PS_i \leftarrow ([r]_i, Alice, GUID)$ /* PS_i Store the tuple */
8 **end**

/* **Stage 3** : Alice and PSs compute the stealth address */
9 $P \leftarrow H_s(rA)G + B$
10 $R \leftarrow rG$

/* **Stage 4** : PS_{k+1} Sign on P, R */
11 $\sigma(R, P) \leftarrow Sign_{sk_\sigma}(R, P)$
12 **return** *Alice: $(r, P, \sigma(R, P))$, $PS_{i \in [k]}$: $GUID$*

6.3 Verifying a Payment Transaction

Before appending a transaction to a block, a miner verifies the validity of the transaction. The verification algorithm includes Monero transaction verification and verification of the signature on the transaction's public key and the stealth addresses. In cases in which one of the above is invalid, the transaction is rejected.

7   Disclosure

Upon lawful interception, the blockchain must be scanned and all of the transactions in which the suspected client was either the sender or the receiver must be provided.

The disclosure procedures (see the sequence diagrams in Figs. 4 and 6) are executed by law enforcement authorities with the cooperation of the PSs. There are two different disclosure processes:

1. The suspected client is one of the receivers of the transaction.
2. The suspected client is the sender of the transaction.

7.1   Disclosure of a Transaction in Which the Suspected Client Is One of the Receivers

In Monero, the client scans the blockchain and for each transaction computes $P = H_s(\alpha R)G + B$ using α and the transaction's public key R. if P equals one of the outputs in the transaction, this means that the client is one of the receivers of this transaction.

Similarly, in FiatChain the legal authority scans the blockchain and for each transaction with public key R it directs k PSs to engage in MPC and compute P (see Fig. 4). The PSs received and verified their shares of the client's private view key α during the client's registration process as described in Sect. 6.1. Note that at no point is the reconstructed private view key α exposed to any of the PSs or the legal authority.

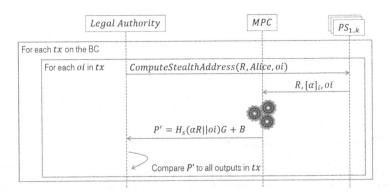

Fig. 4. Sequence diagram of the retrieval of all the transactions (tx) in which the suspected client (Alice) is one of the receivers.

Disclosing the Sender. For every transaction identified in Fig. 4 (where the suspect is one of the receivers), the legal authority is required to disclose the identity of the sender of the transaction. For this purpose, the legal authority engages with k PSs in MPC for every $guid$ in the blockchain (brute force). The input of the legal authority is the transaction's public key R. The input of each PS is the share of r that corresponds to the given $guid$. The output of the MPC is $True$ if the transaction's public key R equals rG and $False$ otherwise.

Algorithm 2. Disclose sender

Input: tx
Output: $sender$
1 **for** $guid \in GetGUIDs()$ **do**
2   **if** $MPC(guid, R)$ **then**
3   **return** $GetOwnerOfGUID()$
4 **end**

Disclosing the Transferred Amount. When the suspect is one of the receivers, the legal authority is also required to disclose the amount transferred to the suspect.

As in Monero, each output in the transaction includes the encrypted amount and a mask value. The legal authority and k PSs engage in MPC to decrypt the amount (see Fig. 5). The inputs of the legal authority to the MPC are R, enc_amount, $mask$ and the index of the output (oi) that is addressed to the suspect. The input of each PS is their share of the suspect's private view key α. The MPC computes the $amount$ and the $blinding\_key$ as follows: $amount \leftarrow enc\_amount - H_n(H_n(H_n(\alpha R||output\_index)))$, $blinding\_key \leftarrow mask - H_n(H_n(\alpha R||output\_index))$

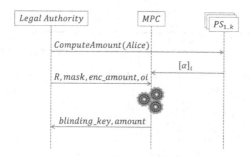

Fig. 5. Sequence diagram of amount disclosure when the suspect (Alice) is one of the receivers.

7.2 Disclosure of a Transaction Where the Suspected Client Is the Sender

In Sect. 6.2, we described the MPC used to compute the public key R and the stealth addresses per each transaction of a client. For every such MPC requested by a client, the PSs store the MPC's GUID, the client's ID and their share of r. As a result, the transaction's public key R encapsulates the identity of the transaction's sender.

During disclosure of a suspected client, the legal authority directs k PSs to compute all the public transaction keys that were computed for the suspected client (see Fig. 6).

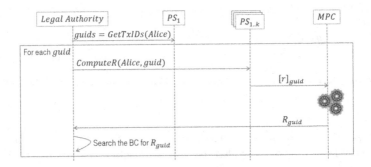

Fig. 6. Sequence diagram of the retrieval of all the transactions where the suspected client (Alice) is the sender.

Disclosing the Receivers. When the suspect is the sender, the legal authority is required to disclose the identities of all of the receivers of the transaction (see Algorithm 3). For every transaction identified in Fig. 6, the legal authority discloses the identities of the receivers by engaging with k PSs in MPC that computes P. The input of each PS is the share of r that corresponds to a given $guid$. The input of the legal authority is a client's identifiers (A, B).

Algorithm 3. Disclose receivers

    Input: $tx, guid$
    Output: $receivers$ (list of clients' identifiers)
1 **for** $oi \in tx.outputs$ **do**
2   **for** $(A, B) \in registered\_clients$ **do**
3           $P' \leftarrow MPC(guid, A, B)$
4   **if** $P' == P$ **then**
5              $receivers.add((A, B))$
6   **end**
7 **end**
8 **return** $receivers$

Disclosing the Transferred Amount. When the suspect is the sender, the legal authority is also required to disclose the amounts transferred to each of the receivers. As in Monero, each output in the transaction includes the encrypted amount and a mask value. The legal authority and k PSs engage in MPC to decrypt the amount (see Fig. 7). The inputs of the legal authority to the MPC are A, enc_amount, $mask$ and the index of the output addressed to the receiver that is identified by the public key A. The input of each PS is their share of the transaction's private key r (according to the given $guid$). The MPC computation reveals the $amount$ and the $blinding\_key$ as follows:

$amount \leftarrow enc\_amount - H_n(H_n(H_n(rA||output\_index)))$,
$blinding\_key \leftarrow mask - H_n(H_n(rA||output\_index))$.

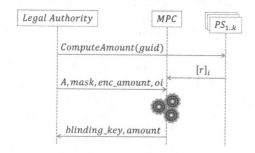

Fig. 7. Sequence diagram of amount disclosure when the suspect (Alice) is a sender.

8   Implementation Details

All of the above mentioned protocols and MPCs were implemented as part of this research. In FiatChain, stealth addresses and transaction keys are computed in the same manner as in Monero, thus ensuring backward compatibility with Monero.

Specifically, Monero utilizes elliptic curve cryptography based on the curve Ed25519 [6] for signatures, stealth addresses, etc.

The protocols discussed in Sect. 6, including elliptic curve operations, Keccak hashing [7], and verifiable secret sharing, were implemented using the FRESCO sMPC framework. This framework provides a suite of protocols for establishing the p2p network between MPC participants and performing the computations. The framework allows different computation engines and settings. In this paper, we use this framework with SPDZ [14,15] and MASCOT [28] preprocessing as the main protocol which relies on Oblivious Transfer (OT) primitive, because it has lower communication complexity.

In the implementation, we addressed the following challenges: (1) The prime in Ed25519 is $2^{255} - 19$. Unfortunately, the current MASCOT and OT modules' implementation in FRESCO only work with a field size whose bit representation length is divisible by eight. (2) Some of the built-in computations in FRESCO (e.g., bit decomposition, equality, and comparison) require additional bits for statistical security. This fact reduces the field of operation to a subset of the field used in FRESCO. Large number operations may utilize the space assigned for security bits and get overwritten.

In order to solve these implementation issues, we increased the number of bits for computations in FRESCO to $\left\lceil \frac{\log_2\left(2^{255}-19\right)^2}{8} + s \right\rceil \cdot 8$, where s is the maximal number of security bits that may be required for a single mathematical operation in FRESCO. This resulted in about 1.5 kbit representations of all of the values used during the sMPC computations. Then, for each operation that is required to work over a finite field, we performed a "public modulo reduction", as described by Ning and Xu [34], on the result of the operation. Finally, implementation of the hash function was done by bit decomposition of the data and the subsequent performance of logical operations on the individual bits, as per the Keccak specification summary.[4]

Unfortunately, the current implementation is not scalable. First, we have ended up working over a huge modulus (~600 bits instead of 256 bits) which results in larger payloads and longer computation time. Second, as a result of performing "public modulo reduction" on every operation, a big overhead was added to even the simplest calculation. Finally, the hash function implementation was naive and no optimizations were applied.

9 Conclusion

In this paper, we present a privacy preserving cryptocurrency with law enforcement capabilities. FiatChain, the proposed cryptocurrency, represents a significant step toward the adoption of the blockchain technology by governments and central banks around the world. Public interest in cryptocurrencies is apparent, but central banks have been reluctant to accept this technology for supporting fiat currency due to fear of money laundering and the inability to track funds in privacy preserving cryptocurrencies such as Monero or Zcash. Telecom operators and other similar organizations obliged to lawful interception face similar problems in adopting privacy preserving blockchain for some of their services. The distributed disclosure procedures proposed in this paper provide a good trade-off between the required ability to enforce KYC and AML regulations and the requirement to maintain clients' for privacy and anonymity. Clients may rest assured that no one, not even their bank, can disclose their transactions without a court order and consent of at least k PSs.

The multi-party computation (MPC) employed provides secrecy of input, selective output disclosure, and correctness.[5] Future research and development are required to provide more efficient sMPC implementations. In particular it is

---

[4] https://keccak.team/keccak_specs_summary.html.
[5] The integrity of the result is guaranteed and malicious parties deviating from the protocol during execution should not be able to force honest parties to output an incorrect result.

required to modify MASCOT and OT implementations in FRESCO to support modulus who's bit length is not divisible by eight, and support bit decomposition and comparison algorithms in FRESCO without the need for statistical security bits.

Past research assessed the susceptibility of Monero to statistical attacks allowing the adversary to link between transactions [29]. In light of these attacks, further analysis of FiatChain is required in order to make sure that protocols implemented by permissioned signers do not significantly increase linkability and traceability.

References

1. The dai stablecoin system. https://makerdao.com/. Accessed 06 Feb 2019
2. Maxwell, G.: Post on bitcoin forum. https://bitcointalk.org/index.php?topic=279249.msg3013970#msg3013970. Accessed 09 Feb 2019
3. Tether: Fiat currencies on the bitcoin blockchain. https://tether.to. Accessed 06 Feb 2019
4. Swiss national bank plans to launch their own cryptocurrency, February 2018. https://www.interactivecrypto.com/swiss-national-bank-plans-launch-cryptocurrency. Accessed 27 Feb 2018
5. Berentsen, A., Schar, F., et al.: The case for central bank electronic money and the non-case for central bank cryptocurrencies. Federal Reserve Bank of St. Louis Review **100**(2), 97–106 (2018)
6. Bernstein, D.J., Duif, N., Lange, T., Schwabe, P., Yang, B.Y.: High-speed high-security signatures. J. Crypt. Eng. **2**(2), 77–89 (2012)
7. Bertoni, G., Daemen, J., Peeters, M., Van Assche, G.: Keccak specifications. Submission to nist (round 2), pp. 320–337 (2009)
8. Biryukov, A., Khovratovich, D., Pustogarov, I.: Deanonymisation of clients in bitcoin p2p network. In: Proceedings of the 2014 ACM SIGSAC Conference on Computer and Communications Security, pp. 15–29. ACM (2014)
9. Bonneau, J., Narayanan, A., Miller, A., Clark, J., Kroll, J.A., Felten, E.W.: Mixcoin: anonymity for bitcoin with accountable mixes. In: Christin, N., Safavi-Naini, R. (eds.) FC 2014. LNCS, vol. 8437, pp. 486–504. Springer, Heidelberg (2014). https://doi.org/10.1007/978-3-662-45472-5_31
10. Buchanan, B.: The bank of England is planning a bitcoin-style virtual currency – but could it really replace cash? January 2018. http://theconversation.com/the-bank-of-england-is-planning-a-bitcoin-style-virtual-currency-but-could-it-really-replace-cash-89585. Accessed 4 Jan 2018
11. Camenisch, J., Hohenberger, S., Lysyanskaya, A.: Balancing accountability and privacy using e-cash (extended abstract). In: De Prisco, R., Yung, M. (eds.) SCN 2006. LNCS, vol. 4116, pp. 141–155. Springer, Heidelberg (2006). https://doi.org/10.1007/11832072_10
12. Camenisch, J., Maurer, U., Stadler, M.: Digital payment systems with passive anonymity-revoking trustees. J. Comput. Secur. **5**(1), 69–89 (1997)
13. Carney, M.: The future of money. In: Scottish Economics Conference. Edinburgh University, March 2018. https://www.bankofengland.co.uk/-/media/boe/files/speech/2018/the-future-of-money-speech-by-mark-carney.pdf. Accessed 2 Mar 2019

14. Damgård, I., Keller, M., Larraia, E., Pastro, V., Scholl, P., Smart, N.P.: Practical covertly secure MPC for dishonest majority – or: breaking the SPDZ limits. In: Crampton, J., Jajodia, S., Mayes, K. (eds.) ESORICS 2013. LNCS, vol. 8134, pp. 1–18. Springer, Heidelberg (2013). https://doi.org/10.1007/978-3-642-40203-6_1

15. Damgård, I., Pastro, V., Smart, N., Zakarias, S.: Multiparty computation from somewhat homomorphic encryption. In: Safavi-Naini, R., Canetti, R. (eds.) CRYPTO 2012. LNCS, vol. 7417, pp. 643–662. Springer, Heidelberg (2012). https://doi.org/10.1007/978-3-642-32009-5_38

16. Danezis, G., Meiklejohn, S.: Centrally banked cryptocurrencies. arXiv preprint arXiv:1505.06895 (2015)

17. De Cristofaro, E., Tsudik, G.: Practical private set intersection protocols with linear complexity. In: Sion, R. (ed.) FC 2010. LNCS, vol. 6052, pp. 143–159. Springer, Heidelberg (2010). https://doi.org/10.1007/978-3-642-14577-3_13

18. Freedman, M.J., Nissim, K., Pinkas, B.: Efficient private matching and set intersection. In: Cachin, C., Camenisch, J.L. (eds.) EUROCRYPT 2004. LNCS, vol. 3027, pp. 1–19. Springer, Heidelberg (2004). https://doi.org/10.1007/978-3-540-24676-3_1

19. Garman, C., Green, M., Miers, I.: Accountable privacy for decentralized anonymous payments. In: Grossklags, J., Preneel, B. (eds.) FC 2016. LNCS, vol. 9603, pp. 81–98. Springer, Heidelberg (2017). https://doi.org/10.1007/978-3-662-54970-4_5

20. Georgacopoulos, C.: Banks and the crypto industry: Asia, April 2018. https://cointelegraph.com/news/banks-and-the-crypto-industry-asia. Accessed 18 Apr 2018

21. Gupta, S., Lauppe, P., Ravishankar, S.: A blockchain-backed central bank cryptocurrency (2017)

22. Harn, L., Lin, C.: Strong (n, t, n) verifiable secret sharing scheme. Inf. Sci. **180**(16), 3059–3064 (2010)

23. Heilman, E., Alshenibr, L., Baldimtsi, F., Scafuro, A., Goldberg, S.: Tumblebit: an untrusted bitcoin-compatible anonymous payment hub. In: Network and Distributed System Security Symposium (2017)

24. Hopwood, D., Bowe, S., Hornby, T., Wilcox, N.: Zcash protocol specification. Technical report, 2016–1.10. Zerocoin Electric Coin Company (2016)

25. Ibrahim, M.H., Ali, I., Ibrahim, I., El-Sawi, A.: A robust threshold elliptic curve digital signature providing a new verifiable secret sharing scheme. In: 2003 IEEE 46th Midwest Symposium on Circuits and Systems, vol. 1, pp. 276–280. IEEE (2003)

26. Jedusor, T.E.: Mimblewimble (2016)

27. Kappos, G., Yousaf, H., Maller, M., Meiklejohn, S.: An empirical analysis of anonymity in zcash. arXiv preprint arXiv:1805.03180 (2018)

28. Keller, M., Orsini, E., Scholl, P.: MASCOT: faster malicious arithmetic secure computation with oblivious transfer. In: Proceedings of the 2016 ACM SIGSAC Conference on Computer and Communications Security, pp. 830–842. ACM (2016)

29. Kumar, A., Fischer, C., Tople, S., Saxena, P.: A traceability analysis of monero's blockchain. In: Foley, S.N., Gollmann, D., Snekkenes, E. (eds.) ESORICS 2017. LNCS, vol. 10493, pp. 153–173. Springer, Cham (2017). https://doi.org/10.1007/978-3-319-66399-9_9

30. Maxwell, G., Poelstra, A.: Borromean ring signatures (2015)

31. Meiklejohn, S., et al.: A fistful of bitcoins: characterizing payments among men with no names. In: Proceedings of the 2013 Conference on Internet Measurement Conference, pp. 127–140. ACM (2013)

32. Miyaji, A., Nishida, S.: A scalable multiparty private set intersection. Network and System Security. LNCS, vol. 9408, pp. 376–385. Springer, Cham (2015). https://doi.org/10.1007/978-3-319-25645-0_26

33. Nakamoto, S.: Bitcoin: A peer-to-peer electronic cash system (2008)

34. Ning, C., Xu, Q.: Multiparty computation for modulo reduction without bit-decomposition and a generalization to bit-decomposition. In: Abe, M. (ed.) ASIACRYPT 2010. LNCS, vol. 6477, pp. 483–500. Springer, Heidelberg (2010). https://doi.org/10.1007/978-3-642-17373-8_28

35. Noether, S., Mackenzie, A., Monero-Core-Team: Ring confidential transactions, February 2016. https://lab.getmonero.org/pubs/MRL-0005.pdf

36. Noether, S., Mackenzie, A., et al.: Ring confidential transactions. Ledger 1, 1–18 (2016)

37. Pedersen, T.P.: Non-interactive and information-theoretic secure verifiable secret sharing. In: Feigenbaum, J. (ed.) CRYPTO 1991. LNCS, vol. 576, pp. 129–140. Springer, Heidelberg (1992). https://doi.org/10.1007/3-540-46766-1_9

38. Quesnelle, J.: On the linkability of zcash transactions. arXiv preprint arXiv:1712.01210 (2017)

39. Ron, D., Shamir, A.: Quantitative analysis of the full bitcoin transaction graph. In: Sadeghi, A.-R. (ed.) FC 2013. LNCS, vol. 7859, pp. 6–24. Springer, Heidelberg (2013). https://doi.org/10.1007/978-3-642-39884-1_2

40. Ruffing, T., Moreno-Sanchez, P., Kate, A.: CoinShuffle: practical decentralized coin mixing for bitcoin. In: Kutyłowski, M., Vaidya, J. (eds.) ESORICS 2014. LNCS, vol. 8713, pp. 345–364. Springer, Cham (2014). https://doi.org/10.1007/978-3-319-11212-1_20

41. van Saberhagen, N.: Cryptonote v 2.0, October 2013. https://cryptonote.org/whitepaper.pdf

42. Sasson, E.B., et al.: Zerocash: decentralized anonymous payments from bitcoin. In: 2014 IEEE Symposium on Security and Privacy (SP), pp. 459–474. IEEE (2014)

43. Suberg, W.: Malaysian central bank: Id now needed for any crypto exchange transaction, February 2018. https://cointelegraph.com/news/malaysian-central-bank-id-now-needed-for-any-crypto-exchange-transaction. Accessed 28 Feb 2018

44. de Vilaca Burgos, A., de Oliveira Filho, J.D., Suares, M.V.C., de Almeida, R.S.: Distributed ledger technical research in central bank of brazil (2017)

45. Wüst, K., Kostiainen, K., Capkun, V., Capkun, S.: PRCash: fast, private and regulated transactions for digital currencies

46. Yao, A.C.: Protocols for secure computations (extended abstract). In: 23rd Annual Symposium on Foundations of Computer Science, pp. 160–164 (1982)

A Relay Attack on a Tamper Detection System (Brief Announcement)

Itai Dinur[(✉)] and Natan Elul

Department of Computer Science, Ben-Gurion University, Beersheba, Israel
dinuri@cs.bgu.ac.il

Abstract. This short paper analyzes a tamper detection system for IoT environments, presented by Bagci et al. at ACSAC 2015. It shows that the system is vulnerable to relay attacks.

1 Introduction

In this paper we analyze a tamper detection system for IoT environments, published by Bagci et al. [1]. The system does not require adding new hardware components to IoT devices, but rather analyzes the signal obtained from an IoT device, assuming that a tamper event has a noticeable effect on the signal's properties. The main challenge in designing such a system is to accurately separate true tamper events from environmental noise.

More specifically, we studied and implemented the recently proposed tamper detection system of Bagci et al., which was shown to detect tamper events with high accuracy in both stable (controlled) and more chaotic uncontrolled environments (such as a busy office). First, we attempted to reproduce the results of Bagci et al. by implementing their proposed system and conducting similar experiments. While our experiments in controlled environments closely matched the ones of Bagci et al., we were not able to obtain the claimed accuracy level in uncontrolled environments. Second, and more importantly, we noticed that the tamper detection system of Bagci et al. is vulnerable to relay attacks. In such attacks, the attacker relocates the IoT device (stripping it from its original functionality) and replaces it with a relay device that acts as a man-in-the-middle between the relocated IoT device and the receivers of the tamper detection system. We implemented the relay attack and were able to deceive the system of Bagci et al. even in controlled environments (in which it is harder to disguise the attack as environmental noise).

2 The Tamper Detection System of Bagci et al. [1]

We briefly describe the tamper detection system for IoT environments suggested by Bagci et al. [1].

The system is comprised of a network that consists of IoT devices (transmitters) and multiple receivers, whose task is to extract a particular object (called

© Springer Nature Switzerland AG 2019
S. Dolev et al. (Eds.): CSCML 2019, LNCS 11527, pp. 198–201, 2019.
https://doi.org/10.1007/978-3-030-20951-3_17

the *channel state information* or *CSI*) from each transmitted WiFi frame. The CSI data from each receiver is sent to a central computer that runs a designated algorithm for recognising tamper events.

In essence, the algorithm utilises the channel state information from each transmitted frame and evaluates the data by translating signal amplitudes to an Euclidean metric distance measure. This measure reflects the distance between a group of history "untampered" samples to the current measured amplitude. Then, a tamper event is detected by a decision procedure if a substantial changes is observed in the metric distance.

The decision procedure as proposed by Bagci et al. distinguishes between two main types of environment, controlled and uncontrolled. In a controlled environment, the physical changes are very limited, and only pre-planned movements are introduced. On the other hand, an uncontrolled environment may consist of arbitrary regular activities of humans at their working place. In both environments, a threshold value is calculated in order to distinguish between untampered and tampered states. The threshold value depends on the environment type, according to the scale of movement and its physical layout. In a controlled environment, the threshold is calculated by finding the maximal change in the Euclidean distance between each two samples of a precalculated untampered dataset. By using this threshold, the algorithm learns the steady state of the environment, and triggers an alarm on CSI values that exceed the threshold. In an uncontrolled environment, due to potential environmental noise, the algorithm calculates the threshold by using both untampered and tampered samples. In this way, it can differentiate between changes in the signal that originate from the environmental movements and those originating from true tamper events.

3 The Relay Attack on the Tamper Detection System

We observe that the proposed system of [1] heavily relies on the assumption that the evaluated signal is originated from the transmitter, and not by another device that may be maliciously controlled by an attacker in a relay attack.

Our relay attack consists of a relay device that operates in the WiFi frequency and located in the original location of a transmitter (i.e., an IoT device), which is moved to a different location. The relay device repeats the transmission of each frame originated by the transmitter. At the same time, we make sure that the signal of the relocated transmitter is masked and does not reach the transmitters. In order to mask the signal, we utilise a Faraday cage which weaken the signal such that it is virtually blocked from the receivers, but is still readable by the relay device which is located in close proximity to the masked transmitter.

The attack is illustrated in Fig. 1. We stress that the relay device is located in the same location as the original transmitter and is implemented using the same type of hardware (in our case, the same model of Raspberry Pi). Therefore, its signal has similar CSI to the original transmitter and the receivers cannot distinguish it from the signal of the original device. We further note that a relay attack is generally required here (rather than merely replacing the transmitter with an attacker-made device), since the original transmitter and receivers may utilize a cryptographic message authentication code (MAC) algorithm to authenticate messages using a key that is unknown to the attacker.

In an additional (more complex) attack scenario, the attacker may move the transmitter to a remote location and relay its packets using additional devices over an arbitrary network such as the Internet. Consequence, the transmitter can be moved to an attacker-controlled environment and the IoT device (e.g., a surveillance camera or a smoke detector) would not fulfill its original task.

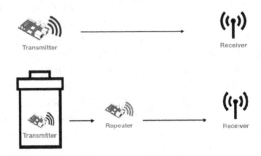

Fig. 1. The relay attack

4 Summary of Results

Our experimental setup consists of: (1) A Raspberry Pi transmitter that simulates a monitored IoT device, (2) Four receivers (industrial computers), equipped with Intel-5300 Network Card Interface (NIC), (3) Main computer (PC) that gathers the data from the receivers and runs the tamper detection algorithm.

We implemented the tamper detection algorithm of [1] in both controlled and uncontrolled environments. Unfortunately, we were not able to reproduce the claimed accuracy level in uncontrolled environments as in [1]. This may be attributed to factors such as the different environments in which experiments were carried out, or the use of different hardware (e.g., [1] implemented the receivers using old laptops, whereas we used industrial computers).

On the other hand, we were able to reproduce similar results to [1] in controlled environments. Consequently, we implemented the relay attack in this environment. This attack was carried out by replacing the transmitter with a relay device, whilst keeping the distance value below the max distance threshold, except for a short period of time as discussed below.

In order to evaluate the attack, we used a similar environment as used in [1]. First, a history dataset was collected when no movement occurs in the environment. In this experiment, an attacker awaits outside the experiment space. Then, at time 200 s, the attacker places the transmitter inside a customised Faraday cage (a metal trashcan), positions the relay device (another Raspberry Pi) in the original position of the transmitter, and powers on the relay device before exiting the space.

Figure 2 shows the Euclidean distance data collected from the first receiver on every received sample (the data collected from other receivers is similar). The outcome is a successful relay that does not trigger a tamper event by the algorithm after the replacement of the receiver. On the other hand, a tamper event is triggered during the replacement (210 s–240 s).

Even though a tamper event is triggered during replacement, the attack should be considered as successful (or at least partially successful), as after the replacement, a tamper event is not triggered, whereas the system is clearly in a tampered state. Of course, the question of whether the attack would be detected in practice depends on how short tamper events are treated. We further note that a highly trained attacker (or a group of attackers) might be able to implement the replacement without triggering an alarm, if replacement is performed in the time period between transmissions (which is 1 s in [1]).

Finally, although we did not implement the attack in an uncontrolled environment (as attacking an inaccurate tamper detection system is pointless), we note that the implementation of the relay attack (on an accurate system) in such an environment should be significantly easier compared to a controlled environment. One reason for this is that in order to separate tamper events from environmental noise, the algorithm of [1] uses time-wise filtering which averages received values over windows of (up to) 60 s. Thus, short fluctuations in CSI values have little effect and would not trigger an alarm. Consequently, it is likely that an attacker would be able to perform the replacement procedure without triggering any tamper event.

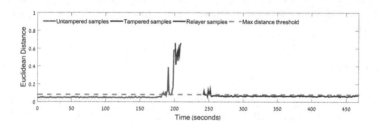

Fig. 2. Euclidean distance vs. Time measurement of receiver 1

Reference

1. Bagci, I.E., Roedig, U., Martinovic, I., Schulz, M., Hollick, M.: Using channel state information for tamper detection in the internet of things. In: ACSAC 2015 (2015)

Amended Cross-Entropy Cost:
An Approach for Encouraging Diversity
in Classification Ensemble
(Brief Announcement)

Ron Shoham[(✉)] and Haim Permuter

Ben-Gurion University, 8410501 Beer-Sheva, Israel
ronshoh@post.bgu.ac.il, haimp@bgu.ac.il

Abstract. In the field of machine learning, the training of an ensemble of models is a very common method for reducing the variance of the prediction, and yields better results. Many researches indicate that diversity between the predictions of the models is important for the ensemble performance. However, for Deep Learning classification tasks there is no explicit way to encourage diversity. Negative Correlation Learning (NCL) is a method for doing so in regression tasks. In this work we develop a novel algorithm inspired by NCL to explicitly encourage diversity in Deep Neural Networks (DNNs) for classification. In the development of the algorithm we first assume that the same training characteristics that hold in NCL must also hold when training an ensemble for classification. We also suggest the Stacked Diversified Mixture of Classifiers (SDMC), which is based on our outcome. SDMC is a layer that aims to replace the final layer of a DNN classifier. It can be easily applied on any model, while the cost in terms of number of parameters and computational power is relatively low.

1 Introduction

Ensemble methods are a simple and efficient way to yield better results by aggregating predictions from multiple models. Many works point out that the key for an ensemble to perform well is to encourage diversity among the models [2,5,6,8,10]. A well known framework for generating a diversified ensemble for regression tasks uses Negative Correlation Learning (NCL) criteria [1,6,8]. In this note we would like to develop a novel analogue framework for the classification problem. For regression, the negative correlation is well motivated from simple decomposition of the error into bias-variance-covariance [1,6]. However, for classification problems such a framework is less clear. Currently, most of the ensembles in DNNs are obtained by training the same architecture multiple times with different seeds. The randomization achieves some diversity but it is done implicitly, without any clear criteria. We suggest an amended cost function for multiple classifiers which encourages diversity between different model predictions.

© Springer Nature Switzerland AG 2019
S. Dolev et al. (Eds.): CSCML 2019, LNCS 11527, pp. 202–207, 2019.
https://doi.org/10.1007/978-3-030-20951-3_18

In general, the cost function used in machine learning can be motivated by several considerations. For instance, cross-entropy can be motivated by a maximum-likelihood criteria, but also by being a "good match" to sigmoid or softmax nodes for binary or multi-class cases, respectively [7]. Using a "good match" to a sigmoid or softmax node is also what motivates us in developing a cost function for ensemble classification. We show that by adding a penalty that encourages increasing the cross-entropy between the predictions of the models we get the same learning characteristics as in NCL.

The novelty of our idea lies in our giving an explicit criterion for simultaneously training multiple models for an ensemble, while encouraging diversity explicitly. One of the benefits of this method is that all models are equally strong. We also suggest a variant called Stacked Diversified Mixture of Classifiers (SDMC), which can be applied on any DNN classifier easily, without increasing the number of parameters and computational power significantly. SDMC is a variant for the vanilla final softmax layer used in DNN, based on our outcome in this article.

2   Regression with Negative Correlation Learning

For regression tasks there is a well known technique for encouraging diversity in ensembles called *Negative Correlation Learning* (NCL) [1,6]. A mathematical analysis shows that reducing the correlation between the regressors in an ensemble might leads to reducing the MSE of the ensemble (bias-variance-covariance decomposition). Its main idea is that by adding a penalty $p_i = (f_i - f_{ens}) \sum_{j \neq i} (f_j - f_{ens})$ for each model cost function, where f_i is the i'th model prediction and $f_{ens} = \frac{1}{M} \sum_{j=1}^{M} f_j$ is the ensemble prediction, we reduce the correlation between the predictors. This yields a new cost function:

$$e_i = \frac{1}{2}(f_i - t)^2 + \gamma p_i, \tag{1}$$

$$= \frac{1}{2}(f_i - t)^2 + \gamma(f_i - f_{ens}) \sum_{j \neq i} (f_j - f_{ens}). \tag{2}$$

When calculating its gradient, and setting $\lambda = 2\gamma(1 - \frac{1}{M})$, we get

$$\frac{\partial e_i}{\partial f_i} = (f_i - t) - \gamma[2(1 - \frac{1}{M})(f_i - f_{ens})] \tag{3}$$

$$= (f_i - t) - \lambda(f_i - f_{ens})$$
$$= (1 - \lambda)(f_i - t) + \lambda(f_{ens} - t). \tag{4}$$

3   Classification

Inspired by the above result, we would like to find a penalty for the classification cost that yields the same characteristics. In order to achieve this, we start from the outcome we got in (4) and integrate it. This procedure is similar to that presented in [7] for finding the cross-entropy as the desired cost function for a sigmoid classifier. The difference between classification and regression is that we use an activation function on the final layer[1]. For binary classification we use the sigmoid function $f_i(z_i) = \frac{1}{1+e^{-z_i}}$, in contrast to regression where $f_i(z_i) = z_i$. Therefore, based on the outcome in (4) we demand

$$\frac{\partial e_i}{\partial z_i} = (1 - \lambda)(f_i - y) + \lambda(f_{ens} - y). \tag{5}$$

By applying the chain rule $\frac{\partial e_i}{\partial z_i} = \frac{\partial e_i}{\partial f_i} \frac{\partial f_i}{\partial z_i}$ and the result $\frac{\partial f_i}{\partial z_i} = f_i(1 - f_i)$, we get

$$\frac{\partial e_i}{\partial f_i} = \frac{(1 - \lambda)(f_i - y) + \lambda(f_{ens} - y)}{f_i(1 - f_i)} \tag{6}$$

$$= \frac{f_i - y}{f_i(1 - f_i)} - \frac{\lambda}{M} \sum_{j \neq i} \frac{f_i - f_j}{f_i(1 - f_i)} \tag{7}$$

$$e_i = \int \frac{\partial e_i}{\partial f_i} df_i \tag{8}$$

$$= -y \log(f_i) - (1 - y) \log(1 - f_i)$$

$$- \frac{\lambda}{M} \sum_{j \neq i} \{ -f_j \log(f_i) - (1 - f_j) \log(1 - f_i) \} \tag{9}$$

$$= H(y, f_i) - \frac{\lambda}{M} \sum_{j \neq i} H(f_j, f_i). \tag{10}$$

H is the cross-entropy function and $y \in \{0, 1\}$ is the true label. Therefore, by adding a penalty $p_i = -\frac{1}{M} \sum_{j \neq i} H(f_j, f_i)$ and choosing $\lambda \in [0, 1]$ we get a method to encourage diversity in classification ensembles explicitly.

4   Stacked Diversified Mixture of Classifiers

In this section we suggest a new architecture inspired by our above outcome and the D-ConvNet architecture [8]. We train a single DNN to generate features, and on top of the net, instead of using a vanilla softmax layer, we use a Stacked Diversified Mixture of Classifiers (SDMC). A SDMC is structure of multiple softmax layers with multiple amended cost functions for each softmax layer. An illustration of this architecture is shown in Fig. 1. The advantage of using this variant is that we do not need to train multiple networks simultaneously, which might significantly increase the training time and the computational power needed. Instead, we only train a single DNN and stack on top of it multiple classifiers. Each classifier has its own set of weights and is jointly optimized with the other classifiers by an amended cost function that penalizes low cross-entropy with others.

---

[1] In this Brief Announcement we demonstrate our idea only on a sigmoid (binary classification), but the proof for softmax is similar and is presented in the full version of this paper.

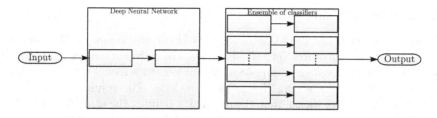

Fig. 1. Diversified mixture of classifiers. First, an input is sent to a DNN. Next, the DNN performs initial processing and feature extraction out of the input. Finally, a pool of classifiers is trained using our suggested cost functions that penalize with respect to the cross-entropy with other classifiers.

5   Results

5.1   MNIST Using Vanilla Diversified Classifiers

The MNIST is a standard toy dataset, where the task is to classify the images into 10 digit classes. Our goal here was to get some proof of concept and to observe training behaviour when using our cross-entropy penalty. Here, we used only our vanilla version and did not apply a SDMS variant. Our architecture was of a single hidden layer DNN with ReLU activation. We set the number of models to be $M = 5$ and changed the values of λ. The results are shown in Table 1. Results include both the accuracy and the cross-entropy of the predictions over the test set. We notice from the results that our method reduces the cross-entropy and get higher accuracy for $\lambda > 0$. We observe that even though the performance of a single net deteriorated when increasing λ, the ensemble performs better.

Table 1. Results on MNIST using our suggested cost function. Ensemble scores refers to the accuracy and cross-entropy (CE) of the ensemble prediction over the test set. Single net scores refers to the scores of the prediction of a single model in the ensemble. Scores are averaged over 6 experiments with a different seed for each λ.

λ	Ensemble scores		Single net scores	
	Accuracy	CE	Accuracy	CE
0	0.9790	0.0669	0.9767	0.0810
0.05	0.9798	0.0663	**0.9770**	0.0809
0.1	0.9799	0.0664	0.9768	**0.0802**
0.3	0.9797	0.0658	0.9767	0.0806
0.5	**0.9802**	**0.0649**	0.9764	0.0842
0.7	0.9800	0.0659	0.9760	0.0866

5.2 CIFAR-10 Using SDMC

We conducted studies of the SDMC over the CIFAR-10 dataset [4]. We used the architecture and code of ResNet 110 [3] and stacked on top of it an ensemble of 10 classifiers. This resulted in adding 5850 parameters to a model with an original size of 1731002, i.e. enlarging the model by 0.34%. The results are shown in Table 2. In the results we see that the optimal λ reduces the error by $\sim 7\%$ with almost no cost in the number of parameters and computational power. We also see that the cross-entropy reduces significantly. We notice that the optimal λ is lower than the vanilla usage of our method.

Table 2. Results on CIFAR-10 test set using SDMC with ResNet 110. M refers to the number of classifiers, and CE stands for cross-entropy. We ran each model 5 times and show "best(mean-std)" as in [3,9].

	$M=1$	$M=10$ $\lambda=0$	$M=10$ $\lambda=0.001$	$M=10$ $\lambda=0.01$	$M=10$ $\lambda=0.05$	$M=10$ $\lambda=0.1$	$M=10$ $\lambda=0.3$	$M=10$ $\lambda=0.5$
Error (%)	6.43	6.2	6.14	6.12	**5.98**	6.09	6.13	6.31
CE		0.3056	0.3102	0.3041	0.3048	0.2968	**0.2918**	0.3137	0.4957

6 Conclusion

In this paper we propose a novel Deep Learning Classification Framework for encouraging diversity explicitly, based on cross-entropy penalties. First, we introduced the idea of using an amended cost function for multiple classifiers based on NCL results. Later, we introduce Stacked Diversified Mixture of Classifiers (SDMC) which aims to improve the capabilities of a model without increasing the number of parameters and computational power significantly.

References

1. Brown, G., Wyatt, J.L., Tiňo, P.: Managing diversity in regression ensembles. J. Mach. Learn. Res. **6**(9), 1621–1650 (2005)
2. Carreira-Perpinan, M.A., Raziperchikolaei, R.: An ensemble diversity approach to supervised binary hashing. In: Lee, D.D., Sugiyama, M., Luxburg, U.V., Guyon, I., Garnett, R. (eds.) Advances in Neural Information Processing Systems 29, pp. 757–765. Curran Associates Inc. (2016)
3. He, K., Zhang, X., Ren, S., Sun, J.: Deep residual learning for image recognition. In: Proceedings of the IEEE Conference on Computer Vision and Pattern Recognition, pp. 770–778 (2016)
4. Krizhevsky, A.: Learning multiple layers of features from tiny images. Technical report, Citeseer (2009)
5. Lee, S., Prakash, S.P.S., Cogswell, M., Ranjan, V., Crandall, D., Batra, D.: Stochastic multiple choice learning for training diverse deep ensembles. In: Lee, D.D., Sugiyama, M., Luxburg, U.V., Guyon, I., Garnett, R. (eds.) Advances in Neural Information Processing Systems 29, pp. 2119–2127. Curran Associates Inc. (2016)

6. Liu, Y., Yao, X.: Ensemble learning via negative correlation. Neural Netw. **12**(10), 1399–1404 (1999)
7. Nielsen, M.A.: Neural Networks and Deep Learning, vol. 25 (2015)
8. Shi, Z., et al.: Crowd counting with deep negative correlation learning (2018)
9. Srivastava, R.K., Greff, K., Schmidhuber, J.: Training very deep networks. In: Advances in Neural Information Processing Systems, pp. 2377–2385 (2015)
10. Zhou, T., Wang, S., Bilmes, J.A.: Diverse ensemble evolution: Curriculum data-model marriage. In: Bengio, S., Wallach, H., Larochelle, H., Grauman, K., Cesa-Bianchi, N., Garnett, R. (eds.) Advances in Neural Information Processing Systems 31, pp. 5909–5920. Curran Associates Inc. (2018)

Governance and Regulations Implications on Machine Learning (Brief Announcement)

Sima Nadler[✉], Orna Raz[✉], and Marcel Zalmanovici[✉]

IBM Research, Haifa, Israel
{sima,ornar,marcel}@il.ibm.com

Abstract. Machine learning systems' efficacy are highly dependent on their training data and the data they receive during production. However, current data governance policies and privacy laws dictate when and how personal and other sensitive data may be used. This affects the amount and quality of personal data included for training, potentially introducing bias and other inaccuracies into the model. Today's mechanisms do not provide (a) a way for the model developer to know about this nor, (b) to alleviate the bias. This paper addresses both of these challenges.

Keywords: Data governance · Implications · Privacy · Machine learning

1 Introduction and Background

More and more of today's computer systems include some kind of machine learning (ML), making them highly dependent on quality training data in order to train and test the model. The ML results are only as good as the data on which they were trained and the data they receive during production. On the other hand, data governance laws and policies dictate when and how personal and other sensitive data may be used. For some purposes it may not be used at all, for others consent is required, and in others it may be used based on contract or legitimate business. In the cases where personal data or other sensitive information cannot be used, or requires consent, the data sets used to train ML models will by definition be a subset of the data. If the data set doesn't include, for example, age, race, or gender, then there is no way to know that the data is not representative of the real target population. This has the potential to introduce bias into the model as well as other inaccuracies — without the solution creator having any idea of the potential problem. Data sets are sometimes augmented with meta data describing what is included in the data set, but currently that meta data has nothing about what has been excluded and why. There are no current methods for alleviating governance induced bias in ML models. **Our work addresses the issues of capturing information about data excluded due to governance regulations and policies and suggests how**

© Springer Nature Switzerland AG 2019
S. Dolev et al. (Eds.): CSCML 2019, LNCS 11527, pp. 208–211, 2019.
https://doi.org/10.1007/978-3-030-20951-3_19

to utilize such information to characterize the governance implications impact on ML and improve the ML models. We are unaware of any work that does that. There is a lot of work about capturing data governance, privacy policies, proper consent management, and identification and handling of bias in ML. There are also various data governance tools available. A summary of such works can be found in the technical report [2] that complements this paper.

We provide a short background on governance laws and policies and their potential impact on ML. Countries and industries have differing laws regulating how data, especially personal and other types of sensitive data, may be used. Europe's General Data Protection Regulation (GDPR) aims to strengthen data subject privacy protection, unify the data regulations across the member states, and broaden the territorial scope of the companies that fall under its jurisdiction to address non-EU companies who provide services to EU residents. In the United States privacy laws have typically been industry based with, for example, HIPAA governing the health care industry as it relates to digital health data. However, in June 2018 the state of California passed a new privacy law that will go into effect in 2020. Since each state could theoretically do the same, the US could find itself with 50 different privacy laws. As a result there are now discussions about creating a federal privacy law in the United States. Similar trends can be seen in other countries around the world. While the laws and standards differ, they tend to be similar in their goals.

When creating a ML system, the goal which it aims to achieve is in essence the purpose. If personal or other regulated data is needed to train and/or use the ML system, either all or a subset of the original data will be made available based on the purpose. Likely this will vary from country to country and/or state to state, based on local regulations and company regulations. For example, if one is creating a model to predict the need for public transportation in a given neighborhood one could use information from current public transportation use, population size, and other relevant data. However, there may be laws restricting the use, for example, of location data and transportation uses by minors. Thus, the training set for the ML-based solution for transportation planning would not include data about people under the age of 18. This introduces bias into the model, since the transportation patterns of children would not be included. There are many other well known fields where such bias is introduced. When the bias introduction is known, it can be accounted for and corrected. A well known example is the pharmaceutical industry, where pregnant women and children are rarely included in clinical trials for drug development. Another example, in which bias was not known in advance, is automated resume review systems (e.g., [1]), where the populations currently employed are the ones for which the ML system naturally is biased.

In this paper we propose to alleviate governance induced bias in ML models by first capturing, and providing as meta data by a governance enforcement engine, information about what has been excluded and why. Then, such information can be used to identify and alleviate governance implications on ML models.

2   Method, Feasibility Results and Summary

Method. We define governance implications and suggest to implement them as
meta data to be added to the output of governance enforcement tools. There
are two major types of excluded data: excluded records and excluded features.
These types differ in terms of how they can be identified and alleviated.

The role of data governance is to enforce proper usage of personal and/or
sensitive data as defined by policies and data subject preferences. As data is
accessed, stored, or transferred the governance module is responsible for invoking
the governance policies on the data. Such function might be to filter out certain
data, obfuscate the data, or allow the data to be used as is. While doing this the
governance module logs what it has done and on what the decision was based.

To create the governance implication summary we parse the governance decisions log, and generate a summary containing: original vs derived data set size,
list of features removed from the data set and the removal reasons (policies),
percentage of data subjects included in the derived data set, and affect on features included in the derived data set — ex: x% of people over age 60, y% of
people from California.

The governance impact summary then provides important additional information which is taken into account when building and running ML models.

Details about governance implications data, impact summary and their
extraction from a governance engine can be found in [2]. That report also
describes in more detail the feasibility analysis which we summarize next.

Feasibility Results. We demonstrate the feasibility of our approach on a US
government Census data set. Our experiments show that it is possible to extract
governance implications from a governance enforcement engine and encode them
as meta data. These governance implications can be effectively utilized to alert
on data issues that negatively affect the ML model trained on the governed data
subset. We demonstrate this for excluded data records, simulating no-consent situations. We defined example governance policies. (1) California residents information was excluded due to new strict privacy law. (2) People over 60 nationwide
tended not to provide consent for their information to be included in the public
data. (3) Granular location codes were excluded entirely to prevent easy cross
reference.

When accessing or sharing data, a data governance enforcement point generates a compliant subset of the original data based on (1) the purpose for which
the data will be used, (2) the geography which determines the relevant policies
and laws. The enforcement point filters and transforms the full data set based
on the policies and data subject preferences. During this process, all decisions
about which data is included and excluded are logged. For each feature there is
an entry in the governance decision log. We parse the log, creating an interim
data structure. From this interim data we generate a summary about what data
was included and excluded. However, information about important features may
be missing, such as geography and other personal information which may not be
part of the source data set, but could influence the ML model's results. If such

information exists in a profile management system that can be cross referenced, we can further generate this data by taking the interim summary and correlating it with information from the profile system. To the governance impact summary we then add the list of profile features, indicating for each the percentage excluded for each data item. The final summary is shown in Fig. 1.

```
{
  "purpose_id": int,
  "percent_data_subjects_included": float,
  "data_items_completely_excluded": [ { "data_item_id": int } ],
  "data_items_included": [{
    "percent_included": float,
    "exclusions" : [
      {
        "num_data_subjects_excluded": int,
        "exclusion_reason_codes": [
          { "reason_code": int,
            "num_excluded_for_reason": int }
        ],
        "profile_feature_exclusions:": [
          feature: {
            profile_feature_id: int,
            percent_excluded: float
          }]
      }],
    "inclusions" : [
      {
        "num_data_subjects_included": int,
        "inclusion_reason_codes": [
          { "reason_code": int,
            "num_included_for_reason": int }
        ],
        "profile_feature_inclusions:": [
          feature: {
            profile_feature_id: int,
            percent_included: float
          }]
      }]
  }]
}
```

Fig. 1. Final governance impact summary.

```
Model features
Index(['SPORDER', 'ST', 'ADJINC', 'PWGTP', 'AGEP', 'CIT', 'COW', 'DDRS', 'DEAR', 'DEYE',
       ...
       'FSEMP', 'FSEXP', 'FSSIP', 'FSSP', 'FWAGP', 'FWKHP', 'FWKLP', 'FWKWP', 'FWRKP',
       'FVOEP'], dtype='object', length=155)

Redacted features (Governance)
{'AGEP', 'ST', 'PUMA', 'POWPUMA'}

WARNING
Dominant model features are under-represented: {'AGEP', 'ST'}
WARNING
```

Fig. 2. Intersection of ML model important features and governance implications features results in a warning about potential implications.

We demonstrate that the governance implications summary can be effectively utilized to raise alerts regarding potential ML model under-performance. We trained a random forest classifier over the US Census data, where the target was the transportation means. Figure 2 shows the results of analyzing the model important features and intersecting the resulting group of features with the features that the governance implication method marked as affected. This method is relevant when the features exist in the data provided for training. The resulting features are indeed two of the features that were under-represented as a result of simulating governance policies on the full data: age (people over 60) and state (California). Because the model owners now know the important features that were under-represented, they know in advance that it is highly likely that the model is biased and can run existing bias detection and alleviation techniques.

References

1. GIZMODO: Amazon's secret ai hiring tool reportedly 'penalized' resumes with the word 'women's'. One of many reports on the topic (2018). gizmodo.com/amazons-secret-ai-hiring-tool-reportedly-penalized-resu-1829649346
2. Sima Nadler, O.R., Zalmanovici, M.: Governance and regulations implications on machine learning. http://www.research.ibm.com/haifa/dept/vst/papers/Data_Governance.pdf

Simulating Homomorphic Evaluation
of Deep Learning Predictions

Christina Boura[1,4], Nicolas Gama[1,2], Mariya Georgieva[2,3(✉)],
and Dimitar Jetchev[2,3]

[1] Laboratoire de Mathématiques de Versailles, UVSQ, CNRS,
Université Paris-Saclay, Versailles, France
`christina.boura@uvsq.fr`
[2] Inpher, Lausanne, Switzerland
`{nicolas,mariya,dimitar}@inpher.io`
[3] EPFL, Lausanne, Switzerland
[4] Inria, Paris, France

Abstract. Convolutional neural networks (CNNs) is a category of deep neural networks that are primarily used for classifying image data. Yet, their continuous gain in popularity poses important privacy concerns for the potentially sensitive data that they process. A solution to this problem is to combine CNNs with Fully Homomorphic Encryption (FHE) techniques. In this work, we study this approach by focusing on two popular FHE schemes, TFHE and HEAAN, that can work in the approximated computational model. We start by providing an analysis of the noise after each principal homomorphic operation, i.e. multiplication, linear combination, rotation and bootstrapping. Then, we provide a theoretical study on how the most important non-linear operations of a CNN (i.e. max, `Abs`, `ReLU`), can be evaluated in each scheme. Finally, we measure via practical experiments on the plaintext the robustness of different neural networks against perturbations of their internal weights that could potentially result from the propagation of large homomorphic noise. This allows us to simulate homomorphic evaluations with large amounts of noise and to predict the effect on the classification accuracy without a real evaluation of heavy and time-consuming homomorphic operations. In addition, this approach enables us to correctly choose smaller and more efficient parameter sets for both schemes.

Keywords: Neural networks · Homomorphic encryption · TFHE · HEAAN

1 Introduction

Neural networks (NN) are extremely powerful machine learning algorithms for classification or recognition of complex data such as images, handwriting or speech. These algorithms are used in many domains and so, they often treat highly sensitive data like medical records or confidential financial information.

© Springer Nature Switzerland AG 2019
S. Dolev et al. (Eds.): CSCML 2019, LNCS 11527, pp. 212–230, 2019.
https://doi.org/10.1007/978-3-030-20951-3_20

One of the most popular choices for achieving privacy guarantee in these settings is Fully Homomorphic Encryption (FHE) [7,25]. FHE schemes allow for computing on encrypted data in the sense that decrypting the encrypted result yields the result that would have been produced if the computation had been performed on the plaintext. Compared to other privacy-preserving solutions (e.g. Multiparty Computation (MPC)), FHE operations are non-interactive and thus, they save on communication costs. Second, MPC schemes require non-collusion assumptions on the computing parties in order to achieve privacy and such assumptions can often be challenging. In FHE applications, no such assumptions are needed.

The three FHE schemes B/FV [8,12,20], TFHE [16,17], based on [18,21] and HEAAN [14,15], all based on the Ring-LWE problem, are currently among the most efficient constructions. For all of them, a homomorphic noise is added on the top of the plaintext. The scheme B/FV was initially designed to perform exact SIMD operations modulo a prime. Thus, for B/FV the added noise does not affect the outcome of the decryption in the sense that the decrypted value is exactly the plaintext. In this context the noise quantifies how many operations can be homomorphically executed with the decrypted value remaining correct. The notion of bootstrapping in B/FV has therefore the meaning of "noise reduction".

On the other hand, in HEAAN, homomorphic operations are floating-point operations where the least-significant bits of the mantissa are randomly rounded at each arithmetic operation to a value that is close to the exact result. The entropy in the errors induced by these least-significant roundings arise from many factors such as the randomness of the ciphertexts as well as the randomness of the large evaluation keys. These errors, unpredictable to the users, are corrected by neither decryption nor bootstrapping (the decryption of the encryption is not the original message) and accumulate throughout the whole computation.

There is still a notion of the maximum number of homomorphic operations, or *multiplicative level*, that designs the maximum number of operations that can be applied on a given ciphertext: if we do less operations than this level, the decryption produces an approximate result (as opposed to the exact result in B/FV); if we exceed this level, the decryption fails completely in an undefined behaviour manner. The bootstrapping of HEAAN can still extend this level to allow further computations, but it does not reduce noise. As shown in [6], TFHE (the last of the above-mentioned schemes) can be interfaced with both B/FV and HEAAN, and thus, supports both exact or approximated arithmetic: in this paper, we only consider the approximate mode of operation.

For evaluating CNNs with FHE, one can either select one scheme over the other, or propose a hybrid solution combining HEAAN and TFHE. Indeed, some of the computations performed during a CNN evaluation are easier with TFHE while some others are more natural with HEAAN. For instance, in the case when many approximated computations have to be performed and a decision must be taken on the result, it is optimal to use the HEAAN scheme for the first part and switch to TFHE for evaluating the decision function. This hybrid approach based on the Chimera framework has already been used by one of the solutions proposed to the Idash'18 Track 2 [2,10] competition on designing homomorphic solutions for semi-parallel Genome Wide Association Studies (GWAS) based on logistic regression using homomorphically encrypted data. Here, the logistic regression requiring many iterations was performed with TFHE in order to use a fast bootstrapping to reduce the noise, whereas the linear algebra computations on matrix of large dimensions was performed with HEAAN using massively vectorized SIMD computations offered by the scheme.

Our Contributions. The goal of this paper is to efficienty simulate homomorphic evaluation of neural network predictions (in particular, CNN predictions) in order to analyze the stability of the performance (evaluation accuracy) of neural networks in the presence of noise due to FHE decryptions (what we refer to as the approximated computational model). Performing such an analysis on encrypted data can be extremely time consuming, the reason why we choose to do our analysis on the plaintext and simulate the noise resulting from the homomorphic computations and the function approximations.

In order to perform our experiments on approximate operations, we have chosen exclusively the HEAAN and TFHE schemes implemented in the context of the Chimera [6] framework. After analyzing the noise in the homomorphic operations in Sect. 2 and explaining how/why this noise can be modeled with Gaussian distributions in the context of both TFHE and HEAAN, we show in Sect. 3 how one can homomorphically evaluate various commonly used functions for deep learning (e.g., Abs, Sign, max and ReLU) with TFHE and HEAAN and discuss the potential difficulties of such an approach. We remark that the choice of a scheme also depends on the desired level of precision in the output. Through the simulation approach, one is able to efficiently determine the best CNN structure and the smallest FHE parameters required during a preliminary study phase.

We performed experiments with perturbations on three distinct convolutional neural networks of small (LeNet-5), medium (cat-and-dog-9) and large (ResNet-34) size and observed that all these networks support large relative errors of at least 10% without almost any impact on the global accuracy (see Sect. 2). This means, as we show, that only 4 bits of precision (instead of 20 to 40 bits usually) are needed on all fixed-point operations throughout the network, which yields very small parameter sets and fast homomorphic operations. Finally, these experiments allowed to make useful deductions about the stability of some common CNN operations (e.g., different pooling functions). As we show, all operations are not equally stable and thus, some of them should be preferred when used in a FHE context.

Outline. In Sect. 2 we recall the homomorphic schemes TFHE and HEAAN and we analyse the noise propagation for basic arithmetic (linear combination, multiplication, rotation/permutation and bootstrapping). In Sect. 3, we show how to tweak the bootstrapping to evaluate the activation functions of the CNN. Finally, in Sect. 4, we simulate the noise propagation during the homomorphic evaluation and measure its effect on the CNN prediction accuracy.

2   Homomorphic RLWE Encryption Schemes and Noise Propagation

The goal of this section is to introduce the key concepts concerning both the TFHE and HEAAN schemes that are necessary to understand the core of this article. As explained earlier, both schemes will be introduced via the Chimera framework [6] that provides a unified representation of these schemes as well as a uniform noise analysis. We start by introducing some necessary notation.

Notation. Let $\mathbb{T} = \mathbb{R}/\mathbb{Z}$ be the real torus, that is the set of real numbers modulo 1. We denote further by $\mathbb{Z}_N[X] = \mathbb{Z}[X]/(X^N + 1)$ the ring of polynomials with integer coefficients modulo $X^N + 1$. Respectively, $\mathbb{R}_N[X] = \mathbb{R}[X]/(X^N + 1)$ is the ring of real polynomials modulo $X^N + 1$. Informally, the elements of $\mathbb{Z}_N[X]$ are seen as integer polynomials with N coefficients whereas the elements of $\mathbb{R}_N[X]$ are seen as real polynomials with N coefficients.

In order to introduce the notion of slots (real or complex), we use the following two isomorphisms of $\mathbb{R}$-vector spaces:

$$\mathbb{R}[X]/(X^N + 1) \simeq \mathbb{R}^N, \qquad f = a_0 + \cdots + a_{N-1}X^{N-1} \mapsto (a_0, \ldots, a_N), \quad (1)$$

and

$$\mathbb{R}[X]/(X^N + 1) \simeq \mathbb{C}^{N/2}, \qquad f \mapsto (f(\zeta), f(\zeta^3), \ldots, f(\zeta^{N-1})). \quad (2)$$

Here $\zeta = e^{\pi i/N}$ is a primitive root of $X^N + 1$. Representation (1) corresponds to what is called the *coefficient packing* and representation (2) corresponds to what is called the *slot packing*.

2.1   HEAAN and TFHE Through the Chimera Framework

The Chimera framework introduced in [6] allows to apply elementary operations either from the HEAAN or the TFHE library to RLWE ciphertexts [29] within the same FHE computation. Both use the same ciphertext space.

In this work, we describe these libraries mostly from the user point of view without going into the details of their internal representation. In particular, we view an RLWE ciphertext as an encryption of a plaintext in $\mathbb{C}^{N/2}$ (i.e., $N/2$ complex plaintext slots under the isomorphism (2)) on which one can perform approximated arithmetic. The coefficients to slots representation and slots to coefficients representation can be used at any moment to switch between a slot-based representation in $\mathbb{C}^{N/2}$ and a coefficient-based representation in $\mathbb{R}^N$.

The slots in a given ciphertext vector have a fixed public precision $\rho > 0$ in the following sense: the complex coordinates of the vector are all of the form $(x + iy) \cdot 2^\tau$ for some public exponent $\tau > 0$ (uniform across all the coordinates and precomputed in advance) and some secret $x, y \in [-1, 1]$. In addition, both x and y are assumed to have ρ fractional bits of precision (i.e., the size of the mantissa is exactly ρ bits, where ρ is usually a fixed constant across the entire computation).

During the FHE computation, only the ρ-bits of the mantissa are secret and are the only ones that are homomorphically evaluated.

In a pure floating-point model, the result of some operations cannot always be exactly represented on the target precision: these results are usually rounded to the nearest mantissa. In FHE, these roundings are more random and difficult to predict and we modelize this via a noise propagation model, whose mean and standard deviation depend on the elementary operation.

We will only refer to the internal cryptographic representation of the ciphertexts in the section where we define our noise propagation model. Namely, both TFHE and HEAAN schemes use RLWE ciphertexts in $\mathbb{R}_N[X]^2$ mod 1 (or $\mathbb{R}_N[X]^2$ mod q), the same key space $\mathbb{Z}_N[X]$ with small coefficients and the same phase function $\varphi_s(a, b) = b - s \cdot a$ introduced in [16]. In this framework, the approximated decryption, common to HEAAN and TFHE, considers that the phase is always close to the actual message and is a good enough approximation thereof. Then, accumulated errors are not corrected by the cryptosystem but rather by the numerical stability of the homomorphically evaluated algorithm.

Finally, the notion of level common to TFHE and HEAAN is defined as the maximal multiplicative depth supported by the ciphertext. Each homomorphic product reduces the level of the resulting ciphertext; when the level 0 is reached, the ciphertext must be bootstrapped to continue operating on it.

Consider a security parameter λ, a maximal level L and a target precision ρ, then these parameters implicitly define a minimal key size N. For more details see the FHE standardization workshop security document [3].

Below, we describe the algorithms for encryption and decryption that are used in TFHE and HEAAN, both enabling error-tolerant decryption functions, and hence approximated arithmetic.

KeyGen: A uniformly random binary key $s \in \mathbb{Z}_N[X]$ (with small coefficients). In order to support non-linear operations, **KeyGen** also needs to generate various encryptions of s, such as evaluation, key-switching or bootstrapping keys, which are not essential to this paper (see [9,15,20] for more details).

EncryptAtLevel$_{\tau,L}(x, s)$: The plaintext x is in $\mathbb{C}^{N/2}$ (complex slots bounded by $|x| \leq 2^\tau$). Divide x by $2^{\tau+L}$ and apply the isomorphism (1) to obtain a small real polynomial μ bounded by 2^{-L}. Then, pick a uniformly random $a \in \mathbb{R}_N[X]$ mod 1, and a small Gaussian error e with standard deviation $2^{-L-\rho}$, and return $(a, s \cdot a + \mu + e)$.

DecryptApproxAtLevel$_{\tau,L}(c, s)$: Compute the phase $\varphi_s(c) = b - s \cdot a$ mod 1, lift all its coefficients to the real field in the interval $[-\frac{1}{2}, \frac{1}{2})$ which recovers an approximation of μ, then apply the isomorphism (1) and multiply by $2^{\tau+L}$ to recover the slots x (up to an error $2^{\tau-\rho}$).

Remark 1. Here we describe only a symmetric key version. Note however that the public key version is obtained by evaluation of constant functions using the secret key.

2.2   Noise Models for Homomorphic Operations

We now analyze the resulting output noise of the main homomorphic operations for TFHE and HEAAN. The most common operations are linear combinations, multiplications, slot permutations as well as functional bootstrapping.

Linear Combination. Let $\sum_{i=1}^{k} \alpha_i c_i$ be a linear combination, where the c_i are RLWE ciphertexts that encrypt the plaintexts x_i and $\alpha_i \in \mathbb{Z}$ are small integers. Given independent normally distributed Gaussian noises $e_i \in \mathbb{C}^{N/2}$ (slot representation) with multivariate normal distribution $N(x_i, \sigma_i^2)$ ($x_i \in \mathbb{C}^{N/2}$ is the mean and $\sigma_i \in \mathbb{C}^{N/2 \times N/2}$ is the covariance matrix), the noise of the decryption of $\sum_{i=1}^{k} \alpha_i c_i$ is $\sum_{i=1}^{k} \alpha_i e_i$ which is normally distributed with multivariate distribution $N\left(\sum_{i=1}^{k} \alpha_i \mu_i, \sum_{i=1}^{k} \alpha_i^2 \sigma_i^2\right)$.

We can thus simulate this noise by computing the exact result $\sum_{i=1}^{k} \alpha_i x_i$, applying a random multivariate (discrete) Gaussian noise of amplitude $\sum \alpha_i 2^{\tau_i - \rho}$ and expressing the outcome as an exact multiple of $2^{\tau - \rho}$.

Multiplication. The homomorphic evaluation of a multiplication corresponds to the internal product of ciphertexts of HEAAN [15] or to the external product of Chimera/TFHE [6,17] if one of the operands is a fresh ciphertext.

Assuming that c_1 and c_2 are ciphertexts corresponding to the two plaintexts x_1, x_2 and assuming that the noise parameters $e_1, e_2 \in \mathbb{C}^{N/2}$ in the decryptions of c_1 and c_2, respectively, are independent and normally distributed according to $N(\mu_i, \sigma_i)$, then the distribution of the noise parameter for the decryption of the product $c_1 c_2$ can be approximated with a normal distribution. Indeed, note that,

$$(x_1 + e_1)(x_2 + e_2) = x_1 x_2 + x_1 e_2 + x_2 e_1 + e_1 e_2.$$

Now, for fixed x_1, the terms $x_1 e_2$ and $x_2 e_1$ are clearly normally distributed and $e_1 e_2$ is negligible, so the distribution of the noise in the decryption of the product can be approximated with the normal distribution for $x_1 e_2 + x_2 e_1$. This has already been studied (see e.g. [15,16]). Thus, when multiplying homomorphically two ciphertexts c_1, c_2 representing plaintexts x_1, x_2 with public exponents τ_1, τ_2 and precision ρ, we obtain a ciphertext c with exponent $\tau = \tau_1 + \tau_2$ and precision ρ, which can be modeled as follows: compute the exact product $x_1 x_2$, add a random (discrete) multivariate Gaussian noise of amplitude $2^{\tau_i - \rho}$ and express the outcome as an exact multiple of $2^{\tau - \rho}$.

Rotations/Permutations. One of the possibilities for permuting or rotating the elements in the slot representation is to switch to the coefficient packing. This last operation is easy. Knowing that the transformation between coefficients to slots representation and inversely corresponds to applying an orthogonal (or hermitian) matrix, the effect on the noise is numerically stable and it preserves the Gaussian noise amount. However, this consumes (at least) one homomorphic multiplicative level, because the transformation involves a homomorphic evaluation of a Discrete Fourier Transformation.

Bootstrapping. Traditionally, a bootstrapping applies homomorphically the identity function to the plaintext and resets the multiplicative level to a high value. Here, we omit the noise-reduction part which does not occur in the floating-point mode [14]. Complex non-linear functions are traditionally evaluated by interleaving bootstrappings, SIMD additions and multiplications and slot rotations. However, it is not optimal to proceed this way for three reasons: (1) After a costly bootstrapping, one still needs to evaluate the non-linear function which is time consuming, thus sacrificing efficiency. (2) One can approximate the non-linear function by polynomials: if the approximation can be made arbitrarily precise within a fixed range, the degree and the size of the coefficients rapidly diverge for large ranges and the expression gets numerically unstable outside the specified range (Runge's phenomenon). Therefore, any plaintext outlier can destroy the correctness of the result, which leads to a precision sacrifice. (3) Finally, the bootstrapping needs to raise the multiplicative level very high to leave room for the homomorphic function evaluation, thus requiring excessively large parameters (again, sacrificing efficiency). In the cases of both TFHE and HEAAN, we thus focus on a more numerically stable strategy where the bootstrapping includes the evaluation of the non-linear function.

Functional Bootstrapping in TFHE. Recall that the TFHE scheme evaluates functions via evaluating lookup tables on discretized input [17, §4.3, Alg. 4]. As such, the bootstrapping of TFHE approximates a given function by a step function (in exactly the same way as one performs Riemann integration) and then evaluates the approximation by a homomorphic lookup table evaluation. For example, the ReLU function $f(x) = \max(0, x)$ for $-1 \leq x \leq 1$ can be approximated by the step function defined as follows:

$$f_\delta(x) = \begin{cases} 0 & \text{if } x \leq 0 \\ k\delta & \text{if } x \in [(k-1)\delta, k\delta), \end{cases}$$

where $k \in \mathbb{Z}$ and $k \leq 1/\delta$ (see Fig. 1 (left)). Thus, given a plaintext x, instead of computing $f(x)$, one obtains the value $f_\delta(x + e_1) + e_2$ where e_1 and e_2 are two error terms, e_2 being Gaussian noise and e_1 corresponding to an internal rounding error (see the rounding in Step 2 of [16, Alg. 3]).

Functional Bootstrapping in HEAAN. In contrast to TFHE, the original version of HEAAN evaluates the sine function by Taylor approximation [14, §3.2]. Moreover, the extension of HEAAN proposed in Chimera generalizes this method to evaluation of Fourier series and thus, evaluation of the given target function via a low-degree Fourier series. Graphically, the target function f is replaced by a smooth function S_f and then a Gaussian noise is added on the top of that (see Fig. 1 (right)). Finally, when the function has a point of singularity (such as the ReLU at the point $x = 0$), the HEAAN approximation is biased at that point (strictly above $x = 0$). It is thus desirable to validate the effect of this biased approximation to the quality of prediction of the trained convolutional neural network.

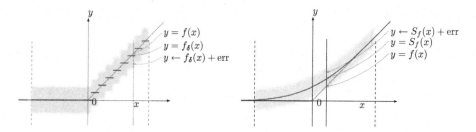

Fig. 1. Functional bootstrap in TFHE for the `ReLU` function (in left) and Functional bootstrap in `HEAAN` for the `ReLU` function (in right). (Color figure online)

In conclusion of this section, since every elementary FHE operation has a Gaussian noise in output, we can omit the input noise from the bootstrapping and merge it with the output noise of the previous operation in our simulation.

3   Evaluation of Nonlinear Functions in Neural Networks

Non-linear functions are central building blocks in deep learning and as such it is important to analyse how to homomorphically evaluate them. Examples of such operations are comparisons, max functions, piecewise functions (e.g. the REctified Linear Unit (`ReLU`) := $\max(0, x)$ activation function), rounding, a decryption function (equivalent to the sign function) or continuous functions such as the sigmoid $\mathsf{sigmoid}(x) = 1/1 + \exp(-x)$.

Note that the `ReLU` and max are easily expressed with the absolute value: for x, y in $(-1/4, 1/4)$, $2\max(x, y) = (x + y) + |x - y|$, and for $2\mathtt{ReLU}(x) = x + |x|$.

3.1   Non-linear Functions in **TFHE**

In TFHE, given a non-linear function $f\colon \mathbb{T} \to \mathbb{T}$, one can compute $f(\varphi_s(c))$ (see Sect. 2.1) for a LWE ciphertext c via functional boostrapping under the following constraints: the domain of the function is restricted to multiples of $1/2N$ where N is the bootstrapping key size (in particular, it is a medium-sized power of 2), and the function must be $(1/2)$-antiperiodic, i.e. $f(x + 1/2) = -f(x)$. On the half-period, the function can be defined pointwise, so its graph can be arbitrary. Some particular functions such as $\mathtt{Abs}(x) - 1/4$ and $\mathtt{Sign}(x)$ already coincide with a $(1/2)$-antiperiodic function over $[-1/2, 1/2]$ (see Fig. 2). More general functions such as $\mathsf{sigmoid}(\gamma x) - 1/2$ can be defined over $[-1/2, 1/2]$ and extended to $\mathbb{R}$ by anti-periodicity.

Once the $(1/2)$-antiperiodic function f to evaluate is chosen, its graph is mapped to the element $\nu = \sum_{i=0}^{N-1} \nu_i X^i \in \mathbb{R}_N[X] \mod 1$ where $\nu_i = f(i/2N)$ and used as a test vector in the bootstrapping of TFHE to evaluate f (see [17, §6.1]). In the output of the bootstrapping, the decrypted value is within a small Gaussian error around $f(x)$ as discussed in Sect. 2.

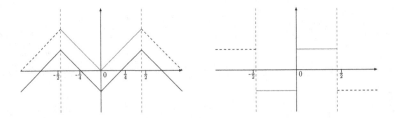

Fig. 2. Absolute (on the left) and Sign (on the right) values TFHE

3.2   Non-linear Functions in HEAAN

In HEAAN, non-linear functions can be evaluated via approximations by either complex-valued polynomials (via traditional products) or trigonometric polynomials (Fourier approach within the bootstrapping).

As explained in [5], Fourier series of smooth and regular functions converge rapidly: for instance, the Fourier series of a C^∞-function converges super-algebraically and if one smooths any periodic function by convolution with a small Gaussian, its Fourier series converges exponentially fast. However, the convergence is slower if the function has discontinuities (pointwise convergence in $\Omega(1/k)$), or discontinuities in its derivative (uniform convergence in $\Omega(1/k^2)$) where k is the number of harmonics used in the series.

For example, the absolute value is a triangular signal on $[-1/2, 1/2]$ which extends naturally to a 1-periodic continuous function (piecewise C^1). Given $N/2$ LWE ciphertexts, we can efficiently pack the complex exponential of their phases $\exp(2i\pi\mu)$ in the slots of a single HEAAN ciphertext. Subsequently, we can evaluate any trigonometric polynomial of small degree and extract the results back to LWE samples. For instance, the triangular signal (corresponding to the absolute value) has the following Fourier series with only cosine terms of odd degrees that converge in $O(k^2)$ and the square signal (corresponding to the sign or decryption function) has only sine terms of odd degrees.

$$\mathtt{Abs}(x) = K_1 \sum_{k=0}^{\infty} \frac{\cos 2\pi(2k+1)x}{(2k+1)^2} + K_2, \; \mathtt{Sign}(x) = K_1 \sum_{k=0}^{\infty} \frac{\sin 2\pi(2k+1)x}{(2k+1)} + K_2$$

Figure 3 shows that the first three (resp. six) terms of the Fourier series of the absolute value and the sign function already provide a good approximation on the interval $[-1/2, 1/2)$.

Compared to classical approximations of functions by polynomials in [11, 22] (i.e. Taylor series or Weierstrass approximation theorem), Fourier series have three main advantages: they do not diverge to ∞ outside of the interval (better numerical stability), the Fourier coefficients are small (square integrable), and the series converge uniformly to the function on any interval that does not contain any discontinuity in the derivative. However, in the particular case of Abs and Sign, the presence of a singularity or discontinuity at $x = 0$ in both graphs implies that the series converge poorly around 0. Unfortunately, native plaintexts in HEAAN ciphertext at level L have by definition tiny phases in the interval $[-1/2^L, 1/2^L)$. We address this problem using the bootstrapping capability of HEAAN: First, we decrease the level $L = 0$ or $L = 1$ (using the algorithm of re-scaling defined in [15]), so that input phases range over a large torus interval $(-1/2, 1/2)$ or $(-1/4, 1/4)$, and then, divide K_1 by 2^L so that the output has level L.

With this bootstrapping trick, HEAAN can at the same time evaluate a non-linear function and bootstrap its output to a level L even higher than its input. Taking this fact into account, instead of writing $\text{ReLU}(x) = \max(0, x)$ as $\frac{1}{2}(|x|+x)$ like in TFHE, where the term $+x/2$ is not bootstrapped, it is actually better to extend the graph of ReLU from a half period $(-1/4, 1/4)$ directly to a 1-periodic continuous function and to decompose the whole graph as a Fourier series. In the latter case, the output level L can be freely set to an arbitrary large value. Figure 3 shows a degree-7 approximation of the odd-even periodic extension of the graph of $\text{ReLU}(x)$. If the ReLU is evaluated via this technique, the output message is the Fourier approximation, and the phase still carries an additional Gaussian noise on top of it, as shown in Sect. 2. In the next section, we also study the robustness of neural networks with this approximation and perturbation model.

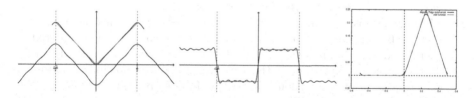

Fig. 3. Abs (on the left), Sign (in the middle) and ReLU (on the right) for HEAAN

4   Predictions for Deep Learning

Neural networks (NN) are computing systems trained to solve among others classification problems. Networks with multiple layers are known as *deep*. *Convolutional neural networks* (CNN) are a special type of deep neural networks that have been proven very successful in image recognition and classification. Preserving the privacy of sensitive data (e.g., medical or financial) while applying machine learning algorithms and still ensuring good performance and high output accuracy is currently a problem of interest to both the cryptographic and the machine learning communities [4, 7, 10, 11, 23, 25, 32]. We briefly describe now the main layers composing a CNN from a FHE point of view.

Convolution: It is an operation that extracts features from the input image (such as lines or borders) and is achieved by computing convolutions (via element-wise products) of the input matrix and a filter. Convolution is viewed as a secret affine function that can be efficiently evaluated using the external product of [6,17].

Non-linearity: To introduce non-linearity, an activation function is then applied to the output of the convolution. Nowadays, this is almost always achieved by the ReLU function. In almost all previous works, the standard approach was to replace the ReLU by a function with a lower multiplicative depth. In [23], ReLU is notably approximated by the square function $f(x) = x^2$, in [7] it is replaced by the sign function, while in [11] the ReLU is approximated by low-degree polynomials.

Pooling: This layer reduces the dimensions of the input by retaining the most important information. This is typically done by a procedure called *max pooling* or more rarely by *average pooling* that compute the maximum (resp. average) value for every disjoint region of the input. Today, no efficient algorithm is known to compute the maximum of a large number of values. On the contrary, average pooling is linear with public coefficients and therefore FHE-friendly. In [23] the authors replace max pooling by sum pooling, while in [11] max pooling is replaced by average pooling.

Fully Connected (FC) Layer: All the neurons of this layer are all connected to all neurons of the previous layer. Their activation is computed by a matrix multiplication plus a bias offset. This is again a secret precomputed affine step that can be achieved via the external product.

Loss Layer: This is normally the last layer of a CNN. During the evaluation, the loss layer becomes an argmax operation. This last step is in general ignored in other homomorphic implementations of neural networks. For example, in [7, 23], the authors simply output the score vectors and the recipient computes the best one after decryption. To do this final step homomorphically, the boolean approach of TFHE seems to be the most suited to this non-SIMD step.

4.1 Robustness Against the FHE Error Models

In this section, we simulate the homomorphic execution of the neural network by replacing the value output of each non-linear layer by a random sample which has the same distribution as the phase of RLWE samples after a homomorphic evaluation of the layer. This approach allows us to simulate a homomorphic evaluation, and to obtain accurate predictions on the outcome without having to run the expensive homomorphic computation. This allows to estimate the largest noise standard deviation α that can be tolerated by the network, and therefore, the smallest FHE parameters required to evaluate it. In our experiments we add Gaussian noise with varying standard deviation and look for the maximal standard deviation of the noise that can be tolerated by the network.

As explained above, in the context of FHE, the training of networks is usually done on the plaintexts without any perturbations occurring, and only then, the network is encrypted to the cloud to protect the privacy of the model during

predictions. In this direction, we carried out many experiments on three different convolutional neural networks structures, using the TFHE and HEAAN noise
models of Sect. 2, in order to measure their robustness against such perturbations. This approach is not new. For example, in [13] the authors studied the
stability of CNNs by applying among others a Gaussian perturbation to the
internal weights inside the convolutional layers. The applied Gaussian was cen-
tered at zero and had a standard deviation relative to the standard deviation of
that layer's original weight distribution. This type of perturbation modifies the
average value of the inputs to the convolutional layer. Even, if the motivation
of this paper is not linked to homomorphic computations, their conclusions and
ours intersect at some points. Indeed, the authors of [13] noticed that the last
convolutional layers are surprisingly stable, while the first convolutional layers
are much more fragile and so the accuracy depends on the level the perturbation
applies. The most surprising result that we obtain in our experiments is that
all the neural networks we tested support quite large relative errors of at least
10% of 2^r, without any impact on the global accuracy. In a TFHE context, rais-
ing the error amplitude from a usually required 2^{-40} negligible amount to 2^{-4}
means that the depth of leveled circuits (number of transitions in automata in
leveled circuits in [17]) can be increased by a factor $(2^{36})^2$ without changing the
parameter sets. This also means that only 4 bits of precision (instead of 20 to 40
bits usually) are needed on all fixed point operations throughout the network,
which results notably in very small parameter sets for HEAAN.

4.2   Experiments

We conducted experiments with three different convolutional neural networks
and for all of them we used the dlib C++ library [26]. The first network is
LeNet-5 [27], that can be trained to recognize handwritten digits, the second-
one is a 9-layer CNN trained to distinguish cat from dog pictures, and the last
one is the ResNet-34 network [24], a deep network of 34 layers able to classify an
input image into one of 1000 objects. We briefly describe each of the networks
and the experiments done on it.

LeNet-5: Recognition of Handwritten Digits. LeNet-5 is a well-known
convolutional 7-layer neural network designed by LeCun et al. in 1998 to recognize handwritten digits [27]. In the original version of the network, the sigmoid
was used as the activation function. In the version that we manipulated (dlib
library [26]), the ReLU activation function is used instead.

We trained this network on the MNIST dataset [28], composed of 60000
training and 10000 testing images, with two different versions of the pooling
algorithm. We first trained the network by using max pool for both pooling layers and at a second stage we re-trained it from scratch by replacing now max
pool by average pool. Our goal was to see how each version reacts to perturbations. In particular, we added to each output value of the activation function
a value drawn from a Gaussian distribution with mean value zero and some
standard deviation σ. This was done for the activation function of all levels. For

our experiments we further used two different activation functions: the original ReLU activation function and then an approximation of the ReLU function by a trigonometric function, depicted in Fig. 3 (right), or in green in Fig. 1 (right) which can be used in HEAAN as a replacement of $\max(0, x)$. Finally, we perturbed the output of the activation function in two different ways. First by a Gaussian distribution of fixed standard deviation σ and in a second experiment by a standard deviation proportional to the input's standard deviation (which can be publicly estimated during training).

The results of these experiments are summarized in Table 1 and Fig. 4. In this example, we pushed standard deviation from 0.0 to 1.0 for both trained CNNs, the one trained with max pool and the other one trained with average pool. In Table 1 we give both the accuracy on the testing set but also on the training set. In order to correctly interpret the right part of Fig. 4 it has to be noted that the mean value of the ReLU entries was measured between 0.4 and 1.91 and the standard deviation between 0.97 and 2.63.

Table 1. Experiments on the LeNet-5 network trained first with max pool and then with average pool. ReLU means that during the evaluation the original ReLU function was used, while $\widetilde{\text{ReLU}}$ signifies that an approximation was used instead.

Pool type	σ	Non-proportional perturbation				Proportional perturbation			
		ReLU		$\widetilde{\text{ReLU}}$		ReLU		$\widetilde{\text{ReLU}}$	
		Train acc.	Test acc.	Train acc.	Test acc.	Train acc.	Test acc.	Train acc.	Test acc.
Max	0.0	0.9999	0.9924	0.9999	0.9924	0.9999	0.9924	0.9999	0.9924
Average		0.9994	0.9903	0.9994	0.9903	0.9994	0.9903	0.9975	0.9903
Max	0.1	0.9998	0.9918	0.9996	0.9916	0.9984	0.9908	0.9980	0.9905
Average		0.9994	0.9903	0.9993	0.9904	0.9977	0.9891	0.9976	0.9892
Max	0.2	0.9990	0.9910	0.9976	0.9899	0.9883	0.9835	0.9842	0.9787
Average		0.9991	0.9901	0.9985	0.9894	0.9897	0.9843	0.9878	0.9826
Max	0.3	0.9966	0.9894	0.9901	0.9833	0.9540	0.9501	0.9199	0.9192
Average		0.9981	0.9898	0.9960	0.9872	0.9699	0.9655	0.9595	0.9581
Max	0.4	0.9919	0.9843	0.9654	0.9610	0.8686	0.8723	0.7695	0.7815
Average		0.9968	0.9884	0.9908	0.9845	0.9308	0.9296	0.9014	0.9039
Max	0.5	0.9823	0.9766	0.8942	0.8966	0.7475	0.7587	0.5901	0.5959
Average		0.9947	0.9869	0.9792	0.9737	0.8728	0.8745	0.8156	0.8214
Max	0.6	0.9626	0.9610	0.7644	0.7737	0.6199	0.6248	0.4325	0.4317
Average		0.9919	0.9842	0.9552	0.9517	0.8007	0.8054	0.7179	0.7245
Max	0.7	0.9284	0.9280	0.6166	0.6288	0.5013	0.5024	0.3233	0.3274
Average		0.9883	0.9816	0.9171	0.917	0.7219	0.7288	0.6212	0.6332
Max	0.8	0.8756	0.8808	0.4809	0.4953	0.4040	0.4056	0.2526	0.2576
Average		0.9843	0.9779	0.8633	0.8698	0.6433	0.6506	0.5295	0.5383
Max	0.9	0.8103	0.8191	0.3826	0.3884	0.3316	0.3322	0.2036	0.2094
Average		0.9779	0.9724	0.8044	0.8135	0.5691	0.5727	0.4498	0.4538
Max	1.0	0.7399	0.7462	0.3179	0.326	0.2757	0.2803	0.1719	0.1732
Average		0.9696	0.9636	0.7434	0.7548	0.4989	0.5062	0.3822	0.3862

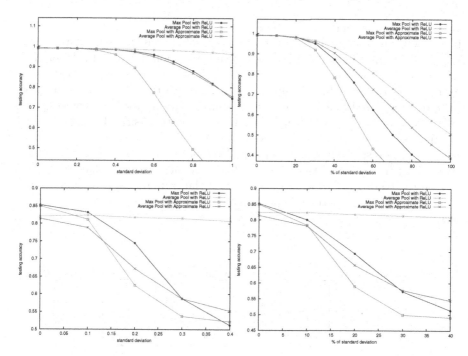

Fig. 4. Experiments with LeNet-5 (up) and the cat versus dog classifier (down). The results with proportional perturbations are on the right, while with non-proportional perturbations on the left.

The first remark that can be done by looking into these experiments is that average pool is much more stable to perturbations than max pool and provides a high accuracy even for large values of the standard deviation. The second remark concerns the accuracy when an approximation of the ReLU function is used instead of the original one. As it can be seen from the left part of Fig. 4, the accuracy for the average pool version is clearly lower when a ReLU approximation is used, but still has a very good score (over 95%) for standard deviations as high as 0.6. Finally, special care has to be taken when interpreting the results corresponding to the application of a proportional perturbation of the input data standard deviation. In the right part of Fig. 4 the x-axis corresponds to a perturbation equal to the percentage of the inputs' standard deviation. Depending on the original deviation of the input distribution, the perturbation can be extremely important and this is why the accuracy shows to drop. Therefore, one has to keep in mind that the perturbation of the right-side figures is in general more important and probably also more meaningful than the one of the left-side figures.

Cats versus Dogs Classifier. In this section we present our results and remarks on a simple 9-layer neural network that was trained to classify pictures as cats or dogs. For this, we used again the `dlib` library [26] and coded with it the 9-layer NN presented in [1]. The structure of this NN is depicted in Fig. 5. This network is composed of 3 convolution layers followed by the ReLU activation function, two fully connected (FC) layers and two pooling layers. In the original net, the max pool operation is used at this step. The 7-th layer is a dropout layer, that is a standard technique for reducing overfitting and consists in ignoring a different randomly chosen part of neurons during the different stages of the training phase [31]. We trained this network on the Asirra dataset [19] used by Microsoft Research in the context of a CAPTCHA (Completely Automated Public Turing test to tell Computers and Humans Apart) challenge. Most of the good CNNs trained to distinguish dogs from cats achieve more than 80% accuracy on the testing set while the accuracy on the training set is usually around 100%. The difference in the two performances is usually due to some overfitting occuring.

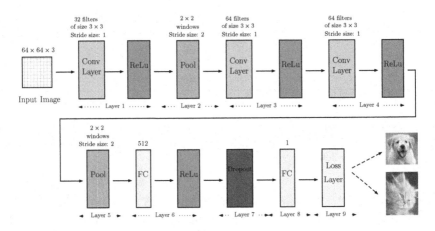

Fig. 5. 9-layer neural network [1] trained to classify pictures as cats or dogs.

We did exactly the same type of experiments for this network and the results can be found in Table 2 or visualized in the lower part of Fig. 4. This network is a little-bit more complex than LeNet-5 and seems to be less stable. For this reason, the higher standard deviation considered here is 0.4. However, globally, the same remarks as for LeNet-5 network result. Again, for correctly interpreting the right part of the table, it has to be noted that the mean value of the inputs of the activation function ranges between 0.0004 and 0.628 and the standard deviation ranges between 0.0067 and 3.51.

ResNet-34. ResNet (Residual Network) is a recent family of very deep convolutional neural networks showed to perform extremely well [24]. The global layer structure is very similar to a classical CNN, however better performances are achieved by the introduction of a shortcut connection, that consists in skipping one or more layers. The version that we used is composed of 34 layers, and is

Table 2. Experiments on a 9-layer CNN trained to distinguish cats from dogs.

Pool type	σ	Non-proportional perturbation			Proportional perturbation	
		ReLU		ReLU͠	ReLU	ReLU͠
		Training acc.	Test acc.	Test acc.	Test acc.	Test acc.
Max	0.0	0.9999	0.8530	0.8500	0.8524	0.85
Average		0.99995	0.8202	0.8138	0.8232	0.814
Max	0.1	0.9944	0.8316	0.8112	0.801	0.784
Average		0.99995	0.8232	0.7880	0.8234	0.7812
Max	0.2	0.8782	0.7446	0.6246	0.6942	0.5892
Average		0.9999	0.8174	0.6726	0.8174	0.6574
Max	0.3	0.6234	0.5872	0.5368	0.5736	0.4996
Average		0.99965	0.8146	0.5868	0.8134	0.5776
Max	0.4	0.5228	0.512	0.5222	0.514	0.4916
Average		0.998	0.8074	0.5522	0.8092	0.5444

abbreviated as ResNet-34. This network, once trained, is able to classify photos of objects into 1000 distinct object categories.

The training of such residual networks is extremely time consuming (two weeks on a 16-GB Titan GPU, and about 20 times more on 16-CPU cores) and because of time constraints we were not able to finish the training on a network where max pooling is replaced by average pooling. Thus, we were only able to perform our experiments on the pre-trained network on the imagenet ILSVRC2015 dataset [30] and the results are reported in Table 3. Top 1 and Top 5 labels report respectively the percentage of the pictures in the validation set that were correctly classified (Top 1) and whose correct label appeared in the five top suggestions provided by the network (Top 5).

Table 3. Experiments on ResNet-34 with max pooling and with perturbations of standard deviation ranging from 0.0 to 0.5. The right columns correspond to perturbations proportional to the input's standard deviation.

Pool type	σ	Non-proportional perturbation				Proportional perturbation			
		ReLU		ReLU͠		ReLU		ReLU͠	
		Top 1	Top 5	Top 1	Top 5	Top 1	Top 5	Top 1	Top 5
Max	0.0	0.7416	0.9158	0.7428	0.9187	0.7439	0.9202	0.7398	0.9166
Max	0.1	0.7357	0.9132	0.7056	0.9165	0.7132	0.8948	0.7586	0.9252
Max	0.2	0.6991	0.8860	0.7056	0.8967	0.1562	0.3294	0.3658	0.6027
Max	0.3	0.5068	0.7267	0.4829	0.7171	0.0019	0.0089	0.0012	0.0079
Max	0.4	0.1500	0.0498	0.1065	0.0817	0.0018	0.0085	0.000	0.0009
Max	0.5	0.0233	0.0608	0.0017	0.0066	0.0001	0.0044	0.000	0.0010

4.3 Conclusion/Discussion

Finally, we summarize the experiments with the three different CNNs, provide links to Sect. 3 and give recommendations on which operation should be performed with which FHE scheme (depending on the given use case).

Max pool versus Average pool: We conducted experiments on LeNet-5 and the 9-layer CNN classifying cats and dogs, by replacing during the training and the evaluation the classical max pooling operation by the average pool. This modification, applied also in [11] and to some extend in [23], offers a significant advantage for all FHE schemes, as this operation is affine with public coefficients, compared to max pool that is non-linear. Our experiments showed that this approach offers a further advantage in FHE, as it is way more stable than max pool to perturbations. This behaviour has a natural mathematical explanation, since the standard deviation of an average of independent samples is smaller than the input standard deviations.

Proportional versus non-proportional perturbations: We applied two types of perturbations to all three networks. The first type of perturbations was the addition at the output of the activation function of a value drawn from a Gaussian distribution with zero mean and a fixed standard deviation. In the second type of perturbations, the value added had a standard deviation proportional to the standard deviation of the input distribution. The second scenario corresponds to the fixed-point arithmetic model, where the public plaintext exponent τ is set to match the amplitude during the training phase, and therefore, the noise α is by definition relative to 2^τ. Surprisingly, without impacting the result, neural networks are able to absorb very large relative errors between 10% and 20% after each ReLU (there are respectively thousands, millions, and billions of them in the three tested networks). This means homomorphic parameters need only to ensure $\rho = 4$ bits of precision on the plaintext, instead of the usually recommended $\rho = 30$.

Approximating the ReLU activation function: The main source of non-linearity of a convolutional neural network is coming from the ReLU function. In TFHE these functions are evaluated exactly either as circuits, or as pointwise-defined arbitrary functions. Approximating the ReLU by something easier is thus a natural approach [7,11,23]. In HEAAN such continuous functions can be approximated accurately by low degree trigonometric polynomials. In our experiments with ResNet-34 (see Table 3) the output accuracy is surprisingly even better with an approximated ReLU of this type than with the classical one, in the presence of small noise, which proves that this approach is realistic.

Number of layers: In the plaintext model, the accuracy can in general be improved by adding more layers, if no overfitting occurs. However, in the homomorphic model, what happens with accuracy is still an open question, because with the number of layers, the complexity of computation grows and the activation function can only be approximated. This generates additional noise that can affect the accuracy.

References

1. Cats and dogs and convolutional neural networks, September 2016. http://www. subsubroutine.com/sub-subroutine/2016/9/30/cats-and-dogs-and-convolutional-neural-networks

2. Track 2: Secure parallel genome wide association studies using homomorphic encryption (2018). www.humangenomeprivacy.org/2018/competition-tasks.html

3. Albrecht, M., et al.: Homomorphic encryption security standard. Technical report, HomomorphicEncryption.org, Toronto, Canada, November 2018

4. Badawi, A.A., et al.: The AlexNet moment for homomorphic encryption: HCNN, the first homomorphic CNN on encrypted data with GPUs. Cryptology ePrint Archive, Report 2018/1056 (2018). https://eprint.iacr.org/2018/1056

5. Boura, C., Chillotti, I., Gama, N., Jetchev, D., Peceny, S., Petric, A.: High-precision privacy-preserving real-valued function evaluation. IACR Cryptology ePrint Archive 2017, 1234 (2017)

6. Boura, C., Gama, N., Georgieva, M.: Chimera: a unified framework for B/FV, TFHE and HEAAN fully homomorphic encryption and predictions for deep learning. Cryptology ePrint Archive, Report 2018/758 (2018)

7. Bourse, F., Minelli, M., Minihold, M., Paillier, P.: Fast homomorphic evaluation of deep discretized neural networks. In: Shacham, H., Boldyreva, A. (eds.) CRYPTO 2018. LNCS, vol. 10993, pp. 483–512. Springer, Cham (2018). https://doi.org/10.1007/978-3-319-96878-0_17

8. Brakerski, Z.: Fully homomorphic encryption without modulus switching from classical GapSVP. In: Safavi-Naini, R., Canetti, R. (eds.) CRYPTO 2012. LNCS, vol. 7417, pp. 868–886. Springer, Heidelberg (2012). https://doi.org/10.1007/978-3-642-32009-5_50

9. Brakerski, Z., Gentry, C., Vaikuntanathan, V.: (Leveled) fully homomorphic encryption without bootstrapping. In: ITCS 2012, pp. 309–325. ACM (2012)

10. Carpov, S., Gama, N., Georgieva, M., Troncoso-Pastoriza, J.R.: Privacy-preserving semi-parallel logistic regression training with fully homomorphic encryption. Cryptology ePrint Archive, Report 2019/101 (2019). https://eprint.iacr.org/2019/101

11. Chabanne, H., de Wargny, A., Milgram, J., Morel, C., Prouff, E.: Privacy-preserving classification on deep neural network. Cryptology ePrint Archive, Report 2017/035 (2017). https://eprint.iacr.org/2017/035

12. Chen, H., Laine, K., Player, R.: Simple encrypted arithmetic library - SEAL v2.1. In: Brenner, M., et al. (eds.) FC 2017. LNCS, vol. 10323, pp. 3–18. Springer, Cham (2017). https://doi.org/10.1007/978-3-319-70278-0_1

13. Cheney, N., Schrimpf, M., Kreiman, G.: On the robustness of convolutional neural networks to internal architecture and weight perturbations. CoRR, abs/1703.08245 (2017)

14. Cheon, J.H., Han, K., Kim, A., Kim, M., Song, Y.: Bootstrapping for approximate homomorphic encryption. In: Nielsen, J.B., Rijmen, V. (eds.) EUROCRYPT 2018. LNCS, vol. 10820, pp. 360–384. Springer, Cham (2018). https://doi.org/10.1007/978-3-319-78381-9_14

15. Cheon, J.H., Kim, A., Kim, M., Song, Y.: Homomorphic encryption for arithmetic of approximate numbers. In: Takagi, T., Peyrin, T. (eds.) ASIACRYPT 2017. LNCS, vol. 10624, pp. 409–437. Springer, Cham (2017). https://doi.org/10.1007/978-3-319-70694-8_15

16. Chillotti, I., Gama, N., Georgieva, M., Izabachène, M.: Faster fully homomorphic encryption: bootstrapping in less than 0.1 seconds. In: Cheon, J.H., Takagi, T. (eds.) ASIACRYPT 2016. LNCS, vol. 10031, pp. 3–33. Springer, Heidelberg (2016). https://doi.org/10.1007/978-3-662-53887-6_1

17. Chillotti, I., Gama, N., Georgieva, M., Izabachène, M.: TFHE: fast fully homomorphic encryption over the torus. Cryptology ePrint Archive, Report 2018/421 (2018). https://eprint.iacr.org/2018/421

18. Ducas, L., Micciancio, D.: FHEW: bootstrapping homomorphic encryption in less than a second. In: Oswald, E., Fischlin, M. (eds.) EUROCRYPT 2015. LNCS, vol. 9056, pp. 617–640. Springer, Heidelberg (2015). https://doi.org/10.1007/978-3-662-46800-5_24

19. Elson, J., Douceur, J.R., Howell, J., Saul. J.: Asirra: a CAPTCHA that exploits interest-aligned manual image categorization. In: Proceedings of the 2007 ACM Security, CCS 2007, pp. 366–374. ACM (2007)

20. Fan, J., Vercauteren, F.: Somewhat practical fully homomorphic encryption. IACR Cryptology ePrint Archive 2012, 144 (2012)

21. Gentry, C., Sahai, A., Waters, B.: Homomorphic encryption from learning with errors: conceptually-simpler, asymptotically-faster, attribute-based. In: Canetti, R., Garay, J.A. (eds.) CRYPTO 2013. LNCS, vol. 8042, pp. 75–92. Springer, Heidelberg (2013). https://doi.org/10.1007/978-3-642-40041-4_5

22. Gilad-Bachrach, R., Dowlin, N., Laine, K., Lauter, K.E., Naehrig, M., Wernsing, J.: CryptoNets: applying neural networks to encrypted data with high throughput and accuracy. In: Proceedings of the 33nd International Conference on Machine Learning, ICML 2016, New York City, NY, USA, 19–24 June 2016, pp. 201–210 (2016)

23. Gilad-Bachrach, R., Dowlin, N., Laine, K., Lauter, K.E., Naehrig, M., Wernsing, J.: CryptoNets: applying neural networks to encrypted data with high throughput and accuracy. In: ICML 2016. JMLR Workshop and Conference Proceedings, vol. 48, pp. 201–210. JMLR.org (2016)

24. He, K., Zhang, X., Ren, S., Sun, J.: Deep residual learning for image recognition. In: CVPR 2016, pp. 770–778. IEEE Computer Society (2016)

25. Jiang, X., Kim, M., Lauter, K.E., Song, Y.: Secure outsourced matrix computation and application to neural networks. In: Proceedings of the 2018 ACM SIGSAC Conference on Computer and Communications Security, CCS 2018, Toronto, ON, Canada, 15–19 October 2018, pp. 1209–1222. ACM (2018)

26. King, D.E.: Dlib-ml: a machine learning toolkit. J. Mach. Learn. Res. **10**, 1755–1758 (2009)

27. Lecun, Y., Bottou, L., Bengio, Y., Haffner, P.: Gradient-based learning applied to document recognition. In: Proceedings of the IEEE, pp. 2278–2324 (1998)

28. Lecun, Y., Cortes, C., Burges, C.J.: The MNIST database of handwritten digits. http://yann.lecun.com/exdb/mnist/

29. Lyubashevsky, V., Peikert, C., Regev, O.: On ideal lattices and learning with errors over rings. In: Gilbert, H. (ed.) EUROCRYPT 2010. LNCS, vol. 6110, pp. 1–23. Springer, Heidelberg (2010). https://doi.org/10.1007/978-3-642-13190-5_1

30. Russakovsky, O., et al.: ImageNet large scale visual recognition challenge. IJCV **115**(3), 211–252 (2015)

31. Srivastava, N., Hinton, G.E., Krizhevsky, A., Sutskever, I., Salakhutdinov, R.: Dropout: a simple way to prevent neural networks from overfitting. J. Mach. Learn. Res. **15**(1), 1929–1958 (2014)

32. Wagh, S., Gupta, D., Chandran, N.: SecureNN: efficient and private neural network training. Cryptology ePrint Archive, Report 2018/442 (2018). https://eprint.iacr.org/2018/442

Everything Is in the Name – A URL Based Approach for Phishing Detection

Harshal Tupsamudre$^{(\boxtimes)}$, Ajeet Kumar Singh, and Sachin Lodha

TCS Research, Pune, India
{harshal.tupsamudre,ajeetk.singh1,sachin.lodha}@tcs.com

Abstract. Phishing attack, in which a user is tricked into revealing sensitive information on a spoofed website, is one of the most common threat to cybersecurity. Most modern web browsers counter phishing attacks using a blacklist of confirmed phishing URLs. However, one major disadvantage of the blacklist method is that it is ineffective against newly generated phishes. Machine learning based techniques that rely on features extracted from URL (*e.g.*, URL length and bag-of-words) or web page (*e.g.*, TF-IDF and form fields) are considered to be more effective in identifying new phishing attacks. The main benefit of using URL based features over page based features is that the machine learning model can classify new URLs on-the-fly even before the page is loaded by the web browser, thus avoiding other potential dangers such as drive-by download attacks and cryptojacking attacks.

In this work, we focus on improving the performance of URL based detection techniques. We show that, although a classifier trained on traditional bag-of-words features (tokenized using special characters) works well in many cases, it fails to recognize a very prevalent class of phishing URLs that combines a popular brand with one or more words (e.g., www.paypalloginsecure.com and paypalhelpservice.simdif.com) among others. To overcome these flaws, we explore various alternative feature extraction techniques based on word segmentation and $n-$grams. We also construct and use a phishylist of popular words that are highly indicative of phishing attacks. We verify the efficacy of each of these feature sets by training a logistic regression classifier on a large dataset consisting of 100,000 URLs. Our experimental results reveal that features based on word segmentation, phishylist and numerical features (*e.g.*, URL length) perform better than all other features, as measured by misclassification and false negative rates.

Keywords: Phishing detection · Machine learning ·
Social engineering attacks

1 Introduction

Phishing is a form of social engineering attack that exploits the weakest link in the security chain, *i.e.*, humans. The attack typically starts with an email

© Springer Nature Switzerland AG 2019
S. Dolev et al. (Eds.): CSCML 2019, LNCS 11527, pp. 231–248, 2019.
https://doi.org/10.1007/978-3-030-20951-3_21

campaign that appears to come from a legitimate entity such as PayPal. The email lures the recipient into clicking a URL, which leads the user to a website designed to look legitimate but is not. When the user enters sensitive data such as passwords or credit card numbers, the fraudulent website records the information and sends it back to the attacker. Phishing attacks are extremely successful. According to 2018 Verizon's data breach investigation report [26], phishing is the third most common threat vector for data breaches and 4% of users click on any given phishing campaign. Phishing attacks are not only increasing in number, but they are also getting more sophisticated every day. The Anti Phishing Work Group (APWG) identified a total of 151,014 unique phishing websites in the third quarter of 2018. About half of these websites (49.4%) were hosted on infrastructure with HTTPS and SSL certificates, whereas at the end of 2016, the number of phishing websites using HTTPS were merely less than 5% [1].

The security community has invested a great deal of effort in developing detection countermeasures against phishing attacks. Most phishing detection techniques can be broadly classified into three categories, blacklist based, heuristics based and machine learning based [14]. Currently, Google Safe Browsing [3] is the most popular blacklisting service and is used by several web browsers including Chrome, Firefox and Safari to prevent users from visiting phishing websites. Microsoft offers similar such service known as SmartScreen and is used in the Internet explorer. The blacklist method is easy to implement, however one major disadvantage of this method is that it lacks the ability to protect against zero-hour phishing attacks. According to one study [25], 63% of the phishing campaigns end within the first two hours, whereas 47% to 83% of phishing URLs appeared in blacklists only after 12 h.

The heuristics based approaches exploit common characteristics found in the previously reported phishing attacks in order to detect new attacks. Few examples of heuristic tests are as follows:

- if the host-name portion of a URL is an IP address, the URL is phishing.
- if an organization's name (*e.g.*, PayPal) is present in a URL path but not in the primary domain, the URL is phishing.
- if hyphen is present in a primary domain, the URL is phishing.
- if password field is present in a web page, the website is phishing.

However, the use of heuristics can be tricky as it requires choosing the right weights for each heuristic check, and if not done properly it runs the risk of misclassifying legitimate websites. Machine learning algorithms, on the other hand, automatically determines best weights for all features (heuristic checks) using a database of training examples. In the machine learning approach, the problem of phishing detection is formulated as a binary classification task with two classes: *phishing* (positive class) and *valid* (negative class). The features required for training the classifier are mainly extracted from the URL [16,17,23] or web page [7,31] or both [14,19]. While the use of web page features may lead to better classification accuracy, the main benefit of using URL based features is that the resulting model can classify new URLs on-the-fly even before the page is loaded by the web browser, thus avoiding other potential dangers like drive-by download and cryptojacking attacks. Further, page based detection techniques suffer from performance issues, as many of these [7,31] work only after the entire web page is rendered, and there is a possibility that users may have divulged sensitive data before the page is detected as phishing.

The term URL is an abbreviation of Uniform Resource Locator, the global address of documents and other resources on the World Wide Web. A URL has three main components: (i) protocol, (ii) hostname, and (iii) path. The hostname specifies the server on which the resource is located and the path specifies the location of the document on the server. The hostname is further divided into two sub-parts: subdomain and domain. The path is also divided into three sub-parts: directory, file name and arguments. An example is shown in Fig. 1. In the figure, the term TLD stands for top-level domain.

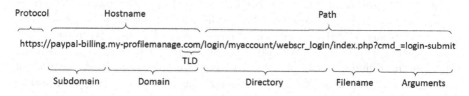

Fig. 1. Different components of a URL

URL features are of two types: *lexical* features and *external* features [16, 17]. Lexical features are those which can be quickly extracted from the URL string such as the length of the URL, the number of dots in the URL and the bag-of-words features. External features, on the other hand, require queries to remote servers (*e.g.*, whois lookup and DNS resolution) which introduces additional overhead and consume more resources at the client, *e.g.*, battery life and bandwidth of devices. Researchers [16] showed that the performance of a classifier that uses only lexical features is comparable to the one that uses full features (lexical + external). Therefore, lexical features are more appropriate for implementing an anti-phishing solution at the client side.

1.1   Contributions

Although a classifier trained on conventional lexical features [16,17] performs well in many cases, in this paper, we demonstrate it fails to recognize an important class of phishing URLs that contain popular brand names concatenated with one or more phishy words. Consequently, we explore various alternative feature extraction techniques to improve the robustness of classifiers. Specifically, our contributions are as follows:

1. We find that the conventional bag-of-words (BoW) feature extraction technique, based solely on special characters ('/', '?', '.', '=', '_', '&' and '-'), is not robust enough to detect all types of phishing URLs. For example, the

BoW features of the URL `paypal.com.secure05.xserver.prishka1.com` extracted using techniques described in [16,17] are $name = \{$`paypal`, `com`, `secure05`, `xserver`, `prishka1`$\}$ and $tld = \{$`com`$\}$. A classifier trained on these conventional BoW features correctly predicts the URL as phishing due to the high frequency of the words `paypal` and `com` in the hostname portion of the phishing URLs dataset. However, the classifier fails to predict the URL `paypalhelpservice.simdif.com` as phishing, based on the BoW features: $name = \{$`paypalhelpservice`, `simdif`$\}$ and $tld = \{$`com`$\}$, as the tokens `paypalhelpservice` and `simdif` do not appear in the phishing dataset.

2. Therefore, to overcome these limitations of conventional bag-of-words (BoW) features, we explore other feature extraction techniques based on word segmentation and $n-$grams. We also build and use a phishy-list to recognize phishing URLs containing brand names along with phishy words.

   (a) In the word segmentation technique, we first split the entire URL string using special characters and then apply word segmentation algorithm on each token to extract segmented bag-of-words features. We refer to this feature set as SBoW. We also make distinction between words appearing in the different parts of the URL. For example, the SBoW features of the URL `paypalhelpservice.simdif.com` are $name = \{$`paypal`, `help`, `service`, `simdif`$\}$ and $tld = \{$`com`$\}$.

   (b) In the $n-$grams technique, we split the URL string using special characters and then extract tri-grams from each resulting token. We refer to this feature set as bag-of-$n$grams (BoN). Again, we make distinction between $n-$grams appearing in the different parts of the URL. For instance, the BoN features of the URL `paypalhelpservice.simdif.com` are $name = \{$`pay`, `ayp`, `ypa`, `pal`, `hel`, `elp`, $\ldots$, `dif`$\}$ and $tld = \{$`com`$\}$.

   (c) Phishing URLs often contain several words such as `login`, `secure`, `help` and `update` which are indicative of phishing attacks. Based on this observation, we retrieve popular tokens from the phishing dataset and create a phishy-list (PL) of these words. We check whether any phishy word appears in the URL and use it as a binary feature in conjunction with BoW features. We refer to this feature set as BoW-PL. For example, if the word `help` is present in the phishy-list, then the BoW-PL features of the URL `paypalhelpservice.simdif.com` are $name = \{$`paypalhelpservice`, `simdif`$\}$, $tld = \{$`com`$\}$ and $phishy\text{-}list = 1$.

3. We evaluate the efficacy of all proposed feature sets on a dataset of 100,000 URLs obtained from PhishTank and DMOZ websites. We find that, a classifier trained on SBoW, phishy-list and numerical features (*e.g.*, URL length) outperforms classifiers trained on other feature sets.

2   Related Work

In this section, we give a brief overview of different anti-phishing countermeasures proposed in the literature. These countermeasures are broadly classified into three categories: *make things invisible*, so that users can focus on their task

instead of worrying about phishing attacks; *provide better interfaces* that assist
users in detecting phishing attacks; and *train users* to proactively recognize and
counter phishing attacks [13].

2.1   Making Things Invisible

Various phishing detection techniques that rely on URL based features or page
based features fall under the make things invisible category. First, we describe
URL based detection techniques (which is the topic of this paper) in detail
followed by page based detection techniques.

URL Based Detection. In [12], Garera *et al.* identified four distinct categories of URL obfuscation techniques that the attackers use to mount phishing
attacks. Further, to identify these phishing URLs, they proposed 18 different
features including those based on Google infrastructure such as page rank and
page quality. They determined the weight of each feature using a logistic regression model trained on a dataset of approximately 2500 URLs. McGrath *et al.*
[20] performed a comparative analysis of phishing and non-phishing URLs and
found that phishing URLs and domains have very different lengths and character
distributions compared to non-phishing URLs and domains. As a consequence,
the features based on URL length and domain length were successfully employed
in classification models constructed in the subsequent studies.

Ma *et al.* [17] described a phishing detection approach that uses (a) lexical features extracted from URL names such as URL length and bag-of-words
(BoW), and (b) external features acquired from queries to remote servers such
as whois lookup. They examined the performance of several batch based learning algorithms on a dataset of 35,500 URLs and found that the use of lexical
features achieved similar classification accuracy without incurring the overhead
of querying remote queries. Later, Le *et al.* [16] performed a focused study on
evaluating a classifier trained only on lexical features vs. a classifier trained
on full features (lexical + external) to detect phishing attacks. They found that
the performance of a classifier trained with only lexical features was similar to
the one trained with full features. Their results were based on around 14,000
phishing URLs. We note that both approaches [16,17] extract BoW features by
tokenizing the URL string using special characters ('/', '?', '.', '=', '_', '&' and
'-') and make distinction between tokens that appear in the domain name, the
top level domain, the directory, and the file extension. An extensive survey of
phishing detection techniques that rely on URL based features can be found in
[23]. Recently, researchers have also proposed the usage of deep neural networks
for feature extraction and classification of malicious URLs [30].

In this work, we focus on improving the detection capabilities of lexical features based classifiers. We explore various lexical features based on word segmentation and $n-$grams. Further, we also construct and use a phishy-list of phishy
words. In [28], Wang *et al.* explored the use of a word segmentation algorithm
to improve the detection of malicious domains containing brand names concatenated with one or more phishy words. They applied the word segmentation

algorithm only on the domain portion of the URL string. However, we observed that phrases containing popular brand names and phishy words appear not only in the domain, but also in other parts of phishing URLs such as subdomain and path. Therefore, in our approach, we first tokenize the entire URL string using special characters ('/', '?', '.', '=', '_', '&' and '-') and then apply a word segmentation algorithm on each token. Further, we distinguish between tokens appearing in the hostname, tld, directory, file name and arguments portion of the URL string. Recently, Verma *et al.* [27] explored the efficacy of unigrams, bigrams and trigrams features and found that classifiers trained on $n-$gram features achieved a higher classification accuracy. While they extract $n-$grams from the URL string directly (without tokenizing), we first tokenize the URL string and then extract $n-$grams from each resulting token. In addition, we make distinction among $n-$grams belonging to hostname, tld, directory, file name and arguments, whereas they do not. We evaluate the effectiveness of each of these feature sets by training a classifier on a large dataset of 100,000 URLs.

Page Based Detection. Other phishing detection techniques rely on page based features. Zhang *et al.* [31] developed a novel content based approach called CANTINA that uses TF-IDF information retrieval algorithm to extract features from the web page. Their evaluation showed that CANTINA achieved a true positive rate of approximately 95%. Whittaker *et al.* [29] described the design of the Google's proprietary machine learning classifier that uses a variety of features such as lexical features, external features, Google Page Rank, and features extracted from the page content, to detect phishing websites. Their approach also achieved a true positive rate of around 95% and a false positive rate of 0.1%. Ardi *et al.* [7] proposed an approach that uses cryptographic hashing of each web page's Document Object Model (DOM) to detect phishing attacks. Their approach yielded a zero false positive rate.

2.2 Better Interfaces and Training

Numerous studies show that users do not pay attention to the security indicators in the browsers [6,10] nor do they adhere to the browser warning messages [11]. Although, modern web browsers have improved the design of their warning pages, many users still struggle to understand and therefore, disregard browser warning messages [22]. As a consequence, researchers have explored various training methods to teach users about the importance of various security indicators and to recognize phishing attacks. For instance, numerous educational games have been developed to educate users about phishing URLs [8,9,24] which mainly focus on teaching users about different URL obfuscation techniques as identified by Garera *et al.* [12]. Although, training users to recognize phishing attacks could complement the machine based phishing detection methods, the actual benefits of using these training techniques in the real world is not yet known.

3   Approach

In this section, we first describe the phishing and valid URL datasets used in our evaluation. Later, we discuss the pros and cons of the traditional lexical features [16,17] and describe various alternative lexical features. Finally, we give a brief overview of the logistic regression model employed to recognize phishing URLs.

3.1   Datasets

Phishing URL Dataset. PhishTank [4], a community-driven phishing URL submission and verification system operated by OpenDNS, is one of the most widely used phishing data source for training URL based classifiers [16–18,27]. A suspicious URL is marked as phish if it is voted by at least two other members of the community. The data submitted to PhishTank is available free of cost to everyone through the PhishTank's website and API. We scraped 55,000 unique verified phishing URLs from the PhishTank website during January 2019.

Valid URL Dataset. DMOZ [2] is a large open human-edited directory of the web containing over five million URLs organized hierarchically in over one million categories. It is one of the most popular source to obtain legitimate URLs [16–18,27] and contains websites from diverse categories such as arts, business, news and sports. We randomly crawled 55,000 unique URLs from the DMOZ website during January 2019.

After the data collection phase, we performed data sanitization and removed all URLs with invalid syntax. Since URL based classifiers require lexical features for predicting a label, we filtered out all short URLs from both datasets. There were no short URLs in the valid dataset, however there were about 2, 000 short URLs in the phishing dataset belonging to 20 different URL shortening services. We also replaced %xx escapes in the URL with their single character equivalent, *e.g.,* %20 is replaced with *space* and %2D is replaced with *hyphen*. From the remaining URLs, we randomly chose a subset of 50,000 URLs in each of the datasets.

3.2   Features

In [12], Garera *et al.* identified four prominent URL obfuscation techniques used by the attacker. These are as follows:

– **Type I.** Obfuscation the host with an IP address: In this attack, the hostname contains an IP address and the organization being phished is placed in the path.
– **Type II.** Obfuscating the host with another domain: In this attack, the URL's hostname contains a valid looking domain name and the organization being phished is placed in the path.
– **Type III.** Obfuscating with large hostnames: In this attack, the organization being phished is present in the subdomain part of the URL.

- **Type IV.** Domain unknown or misspelled: In this attack, the domain name is misspelled or there is no apparent relationship between the organization being phished and the domain name.

Table 1. Commonly used URL obfuscation techniques illustrated using PayPal brand. The first four obfuscation techniques were identified by Garera *et al.* [12] while the Type V obfuscation was identified by Kintis *et al.* [15].

Category	Description	Examples
Type I	IP address	`http://51.77.145.33/www.paypal.com.webapps.mpp.account-selection/`
		`http://159.203.6.191/servicepaypal/`
Type II	Brand in path	`http://kannadamatinee.com/www.paypal.com.us/myaccount/signin`
		`http://a0243562.xsph.ru/servicePayPal/C/`
Type III	Brand in subdomain	`http://paypal.com.secure05.xserver.prishka1.com/`
		`https://paypalhelpservice.simdif.com/`
Type IV	Misspelled brand or unrelated domain	`http://paypa1.com`
		`http://bnkp-bdg.com/login`
Type V	Brand in domain	`http://paypal-account-limit-remove-com.ga/`
		`http://ssl-paypalupdate.com/success`
		`http://paypalnow.de/signin.htm`

Recently, Kintis *et al.* [15] identified a potent URL obfuscation technique known as *combosquatting* in which the organization being phished is present in the domain along with one or more words. We refer to this obfuscation technique as Type V. Table 1 provides illustrative examples for each of these obfuscation techniques.

To improve the classification accuracy of different obfuscating URLs, researchers [16,17] extracted two types of lexical features from the URL name: *bag-of-words* (BoW) features and *numerical* features. Originally researchers focused on detecting only the first four obfuscation techniques proposed by Garera *et al.* [12] as the Type V obfuscation is a more recent one. However, we find that some of these features are also useful in detecting Type V obfuscation. Now, we describe pros and cons of each of these features.

Bag-of-Words (BoW). The bag-of-words features are conventionally extracted by splitting the URL string into multiple tokens using special characters ('/', '?', '.', '=', '-', '&' and '-') [16,17]. Each resulting token constitutes a binary feature, the value of the feature is one if the token is present in the URL, otherwise it is zero. Further, a distinction is made among tokens appearing in the hostname, tld, directory, file name and the argument part of the URL, *i.e.*, the same word appearing in different parts of the URL is treated as a different binary feature. The main purpose of using positional bag-of-words (BoW) features is to detect Type I, Type II and Type III obfuscation techniques where the organization being phished (*e.g.*, `paypal`) or tld (*e.g.*, `com`) or phishy words (*e.g.*, `account`) appear in unexpected parts of the URL. For instance, the word `com` is more likely to appear in the tld part of the URL, however, if it appears in either subdomain or path, then the URL is a potential phish.

Table 2. Examples of BoW, SBoW, BoN and BoW-PL features

Type I URL	`159.203.6.191/servicepaypal/`
BoW	$name = \{159,\ 203,\ 6,\ 191\}$, $tld = \{\}$, $dir = \{$servicepaypal$\}$
SBoW	$name = \{159,\ 203,\ 6,\ 191\}$, $tld = \{\}$, $dir = \{$service, paypal$\}$
BoN	$name = \{159,\ 203,\ 6,\ 191\}$, $tld = \{\}$, $dir = \{$ser, erv, rvi, vic, ice, $\ldots$, pal$\}$
BoW-PL	$name = \{159,\ 203,\ 6,\ 191\}$, $tld = \{\}$, $dir = \{$servicepaypal$\}$, $phishy\text{-}list = 1$
Type II URL	`a0243562.xsph.ru/servicePayPal/C/`
BoW	$name = \{$a0243562, xsph$\}$, $tld = \{$ru$\}$, $dir = \{$servicepaypal, c$\}$
SBoW	$name = \{$a0243562, xsph$\}$, $tld = \{$ru$\}$, $dir = \{$service, paypal, c$\}$
BoN	$name = \{$a02, 024, 243, 435, $\ldots$, sph$\}$, $tld = \{$ru$\}$, $dir = \{$ser, erv, rvi, $\ldots$, c$\}$
BoW-PL	$name = \{$a0243562, xsph$\}$, $tld = \{$ru$\}$, $dir = \{$servicepaypal, c$\}$, $phishy\text{-}list = 1$
Type III URL	`paypalhelpservice.simdif.com`
BoW	$name = \{$paypalhelpservice, simdif$\}$, $tld = \{$com$\}$
SBoW	$name = \{$paypal, help, service, simdif$\}$, $tld = \{$com$\}$
BoN	$name = \{$pay, ayp, ypa, pal, $\ldots$, dif$\}$, $tld = \{$com$\}$
BoW-PL	$name = \{$paypalhelpservice, simdif$\}$, $tld = \{$com$\}$, $phishy\text{-}list = 1$
Type V URL	`ssl-paypalupdate.com/success`
BoW	$name = \{$ssl, paypalupdate$\}$, $tld = \{$com$\}$, $dir = \{$success$\}$
SBoW	$name = \{$ssl, paypal, update$\}$, $tld = \{$com$\}$, $dir = \{$success$\}$
BoN	$name = \{$ssl, pay, ayp, $\ldots$, ate$\}$, $tld = \{$com$\}$, $dir = \{$suc, ucc, cce, ces, ess$\}$
BoW-PL	$name = \{$ssl, paypalupdate$\}$, $tld = \{$com$\}$, $dir = \{$success$\}$, $phishy\text{-}list = 1$

We observed that although a classifier trained on conventional BoW features performs well in many cases, it fails to recognize phishing URLs that combine a popular brand with one or more words. Table 2 shows BoW features for URLs belonging to different obfuscation techniques. Since the tokenization procedure employed in extracting BoW features rely only on special characters, long phrases such as `servicepaypal`, `paypalhelpservice` and `paypalupdate` remain unsegmented in BoW features. The prediction scores of the Type I and Type II URLs could be improved if the token `servicepaypal` in the directory is further segmented into individual words `service` and `paypal`. Similarly, the Type III URL is more likely to be classified correctly, if the token `paypalhelpservice` in the subdomain is further segmented into words `paypal`, `help` and `service`. Therefore, we explore different lexical features based on the word segmentation and n−grams, and use a list of phishy words to improve the prediction of phishing URLs.

Segmented Bag-of-Words (SBoW). We use word segmentation based technique to extract BoW features from the URL string which are more robust against combosquatting URLs. In this technique, we first extract tokens from the URL string using special characters ('/', '?', '.', '=', '_', '&' and '-'). Subsequently, we apply a word segmentation algorithm on each extracted token to recover the individual words. We use Python's WordSegment module [5] for word segmentation which is based on code by Peter Norvig that uses *Google Web Trillion Word Corpus* [21]. Table 2 shows SBoW features for different obfuscated URLs. For example, after applying the word segmentation algorithm, the token `paypalhelpservice` in the Type III URL is now further divided into a set of three words {`paypal`, `help`, `service`}.

Bag-of-ngrams (BoN). We also explore n−gram based features to improve the detection of phishing URLs containing brand names and words. In this technique, we first extract tokens from the URL string using special characters ('/', '?', '.', '=', '_', '&' and '-'). Subsequently, we extract tri-grams from each token and use them as binary features. BoN features for four different obfuscated URLs are given in Table 2. For example, the trigrams of the token `paypalhelpservice` are {pay, ayp, ypa, pal, alh, lhe, hel, elp, lps, pse, ser, erv, rvi, vic, ice}.

Phishy-List (PL). In this technique, we construct a list of popular phishy tokens by analysing URL domains in the phishing dataset. We discard all tokens with *length* ≤ 3 as they contain common URL parts such as `com` and `org`. We remove organization name tokens like `paypal` to keep our phishy-list brand agnostic. The resulting list contains 105 popular words (frequency ≥ 20) indicative of phishing attacks. We refer to this list as *new-PL* (provided in Appendix A). Few examples of popular phishy words are `secure`, `login`, `account`, `update`, `verify` and `service`. We use this phishy-list as a binary feature and check whether any of the phishy tokens appear in the URL. The main purpose of using the phishy-list is to detect phishing URLs that contain brand names concatenated with popular phishy words. The phishy-list feature was also used in [16] (referred as blacklist feature) to address Type IV obfuscation. However, their phishy-list was small and contained only 12 words: `confirm`, `account`, `banking`, `secure`, `ebayisapi`, `webscr`, `login`, `signin`, `paypal`, `free`, `lucky` and `bonus`. We refer to this list as *legacy-PL*. We emphasize that our phishy-list is large and contains 105 popular brand agnostic phishy tokens.

Numerical Features. We also extract various numerical features as described by Le *et al.* [16]. First, the URL string is broken into four parts: domain, directory, file name and arguments. Subsequently, numerical features in each of these parts are retrieved. Table 3 shows different numerical features of a URL.

Table 3. Numerical features of a URL

URL	`paypal-billing.my-profilemanage.com/login/myaccount/webscr_login/index.php ?cmd_=login-submit`
Features	$len = 92$, $n\_dot = 3$
Hostname	`paypal-billing.my-profilemanage.com`
Features	$len = 35$, $IP = 0$, $port = 0$, $n\_token = 5$, $n\_hyphen = 2$, $max\_len = 13$
Directory	`/login/myaccount/webscr_login/`
Features	$len = 30$, $n\_subdir = 3$, $max\_len = 9$, $max\_dot = 0$, $max\_delim = 1$
Filename	`index.php`
Features	$len = 9$, $n\_dot = 1$, $n\_delim = 0$
Arguments	`?cmd_=login-submit`
Features	$len = 18$, $n\_var = 1$, $max\_len = 6$, $max\_delim = 2$

1. *URL related features.* These features include the length of the URL and the number of dots in the URL. These features are used to address Type II obfuscation.

2. *Domain related features.* These features include the length of the domain name, the number of tokens in the domain name, the number of hyphens in the domain name, the length of the longest token and whether an IP address or a port number is present in the domain name. Although, these features are used to address Type I and Type III obfuscation techniques, these features particularly the number of hyphens can also detect few instances of Type V obfuscation.

3. *Directory related features.* These features include the length of the directory, the number of sub-directory tokens, the length of the longest sub-directory token, and the maximum number of dots and other delimiters ('_' and '-') used in a sub-directory token. These features are proposed to address the Type II obfuscation technique.

4. *File name related features.* These features include the length of the file name, and the number of dots and other delimiters ('_' and '-') used in the file name. These features also used to address Type II obfuscation.

5. *Argument related features.* These features include the length of the arguments, the number of variables, the length of the longest variable value, and the maximum number of delimiters ('.', '_' and '-') used in a value.

Thus, a total of 20 numerical features are extracted from different parts of a URL. Table 4 compares the numerical features in valid and phishing datasets. URLs in the phishing dataset are much longer (more than 2x times) and contain more special characters (hyphen, dot) as compared to URLs in the valid dataset. We use these numerical features along with BoW, SBoW and BoN features.

Table 4. Analysis of numerical features in phishing and valid datasets

URL	len	n_dot	blacklist			
Valid	31.31	2.16	0.01			
Phishing	73.45	2.44	0.32			
Hostname	len	IP	port	n_token	n_hyphen	max_len
Valid	18.77	0	0	3.05	0.09	10.07
Phishing	20.99	0.02	0	2.71	0.35	11.17
Directory	len	n_subdir	max_len	max_dot	max_delim	
Valid	2.36	0.31	1.59	0	0.04	
Phishing	20.92	2.09	10.44	0.13	0.34	
File	len	n_dot	n_delim			
Valid	1.76	0.1	0.06			
Phishing	7.02	0.47	0.11			
Arguments	len	n_var	max_len	max_delim		
Valid	0.2	0.02	0.08	0		
Phishing	15.05	0.41	5.78	0.16		

3.3   Logistic Regression for URL Classification

The problem of phishing detection is formulated as a binary classification task with two classes: *phishing* (positive class) and *valid* (negative class). We use logistic regression as it is computationally efficient and improves the performance by retaining only the relevant features. It is a simple parametric model where URLs are classified based on their distance from hyperplane decision boundary. In the binary classification task, we are given $\mathcal{M}$ training instances $\{x_1, x_2, \ldots, x_M\}$, where each x_i is a N dimensional feature vector and $y_i \in \{0, 1\}$ is a class label associated with sample x_i. Logistic regression models the probability distribution of the class label y, given a feature x as follows:

$$p(y = 1|x; \theta) = \sigma(\theta^T x + b) = \frac{1}{1 + \exp^{-(\theta^T x + b)}} \qquad (1)$$

where, $\theta \in \mathbb{R}^N$ and bias b are the parameters of the logistic regression model, and $\sigma(\cdot)$ is the sigmoid function defined as $\sigma(z) = 1/(1 + \exp^{-z})$. This sigmoid function $\sigma(\cdot)$ interprets the distances as probabilities of positive and negative labels.

We train the logistic regression model using maximum likelihood estimation with l_1 regularization. We estimate the weight vector θ and bias b by maximizing the objective function:

$$\mathcal{L}(\theta, b) = \sum_{i=1}^{M} \log p(y_i|x_i) - \lambda \sum_{j=1}^{N} |\theta_j| \qquad (2)$$

The first term in Eq. 2 computes the conditional log-likelihood that the model predicts correct label for all the samples in the training set. The second term in the equation penalizes large magnitude values in the weight vector θ. This is known as l_1 norm regularization and has many beneficial properties over SVM and Naive Bayes estimators while working with large feature dimensions. (i) It serves as a measure against overfitting; (ii) it encourages sparse solutions in which many elements of the weight vector θ are *exactly* zero (iii) it also helps in feature selection by retaining only the most relevant features. Due to these benefits, the logistic regression classifier has been widely used to develop various anti-phishing solutions in the past [12,17,28].

4   Results and Discussion

Now, we evaluate and compare the efficacy of classifiers trained on various feature sets described in Sect. 3. Specifically, we investigate how different feature extraction techniques help in distinguishing phishing URLs from valid URLs. To this end, we train logistic regression classifiers on different feature sets and report their misclassification rate (MCR) and false negative rate (FNR). MCR measures the rate of incorrectly detected valid and phishing instances in relation to all instances, whereas false negative rate (FNR) measures the rate of phishing instances that are incorrectly detected as valid in relation to all phishing instances. Specifically,

$$MCR = \frac{N_{P \to V} + N_{V \to P}}{N_{P \to P} + N_{P \to V} + N_{V \to V} + N_{V \to P}} \tag{3}$$

and,

$$FNR = \frac{N_{P \to V}}{N_{P \to P} + N_{P \to V}} \tag{4}$$

where $N_{P \to P}$ is the number of phishing URLs correctly identified as phishing, $N_{V \to V}$ is the number of valid URLs correctly identified as valid, $N_{P \to V}$ is the number of phishing URLs incorrectly identified as valid and $N_{V \to P}$ is the number of valid URLs incorrectly identified as phishing. Our objective is to minimize both MCR and FNR. For training, we randomly select a subset of 80,000 URLs and use the remaining 20,000 URLs for testing. In our classification tasks, we consider phishing URL as positive class and valid URL as negative class.

We divide our experiments into three parts. Firstly, we investigate the effectiveness of three logistic regression classifiers trained on different bag-of-X representations, namely BoW [16,17], SBoW and BoN. Secondly, we compare the effectiveness of two phishy-lists, legacy-PL [16] and our proposed new-PL. Finally, we determine the potency of combining these different features with numerical features. The list of feature sets used in our classification experiments along with their corresponding MCR and FNR are given in Table 5. The table also shows the total number of extracted features in each feature set, the number of retained (non-zero) features, the number of retained features with positive (+ve) and negative (−ve) weights, and FNR reduction (FNR-Red) with respect to the baseline classifier (trained only on BoW features).

Table 5. Performance of classifiers trained with different feature sets based on MCR, FNR and reduction in FNR. We also report the number of features in each feature set, the number of relevant features, and features with +ve and −ve coefficients. Note that *num* represents numerical features.

Feature set	#Features	#Relevant	+ve	−ve	MCR(%)	FNR(%)	FNR-Red(%)
BoW (baseline)	107,277	2,240	1,767	473	5.04	7.87	–
BoN	108,038	3,987	2,621	1,366	4.18	5.29	32.78
SBoW	88,930	2,692	1,941	751	4.07	5.57	29.22
BoW+legacy-PL	107,278	2,201	1,728	473	5.02	7.84	0.38
BoW+new-PL	107,278	1,885	1,426	459	4.23	5.70	27.57
SBoW+new-PL	88,931	2,318	1,619	699	3.63	4.59	41.67
BoW+legacy-PL+num [16]	107,298	1,809	1,199	610	4.05	5.72	27.31
BoW+new-PL+num	107,298	1,604	1,048	556	3.70	4.83	38.62
BoN+num	108,058	3,428	1,569	1,859	3.44	4.25	45.99
SBoW+new-PL+num	**88,951**	**2,124**	**1,354**	**770**	**3.22**	**4.10**	**47.90**

Bag-of-X. Our experimental results show that a logistic regression classifier trained only on conventional BoW features [16,17] (tokens extracted using special characters) yielded a MCR of 5.04%. However, classifiers trained on BoN (tri-gram) features and SBoW features (tokens extracted using special characters and word segmentation) reduced the MCR to 4.18% and 4.07% respectively. A deeper analysis of the results show that SBoW and BoN features are more robust (low FNR) against all types of phishing URLs as compared to BoW features. Few examples of such URLs are illustrated in Table 6, where the classifier trained on BoW features misclassified the phishing URL as valid whereas classifiers trained on SBoW and BoN did not. For instance, based on BoW features, the Type II URL `al-cap.com/vvb/chaseonline2018` (a spoof of US based *Chase* bank) is labelled as phish with a probability of 0.42. Note that in this case, only the tld token `com` is determined as a relevant feature (and that too negative) by the logistic regression classifier, whereas other tokens such as `cap` and `chaseonline2018` are simply ignored since their corresponding weights are zero. The SBoW features on the other hand extract relevant tokens `chase` and `online` from the phrase `chaseonline2018` which are determined as positive features by the classifier. As a consequence, the URL is classified as phishing with a very high probability (0.99). The classifier trained on BoN features performed similarly to that trained on SBoW features. Consequently, when compared to the BoW model, FNR of BoN reduced by 32.78% and FNR of SBoW reduced by 29.22%. Although FNR of BoN is slightly less than FNR of SBoW, the number of features retained in the BoN model (3,987) is almost 1.5 times more than those retained in the SBoW model (2,692). Therefore, the model trained using SBoW features is simpler than the model trained using BoN features and exhibit comparable performance.

Table 6. Illustrative examples demonstrating the effectiveness of logistic regression classifiers trained on SBoW and BoN features over classifier trained on BoW features.

URL	Features	+ve features	−ve features	Prob
Type II	BoW	—	com	0.42
al-cap.com/vvb/chaseonline2018	SBoW	online, chase	com	0.99
	BoN	cha, has, ase, lin, nli	com, eon, ine	0.99
Type III	BoW	—	blogspot, com	0.19
facebookloginconfirmation.	SBoW	facebook, login, confirmation	blogspot, com	0.99
blogspot.com	BoN	fac, ceb, ebo, boo, con, . . .	log, com, . . .	0.98
Type IV	BoW	account	www, com	0.28
www.amzaon-account.com/	SBoW	am, on, account	www, com	0.68
	BoN	cco, amz, acc, zao	oun, com, www	0.93
Type V	BoW	—	com	0.42
google1mail.com/mi-cuenta	SBoW	mail, cuenta, google	com	0.95
	BoN	nta, mai, ail, cue, ogl	oog, gle, ent, com	0.90

Phishy-Lists. We trained two logistic regression classifiers to determine the quality of two phishy lists, legacy-PL and new-PL. Both classifiers were trained on conventional BoW features, the only difference was that the first classifier considered legacy-PL whereas the second classifier considered new-PL. We note that phishy-list is a binary feature, where we check if any of the words in the phishy-list appear in the URL. Therefore, the total number of features used for training two classifiers were same (107,278). However, after training, we found that the first classifier with legacy-PL retained 2,201 features, whereas the other classifier that used new-PL retained only 1,885 features. Also, MCR of the first classifier with legacy-PL was 5.02%, slightly better than the BoW features (5.04%). Further, there was only a miniscule reduction of 0.38% in FNR. On the other hand, MCR of the second classifier with new-PL was 4.23% and its FNR reduced by 27.57%. Therefore, the use of new-PL resulted in simple model and improved accuracy. Replacing the BoW features with SBoW features and using new-PL, reduced the MCR to 3.63%. Also, its FNR decreased by 41.67%. Hence, as new-PL outperformed legacy-PL, we conduct the remaining experiments using new-PL only.

Full Feature Set. From the experiments above, it can be seen that BoX features, alone, perform very well in classifying phishing URLs. However, these BoX features are not always enough to model the unseen URLs. Hence, we require a set of orthogonal features that complement the BoX features. Therefore, we also consider 20 numerical features to make classifiers more robust. The performance of classifiers trained on the following combination of feature sets (BoX, phishy-list, numerical) is shown in Table 5.

1. BoW + numerical + legacy-PL (state-of-the-art): In this we implemented a logistic regression classifier based on features proposed in [16]. These state-of-the-art features resulted in a MCR of 4.05%. Further, we observed a FNR reduction of 27.31% against the baseline BoW features. However, as shown in Table 5, this feature set is outperformed by all other full feature sets in terms of MCR as well as FNR. Further, the classifier trained only on SBoW and new-BL features (with MCR 3.63% and FNR reduction of 41.67%) performed better than the current classifier that used BoW features, legacy-PL as well as numerical features.

2. BoW + numerical + new-PL: Here, instead of using the legacy-PL consisting of 12 phishy words [16], we used a larger new-PL consisting of 105 brand agnostic phishy words. We obtained a MCR of 3.70% and FNR reduction of 38.62%, both better than the state-of-the-art features proposed in [16]. However, these MCR and FNR are still higher than those achieved using only SBoW and new-PL features.

3. BoN + numerical: After training a logistic regression classifier on tri-gram features and numerical features, we obtained a MCR of 3.44% and FNR reduction of 45.99% on the test set. This is the second best feature set among all other feature sets.

4. SBoW + numerical + new-PL: Here, we used SBoW features, numerical features as well as new-BL. We obtained a MCR of 3.22% and FNR reduction of 47.90%, which is the lowest among all feature sets.

5   Conclusion and Future Work

In this paper, we demonstrated that a classifier trained on conventional lexical features fails to recognize phishing URLs that contain a brand name concatenated with one or more phishy words (*e.g.*, `paypalhelpservice.simdif.com`). To overcome these limitations, we explored different bag-of-X representations including bag-of-words (BoW), segmented bag-of-words (SBoW) and bag-of-ngrams (BoN). We found that a logistic regression classifier trained on SBoW features resulted in lower misclassification rate (MCR) as well as lower false negative rate (FNR) when compared with BoW features. Further, SBoW features yielded a simpler model when compared with BoN features. We also proposed a new phishy-list consisting of 105 brand agnostic words suggestive of phishing attacks and compared its performance against the legacy phishy-list [16]. The results of our experiments suggest that the new phishy-list not only improved the detection of phishing URLs, but also resulted in a simpler model. Further, we found that combining numerical features with SBoW features and new phishy-list outperformed all other combinations of feature sets used for phishing detection.

The feature extraction techniques proposed in this paper are well suited for detecting Type III (brand in subdomain), Type V (brand in domain), and Type II (brand in path) phishing URLs. But still, there is a lot to be desired for Type IV phishing URLs which are composed of unrelated or misspelled domains. We plan to explore the techniques to counter these URLs in our future work.

Appendix A

The phishy-list consisting of 105 words extracted from the phishing dataset is given below:

{limited, securewebsession, confirmation, page, signin, team, sign, access, protection,active, manage, redirectme, http, secure, customer, account, client, information, recovery, verify, secured, busines, refund, help, safe, bank, event, promo, webservis, giveaway, card, webspace, user, notify, servico, store, device, payment, webnode, drive, shop, gold, violation, random, upgrade, webapp, dispute, setting, banking, activity, startup, review, email, approval, admin, browser, webapp, billing, advert, protect, case, temporary, alert, portal, login, servehttp, center, client, restore, secure, blob, smart, fortune, gift, server, security, page, confirm, notification, core, host, central, service, account, servise, support, apps, form, info, compute, verification, check, storage, setting, digital, update, token, required, resolution, ebayisapi, webscr, login, free, lucky, bonus}

References

1. APWG, February 2019. http://docs.apwg.org/reports/apwg_trends_report_q3_2018.pdf
2. DMOZ, February 2019. http://dmoz-odp.org/
3. Google Safe Browsing, February 2019. https://safebrowsing.google.com/
4. PhishTank, February 2019. https://www.antiphishing.org/resources/apwg-reports/
5. Python Word Segmentation, February 2019. http://www.grantjenks.com/docs/wordsegment/
6. Alsharnouby, M., Alaca, F., Chiasson, S.: Why phishing still works: user strategies for combating phishing attacks. Int. J. Hum.-Comput. Stud. **82**, 69–82 (2015)
7. Ardi, C., Heidemann, J.: Auntietuna: personalized content-based phishing detection. In: Proceedings of the NDSS Workshop on Usable Security. The Internet Society, San Diego, California, USA, February 2016. http://www.isi.edu/%7ejohnh/PAPERS/Ardi16a.html
8. Canova, G., Volkamer, M., Bergmann, C., Reinheimer, B.: NoPhish app evaluation: lab and retention study. Internet Society, USEC (2015)
9. CJ, G., Pandit, S., Vaddepalli, S., Tupsamudre, H., Banahatti, V., Lodha, S.: Phishy - a serious game to train enterprise users on phishing awareness. In: Proceedings of the 2018 Annual Symposium on Computer-Human Interaction in Play Companion Extended Abstracts, CHI PLAY 2018, pp. 169–181. ACM, New York (2018). https://doi.org/10.1145/3270316.3273042
10. Dhamija, R., Tygar, J.D., Hearst, M.: Why phishing works. In: Proceedings of the SIGCHI Conference on Human Factors in Computing Systems, CHI 2006, pp. 581–590. ACM, New York (2006). https://doi.org/10.1145/1124772.1124861
11. Felt, A.P., et al.: Improving SSL warnings: comprehension and adherence. In: Proceedings of the 33rd Annual ACM Conference on Human Factors in Computing Systems, CHI 2015, pp. 2893–2902. ACM, New York (2015). https://doi.org/10.1145/2702123.2702442
12. Garera, S., Provos, N., Chew, M., Rubin, A.D.: A framework for detection and measurement of phishing attacks. In: Proceedings of the 2007 ACM Workshop on Recurring Malcode, WORM 2007, pp. 1–8. ACM, New York (2007). https://doi.org/10.1145/1314389.1314391
13. Hong, J.: The state of phishing attacks. Commun. ACM **55**(1), 74–81 (2012). https://doi.org/10.1145/2063176.2063197
14. Khonji, M., Iraqi, Y., Jones, A.: Phishing detection: a literature survey. IEEE Commun. Surv. Tutor. **15**(4), 2091–2121 (2013). https://doi.org/10.1109/SURV.2013.032213.00009
15. Kintis, P., et al.: Hiding in plain sight: a longitudinal study of combosquatting abuse. In: Proceedings of the 2017 ACM SIGSAC Conference on Computer and Communications Security, CCS 2017, pp. 569–586. ACM, New York (2017). https://doi.org/10.1145/3133956.3134002
16. Le, A., Markopoulou, A., Faloutsos, M.: PhishDef: URL names say it all. In: 2011 Proceedings IEEE INFOCOM, pp. 191–195, April 2011. https://doi.org/10.1109/INFCOM.2011.5934995
17. Ma, J., Saul, L.K., Savage, S., Voelker, G.M.: Beyond blacklists: learning to detect malicious web sites from suspicious URLs. In: Proceedings of the 15th ACM SIGKDD International Conference on Knowledge Discovery and Data Mining, KDD 2009, pp. 1245–1254. ACM, New York (2009). https://doi.org/10.1145/1557019.1557153

18. Marchal, S., François, J., State, R., Engel, T.: Phishstorm: detecting phishing with streaming analytics. IEEE Trans. Netw. Serv. Manag. **11**(4), 458–471 (2014). https://doi.org/10.1109/TNSM.2014.2377295

19. Marchal, S., Saari, K., Singh, N., Asokan, N.: Know your phish: novel techniques for detecting phishing sites and their targets. In: 2016 IEEE 36th International Conference on Distributed Computing Systems (ICDCS), pp. 323–333, June 2016. https://doi.org/10.1109/ICDCS.2016.10

20. McGrath, D.K., Gupta, M.: Behind phishing: an examination of phisher modi operandi. In: Proceedings of the 1st Usenix Workshop on Large-Scale Exploits and Emergent Threats, LEET 2008, pp. 4:1–4:8. USENIX Association, Berkeley, CA, USA (2008). http://dl.acm.org/citation.cfm?id=1387709.1387713

21. Norvig, P.: Natural Language Corpus Data: Beautiful Data, February 2019. http://norvig.com/ngrams/

22. Reeder, R.W., Felt, A.P., Consolvo, S., Malkin, N., Thompson, C., Egelman, S.: An experience sampling study of user reactions to browser warnings in the field. In: Proceedings of the 2018 CHI Conference on Human Factors in Computing Systems, CHI 2018, pp. 512:1–512:13. ACM, New York (2018). https://doi.org/10.1145/3173574.3174086

23. Sahoo, D., Liu, C., Hoi, S.C.: Malicious URL detection using machine learning: a survey. arXiv preprint arXiv:1701.07179 (2017)

24. Sheng, S., et al.: Anti-phishing phil: the design and evaluation of a game that teaches people not to fall for phish. In: Proceedings of the 3rd Symposium on Usable Privacy and Security, SOUPS 2007, pp. 88–99. ACM, New York (2007). https://doi.org/10.1145/1280680.1280692

25. Sheng, S., Wardman, B., Warner, G., Cranor, L., Hong, J., Zhang, C.: An empirical analysis of phishing blacklists. In: Sixth Conference on Email and Anti-Spam (CEAS), California, USA (2009)

26. Verizon: 2018 data breach investigations report, February 2019. http://www.verizonenterprise.com/resources/reports/rp_DBIR_2018_Report_en_xg.pdf

27. Verma, R., Das, A.: What's in a URL: fast feature extraction and malicious URL detection. In: Proceedings of the 3rd ACM on International Workshop on Security and Privacy Analytics, IWSPA 2017, pp. 55–63. ACM, New York (2017). https://doi.org/10.1145/3041008.3041016

28. Wang, W., Shirley, K.: Breaking bad: detecting malicious domains using word segmentation. arXiv preprint arXiv:1506.04111 (2015)

29. Whittaker, C., Ryner, B., Nazif, M.: Large-scale automatic classification of phishing pages. In: NDSS 2010 (2010). http://www.isoc.org/isoc/conferences/ndss/10/pdf/08.pdf

30. Yang, W., Zuo, W., Cui, B.: Detecting malicious urls via a keyword-based convolutional gated-recurrent-unit neural network. IEEE Access **7**, 29891–29900 (2019). https://doi.org/10.1109/ACCESS.2019.2895751

31. Zhang, Y., Hong, J.I., Cranor, L.F.: Cantina: a content-based approach to detecting phishing web sites. In: Proceedings of the 16th International Conference on World Wide Web, WWW 2007, pp. 639–648. ACM, New York (2007). https://doi.org/10.1145/1242572.1242659

Network Cloudification
(Extended Abstract)

Yefim Dinitz[1], Shlomi Dolev[1], Sergey Frenkel[1,2], Alex Binun[1],
and Daniel Khankin[1(✉)]

[1] Department of Computer Science, Ben-Gurion University of the Negev,
Beersheba, Israel
{dinitz,dolev}@cs.bgu.ac.il, {binun,danielkh}@post.bgu.ac.il
[2] Institute of Informatics Problems of FRC "Computer Science and Control",
Moscow, Russia
fsergei51@gmail.com

Abstract. An automatic cloudification scheme for Software-Defined Networks (SDN) is presented. An existing network consisting of communicating network elements and network functions should be served by several cloud suppliers. The costs of cloudifying each element and each function at each cloud and the costs of transferring a unit of information between and inside clouds are given. The scheme selects in which cloud to locate each element and function in a way that minimizes the total cost of cloudifying and communication. As well, an online distributed protocol of seamless transformation of the existing network communication to the clouds is presented.

1 Introduction

The migration of an entire network including all of the network elements and functions in a cost efficient and seamless manner, is becoming a standard operation. Such *network cloudification* is motivated by the need for maintenance of the original network, as well as a technique for mitigating cyber-attacks by moving the attack target upfront prior to an anticipated attack.

Network Virtualization (NV), which is the abstraction of a network from the underlying physical viewpoint, allows customized routing, multiple network architectures, efficient utilization of infrastructure resources, and customized infrastructure-abstracted services.

In *Software-Defined Networking* the control plane and the data plane are separated. The control logic is centralized in a software-based entity called the *controller*, which communicates with switches using a standardized protocol, such as OpenFlow [9]. SDN can serve as a platform for flexible creation of directly programmable virtual networks with custom control logic. As a complementary technology, SDN advents NV and *Network Functions Virtualization*

Research supported by Neptune - The Israeli Network Consortium, and partially supported by Rita Altura trust chair in Computer Science.

S. Dolev et al. (Eds.): CSCML 2019, LNCS 11527, pp. 249–259, 2019.
https://doi.org/10.1007/978-3-030-20951-3_22

(NFV), which allows the implementation of network functions in software. The significant advantage of NFV is the reduction in the number of middleboxes [8]. This results in increased flexibility, network resilience, on-demand network services, and service reliability.

Related Work. In the scope of SDN and NFV, several papers proposed methods for seamless network re-configurations. The works [1,2] proposed multicast-based methods for route updates, introducing the Make&Activate-Before-Break approach (MABB). Using MABB, the original configuration remains active until the correct working of the new configuration is achieved and verified, and only then the old configuration is dismantled. So, it may occur that two configurations may exist simultaneously, thus providing a seamless user experience during the configuration update. Further, the above-mentioned papers were extended to several, dependent via shared links, pairs of routes in [3] and to policy preserving routes updates in [4]. Moreover, paper [3] described a high-level protocol for network updates in MABB, which serves as a guideline for the protocol in this paper. Paper [4] suggested the Route Readiness Verifier (RRV) tool for implementing the high-level protocol for MABB on the low level of OpenFlow specifications.

The paper [5] demonstrates a dynamic construction of a virtual network with custom routing in the context of SDN. Thus, showing the possibility of using SDN for creating virtual network on-demand for virtualized services. The paper [10] considers virtual network embedding via path splitting and path migration. In this work, we do not consider path mapping but assume that network connectivity remains unchanged. Also, we do not map virtual nodes to bundles of physical nodes but *virtualize* each node to its designated cloud.

Problem Description. We represent the original communication network by weighted graph $G = (V, E, w)$. The set of vertices V represents the network elements, e.g., a router or a *Network Function* (NF). The set of edges E represents the network links connecting network elements. The weight function on the graph edges represents the communication load between the network elements.

We are given a fixed set of cloud providers, denoted by $CP = \{CP_i\}$, in which we can virtualize the network elements. For each cloud provider, we are given a *price list*, which includes a cost for hosting (virtualizing) each network element. The communication cost per unit varies, depending on whether the connected network elements reside in the same cloud or in different clouds, and on the concrete clouds that the elements belong to.

The first goal of our research is to achieve the lowest cost for virtualizing the given network. See Fig. 1 for an example. Figure 1a shows a possible given network that we are required to cloudify. Figure 1b shows the graph representation of the network in Fig. 1a. Figure 2 shows a possible cloudification outcome of the network in Fig. 1b.

Note that putting network elements in the same cloud may reduce the communication cost between them, but might increase the communication cost with other elements. For example, consider Fig. 2. Assume that we move the cloud image of node e from CP_3 to CP_1. On one hand, it may be that hosting e at CP_1

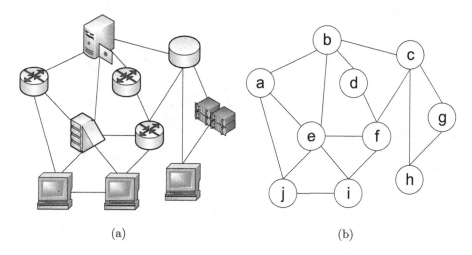

(a)   (b)

Fig. 1. Example of the original network and its graph representation.

is cheaper, and the communication costs between e and nodes a and b already residing in CP_1 would be decreased. On the other hand, the communication cost between e and nodes i and j that stay in CP_3, and maybe also between e and the elements in other cloud providers would increase.

The second goal of our research is developing a seamless way of on-line replacement of the data transfer and processing from the original network to its cloudified image. The trivial approach may be to stop transmitting the flow, to wait until all sent packets have been processed by the original network and reach their destination, to copy the states of all network functions to their cloud images, and only then to resume transmitting the flow via the clouds. However, this would involve a considerable delay. Therefore, we need to develop a communication protocol between the SDN controller and the network elements and functions during the replacement process, so that the user will not feel any delay in the transmission and processing of the flow, as much as possible. Of course, the FIFO order of processing flow packets by network functions, and the order of the arrival of packets at their destination should be preserved during the on-line replacement process.

Paper Outline. In this work, we suggest two ways of finding optimal/near-optimal cloudification of a given network to a given set of clouds. In addition, we describe a high-level protocol for seamless on-line data transfer and processing from the original network to its, previously chosen, cloudified version.

In Sect. 2, we formalize our optimization problem and describe its reduction to Integer Linear Programming (ILP), while referring to a recognized ILP solver. Section 3 suggests a heuristic method for finding a near-optimal cloudification solution. Section 4 describes a high-level protocol for seamless on-line transfer from the original network to its given cloudified version.

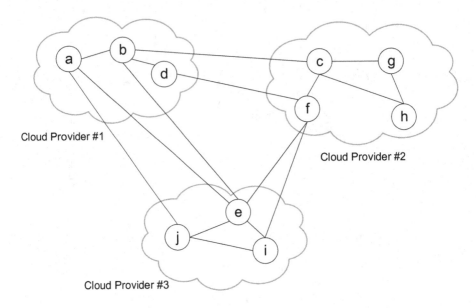

Fig. 2. Possible cloudification of the network in Fig. 1b.

2   Formal Problem Statement and Its Reduction to ILP

The formal cloudification problem instance is defined:

– by graph $G = (V, E, w)$ of the network to be cloudified, with the function w of link loads,
– by the set $\mathcal{P} = \{CP_p\}$ of the cloud providers,
– by the "entrance fee" costs $c_p \geq 0$ of using cloud CP_p,
– by the costs $c_{vp} \geq 0$ of virtualizing node $v \in V$ to cloud CP_p, and
– by the costs $c_{pq}^t \geq 0$ of transferring a unit of data from cloud CP_p to cloud CP_q (including the case $p = q$).

Our goal is to find a minimal total cost cloudification function $f : V \to \mathcal{P}$.

The cloudification problem is NP-hard, by the following reduction of one of the versions of the k-way cut problem to it. As a consequence, we cannot hope to find an effective algorithm for solving the cloudification problem.

The basic version of k-way cut problem is as follows. Given an undirected graph $G = (V, E)$ with an assignment of weights to the edges $w : E \to N$ and an integer $k \in \{2, 3, \ldots, |V|\}$, a k-way cut is a partition of V into k disjoint sets $C_1, C_2, \ldots, C_k$; its weight is

$$\sum_{i=1}^{k-1} \sum_{j=i+1}^{k} \sum_{(u,v) \in E, u \in C_i, v \in C_j} w(v_1, v_2).$$

We look for a k-way cut of the minimal weight. In the problem version that we choose, we also specify k vertices and ask for the minimum k-cut which separates these vertices among each of the sets. The NP-hardness of this version of the k-way cut problem is proved in [6].

For any instance of the chosen version of k-way cut problem (with the notion as above), we define the corresponding instance of the cloudification problem as follows. Let us denote the specified k vertices by v_i, $1 \leq i \leq k$. Let us set $M = \sum_{e \in E} w(e) + 1$. The cloud providers CP_p correspond to C_p, $1 \leq p \leq k$, all costs c_p are 0, all costs c_{vp} equal M, except for all $c_{v_p p}$ which are 0, all costs c^t_{pq} are 1, except for the case $p = q$ where they are 0. The equivalence of the above two problem instances is implied by the following two observations:

1. For all mappings f satisfying $f(v_p) = C_p$ for all p, the pre-images of C_p form a k-way cut as required, and vice versa, so that the cost of f equals the weight of that k-way cut and that common weight is at most $M - 1$.
2. For all other mappings, the cost of f is at least M.

We suggest a reduction to Integer Linear Programming (ILP) in order to solve the cloudification problem. The motivation for our choice is as follows. One of the currently widely used ways to solve hard problems is via a recognized solver, which works successfully for many large problem instances in a reasonable time. The most known solvers of this kind are those for SAT (satisfiability) and LP (linear programming) problems. Also software Gurobi [7] is known to work quite efficiently in many large ILP instances.

In what follows, we describe the ILP problem instance that finds an optimal cloudification function. The variable set is composed of the three following groups of Boolean variables:

- $\{x_{vp}\}$, $v \in V, CP_p \in \mathcal{P}$, where $x_{vp} = 1$ iff $f(v) = CP_p$;
- $\{y_{epq}\}$, $e = (v, v') \in E, CP_p, CP_q \in \mathcal{P}$, where $y_{epq} = 1$ iff $f(v) = CP_p$, $f(v') = CP_q$.
- $\{z_p\}$, $CP_p \in \mathcal{P}$, where $z_p = 1$ iff cloud CP_p is used by f at least once.

The goal function and the restrictions are as follows:

$$\text{Minimize} \sum_{v \in V, CP_p \in \mathcal{P}} c_{vp} \cdot x_{vp} + \sum_{e \in E \ CP_p, CP_q \in \mathcal{P}} c^t_{pq} \cdot y_{epq} + \sum_{CP_p \in \mathcal{P}} c_p \cdot z_p, \quad (1)$$

subject to:

$$\sum_{CP_p \in \mathcal{P}} x_{vp} = 1 \qquad (v \in V),$$

$$\sum_{CP_q \in \mathcal{P}} y_{epq} = x_{vp} \qquad (e = (v, v') \in E, \ CP_p \in \mathcal{P}),$$

$$\sum_{CP_p \in \mathcal{P}} y_{epq} = x_{v'q} \qquad (e = (v, v') \in E, \ CP_q \in \mathcal{P}),$$

$$x_{vp} \leq z_p \qquad (v \in V, \ CP_p \in \mathcal{P}),$$

Let us show that the above ILP problem instance is equivalent to the given optimization problem instance. Pay attention that all the variables have values either 0 or 1, as required by their meanings. The first equation implies that each network node is mapped to exactly one cloud. The second and third equations imply that each network link (v, v') goes from the cloud image of node v to the cloud image of node v'. The inequality $x_{vp} \leq z_p$ implies that the flag z_p is set to 1 if at least one network node is mapped to cloud CP_p. Subject to all those conditions, the set of feasible solutions and goal function of the ILP problem instance correspond exactly to those of the original problem instance, as required.

3   Heuristic Approach

It might be that the ILP solution is computationally too expensive. For example, for very large networks it will take a very long time to find a solution. We propose the following heuristic approach for such instances.

The heuristic is based on repeated random choice of a feasible solution. Each time a random solution is selected, a greedy algorithm is used to move to a *neighboring* configuration with minimal cost, until a solution with (local) minimum cost is reached. A solution is *neighbor* to another solution iff there exists exactly one element or function (e.g., firewall) instance that is assigned to a different cloud, while all other element or function instances are identically located in both solutions. Note that the number of (solution) neighbors is proportional to the number of cloud suppliers multiplied by the number of elements and functions. Moreover, the cost of configuring neighboring solutions can be easily computed based on the cost of the configuration.

The heuristic stops when successive k randomly chosen solutions and following greedy traces from the chosen solution do not improve the already known minimum cost. There, k is a constant chosen in-advance.

Another possible criteria for terminating the heuristic is the ratio of a lower bound on the total cost. An obvious cost lower bound is the sum of the minimal costs of the function instances (according to the cost lists of the cloud suppliers) discarding the communication costs among the function instances. After each iteration of the heuristic, one can compute the ratio between the minimal cost found by the heuristic so far and the lower bound. The heuristic stops when either no improvement in the cost can be obtained in k successive iterations or the ratio of a lower bound is good enough prior to reaching k.

4   Launching the Cloudified Version

In this section, we assume that the cloudified configuration N_C of the original network N is already chosen. Moreover, that the cloud controllers already sent instructions to the corresponding cloud elements to begin working together as a virtual copy of N. The remaining task is arranging a seamless ("smooth") way of launching the virtual version N_C instead of N. The challenge is to arrange the replacement process so that sources and destinations of the flows transferred via N would not feel any trouble from changing the flow route from N to N_C, except for as small as possible temporary delays in arriving packets during the update period.

We assume that the clouds have sufficient resources, so that no congestion on links and routers can be expected. In such case, we can execute re-routing of all flows independently in-parallel. In what follows, we suggest the launching protocol for the case of a single flow. By the above assumption, treating all flows accordingly to the same protocol would solve the re-routing problem as above in the general case. In order to simplify the presentation, we assume that there is a single controller C instructing the entire cloudified configuration N_C, which is in contact with elements of N, when needed; in the general case of several controllers, they should be synchronized.

Let us denote the flow by F, its source by s, its destination by d, its current route from s to d by R, and its new (cloudified) route from the cloud image s_C of s to the cloud image d_C of d by R_C. Source s is linked to s_C and d_C is linked to destination d. Each one of R and R_C contains the same (virtual) network functions processing the packets in F. It is essential that all packets in F: a) will arrive at d in the original order of their sending from s, and b) will be processed by each network function in the same order. Moreover, the protocol should be arranged so that the state of any network function NF_C on R_C when processing each packet p would be the same as if all packets sent before p were processed by its prototype NF on R. The delays in transferring the packets should be made as minimal as possible.

A special challenge is as follows. We assume that when the cloudified route R_C is ready and packets of F begin to be sent along it, their transfer along R_C might be slow at the beginning and will be accelerated to a reasonable level only after some period of time. In order to avoid delays in the packets transfer to d, we would like to duplicate F along both routes R and R_C during the stabilization period at R_C. During that period, the packets arriving at d along R_C will be ignored. Only when the transfer rate along R_C would stabilize, the flow transfer along R could be canceled.

For illustration see Fig. 3. In the figure, we assume that R contains network functions $NF1$ and $NF2$ and that R_C contains their copies $NF1_C$ and $NF2_C$.

Launching Protocol. In the following protocol, we use the notion of a "marker". It is a special packet labeled as belonging to F, with some instructions provided by C on its specific processing by certain routers on its way. Anytime when sending instructions to s by C is mentioned, it means interacting with s via its image s_C; similarly on sending messages to C by d, made via d_c. The protocol items are executed in the logical order.

- The controller C sends marker m_0 to s, to be forwarded along R_C and to be returned to C by d.
- When m_0 arrives at C, the controller C instructs d_C: (a) to buffer all packets of F arriving via the last link of R_C, and (b) to inform the controller permanently on the rate of arrival of such packets.

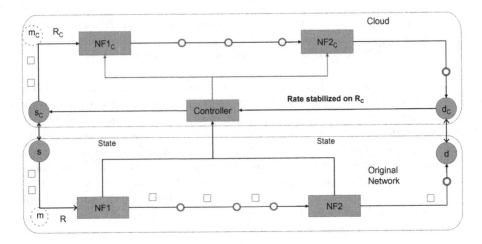

Fig. 3. Illustration to the launching protocol

- The controller C sends marker m along R, to be returned to C by d, and marker m_C to s, to be forwarded along R_C and to be returned to C by d_C. The controller instructs s to duplicate all packets of flow F to the first link of R_C, while keeping sending them along R.
- When marker m arrives at some network function NF, a special instruction at m commands NF to send its state S to C. When state S arrives at C, it is forwarded to the cloudified copy NF_C of NF.
- When marker m_C arrives at copy NF_C of some network function NF, a special instruction at m_C commands NF_C to suspend processing the packets of F, by buffering them up to receiving the state of NF from C. When that state is received, it is installed at NF_C. After that, processing of F at NF_C is released: the buffered packets of F are processed first, and when the buffer becomes empty, the buffering of F at NF_C is canceled.
- After marker m arrives at C, and C also decides that the packets arrival rate on R_C is stabilized at a reasonable level, the controller does the following. It sends: (a) marker m' along R, to be returned to C by d, and (b) marker m'_C to s to be forwarded along R_C and to be buffered at d_C as all other packets of F, with informing C on its buffering. Besides, it instructs s to cancel the duplication of F, sending the further packets of F on R_C only.
- When marker m' arrives at C, and C is also informed by d_C on the buffering of m'_C, the controller C instructs d_C: (a) to erase all the packets up to m'_C, included, from the buffer of F, and (b) to release forwarding the packets of F to d: the buffered packets of F are processed first, and when the buffer becomes empty, the buffering of F at d_C is canceled.

Let us briefly show the correctness and efficiency of the protocol.

- When m_0 arrives at C, the entire route R_C is known to be ready for using it for F. The controller waits for that moment before beginning the usage of R_C in order to ensure real transmitting along R_C.

- When marker m arrives at some network function NF, this means that all packets sent along R before the beginning of duplication were already processed by NF. At that moment, the current state of NF is exactly the state that NF_C should begin processing the packets of flow F from. Accordingly, the suspending and releasing processing at NF_C as in the protocol is exactly what is needed for the correctness of the processing of flow F at NF_C. Besides, the way of state transferring as in the protocol is as efficient as possible in SDN.
- Waiting for both the arrival of marker m at C, meaning that all packets of F sent along R before the beginning of duplication at s were already accepted at d, and for the report on stabilization of the arrival rate of F on R_C is exactly what is needed to C for initializing dismantling route R at the earliest possible moment.
- The arrival of marker m' at C means that all packets of F sent along R before the finishing of duplication at s were already accepted at d. After that, the report of d_C on buffering m'_C means that the packets of F arriving at d_C after m'_C (i.e., those sent along R_C after canceling the duplication) should be forwarded to d. Exactly this is arranged at d_C by the protocol.

Launching Variants and Discussion. Let us describe briefly two specific cases, implying some changes in arranging the launching of the cloudified route of F.

1. It may happen that we are sure that the transfer rate on route R_C will be reasonable from the very beginning of its work. Then, we could cancel the duplication of packets of F as above, so that each packet of F will arrive at d only once. In order to keep the FIFO order of processing of F at d, the controller instructs d to buffer all packets of F arriving on R_C. This buffering will be canceled by the controller only when marker m will arrive at C. After that, processing of the packets of F arriving at d_C via R_C is released: the buffered packets, if any, are processed first, and when the buffer becomes empty, the buffering is canceled.
2. It may happen that processing of F by (some of) network functions on R involves changes in some global data base, so that the double processing of packets by both those functions and their cloudified versions would be wrong. In such a case, we can send the copies of real packets of F on R_C with a special instruction not to process them by the copies of such network functions. If also this would not be possible, we can send dummy packets of F along R_C, waiting for the stabilization rate of their arrival at d_C. (Note that it might happen that canceling the processing of packets of F at network functions at R_C would imply a not so adequate measuring of the arrival rate of those packets at d_C.)

We would like to mention that the protocol provided in Sect. 4 is a high-level one not only for saving place in the paper and attention of the reader. The OpenFlow protocol suffers from the lack of feedback from switches/routers to the controller on finishing the execution of operations. Therefore, composing a low level protocol as above based OpenFlow encounters problems. This results in a need of including sometimes heavy and/or time-consuming additions to the protocol and even a need of enhancing OpenFlow specifications. See [4] for some suggestions in this direction.

5   Conclusions

We presented the first seamless network cloudification scheme. The scheme is composed of: (1) techniques for determining an optimal assignment of network elements and functions to cloud suppliers, and (2) an on-line communication protocol for re-routing to the chosen cloud virtual elements and functions during regular operation in a seamless manner.

In the framework of future work on our research, it would be useful to take a deeper look at whether the cloudification problem has similarities with other known optimization problems related to the cloud, in what concerns definitions and used methods of solution. Besides, an experimentation related to our results is needed. The restrictions on the problem size implied by the current ILP solvers could be cleared up. An investigation that shows how good is the suggested heuristic in practice could be made. The comparison of the results achieved by the suggested heuristic and by ILP solvers could be made too.

References

1. Delaët, S., Dolev, S., Khankin, D., Tzur-David, S., Godinger, T.: Seamless SDN route updates. In: 2015 IEEE 14th International Symposium on Network Computing and Applications, pp. 120–125 (2015). https://doi.org/10.1109/NCA.2015.24

2. Delaët, S., Dolev, S., Khankin, D., Tzur-David, S.: Make&activate-before-break for seamless SDN route updates. Comput. Netw. **147**, 81–97 (2018). https://doi.org/10.1016/j.comnet.2018.10.005

3. Dinitz, Y., Dolev, S., Khankin, D.: Dependence graph and master switch for seamless dependent routes replacement in SDN (extended abstract). In: 2017 IEEE 16th International Symposium on Network Computing and Applications (NCA), pp. 1–7. https://doi.org/10.1109/NCA.2017.8171386

4. Dinitz, Y., Dolev, S., Khankin, D.: Make&activate-before-break: policy preserving seamless routes replacement in SDN. In: Lotker, Z., Patt-Shamir, B. (eds.) SIROCCO 2018. LNCS, vol. 11085, pp. 34–37. Springer, Cham (2018). https://doi.org/10.1007/978-3-030-01325-7_6

5. Dolev, S., Khankin, D.: Monitorability bounds via expander, sparsifier and random walks. In: El Abbadi, A., Garbinato, B. (eds.) NETYS 2017. LNCS, vol. 10299, pp. 307–321. Springer, Cham (2017). https://doi.org/10.1007/978-3-319-59647-1_23

6. Goldschmidt, O., Hochbaum, D.S.: Polynomial algorithm for the k-cut problem. In: 1998 29th Annual IEEE Symposium on Foundations of Computer Science (FOCS 1988), pp. 444–451 (1988)

7. Gurobi Optimization: Gurobi optimizer, 2019 (2019). http://www.gurobi.com

8. Kreutz, D., Ramos, F.M., Verissimo, P.E., Rothenberg, C.E., Azodolmolky, S., Uhlig, S.: Software-defined networking: a comprehensive survey. Proc. IEEE **103**(1), 14–76 (2015)

9. ONF: OpenFlow Switch Specification Ver 1.5.1. Open Networking Foundation. https://www.opennetworking.org/software-defined-standards/specifications/

10. Yu, M., Yi, Y., Rexford, J., Chiang, M.: Rethinking virtual network embedding: Substrate support for path splitting and migration. SIGCOMM Comput. Commun. Rev. **38**(2), 17–29 (2008). https://doi.org/10.1145/1355734.1355737

New Goal Recognition Algorithms
Using Attack Graphs

Reuth Mirsky[✉], Ya'ar Shalom[✉], Ahmad Majadly[✉], Kobi Gal[✉],
Rami Puzis[✉], and Ariel Felner[✉]

Ben-Gurion University of the Negev, Beersheba, Israel
{dekelr,yaarsh,ahmadmaj,kobig,puzis,felner}@bgu.ac.il

Abstract. Goal recognition is the task of inferring the goal of an actor given its observed actions. Attack graphs are a common representation of assets, vulnerabilities, and exploits used for analysis of potential intrusions in computer networks. This paper introduces new goal recognition algorithms on attack graphs. The main challenges involving goal recognition in cyber security include dealing with noisy and partial observations as well as the need for fast, near-real-time performance. To this end we propose improvements to existing planning-based algorithms for goal recognition, reducing their time complexity and allowing them to handle noisy observations. We also introduce two new metric-based algorithms for goal recognition. Experimental results show that the metric based algorithms improve performance when compared to the planning based algorithms, in terms of accuracy and runtime, thus enabling goal recognition to be carried out in near-real-time. These algorithms can potentially improve both risk management and alert correlation mechanisms for intrusion detection.

1 Introduction

Attack Graphs combine vulnerabilities, exploits, assets, and connectivity among the nodes in a computer network into a singe concise model that encompasses all attack scenarios where an attacker can reach its goal [4,30]. Attack graphs have been used in past to asses the security risk of a computer network [33], improve resilience of the network by patching vulnerabilities that are the most important for the overall network security, optimize sensors placement [29], correlate alerts for efficient intrusion detection [37], penetration testing [39] and more.

One of the most challenging and yet important problems in security operations management is reconstructing the attack scenario to understand how did the attacker breach the network and recognizing the adversary's goals to anticipate his future actions [2,22,34]. Goal recognition is a key AI problem that deals with reasoning about an actor's goals according to a sequence of observed actions [45]. This paper studies the goal recognition problem for time-critical security settings where up to date insights about the possible attack goals and yet unobserved attacker's actions should be presented to the analyst by the recognizer.

© Springer Nature Switzerland AG 2019
S. Dolev et al. (Eds.): CSCML 2019, LNCS 11527, pp. 260–278, 2019.
https://doi.org/10.1007/978-3-030-20951-3_23

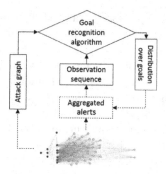

Fig. 1. Components of the proposed approach.

Consider an attacker that aims to take control of a target node in a communication network. Following the initial penetration an attacker establishes presence in the victim computer network and perform a series of actions consisting of lateral movements, privilege escalations, etc. up until reaching the target node. These actions represent its attack plan. An Intrusion Detection System (IDS) monitors the nodes in the network and detects malicious behavior of potential attackers in with certain accuracy. The alerts produced by IDS are mapped to their respective hosts. Preliminary inspection of logs and sensory information may infer the tools and exploits used in the course of attack execution. Given these (noisy) observations the goal recognition task is to infer the most probable goal (target node) of the attacker as well as its plan for achieving this goal.

There are two challenges facing goal recognition in this setting. First, the recognition must be done in near real time in order to be able to counter the attack as soon as possible. Thus, we seek algorithms with short running times. However, existing plan recognizers rely on making calls to costly planning algorithms during runtime. Second, the incorrect observations, including false positive/false negative alerts, hinder the goal recognition task using standard algorithms, thus the proposed goal recognition algorithm must be robust to noisy and partial observations.

While several works have tried to reason about probabilistic goal recognition for cyber security, they were evaluated theoretically [13,15] or using toy problems [6,25], all using various relaxations that do not apply to real time settings. In addition, while there exist planning algorithms for goal recognition [32,35,42,45], they require running off-the-shelf planners online as part of the recognition task of determining the most likely goals. The planner, which is the computational bottleneck of these approaches, is called at least once for each goal so as to be able to compare the observed actions to the optimal plan to that goal. This paper enhances existing approaches as well as introduces new approaches for goal recognition, which reduce the number of times the planner is called, making them significantly more efficient, without hindering their empirical performance. The main advantage of our new approaches is that they reduce and even eliminate the need to call planners online.

Figure 1 summarizes our proposed framework, working in a pipeline with existing intrusion detection approaches that correlate and aggregate alerts [1, 8]. A PDDL representation of the attack graph (Fig. 1 left) is generated from the network (Fig. 1 bottom). Alerts generated by an IDS deployed within the network are compiled into observations (Fig. 1 middle). The inputs for the goal recognition algorithm (Fig. 1 top) are the attack graphs and the alerts. The goal recognition algorithm outputs a distribution over the goals of the potential attacker (Fig. 1 right), which can be potentially used by the IDS to refine future alerts. The components presented in this work are represented with solid lines, where other components are represented using dashed lines.

This paper makes the following contributions:

1. We enhance the benchmark planning-based algorithm for goal recognition [35] to real time settings by reducing its time complexity and allowing it to better handle noisy and missing observations. This is described in Sect. 4;
2. In Sect. 5 we introduce a new family of goal recognition algorithms that completely avoid running planners in the recognition phase. Importantly, our algorithms execute such planners in a preprocessing phase and their output can be shared by many online queries on the same network. We describe novel metrics to compute the distance between the actor's observed actions and the optimal plan to the goal (calculated in the preprocessing phase);
3. Finally (in Sect. 6) we experimented with of all these algorithms on attack graphs representing a real world network and analyze the pros and cons of each of the approaches. Our metric-based algorithms always run faster than the planning-based approaches, even on noisy observations. In addition, they provide equal or better predictions except for input with missing observations, where the planning-based approaches are superior.

2   Goal Recognition

We follow a recent line of research known as *goal recognition as planning* [35]. The input is a planning theory, usually described in PDDL, and a set of possible goals. The output is one of the goals or a distribution over all possible goals. This opened a line of algorithms that execute planners to find plans to the goal with or without the observations [12,23,36,41,42,44]. Some works added landmark-based heuristics [31] and cost propagation [10] to the planning algorithms.

We next briefly mention some basic concepts in this research direction, as presented by Ramírez and Geffner [35], simplified for brevity. In a goal recognition problem, there is an observer and an actor, and the observer needs to infer the goal of the actor. The input to the observer is a theory description and a sequence of observations.

Definition 1. *A* **Theory Description** *(D) is a tuple* $D = \langle S, A, G, I, C \rangle$, *where S is a set of states, A is a set of actions representing transitions from state to state, $G \subseteq S$ is the goals the actor can achieve and $I \in S$ is the initial state. C is a cost function mapping any action in A to a real number.*

Each state in S is represented by a set of predicates. All predicates in the state are assumed to hold true in the environment, and predicates that do not appear in the state are assumed to be false. Each action a in A has preconditions and effects, describing what should be true in the state before executing a and after its execution, respectively. They are both represented as a set of predicates. The actor is assumed to plan by choosing a goal and then carrying out a plan for reaching this goal.

Definition 2. *A plan for achieving a goal $g \in G$ is a sequence of actions $a_1, \ldots, a_n$ such that:*

- *The execution starts at I (the predicates in the precondition of the first action are all in I).*
- *For each $a_i \in A$, the state before the execution contains all of the predicates in a_i's precondition.*
- *After executing all actions in the sequence, all the predicates in g are true.*

Given a theory with n possible goals, $g_1, \ldots, g_n$ and an observation sequence $O = o_1, \ldots, o_t$, a solution to the goal recognition problem is a distribution over the goals such that $p(g_i \mid O)$ is the likelihood that the actor is pursuing goal g_i given O.

In order to suit a real world scenario we make the following assumptions. First, we allow noisy observation sequences by assuming that it contains false alerts, i.e., the input may falsely contain some observed actions. Second, we assume that there are some missing observations, i.e., some actions of the actor are not reported in the input sequence.

2.1   Other Goal Recognition Works

While we use the *goal recognition as planning approach*, we note that there are different approaches to represent a theory in goal recognition, including policy-based, library-based and others [3,45].

For example, YAPPR [14] takes as input a plan library and can output both a distribution over the goals of the actor and predictions about future actions. DOPLAR [20] extended YAPPR using probabilistic reasoning to reach better performance, at the cost of completeness.

These works require to model the settings using a plan library, which is difficult to elicit and susceptible to faults. Bui [7] uses particle filtering to provide approximate solutions to goal recognition problems. These works all rely on a model of the plans or strategies that the actor can execute.

While adversarial goal recognition was investigated in the past [13,21,22,25], none of the works mentioned above have combined a PDDL description that can represent an attack graph in order to recognize the goals of an attacker. Masters and Sardina [24] recently presented an intersection of deception with goal recognition in the context of path-planning. We next dive deeper into the attack graph representation.

3 Attack Graphs

3.1 Definitions and Background

An attack graph is a description of a network that comprises hosts, their vulnerabilities, and their connectivity to one another [5]. Formally,

Definition 3. *An attack graph A is an undirected graph $A = \langle V, E \rangle$ where:*

- *V is a set of vertices, such that each $v \in V$ represents a single host in the network. Each host has a single operating system (OS) and it contains a list of installed software. Each piece of such software can hold a vulnerability, which can be exploited by an attacker to gain control over the host.*
- *E is a set of edges, representing the connectivity of the hosts.*

A potential attacker traverses over the network by reaching a host and gaining control over it. After gaining control over a host, all of its neighbors become accessible to the attacker. The attacker then may choose to traverse one of these edges and try to take control over the corresponding neighbor. Gaining control requires to exploit a specific vulnerability, which depends on a combination of the OS and software available on that host. In the real world, vulnerabilities might be different from one computer to another even if they share similar OS and software, and there is no way to detect the specific vulnerabilities in advance.

Swiler et al. [43] presented an automatic tool for generating an attack graph representation of a computer network. This work has been extended to handle networks at a larger scale [27]. Later, Noel and Jajodia [29] presented a method for optimizing the placement of intrusion detection system (IDS) sensors and prioritizing IDS alerts using attack graph analysis.

Recent studies continued improving the attack graph generation and analysis approaches toward automated pentesting [9,16,18,40].

Hoffmann [18] discusses the suitability of the "CyberSecurity" benchmark at the International Planning Competition (IPC) and analyzes the importance of factoring uncertainty when it comes to understanding the behavior of potential hacking actors. However, analysis of an attack graph has only focused on mapping of vulnerabilities and pentesting, rather than on realtime intrusion detection.

A different line of research does utilize the attack graphs for prioritizing alerts generated by IDS. These works use attack graphs for alert correlations [28,37,46,47]. Modern attacks are getting more complex and the number of alerts emerging from the system increases significantly. Reasoning about temporal order and causality of alerts, allows detecting false negative and false positive alerts more efficiently [28,37]. This line of research has done a great deal in refining the alerts, but did not reason about the ultimate goal of the attacker.

In this work, we feed the alerts as observations into a goal recognizer with the attack graph as the underlying theory description. Thus, the attack graph is used directly for online goal recognition. Under these settings, the attacker might wish to obfuscate the attack by executing irrelevant actions, or the alert aggregation might produce false positive alerts which are not part of a valid attack.

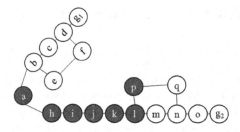

Fig. 2. Simple network example.

3.2   Attack Graphs as PDDL

The theory we use is based on the work of Shmaryahu [38], and was compiled to match the requirements of our goal recognition algorithms. The theory has 4 types of variables, $host, os, sw, vuln$, representing hosts, operating systems, software and vulnerabilities respectively.

These types are used to define 7 parameterized predicates:

1. (LNK, h_1, h_2) - true if h_1 and h_2 are linked by an edge on the attack graph.
2. $(CNTRL, h)$ - true if the attacker controls h.
3. (SW, h, s) - true if the software s is installed on the host h.
4. (OS, h, o) - true if host h runs operating system o.
5. $(VLNR, v, h)$ - true if vulnerability v exists in host h.
6. $(MATCH, o, s, v)$ - true if vulnerability v exists in software s under operating system o.
7. $(ACCESS, h)$ - true if host h is accessible by the attacker.

In addition, the PDDL theory defines the actions the attacker can perform:

- $GetAccess(h_1, h_2)$, which has the preconditions that h_1 and h_2 are linked and that the attacker is controlling h_1. The effect is that host h_2 is now accessible to the attacker.
- $RunSW(h, sw, os, v)$ is the action used to run some software sw on the system os of host h, that might exploit a vulnerability v. This combination might be a valid software usage, or an exploit.

Using these actions, reaching a goal is a process of traversing to a host, then running some software on it in order to gain control over it. This is done repeatedly, until taking control on a connected path to the goal host.

Throughout the paper we will use the following running example from Fig. 2. This example includes a network with 18 nodes, each node represents a host in the network, and edges represent connectivity between nodes. An attacker commences at host a, with the goal of attacking node g_1 or g_2. Observations (hosts that are controlled by the attacker) are shown as dark nodes. The cost of connecting ($GetAccess$ action) and gaining control over a node ($RunSW$ action) is 1. Note that there is no notion of backtracking because there is no need to undo a connection. Once control has been established for a given node, it can always be used to connect to hosts at adjacent nodes.

4 Planning-Based Algorithms for GR

All of the methods we present rely on calling a planning algorithm to compute the cost of potential plans that the actor may be pursuing. Running the planner is the computational bottleneck of all these approaches, especially in realtime systems as the one that is the focus of this paper. The main advantage of our new approaches is that they reduce and even eliminate the need to call such planners online. We distinguish between calls to the planner that are done *offline*, that is in a preprocessing phase before observations have been received and *online*, during recognition.

We first describe two variants of the benchmark planning-based algorithm by Ramírez and Geffner [35] (denoted R&G). Then, we will introduce our further enhancement to this approach. In the next section we will introduce a new metric-based approach for GR.

Table 1. Number of calls to planner by each method

	offline	online
R&G		$2|G|$
M&S	$|G|$	$|G|$
R&G+	$|G|$	$|G|$
PED	$|G|$	
APC	$|G|$	

4.1 The R&G Approach

Ramírez and Geffner [35] introduced the first planning-based algorithm for goal recognition (R&G).

Given a theory D and an observation sequence O, R&G introduces a modified theory that takes into account O:

Definition 4. *A **Modified Theory** (D') given D and O is a tuple $D' = \langle S, A', G, I, C \rangle$, where for each action $a \in A$, there is a parallel action in A' with a possible extra predicate in its effects list: p_a when a is the first observation in O and $p_b \rightarrow p_a$ when b is the action that immediately precedes a in O.*

In a transformed theory and given a plan π, the fluent p_a is true after executing π if and only if π satisfies all observations in O until a. Using D', R&G use an off-the-shelf classical planner in order to calculate the following two quantities:

1. The minimal cost of achieving the goal g_i such that the plan satisfies all observations in O. This cost is denoted $C_i(O)$;

2. The minimal cost of achieving the goal g_i such that it does not satisfy the observation sequence O. This cost is denoted $C_i(\neg O)$.

The term $L(g_i \mid O)$ measures the proximity (in terms of cost) between a plan that is directly based on the observations and the optimal plan for reaching g_i and is defined to be:

$$L(g_i \mid O) = C_i(O) - C_i(\neg O) \tag{1}$$

Intuitively, as the difference grows larger, this increases the likelihood of goal g_i given O. Given a set of observations $O = \{o_1, \ldots, o_t\}$, the R&G algorithm computes the terms $C_i(O)$ and $C_i(\neg O)$ by calling the planner once for each goal g_i given O during the recognition phase. For full details we refer to their paper. The total number of calls to the planner is $2|G|$ (see Table 1).

The score given for goal g_i given the observation sequence O is defined as:

$$p(g_i \mid O) \cong \frac{1}{e^{\beta \cdot L(g_i \mid O)} + 1} \tag{2}$$

Where $0 \leq \beta \leq 1$ is used to soften the impact of observations that deviate from the optimal plan. After $p(g_i \mid O)$ is calculated for all $g_i \in G$, they are normalized to provide a valid probability distribution.

Consider the running example from Fig. 2 and the observation sequence $O = \{a, h, i, j, k, l, p\}$. The optimal plan for g_1 is $P_1 = \{a, b, c, d, g_1\}$. P_1 is also the optimal plan that does not fully follow O (it does not visit any node in O except a). Similarly, the optimal plan for g_2 is $P_2 = \{a, h, i, j, k, l, m, n, o, g_2\}$. P_2 is also the optimal plan that does not fully follow O (it does not visit node p). We assume a stardard cost of 1 for gaining control over each of the nodes. Thus we have that $C_1(P_1) = 5$ and $C_2(P_2) = 10$. Assuming $\beta = 1$ (for the sake of the example), we get the following values:

$$L(g_1 \mid O) = C_1(O \cup \{b, c, d, g_1\}) - C_1(P_1) = 6$$
$$L(g_2 \mid O) = C_2(O \cup \{q, n, o, g_2\}) - C_2(P_2) = 1$$
$$p(g_1 \mid O) \cong \frac{1}{e^6 + 1} = 0.002, \quad p(g_2 \mid O) \cong \frac{1}{e^1 + 1} = 0.269$$

After normalization we get the goal probabilities $p(g_1 \mid O) = 0.007$ and $p(g_2 \mid O) = 0.993$.

4.2   The M&S Approach

Masters and Sardina [23] (M&S) suggested replacing the $C_i(\neg O)$ term with C_i, the minimal cost of achieving the goal g_i without reference to the observations. This term can be computed by calling the planner offline without referencing the observations. The resulting likelihood formula is as follows:

$$L(g_i \mid O) = C_i(O) - C_i \tag{3}$$

For example, in Fig. 2, C_2 is simply the cost of the optimal plan $C_2(P_2)$. The number of calls to the planner in this approach includes $|G|$ offline calls, for computing C_i for each goal, and $|G|$ online calls, for computing $C_i(O)$ for each goal (see Table 1). M&S showed that using this approach significantly improves computation time with similar performance to R&G.

In our example, given the same observation sequence O, we get the same probability measures for the goal likelihoods of g_1 and g_2.

4.3   Improvement 1: Realtime Reasoning and Generalization (R&G+)

We can use the insight from M&S to improve the R&G approach for the case in which there is a single optimal plan. Let P_i be the optimal plan that is associated with C_i and computed offline. During the recognition process, we distinguish between two cases.

1. If $O \subseteq P_i$, that is, the observations in O are part of the optimal plan, then by definition of $C_i(O)$, we get that $C_i(O) = C_i$.
2. Otherwise, there is at least one observation in O that is not in the optimal plan. By definition of $C_i(\neg O)$ we get that $C_i(\neg O) = C_i$.

Note that it is always the case that C_i is a lower bound for both $C_i(O)$ and $C_i(\neg O)$.

We use the above insight to compute $L(g_i \mid O)$ using Eq. 1. We make a single offline call to the planner to compute C_i and a single online call to compute $C_i(O)$ or $C_i(\neg O)$ as needed (see Table 1). Determining whether $O \subseteq P_i$ can be done in linear time.

In our running example, suppose $O = \{a, h, i, j, k, l\}$. M&S will output the same plan P_2 twice, once for calculating C_2 (offline) and once for calculating $C_2(O)$ (online). Our new improvement will get that P_2 is in fact a plan that contains all observations from O, and will choose to calculate $C_2(\neg O)$, thus will be able to produce the same probability distribution as R&G, with the improved online runtime of M&S.

4.4   Improvement 2: Sunk Cost (SC)

In this approach we vary the R&G algorithm to consider the cost already attributed to the actor from executing the actions in O. Consider the following two scenarios based on the example in Fig. 2. In the first scenario, the observation sequence O includes the first six steps of a plan $\{a, h, i, j, k, l\}$, and a seventh observation $\{p\}$ that is not a part of the optimal plan (shown in the figure). Such an action may possibly be the cause of a faulty alert or due to a strategic actor (in Sect. 6 we consider the effect of noise on our algorithms). Here, we get that $C_2(O) = 11$ and $C_2(\neg O) = 10$ and the likelihood $L(g_2 \mid O)$ of goal g_2 is 1 (Eq. 1).

In the second scenario, an observation sequence O' includes $\{a\}$, the first out of the ten steps of the optimal plan for g_2, and then a non-related action $\{b\}$. We get that $C_2(O') = 6$, $C_2(\neg O') = 5$ and the likelihood $L(g_2 \mid O') = 1$. In both scenarios, the observation sequence includes a single non-related action, and the score of goal g_2 is the same $p(g_2 \mid O) = p(g_2 \mid O') = 0.27$. However, if an actor has already put the effort and executed six out of ten steps, it is more plausible that g_2 is the goal, compared to the case when only one action was executed.

We can augment the original R&G formalism to reason about the cost that is already incurred by the actor to carry out the actions in the observation sequence. To this end we vary the β parameter, which was a constant value in the original R&G approach, as follows:

$$\beta = \frac{1}{min(C_i(\neg O), C_i(O))}. \tag{4}$$

Using this measure to compute the likelihood in Eq. 1 reduces the effect of noisy actions in a way that considers their proportion to the optimal plan and the observation sequence. Given this modification, we get a revised score over the goals by which goal g_2 is more likely under O than O'. ($p(g_2 \mid O) = 0.56, p(g_2 \mid O') = 0.44$).

Because all of the above approaches used Eq. 1 to compute the goal probability, we can modify the β parameter in any of them. In the empirical results we use R&G+ with the sunk-cost β.

5   Metric-Based Algorithms for GR

All of the three methods of the R&G family described above must run a planner at least once online, during the recognition phase. We propose a new paradigm for goal recognition that is based on distance metrics between the optimal plan (that is computed offline) and the observation sequence. It does not require online planner executions and so its online performance is much faster. Furthermore, as we show in the Empirical Section, in many cases their recognition is better than the R&G family. We begin with a naive distance metric.

5.1   Plan Edit Distance (PED)

The term *edit distance* usually refers to distance between sequences or sets by counting the number of edit actions needed to transform one sequence to the other. Here, we define an edit distance metric between action sequences which can be partial or complete plans.

The edit distance between two action sequences A and A' is defined as the number of actions that separate them.

$$D_{edit}(A, A') = |A \Delta A'| \tag{5}$$

Given an observation sequence O and a goal g_i we define a distance metric that only depends on the number of actions.

$$D(g_i, O) = D_{edit}(P_i, O) \tag{6}$$

where P_i and O are the action sequences in the optimal plan for achieving g_i (computed offline) and an observation sequence O, respectively. This metric prefers plans which have executed more steps that are part of the optimal plan. It is naive, as it does not reason about the order by which the actions have taken place, or the actual cost of executing the different actions. However, as we show in the Empirical Section, in some cases this metric can be effective.

The score of goal g_i (given O) is defined as:

$$p(g_i \mid O) \cong \frac{1}{D(P_i, O) + 1} \tag{7}$$

We normalize to get a probability distribution. We label this algorithm by Plan Edit Distance (PED).

To summarize, we need to call the planner $|G|$ times offline to compute the optimal plan P_i. Computing $D(g_i, O)$ can thus be done in linear time online.

Using this metric for the same sequence in the running example, $O = \{a, h, i, j, k, l, p\}$, we get that $D(O, P_1) = 10, D(O, P_2) = 5$ and the goal probabilities are $p(g_1 \mid O) = 0.352$ and $p(g_2 \mid O) = 0.647$.

5.2   Alternative Plan Cost

A more informed distance metric between the observations and the optimal plan is based on the Alternative Plan Cost (APC) of Felner et al. [11]. Their approach finds a minimal mapping from the states visited when executing O and the states visited when executing the optimal plan for a given goal g_i.

Let $S = (s_1, \ldots, s_n)$ and $S' = (s'_1, \ldots, s'_m)$ be two sequences of states. Out of the several mappings suggested by Felner et al. [11], we chose a Time Dimension Mapping $M(S, S')$ from the states in S to the states in S'. A time dimension mapping is monotonic, meaning that given a mapping M with $M(s_i) = s'_j$ and $M(s_{i+l}) = s'_k$ (for some $l > 0$), it must hold that $j < k$. This property guarantees consistency over the order in which the states are visited in S and S'.

Given some distance measure between individual states termed D_{base}, we choose the minimal monotonic mapping M that minimizes the average distance between S and S':

$$D_\rightarrow(S, S') = \min_{M: S \rightarrow S'} \frac{\sum_{i=1}^{|S|} D_{base}(s_i, M(s_i))}{|S|} \tag{8}$$

The APC approach can capture more complex relationships than PED, depending on the D_{base} metric that is selected to measure distance between states. Given an observation sequence O and a goal g_i, let S to be the sequence of states visited while executing O and S' be the sequence of stated visited while executing P_i (the optimal plan to g_i). The distance between O and P_i is defined as:

$$D_\rightarrow(g_i \mid O) = D_\rightarrow(S, S') \tag{9}$$

Consider the running example from Fig. 2. Reaching each node x is associated with a state s_x. The set of states in S is $\{s_a, s_h, s_i, s_j, s_k, s_l, s_p\}$ such that each $s_i \in S$ corresponds to observation $o_i \in O$. The set of states in S' is $\{s_a, s_h, s_i, s_j, s_k, s_l, s_m, s_n, s_o, s_{g_2}\}$ such that each $s_i \in S'$ corresponds to action p_i in the optimal plan P_2. The distance D_{base} between individual states is defined as the cost of the shortest path between one state to the other. The minimal time dimension mapping from O to P_2 maps any state that also exists in the optimal plan to itself, and the state s_p that deviates from the optimal plan is mapped to s_m.

$$\forall s \in \{s_a, s_h, s_i, s_j, s_k, s_l\}, \quad M(s) = s$$
$$M(s_p) = s_m$$

We have that $D_\rightarrow(g_i \mid O) = 2/7$, because $D_{base}(s_p, s_m) = 2$ and 0 for all other s, and $|O| = 7$.

One issue with the definition $D_\rightarrow$ is that it does not reason about the differences in the size of the optimal plan and the observation sequence. In the above example, if the goal of the actor was m, we get the same mapping $D_\rightarrow$ as for goal g_2. To account for this issue we also need to consider the reverse mapping $D_\leftarrow(g_i|O)$ from S' to S. The APC distance metric between O and g_i averages both measures:

$$APC(g_i \mid O) = (D_\rightarrow(g_i \mid O) + D_\leftarrow(g_i \mid O))/2 \tag{10}$$

Each of the two mappings maintains the monotonicity property. Finally, the score of a goal g_i given an observation sequence O is

$$p(g_i \mid O) \cong \frac{1}{APC(g_i \mid O) + 1} \tag{11}$$

Again, this is normalized to get a probability distribution.

The minimal time dimension mapping from P_2 to O maps any state in the optimal plan that exists in the observation sequence to itself, otherwise it is mapped to s_p (which preserves monotonicity).

$$\forall s \in \{s_a, s_h, s_i, s_j, s_k, s_l\}, \quad M(s) = s$$
$$\forall s \in \{s_m, s_n, s_o, s_{g_2}\}, \quad M(s) = s_p$$

Thus, we get that the mapping cost from O to P_2 is 2/7 and the mapping cost from P_2 to O is 10/10 (because the distance between p and o, for example, is 3 – one need to reach m, n, o in order to reach o, since l was already reached or alternatively reach q, n, o and $|P_2| = 10$), and together $APC(g_2 \mid O) = 2/7 + 10/10 = 1.29$.

For this method, we need $|G|$ offline calls to the planner to compute the optimal plan for each goal. Also we can build the D_{base} metric offline. The online component of this approach is to find the mapping between the observation sequence and the optimal plan, which takes $\mathcal{O}(|O| \times |P_i|)$ for each goal $g_i \in G$ (Fig. 3).

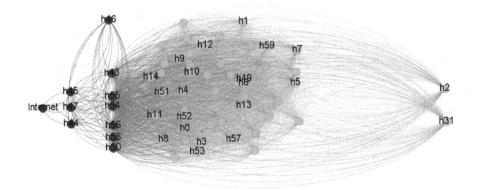

Fig. 3. An illustration of the network used in this work

6 Empirical Evaluation

In this section we provide an empirical comparison between the different goal recognition algorithms. The specific attack graph we use in our evaluations contains 60 hosts. The network architecture as well as the operating systems and software ran by each host was aggregated directly from a real network, that of a large research university.

The vulnerabilities data was randomly generated such that each host has 15 possible vulnerabilities. The initial state in the network is labeled "Internet" and is the entry to all connections in the system. We fixed nodes h_2 and h_{31} as two possible goals for the attacker. The theory was encoded in PDDL as described in Sect. 3.2.

All of the algorithms were implemented in Python, calling the FF planner [17] when required. The algorithms are R&G, M&S, R&G+SC (R&G+ with our varied β), Plan Edit Distance (denoted PED). For the Alternative Plan Cost (denoted APC) algorithm, we used the landmark-based distance suggested by Hoffmann et al. [19].

We simulated attacks targeting host #31 using optimal plans to the goals generated by the FF planner [17]. First, we deleted actions from these plans. Then, we added noisy data to simulate false positive alerts by adding some actions that are not part of the plan.

6.1 Prediction Quality

First, we examined whether the goal with the highest probability predicted is indeed the actual goal. Figure 4 shows the probability distribution on our two goals. The left blue bar is the probability predicted for the real goal (#31) while the right orange bar is for the other goal (#2). As seen in this figure, all of the algorithms gave goal #31 the highest probability, meaning that they managed to capture the true goal. APC gave the highest probability, while PED was close behind it.

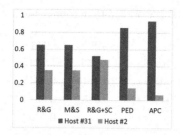

Fig. 4. Probability distribution for multiple goals

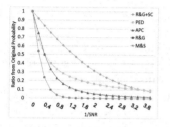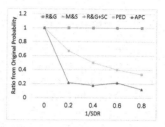

Fig. 5. Probability decline with noisy observations on left (False Positives) and missing observations on right (False Negatives)

The planning-based algorithms gave the true goal the same score (before normalization), but R&G+SC gave the other goal a higher score, thus after the normalization, the true goal's probability declined. This highlights the drawback in giving more influence to the β parameter, which has a dampening effect – while it is beneficial to reduce the decline in probability given noisy observations, it also give high probability to less likely plans.

6.2   Noisy Observations

Next, we looked at different false information that can interrupt the recognition process. When trying to perform an intrusion, an attacker is likely to try and obfuscate the attack. These efforts can lead to False Positive alerts.

Figure 5 (left) shows the probability decline for all recognition algorithms as more observations are noisy. The x-axis shows the Signal to Noise Ratio (SNR) which represents the number of false observations that were injected to the original plan in comparison to the length of the original plan, and the y-axis represents the relative decline in probability as more noise is introduced. As seen from this figure, R&G and M&S give the exact same values and are the less robust to noise and the probability declines fast when introducing noisy observations. R&G+SC is the best to deal with noise due to the plan-length normalization of the cost. PED and APC both perform better than R&G and M&S. Thus, all our new three algorithms outperformed the previous ones along this measure.

Table 2. Runtime comparison

	Offline	Online
R&G	0	1.7237
M&S	0.8210	0.8345
R&G+SC	0.6451	0.6578
PED	0.7251	0.0002
APC	686.7375	0.3246

6.3   Missing Observations

The second property examined is the algorithms' sensitivity to actions that are missing from the observations. This can be either because some of the actions of the attacker were not recognized or because the attacker managed to hide its actions from the alert system, or due to the fact that the attack is still ongoing and not all of the attack steps have yet been executed. Figure 5 (right) shows the probability decline for all recognition algorithms as more actions are missing. The x-axis is Signal Drop Ratio (SDR), representing relative proportion of the number of actions that were removed from the original plan, and the y-axis represents the relative decline (the original probability was normalized to 1) in probability of the goal as more data is missing. The planning-based algorithms give the same results and are more robust to missing observations, as they complete the needed missing actions anyway as part of their solution.

By contrast, both PED and APC reason about the proportion of the plan that was executed. This results in a decline in the probability returned by these algorithms.

6.4   Running Times

Finally, a desired attribute of a goal recognizer in an intrusion detection system is the ability to make a recognition in real-time. Table 2 shows the online and offline runtimes (measured in seconds) of each algorithm. They reflect the differences in computation between the algorithms: R&G and R&G+SC require to run the planner once more per goal, to compute an alternative plan given the observations. PED is the lightest and requires to compute the difference between the actions in the optimal plan and the observation sequence. APC requires to find the landmarks achieved in the observation sequence (a traversal over the list of landmarks) and then to compute the edit distance of two sequences of predicates. This makes it the slowest method during offline planning. PED is the fastest and APC is about an order of magnitude faster than R&G and SC, as it does not require to run a planner during recognition. Thus, both new distance-based algorithms are much faster but have an internal tradeoff. PED is faster but is less robust to noise and its prediction quality (See Fig. 4). Each algorithm has also a different cost in its preprocessing: all algorithms require to find an optimal plan for each goal. Additionally, APC requires to extract the set of landmarks for each goal, a process that takes more than an order of magnitude longer than the other algorithms, but is performed offline.

7   Summary, Discussion and Conclusions

This paper presented goal recognition algorithms on attack graphs for intrusion detection. It utilizes state-of-the-art goal recognition algorithms using planning, proposed a new algorithm to this family that is more adjusted to the challenges of attack graphs, and then proposed a new approach for goal recognition and offers two algorithms to tackle specific challenges that are interesting in the context of an intrusion detection system. All of the algorithms are evaluated on a real-world network and simulated attacks.

The empirical results show that all algorithms manage to deal with missing observations and false positives, while having the highest probability always assigned to the correct goal. However, there is a clear tradeoff between the algorithms in terms of robustness to noise and time.

The first group of presented algorithms (R&G, M&S and R&G+SC) handle missing observations by extrapolating the observation sequence. This means that they are robust to missing observations, but this comes at the cost of runtime. The PED and APC algorithms do not require to run a planner on the observation sequence, thus in real-time the running costs are smaller. The latter does require the extraction of all possible landmarks, but it can be performed offline. They are even better than the previous planning-based algorithms in their online runtime and the prediction quality.

One limitation of the study is that it assumes a deterministic planner that returns a single optimal plan. In many cases k (optimal) plans exist. To find k-optimal or k-best plans one needs to execute a planner k times. This becomes costly in terms of time [42], which is less desirable for real-time intrusion detection. Furthermore, finding k plans may not be cost-effective in our case as k-best plans to the same goal have many overlaps and are very similar, as opposed to plans to different goals which have much fewer overlaps if any [26].

An interesting research direction is to find new algorithms for real-time goal recognition that take advantage of the network structure given by the attack graph. The authors believe that this structure can be used to enhance the distance metric between states, and later be used with the alternative plan cost calculation presented in Felner et al. [11].

References

1. Al-Mamory, S., Zhang, H.: A survey on IDS alerts processing techniques. In: The 6th WSEAS International Conference on Information Security and Privacy (2007)
2. Ang, S., Chan, H., Jiang, A.X., Yeoh, W.: Game-theoretic goal recognition models with applications to security domains. In: Rass, S., An, B., Kiekintveld, C., Fang, F., Schauer, S. (eds.) Decision and Game Theory for Security. LNCS, vol. 10575, pp. 256–272. Springer, Cham (2017). https://doi.org/10.1007/978-3-319-68711-7_14

3. Avrahami-Zilberbrand, D., Kaminka, G.: Fast and complete symbolic plan recognition. In: International Joint Conference on Artificial Intelligence (2005)
4. Azer, M.A., El-Kassas, S.M., El-Soudani, M.S.: Security in ad hoc networks: from vulnerability to risk management. In: 2009 Third International Conference on Emerging Security Information, Systems and Technologies, SECURWARE 2009, pp. 203–209. IEEE (2009)
5. Backes, M., Hoffmann, J., Künnemann, R., Speicher, P., Steinmetz, M.: Simulated penetration testing and mitigation analysis. arXiv preprint arXiv:1705.05088 (2017)
6. Bisson, F., Kabanza, F., Benaskeur, A.R., Irandoust, H.: Provoking opponents to facilitate the recognition of their intentions. In: AAAI (2011)
7. Bui, H.: A general model for online probabilistic plan recognition. In: International Joint Conference on Artificial Intelligence, vol. 3, pp. 1309–1315 (2003)
8. Chyssler, T., Burschka, S., Semling, M., Lingvall, T., Burbeck, K.: Alarm reduction and correlation in intrusion detection systems. In: DIMVA, pp. 9–24 (2004)
9. Durkota, K., Lisý, V., Bosanský, B., Kiekintveld, C.: Optimal network security hardening using attack graph games. In: International Joint Conference on Artificial Intelligence, pp. 526–532 (2015)
10. E-Martin, Y., R-Moreno, M., Smith, D.: A fast goal recognition technique based on interaction estimates. In: Twenty-Fourth International Joint Conference on Artificial Intelligence (2015)
11. Felner, A., Stern, R., Rosenschein, J., Pomeransky, A.: Searching for close alternative plans. AAMAS **14**, 211–237 (2007). https://doi.org/10.1007/s10458-006-9006-1
12. Freedman, R., Zilberstein, S.: Integration of planning with recognition for responsive interaction using classical planners. In: AAAI, pp. 4581–4588 (2017)
13. Geib, C., Goldman, R.: Plan recognition in intrusion detection systems. In: 2001 Proceedings of the DARPA Information Survivability Conference and Exposition II, DISCEX 2001, vol. 1, pp. 46–55. IEEE (2001)
14. Geib, C., Maraist, J., Goldman, R.: A new probabilistic plan recognition algorithm based on string rewriting. In: ICAPS, pp. 91–98 (2008)
15. Goldman, R., Friedman, S., Rye, J.: Plan recognition for network analysis: preliminary report. In: AAAI Workshops on PAIR (2018)
16. Gonda, T., Shani, G., Puzis, R., Shapira, B.: Ranking vulnerability fixes using planning graph analysis. In: IWAISe: First International Workshop on Artificial Intelligence in Security, p. 41 (2017)
17. Hoffmann, J.: FF: the fast-forward planning system. AI Mag. **22**(3), 57 (2001)
18. Hoffmann, J.: Simulated penetration testing: from "Dijkstra" to "Turing Test++". In: ICAPS, pp. 364–372 (2015)
19. Hoffmann, J., Porteous, J., Sebastia, L.: Ordered landmarks in planning. J. Artif. Intell. Res. **22**, 215–278 (2004)
20. Kabanza, F., Filion, J., Benaskeur, A.R., Irandoust, H.: Controlling the hypothesis space in probabilistic plan recognition. In: International Joint Conference on Artificial Intelligence, pp. 2306–2312 (2013)
21. Le Guillarme, N., Mouaddib, A., Gatepaille, S., Bellenger, A.: Adversarial intention recognition as inverse game-theoretic planning for threat assessment. In: ICTAI, pp. 698–705. IEEE (2016)
22. Lisý, V., Píbil, R., Stiborek, J., Bošanský, B., Pěchouček, M.: Game-theoretic approach to adversarial plan recognition. In: ECAI, pp. 546–551. IOS Press (2012)
23. Masters, P., Sardina, S.: Cost-based goal recognition for path-planning. In: AAMAS, pp. 750–758 (2017)

24. Masters, P., Sardina, S.: Deceptive path-planning. In: International Joint Conference on Artificial Intelligence 2017, pp. 4368–4375. AAAI Press (2017)
25. Mirsky, R., Gal, Y., Tolpin, D.: Session analysis using plan recognition. In: Workshop on User Interfaces and Scheduling and Planning (UISP) (2017)
26. Mirsky, R., Stern, R., Gal, Y., Kalech, M.: Plan recognition design. In: AAAI, pp. 4971–4972 (2017)
27. Noel, S., Jajodia, S.: Managing attack graph complexity through visual hierarchical aggregation. In: Workshop on Visualization and Data Mining for Computer Security, pp. 109–118. ACM (2004)
28. Noel, S., Robertson, E., Jajodia, S.: Correlating intrusion events and building attack scenarios through attack graph distances. In: Computer Security Applications Conference (2004)
29. Noel, S., Jajodia, S.: Optimal IDS sensor placement and alert prioritization using attack graphs. J. Netw. Syst. Manag. **16**(3), 259–275 (2008)
30. Ou, X., Govindavajhala, S.: MulVAL: a logic-based network security analyzer. In: 14th USENIX Security Symposium. Citeseer (2005)
31. Pereira, R., Oren, N., Meneguzzi, F.: Landmark-based heuristics for goal recognition. In: AAAI (2017)
32. Pereira, R., Oren, N., Meneguzzi, F.: Plan optimality monitoring using landmarks and planning heuristics. In: PAIR Workshop in AAAI (2017)
33. Poolsappasit, N., Dewri, R., Ray, I.: Dynamic security risk management using Bayesian attack graphs. IEEE Trans. Dependable Secur. Comput. **9**, 61–74 (2012)
34. Qin, X., Lee, W.: Attack plan recognition and prediction using causal networks. In: 2004 20th Annual Computer Security Applications Conference, pp. 370–379. IEEE (2004)
35. Ramírez, M., Geffner, H.: Plan recognition as planning. In: AAAI (2009)
36. Ramírez, M., Geffner, H.: Probabilistic plan recognition using off-the-shelf classical planners. In: AAAI (2010)
37. Roschke, S., Cheng, F., Meinel, C.: A new alert correlation algorithm based on attack graph. In: Herrero, Á., Corchado, E. (eds.) CISIS 2011. LNCS, vol. 6694, pp. 58–67. Springer, Heidelberg (2011). https://doi.org/10.1007/978-3-642-21323-6_8
38. Shmaryahu, D.: Constructing plan trees for simulated penetration testing. In: ICAPS (2016)
39. Shmaryahu, D., Shani, G., Hoffmann, J., Steinmetz, M.: Partially observable contingent planning for penetration testing. In: IWAISe: First International Workshop on Artificial Intelligence in Security, p. 33 (2017)
40. Shmaryahu, D., Shani, G., Hoffmann, J., Steinmetz, M.: Simulated penetration testing as contingent planning. In: ICAPS (2018)
41. Shvo, M., Sohrabi, S., McIlraith, S.: An AI planning-based approach to the multi-agent plan recognition problem. In: PAIR Workshop in AAAI (2017)
42. Sohrabi, S., Riabov, A., Udrea, O.: Plan recognition as planning revisited. In: International Joint Conference on Artificial Intelligence, pp. 3258–3264 (2016)
43. Swiler, L., Phillips, C., Ellis, D., Chakerian, S.: Computer-attack graph generation tool. In: DISCEX, p. 1307. IEEE (2001)
44. Vered, M., Kaminka, G.: Heuristic online goal recognition in continuous domains. In: International Joint Conference on Artificial Intelligence, pp. 4447–4454 (2017)

45. Vered, M., Pereira, R., Magnaguagno, M., Kaminka, G., Meneguzzi, F.: Towards online goal recognition combining goal mirroring and landmarks. In: AAMAS (2018)
46. Wang, L., Liu, A., Jajodia, S.: Using attack graphs for correlating, hypothesizing, and predicting intrusion alerts. Comput. Commun. **29**(15), 2917–2933 (2006)
47. Zhang, S., Li, J., Chen, X., Fan, L.: Building network attack graph for alert causal correlation. Comput. Secur. **27**(5–6), 188–196 (2008)

PeerClear: Peer-to-Peer Bot-net Detection

Amit Kumar, Nitesh Kumar, Anand Handa$^{(\boxtimes)}$, and Sandeep Kumar Shukla

C3I Center, Department of CSE, Indian Institute of Technology, Kanpur,
Kanpur, India
{amitkr,niteshkr,ahanda,sandeeps}@cse.iitk.ac.in

Abstract. A *bot-net* is a network of infected hosts (bots) that works independently under the control of a *Botmaster (Bot herder)*, which issues commands to bots using *command and control (C&C)* servers. Bot-net architectures have advanced over time, to evade detection and disruption. Traditionally, bot-nets used a *centralized client-server architecture* which had a single point of failure but with the advent of peer-to-peer technology, the problem of single point of failure seems to have been resolved. Gaining advantage of the decentralized nature of the P2P architecture, botmasters started using P2P based communication mechanism. *P2P bot-nets* are highly resilient against detection even after some bots are identified or taken down. P2P bot-nets provide central frameworks for different cyber-crimes which include DDoS (Distributed Denial of Service), email spam, phishing, password sniffing, etc. In this paper, we propose *PeerClear*, an approach for identifying P2P bot-nets using network traffic analysis. *PeerClear* uses a two-step process for identifying P2P bots. In the first step, the hosts involved in P2P traffic are detected and in the second step, the detected hosts are further analyzed to detect bot-nets. Our evaluation shows that our approach *PeerClear* outperformed several recent approaches and achieves a high detection rate of 99.85%. We also implement multiple new approaches reported in the literature and test on the same dataset to evaluate their relative performance.

Keywords: Bot-net · Dynamic analysis · Machine learning ·
Malware detection

1 Introduction

According to world Internet user statistics [1], almost 50% of the world population is connected to the Internet. Individuals use it for communication, banking transaction, information seeking, leisure purpose, etc. Organizations use it for their business, connecting with their customers, partners, suppliers, etc. Such widespread usage of the Internet leads us to the new era of cyber crimes. According to IANS (Indo-Asian News Service), cyber crimes in India rose 19 times between 2005 to 2014 and this is based only on the attacks that have been exposed. Currently, there is a combat between hackers and defense agencies.

© Springer Nature Switzerland AG 2019
S. Dolev et al. (Eds.): CSCML 2019, LNCS 11527, pp. 279–295, 2019.
https://doi.org/10.1007/978-3-030-20951-3_24

Among all the cyber attacks, the bots seem to be one of the biggest players in many cyber crimes. Bots are infected machines under the control of an attacker and the network of such infected machines constitutes the bot-net [23]. Bot malware turns the computer into a robot that carries out tasks based on the commands sent to it over the Internet. Bot-nets provide a number of resources to the attackers such as bandwidth, computing power, IP diversity, etc., which allow attackers to commit cyber crimes on a larger scale. According to Vinton Gray Cerf known as the "Father of the Internet", one-quarter of all world computers are part of one or the other bot-net [4].

Realizing the gravity of bot-nets, researchers started studying bot-nets and methods to mitigate them. Traditionally bot-nets used client-server architecture to communicate among themselves, which has a single point of failure and is easier to detect. To make the bot-net resilient against detection, cyber criminals started using new architectures for bot-net communication. Peer-to-Peer (P2P) architecture for bot-net communication comes out to be the most prominent one, avoiding the single point of failure problem of the client-server architecture. One such bot-net is Zeus or Zbot that had become the largest bot-net in the world estimated to affect 3.6 million PCs around the globe according to Damballa [8]. In this paper, we present a new method for P2P bot-net detection and carry out experiments to compare the performance of our method against recently reported methods in the literature.

To summarize our contributions:

- We propose a novel approach, *PeerClear* to detect P2P bot-net over the network using a flow-based approach.
- We have used a two-phase P2P bot-net detection scheme. In the first phase, we identify the P2P hosts on the network and in the second phase, the identified hosts are further analysed to detect P2P bot-nets from P2P-benign applications.
- Our experimental analysis shows that *PeerClear* achieves high detection accuracy of 99.85% which is better as compared to the other authors' work.

In the next section, we discuss the background study of the research. In Sect. 3, we discuss the related work. Section 4 depicts our approach to detect P2P bot-nets. We summarise our results in Sect. 5 and lastly, Sect. 6 concludes the paper.

2   Background

Bot-net is derived from the word *"Robot"* and *"Network."* It is a network of infected hosts or zombies that run automatically and autonomously under the control of an individual or organization. Generally, a bot-net has three working components, first is the attacker, referred to as *botmaster* or *bot herder*, second is the *Bot*, and third is the *Command & Control (C&C)* server.

In bot-nets, the Botmasters directly communicate with the bots using C&C servers. The botmasters are directly connected to the bots because they have a smaller attack domain. However, for bots having larger attack domain such as Zeus [15], Waledac [18], etc., botmaster is connected to the bots through intermediate hosts. These intermediate hosts act as a C&C servers. Nowadays most of the researchers are interested in tracking C&C servers for identifying structures of the bot-net, and these intermediate hosts complicate the process of tracing back the botmaster from detected bots. The most important component in a bot-net is the structure of its command and control channel that prevents the bot-net from being dismantled easily. The communication used among C&C servers and bots can be of the following two types:

- *Push-Based Approach:* In the push based approach, the botmaster pushes the commands into the bots to attack. The advantage of this approach is that the botmaster can instantaneously perform certain tasks through bots. Thus botmaster has higher control over the bots. The main disadvantage of this approach is that the amount of traffic generated is high and two bots infected by the same bot-net, thus having similar traffic patterns, may lead to an easier detection of bots.
- *Pull-Based Approach:* In the pull based approach, the bots periodically receive commands from the server. The server can introduce a random delay while delivering commands, so the bot-net has control over generated traffic. This prevents easy detection of bots and servers. In this approach, instantaneous execution of the command is not possible.

In this work, we are more concerned with P2P bot-net detection, which is a collection of heterogeneously distributed resources connected by a network. The most distinctive difference between client server networking and P2P networking is the existence of *servents* (host that may act both as a server and a client at the same time) [22].

Peer-to-Peer (P2P) Bot-net: P2P bot-nets are the most complex bot-net known so far. The primary objective of P2P bot-nets is to remove or minimize single point of failure problem of the IRC (Internet Relay Chat) /Web bot-nets [21]. In P2P bot-nets, all bots form a P2P network which enables them to communicate and share files across the bot-net. P2P bot-nets help the attacker to inject commands at any point in the network by routing it to all the bots. This activity needs commands to be authenticated to prevent unauthorized injection of commands. Authentication mechanisms such as public key cryptography are often used. The bots need to have access to atleast one other active node to remain connected to a P2P bot-net. For this purpose, some bot-nets use hard-coded lists of peers while some others use network scanning. Examples of P2P bot-net include storm bot-net, first identified around January 2007 [12]. This bot-net infected around 50 million systems worldwide.

3   Related Work

In 2014 Yin et al. proposed a node based detection approach for detecting P2P bot-nets [24]. They extracted network characteristics of individual hosts with time intervals of 10, 20, 30, 60, 180 min. The captured data is sampled for reducing the overhead of the defense system. They have used decision tree classifiers because of its low computational complexity and high performance. They have used only offline traffic and did not evaluate the performance of their approach on online traffic.

Rodriguez-Gomez et al. proposed an approach to detect malicious applications associated with P2P bot-nets based on resources shared by the number of peers in a P2P network [20]. The bot-net resources are the popular resources and have a shorter lifetime as compared to legitimate resources. Therefore, the main inspiration behind the approach is that the resources shared by bots in a P2P network (bot-net resources) will be accessed in a different way than the resources shared by the legitimate users in the P2P network. They trained two models, one for legitimate and other for bot-net resources. Using these models, they have found potential bot-net resources in the P2P network.

Peerminor [13], a pure behavioural system for classifying P2P bots into families, was presented by Kheir et al. They have used a two-stage classifier for this purpose. In the first stage, they have built a classifier to ignore benign P2P traffic and considered only malicious P2P traffic to reduce packet monitoring overhead. In the second stage, they have built one class classifier for known P2P bot families to classify the detected bots into respective families further. *Peerminor* used flow-based features e.g, number of packets sent and received, number of bytes sent and received, flow duration and protocols used. It is the first detection approach that gave information about the type of bot-net infecting the systems. Their training data-set has 794 benign P2P clusters and 1445 malicious P2P clusters. *Peerminor* achieves 97% accuracy for all classes collectively.

Dilon designed a P2P bot detection algorithm using live NetFlow data [10]. NetFlow is a network protocol analyzer for observing network traffic and gathering IP traffic data developed by Cisco. In this work, the Zeus bot-net network traffic was considered and aimed at the detection of individual P2P bots within a network perimeter. For this, they have filtered P2P traffic, the hosts with more than four failed connection is considered as P2P host, and others are discarded. For detecting Zeus, they have used two major features. Firstly, they have used packet ratio, up packets divided by down packets with a threshold of 0.4. Secondly, they have used the traffic patterns. The Zeus bot-net control loop periodically wakes up and contacts peers for P2P network configuration and can be detected by the traffic pattern.

Narang et al. have presented, *PeerShark* [17] for detecting P2P bot-net in the stealthier state (a state where bot-net network activity is almost negligible). *PeerShark* does not require Deep Packet Inspection (DPI). Rather than using the traditional 5-tuple (source IP, source port, destination IP, destination port, protocol) based approaches, they have used a two tuple (port oblivious and protocol oblivious) conversation based approach. They have the following four modules in their model. Firstly, Packet Filtering Module that filter IPv4 packets from network traffic. Secondly, the conversation creation module that creates a list of conversations. Then the conversation aggregation module aggregates conversations into single conversations based on some higher flow-gap value. Finally, the classification module that used supervised machine learning algorithms to train their model. Their training data-set consisted of 50,000 conversations. *PeerShark* used the packet header information of TCP/UDP/IP to extract a set of features such as the duration of the conversation, the inter-arrival time of packets, the amount of data exchanged, a median value of inter-arrival time to classify various P2P applications with an approximate accuracy of 97%.

In another approach, Hojjat et al. [6] proposed a botnet detection based on behavioral analysis of the traffic. The proposed model detects P2P botnets in the command and control phase of the life cycle of the botnet. In this phase, the bot tries to set up a connection to its command and control server and then communicates with the botnet. The proposed model is based on the inferences that bots of a botnet have uniform traffic behavior and bears specific traffic patterns during communication. Hence, the methodology is independent of the content and can also detect P2P botnets which use encrypted traffic. The authors have considered a total of 9930 botnet traffic packets with 3296 extracted flows and 14680 normal traffic packets with 1233 extracted flows. They have used various classifiers such as Bayesian Network Classifier, Naive Bayes Classifier, Support Vector Machine, J48 Decision Tree Classifier, and Random Forest Classifier. The maximum botnet detection accuracy achieved was 99.26% using Random Forest Classifier.

Himanshi et al. [9] proposed a model based on the bot behavior. A two-tier framework was implemented to detect parasitic P2P bots. There are three stages in a P2P botnet lifecycle namely – infection stage, waiting stage, and execution stage. The proposed model detects the bot in the waiting stage i.e. before going into the execution stage. Hence, it did not require any bot signatures. The proposed model considered the features like bot's lifetime in the P2P network, search request intensities, and time correlated behavior for detection of the botnet. The authors have considered 41,941,536 malicious P2P data packets and 25,913,400 Benign Peers packets. The maximum detection accuracy achieved by the proposed model was approx 99%.

In 2016, Alauthaman et al. [5] came up with another P2P botnet detection method which implemented an adaptive multilayer feed-forward NN (Neural Network) using Decision Trees. A network traffic reduction mechanism was introduced to increase the performance. It being a connection-oriented method did not require any Deep Packet Inspection (DPI). Hence, the model was independent of payload and used only the header information of TCP control packets. For feature selection, a classification and regression tree method was used. From these features, a multilayer feed-forward NN was trained using back propagation learning algorithm. The model achieved an accuracy of 99.20%.

Although the above approaches are able to classify or detect the P2P botnet with high accuracy but none of them have sophisticated P2P traffic categorization methodology. They have used a more straight forward approach for categorizing P2P traffic like failed connections threshold, destination diversity threshold, etc. To note that *PeerShark*, the authors have used conversation based approach and they have not differentiated the P2P and non-P2P traffic that we have used in our work. Discarding non-P2P traffic have a greater impact on the computational overhead of the developed system as less traffic needs to be monitored. They have a good P2P traffic categorization method, but they are using the same approach for classifying botnet as used for P2P traffic categorization. Therefore there is a need for a system which can categorize P2P traffic using all properties shown by P2P hosts and has a separate P2P bot detection module for detecting bots using distinctive features shown by P2P botnets. Since the dataset on which these authors calibrated their methods may be different, we have implemented the models reported in [5,6,9,17] and evaluated them on our dataset to obtain a fair comparison.

4   Our Approach

In the previous section, we have discussed various P2P bot-net detection methods proposed by multiple researchers. Studying their approaches, detection methods, and future work, we propose a two-step approach to detect P2P bot-net in the stealthy state (a state where bot-net network activity is almost negligible). Firstly, we have identified all the hosts which are involved in the P2P activity and secondly, we have detected P2P bots in the identified P2P hosts as shown in Fig. 1.

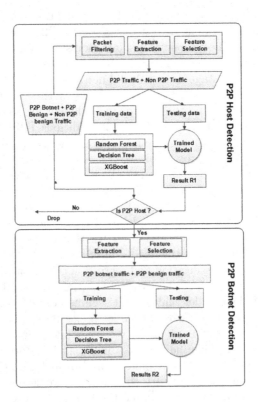

Fig. 1. Flow chart of our approach to detect P2P bot-net.

Dataset. For our experiment we have collected three types of data, i.e., *P2P-Benign, P2P bot-net* and *Non-P2P* network traffic.

- *P2P-Benign network Traffic:* It was collected by 11 distinct hosts which executed five different P2P benign applications (Skype, eMule, μ-Torrent, Frostwire, and Vuze.) for several days.
- *P2P bot-net Traffic:* This data was collected from *Peerrush* [2] dataset which contains the P2P bot-net traffic of Storm [12], Waledac [18], and Zeus [15] and also the P2P bot-net traffic generated from *Vinchuca* bot-net [16].
- *Non-P2P Traffic:* It was obtained from the departmental network which was being observed over five days. Network sniffing tool based on *libpcap* was used to capture the packets.

All the above data was captured in the form of a .pcap file which contains the network information.

4.1 P2P Host Detection

The main aim of this phase is to detect all the hosts which were engaged in P2P activity. It consists of four modules namely packet filter, feature extraction, feature selection and classification.

Packet Filter. In this module, unwanted packets such as multicast, broadcast and DNS generated traffic (P2P network does not use DNS) were filtered out and the rest was sent to feature extraction module as shown in Fig. 2. This filtering reduce the packet monitoring overhead and the processing time.

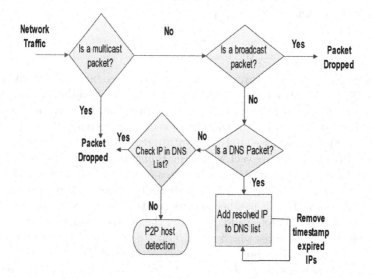

Fig. 2. Packet filter module.

Feature Extraction. To find out the prominent features for the detection of P2P hosts, the distinctive properties shown by the hosts engaged in the P2P activity as opposed to the hosts with Non-P2P activities were studied and discussed as follows:

- *Failed Connections:* In the P2P network, nodes may continuously join and leave the network. To remain connected, the peers must be connected to at least one of the peers. So peers in the P2P network continuously search for new peers. While searching for new peers, many peers may not be available in P2P network because of the continuous process of joining and leaving, so the number of failed connection attempts in the P2P network is usually higher. Regular Internet traffic did not encounter such a high number of failed connection attempts.
- *DNS filter:* Peers in the P2P network operate outside of the DNS system. Peers did not use the DNS queries to search other peers. They get it directly from the overlay network's routing table. Although for connecting to the central server, they may need to make a DNS request, which was very rare. A regular Internet user usually uses the Internet browser to visit some popular websites which were mostly resolved by DNS requests. We implemented this component in the packet filter module.
- *Destination diversity:* Since the IPs of the peers are usually scattered across many different networks, the diversity of IPs (IP domain) contacted by P2P peers in the P2P network is typically large. For all the IPs contacted by a peer, we have computed a set of/16 prefix of each destination IP. It gives an approximate idea of IP domains visited by the peer. The size of this set is the destination diversity of the peer. We have also used *destination diversity ratio* calculated by dividing destination diversity with the total number of distinct IPs contacted by the peers.

Based on the above properties, we have used *tshark* (a network protocol analyzer) [3] tool to extract the features from pcap files (Table 1).

Feature Selection. In feature extraction, we have extracted fourteen features based on the P2P host behavior. However, we found that all the features are not important while training the classifiers. There may be some features which do not affect the performance of the classification or perhaps make the results worse. Therefore, in this section, we apply the feature reduction technique to reduce the dimensionality of the feature vector. Information gain algorithm is used as a measure for feature reduction. As shown in Fig. 3, top 2 to 14 features with highest info-gain score were selected for classification. The final feature vectors consist of the extracted top 10 features because we ran the classifiers on top 2 to 14 features and then ten-fold cross validation, and the accuracy comes out to be maximum for the top 10 features which are demonstrated in Fig. 4. Fourteen features (Table 1) based on the P2P host behavior were extracted. The final feature vector used for the classification is: $<F_2, F_3, F_4, F_5, F_8, F_9, F_{11}, F_{12}, F_{13}, F_{14}, label>$

Table 1. Extracted network traffic features for P2P host detection

Feature_Id	Feature	Description
F_1	ret_count	Retransmitted packet count
F_2	diversity	Destination diversity
F_3	diversity_ratio	Destination diversity ratio
F_4	no_pkt_out	Number of connection attempts made on distinct port
F_5	distinct_ip	Number of distinct IPs contacted
F_6	reset	Reset packets count
F_7	out_of_ord	Out of order packets count
F_8	icmp	ICMP destination unreachable packets count
F_9	flows	Number of packets sent and received
F_10	byte_in	Bytes per packet in forward direction
F_11	byte_out	Bytes per packet in backward direction
F_12	dis_ret_count	Average retransmitted packets per host count
F_13	dup_ack	Duplicate ack packets count
F_14	ctrl_pkt	Total number of control packets (packet without data) sent and received

Classification. The collected traffic data were categorised into two groups, first group is used to train the classifier, and the other group is used to test the classifier. The training group consisted of 70% of the instances, and our testing group consisted of 30% of the instances. For the selection of classification model, we have used 10-fold cross validation on Random forest [11], Decision Tree [19] and XGBoost [7] classifiers to detect P2P hosts from the captured traffic.

For P2P host detection, the data were extracted for three different time windows of 10 min duration and the results are shown in Table 2. The results in terms of true-positive rate (TPR), false-positive rate (FPR), precision and accuracy are summarized in Table 2.

Table 2. P2P host detection results (R1)

Classifier	TPR	FPR	Precision	Accuracy
Random forest	99.91%	0.003%	99.98%	99.93%
Decision tree	99.89%	0.001%	99.92%	99.88%
XGBoost	99.73%	0.001%	99.92%	99.78%

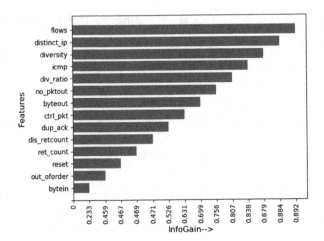

Fig. 3. Information gain

4.2 P2P Bot-net Detection

After the identification of P2P hosts over the network, in this phase, the bot-net was detected from the identified P2P hosts. This phase consists of three modules, i.e., feature extraction, feature selection and classification.

Feature Extraction. For the P2P bot-net detection, the flow-based approach was used and the data was extracted for 1-hour time window, to trace the stealthier nature of P2P bots. A network flow is a set of packets exchanged between two hosts. Network traffic flow is uniquely identified by five tuples ⟨source IP, source port, destination IP, destination port, protocol⟩. The conversation is defined by the help of binary tuple ⟨source IP, destination IP⟩ and vice versa. All the conversations are categorized as port and protocol oblivious. In this work, we have used only flow-based features.

P2P protocols use transport layer protocols to share the files, so both the TCP and UDP traffic are captured for our experimental analysis. To distinguish between the P2P benign traffic and the P2P bot-net traffic, we have focused on *management flows*, i.e., the network traffic which is used to maintain the updated information about the network. Once the bot-net infects any host, in order to remain connected to that host, bot-net continuously sends the control packets as keep-alive messages to the bot. Bots' communication in the waiting state is quite stealthy. These control packets provide useful insights into the bot-net communication pattern.

Moreover, the management flow depends on the protocol design whereas the data flow depends on the user. The data flows are usually regulated by the user interaction with the P2P applications. The usage of the P2P applications varies from user to user. Relying on the management flows allow more universally, user-independent P2P bot-net detection approach. We have not completely discarded the data flows. Some of the features were also obtained from the data flows as well.

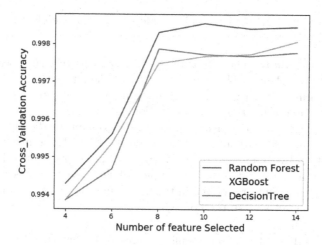

Fig. 4. Ten-fold cross validation

Now the question arises, how to separate the management and data packets. This is because management packets are generally embedded inside the data packets, and sometimes are sent separately. Below are few heuristics considered to separate management from data packets.

- *Inter packet time:* The management packets are exchanged periodically whereas the data packets are sent continuously one after another. Therefore, inter packet time between the data packets are usually very small. On the other hand in the management packets inter packet time is large. We consider only those flows in which inter packet time was greater than a particular threshold θ. For example, consider a packet P_i and packets seen before and after P_i as P_{i-1} and P_{i+1}. Now say inter packet time between packets P_i and P_{i-1} was Δ_{i-1} and that of between P_i and P_{i+11} was Δ_{i+1} then we consider P_i as management packet if Δ_{i-1} and Δ_{i+1} both are greater than θ.
- *Duration of Flow:* P2P network flows are generally long-lasting. Instead of creating a new connection, peers exchange the management packets to keep the connection alive. Same as in the case of the P2P bot-net, to prevent losing connection with a bot, they periodically exchange control messages.

Our main concern is to extract those features which distinguish the P2P bot-net from P2P benign traffic. The communications used by P2P bot are low in volume because the bots are controlled by the bot-master and they continuously communicate with each other to remain connected. Hence, the duration of this communication is large. For P2P benign applications like μ-Torrent, users generally download large files such as music, videos, etc. On the other hand, Bots do not download such large files. Rather they continuously send information to the bot-master. Also, the inter-arrival time between the packets for bots is more as compared to P2P benign applications, because of the reasons discussed above. Therefore by using these features, we can prominently distinguish P2P bot-net traffic from P2P-benign traffic. Table 3 shows the used features captured by *pyshark* [14].

- *Host Access Features:* These features were used to capture the host accessing pattern of the bot-nets. These include features like inter-arrival time of packets, maximum inter-arrival time, minimum inter-arrival time, etc. to capture the distribution of inter-arrival time of flow at any host.
- *Flow Size Features:* These features were used to capture the distribution of both incoming and outgoing flows at a specific host. These include features like packets or bytes sent and received in the flow, to capture their distribution of the flow at any host. Other examples of flow size features include the number of bytes sent or received in the flow, smallest packet seen in the flow, the largest packet seen in the flow, etc.

Table 3. Extracted network traffic features for P2P bot-net detection

ID	Features	Description
F1	mean_inter_time	Mean of the Inter-arrival time between packets
F2	fwd_pkt	Number of packets sent in flow
F3	bkd_pkt	Number of packets received in flow
F4	frwd_bytes	Number of Bytes sent in flow
F5	bkd_bytes	Number of Bytes Received in flow
F6	total_data	Total data sent and received in flow including headers
F7	small_pkt	Smallest packet in flow
F8	large_pkt	Largest packet in flow
F9	max_inter_time	Maximum Inter-arrival time between any two packets in flow
F10	min_inter_time	Minimum Inter-arrival time between any two packets in flow
F11	total_duration	Total duration of flow
F12	pkt_frequency	Packet frequency (flow duration/ number of packets in flow)
F13	mean_fwd_inter_time	Mean inter-time between packets sent in forward direction
F14	mean_bkd_inter_time	Mean inter-time between packets sent in backward direction
F15	max_fwd_inter_time	Maximum inter-time between packets sent in forward direction
F16	min_frwd_inter_time	Minimum inter-time between packets sent in forward direction
F17	max_bkd_inter_time	Maximum inter-time between packets sent in backward direction
F18	min_bkd_inter_time	Minimum inter-time between packets sent in backward direction

Feature Selection. The extracted 18 features based on host access patterns and flow size features were further reduced for bot-net detection. We have used information gain feature selection algorithm to reduce the dimensionality of the feature vector. The top 2 to 18 features with highest info-gain scores were selected (Fig. 5) and respectively used for the classification.

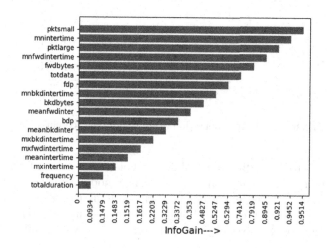

Fig. 5. Information gain

Bot-net Classification. For P2P bot-net detection, we have used the same classification algorithm used in P2P host detection (Random forest, Decision tree, and XGBooost) for the classification of P2P botnet detection. To find the best number of features for the best performance of all selected classifiers, we ran classifiers on 2 to 18 features with the highest info-gain score and obtained results are shown in Fig. 6 and Table 4. The observation of results shows that all the classifier performs with more than 99% accuracy and among them, Random forest outperformed with 99.99% accuracy while using only top 6 features.

Table 4. P2P bot-net detection result (R2)

Classifiers	TPR	FPR	Precision	Accuracy
Random forest	99.98%	0.002%	99.99%	99.99%
Decision tree	99.97%	0.004%	99.97%	99.97%
XGBoost	99.77%	0.024%	99.97%	99.88%

We have also trained the model for P2P bot-net detection using traffic from three bot-nets namely Waledac, Vinchuca, and Zeus. For P2P benign applications, we have used traffic from Skype, eMule, Frostwire, and Vuze. The model

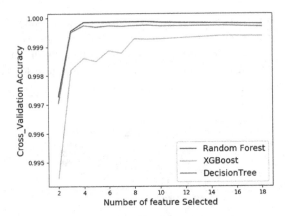

Fig. 6. P2P botnet detection accuracy of selected classifiers

is tested using unseen traffic from a different bot-net i.e. Storm for P2P bot-net and μ-Torrent for P2P benign applications. The model achieves an accuracy of 97% for above-mentioned experiments. This leads us to believe that the approach can be generalized for other bot-net detection. This is perhaps due to the fact that traffic flow features of most P2P bot-nets are very similar.

5   Results and Comparison with Past Work

The overall performance of our system is determined by passing the entire traffic into P2P host detection module. The entire traffic consists of non P2P traffic and P2P traffic. The first module filters P2P hosts from non-P2P hosts. The filtered P2P hosts can be P2P bot-net hosts or P2P benign hosts. This traffic is now fed into the other module i.e. P2P bot-net detection module. P2P Bot-net detection module differentiates P2P bot-nets from P2P benign traffic. The overall accuracy of the system as a whole is 99.85%. The results show that our approach outperforms the results reported previously in the literature. We have also performed experiments using other proposed approaches on our traffic flows to check how much better is our proposed model in terms of accuracy. It shows that our model performs better as compared to their models and achieves better accuracy. We have considered the most recent models discussed in the literature. The results presented in their papers and the ones obtained by using their approach on our dataset are summarised in Table 5.

In our proposed model, there are 7,11,149 P2P botnets, and 8,15,659 benign P2P traffic flows taken into account. Table 5 shows the exact amount of traffic flows, conversations, and packets considered by the different authors. In [9] and [5], the authors notified the packets but not the flows. Similarly, in [17] authors notified the number of conversations. We want to mention here that there were few other work discussed in Sect. 3, but we did not compare them as the information about the features, or the statistical methods was missing from their papers to faithfully reimplement them (Fig. 7).

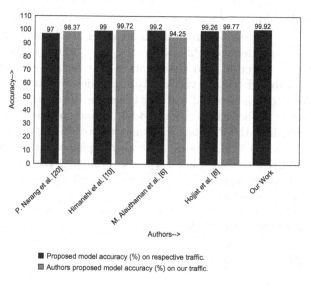

Fig. 7. Accuracy(%) of Authors' proposed model on their's and as well as on our traffic.

Table 5. Accuracy (%) comparison.

Authors	Dataset	Approach	Author reported accuracy %	Authors proposed model accuracy on our traffic
Narang et al. [17]	P2P Botnet Conversations - 50000 P2P Benign Conversations - 50000	Conversation-based	Approx 97%	98.37%
Hojjat et al. [6]	P2P Botnet Flows - 3296 P2P Benign Flows - 1233	Flow based	99.26%	99.77%
Himanshi et al. [9]	P2P Botnet Packets - 41941536 P2P Benign packets - 25913400	Flow based	Approx 99%	99.72%
Alauthaman et al. [5]	P2P Botnet Control packets - 114087 P2P Benign Control packets - 331526	Flow based	99.20%	94.25%
Our approach	P2P Botnet flows - 711149 P2P Benign flows - 815659	Flow based	99.85%	N/A

6   Conclusion

In this work, we have discussed *PeerClear*, an approach for detecting P2P bot-nets using network traffic analysis. The detection of bots was done in two steps, i.e., P2P host detection and P2P bot-net detection. In P2P host detection phase, we have performed packet filtering, feature extraction, and classification. Packet filtering module filters unwanted packets which were not contributing to the classification. Feature extraction module converts network traffic into the host-based feature vectors. Classification module uses decision tree for classification of extracted feature vectors into P2P or non-P2P. After the identification of P2P hosts, we have detected P2P bot-net by three other modules i.e., feature extraction, feature selection, and classification. The feature extraction module extracts the flow-based feature vectors from the network traffic. The feature selection module selects essential features based on the information gain ratio algorithm. Finally in the classification module, Random Forest, XGBoost and decision tree, classified the P2P bot with more than 99% of accuracy. The overall accuracy of *PeerClear* is (99.85%). We also implemented methods for P2P bot-net detection reported in other papers an evaluated them on our dataset. The results indicate our approach does better than others on the same dataset.

Acknowledgement. This work was partially funded by Science and Engineering Research Board, Government of India.

References

1. Internet world stats (2018). https://www.internetworldstats.com/stats.htm
2. Peerrush (2018). http://peerrush.cs.uga.edu/peerrush/
3. Tshark - Dump and Analyze Network Traffic, March 2018. https://www.wireshark.org/docs/man-pages/tshark.html
4. Vint Cerf: One Quarter of All Computers part of a Botnet (2018). http://www.tmttlt.com/archives/5289/
5. Alauthaman, M., Aslam, N., Zhang, L., Alasem, R., Hossain, M.A.: A P2P botnet detection scheme based on decision tree and adaptive multilayer neural networks. Neural Comput. Appl. **29**(11), 991–1004 (2018)
6. Beiknejad, H., Vahdat-Nejad, H., Moodi, H.: P2P botnet detection based on traffic behavior analysis and classification. Int. J. Comput. Inf. Technol. **6**(1), 01–12 (2018)
7. Chen, T., Guestrin, C.: XGBoost: a scalable tree boosting system. In: Proceedings of the 22nd ACM SIGKDD International Conference on Knowledge Discovery and Data Mining, pp. 785–794. ACM (2016)
8. Comodo: Latest malware attacks, May 2018. https://enterprise.comodo.com/blog/tag/latest-malware-attacks/
9. Dhayal, H., Kumar, J.: Peer-to-Peer botnet detection based on bot behaviour. Int. J. Adv. Res. Comput. Sci. **8**(3), 172–175 (2017)
10. Dillon, C.: Peer-to-Peer botnet detection using NetFlow. Master's thesis, University of Amsterdam (2014)
11. Donges, N.: The Random Forest Algorithm (2018). https://towardsdatascience.com/the-random-forest-algorithm-d457d499ffcd
12. Holz, T., Steiner, M., Dahl, F., Biersack, E., Freiling, F.: Measurements and mitigation of peer-to-peer-based botnets: a case study on storm worm. In: Proceedings of the 1st Usenix Workshop on Large-Scale Exploits and Emergent Threats (2008)
13. Kheir, N., Han, X., Wolley, C.: Behavioral fine-grained detection and classification of P2P bots. J. Comput. Virol. Hacking Tech. **11**(4), 217–233 (2015)
14. KimiNewt: Python wrapper for tshark, allowing python packet parsing using wireshark dissectors, June 2018. https://github.com/KimiNewt/pyshark

15. Lelli, A.: Zeusbot/Spyeye P2P Updated, Fortifying the Botnet (2018). https://www.symantec.com/connect/blogs/zeusbotspyeye-p2p-updated-fortifying-botnet
16. Lontivero: A Resilient Peer-to-Peer Botnet Agent in.NET, April 2017. https://github.com/lontivero/vinchuca
17. Narang, P., Ray, S., Hota, C.: PeerShark: detecting peer-to-peer botnets by tracking conversations. In: IEEE Security and Privacy Workshops (2014)
18. Nunnery, C., Sinclair, G., Kang, B.B.: Tumbling down the rabbit hole: exploring the idiosyncrasies of botmaster systems in a multi-tier botnet infrastructure. In: Proceedings of the 3rd USENIX Conference on Large-Scale Exploits and Emergent Threats: Botnets, Spyware, Worms, and More (2010)
19. Quinlan, J.R.: Induction of decision trees. Mach. Learn. **1**(1), 81–106 (1986)
20. Rodriguez-Gomez, R.A., Macia-Fernandez, G., García-Teodoroa, P., Steiner, M., Balzarotti, D.: Resource monitoring for detection of parasite P2P botnets. Comput. Netw. **70**, 302–3011 (2014)
21. Saiyod, S., Chanthakoummane, Y., Benjamas, N., Khamphakdee, N., Chaicha-wananit, J.: Improving intrusion detection on snort rules for botnet detection. Softw. Netw. **2018**(1), 191–212 (2018)
22. Schollmeier, R.: A definition of peer-to-peer networking for the classification of peer-to-peer architectures and applications. In: First International Conference on Peer-to-Peer Computing (2002)
23. Singh, S.C.: High-tech and computer crimes: global challenges, global responses. In: Nirmal, B., Singh, R. (eds.) Contemporary Issues in International Law, pp. 413–437. Springer, Singapore (2018). https://doi.org/10.1007/978-981-10-6277-3_30
24. Yin, C.: Towards accurate node-based detection of P2P botnets. Sci. World J. **2014**, 10 p. (2014)

Rethinking Identification Protocols from the Point of View of the GDPR

Mirosław Kutyłowski[1,2]($\boxtimes$), Lukasz Krzywiecki[1], and Xiaofeng Chen[2]

[1] Department of Computer Science, Faculty of Fundamental Problems of Technology,
Wrocław University of Technology, Wrocław, Poland
miroslaw.kutylowski@pwr.edu.pl

[2] School of Cyber Engineering, Xidian University, Xi'an, People's Republic of China

Abstract. An identification protocol has to deliver a proof that the protocol participants are who they claim to be. Related to the circumstances, the proof must be sufficiently convincing for the addressee. On the other hand, as long as the data minimality principle is concerned, the proof should be useless for any party that is not the intended addressee. While the first goal has attracted a lot of attention, the second one has been rather neglected.

In this paper we discuss requirements for identification protocols from the point of view of privacy protection requirements of the GDPR regulation introduced in Europe. We concern the problem of cryptographic data created by identification protocols and misusing them as an evidence presented to third parties. We concern in particular the case when it appears that a malicious participant follows the protocol, however the privacy protection guarantees supposedly provided by the scheme are effectively broken.

We show that from the point of view of GDPR the classical schemes like static Diffie-Hellman, Schnorr, Wu, Stinson-Wu, and Di Raimondo-Gennaro fail to comply with the EU Regulation even if they are *deniable*.

Keywords: Identification scheme · Privacy protection · GDPR · Attack · Deniability · Simulatability

1 Introduction

By executing an identification protocol, the party called here the *Prover* has to convince the other party, called the *Verifier*, about their identity. Identification is usually one of the first steps executed when communication is started between two actors of a system. More and more frequently, this process concerns not

---

This work has been initiated under support of the Polish National Science Centre, contract OPUS no 2014/15/B/ST6/02837, and later supported by grant S50129/K1102 at Wrocław University of Science and Technology. This work was also partially supported by China 111 Project (No. B16037) and Key Project of Natural Science Basic Research Plan in Shaanxi Province of China (No. 2016JZ021).

S. Dolev et al. (Eds.): CSCML 2019, LNCS 11527, pp. 296–315, 2019.
https://doi.org/10.1007/978-3-030-20951-3_25

only identification of physical persons (holding some electronic artefacts), but also identification of IoT devices in ad hoc systems.

Identification is a process run either independently from establishing a session key or it is integrated with this process. One of the options is to run identification separately after establishing a secure channel (i.e. via Diffie-Hellman Key Exchange), then an eavesdropper does not learn who is communicating with whom. Sometimes, identification is run before session keys are derived, and its output is used for the key exchange protocol. If both functionalities are integrated into a monolithic protocol – *Authenticated Key Establishment (AKE)* – then it might be difficult to separate the identification process from the key exchange activities.

Here, we need to state that in some scenarios identification is enough and establishing shared keys is unnecessary (or even should be avoided as a potential threat). A convincing example is a physical access control mechanism in a building. In this case, an identification token interacts with a door lock and once the token becomes authenticated the holder of the token may pass through the door. (The verification of the holder's rights may be performed according to an Access Control List, with certificates or any other mechanism that is outside the scope of the identification protocol.) No further communication between the token and the door lock is necessary. For this scenario, we have to respect the data minimality principle: no data should be created and processed in the system that is not necessary for realization of the required functionalities. For example, if such a system of physical access control becomes deployed, say, in the Pentagon building, then leaking the data which token has been used to open which door might pose a serious threat to the US national security. If the leaked identification protocol transcripts additionally provide strong cryptographic arguments that the leaked data are authentic, then it is more likely to sell the data to, say, terrorists or foreign intelligence. Note that in this case the threat becomes much higher despite that application of a strong cryptography could have been intended to lower the risks.

The research and development of identification protocols is a process initiated by the seminal work of Diffie and Hellman [1]. It has been followed by a number of proposals motivated by discovering new attack scenarios and corresponding weaknesses of the previous schemes. Gradually, this heuristic approach has been replaced by a more formal treatment, where security models are formulated and the protocols are analyzed with respect to these models. Such an approach makes it easier to compare the schemes and enables better understanding of their features. On the other hand, it has been stated many times that a formal model may fail to reflect the real attack scenarios and therefore formal security proofs may provide false security feelings (see e.g. [2]).

2   GDPR and Privacy Protection Principles for Identification Protocols

Recent General Data Protection Regulation introduced in Europe [3] creates a new framework of legal requirements for the design and implementation of the IT systems. Its heavy impact is due to a couple of factors, where the most important for the system designers might be the following ones:

- privacy-by-design principle,
- demonstrability of security and privacy features,
- heavy financial responsibility of the parties processing personal data not only for damages (material and immaterial), but also for failures to comply with the GDPR regulation.

2.1 Scope

Personal Data. Even if the same or similar technical measures might be appropriate in other areas, GDPR concerns exclusively processing of personal data. However, unlike in the USA, the definition of personal data is very broad:

> *'personal data' means any information relating to an identified or identifiable natural person ('data subject'); an identifiable natural person is one who can be identified, directly or indirectly,*

First, the purpose of an identification protocol is to identify a protocol participant in reliable way. Therefore all data exchanged become the legal status of *personal data.* Even if some of those data are apparently useless for anybody, the other like the location and the time of interaction deserve careful protection (preventing tracing).

Of course, GDPR applies directly, if electronic identification is used to identify a physical person holding the device participating in electronic communication ('natural person' in the legal language). It does not apply directly to IoT devices and their mutual identification. However, the IoT devices may frequently be linked to natural persons – this concerns for instance wearable medical devices, electric scooters, electronic keys and tokens, etc.. Making a decision whether a given artefact creates data about identifiable natural person, might be difficult, especially if the answer has to be created in a fully automated way. Last not least, creating separate identification protocols for natural and 'virtual' persons seems to be irrational from the technical point of view. A pragmatic solution would be to create schemes where privacy protection is granted by design and apply them irrespectively of whether the person identified is natural or 'virtual'.

Material Scope. Due to Article 2, GDPR applies among others to "processing of personal data wholly or partly by automated means". As we are talking about electronic identification, the process is at least partly automatic (possibly with some manual operations like inserting a password).

There are two notable exceptions from applying GDPR. The first one is processing personal data

> *by a natural person in the course of a purely personal or household activity.*

So, for instance a hobbyist creating a smart home solutions for own household need not to worry about GDPR and can deploy any identification scheme of his choice. The second exemption is processing

> *by competent authorities for the purposes of the prevention, investigation, detection or prosecution of criminal offenses or the execution of criminal penalties, including the safeguarding against and the prevention of threats to public security*

It says, among others, that a manufacturer can install trapdoors enabling "competent authorities" to break privacy where otherwise the product concerned satisfies the "privacy-by-design" principles.

Territorial Scope. The rules concerned in the GDPR have to be applied to entities processing data having their establishment in the Union, regardless of the place of processing. It means that an European company providing an identification system must respect the requirements of GDPR. The second case is dual and concerns processing by entities having their establishment outside the Union (so in general not in the scope of the Union's law). In this case again the GDPR applies, but limited to processing of data concerning activities that take place in the Union as long as the processing concerns:

> *(a) the offering of goods or services, irrespective of whether a payment of the data subject is required, to such data subjects in the Union; or*
> *(b) the monitoring of their behavior as far as their behavior takes place within the Union.*

In case of any system offering identification means it would be hard to claim that it does not *provide services*. Therefore a designer of an identification system has to choose either to comply with the requirements of GDPR, or to offer its products only for the use outside the Union. In the case of a global market such customization of products is costly.

Moreover, the legal impact of GDPR is not limited to the European Union, quite many countries adopt very similar regulations. Some countries (among others Israel) have been recognized by the Union to have appropriate legal standard concerning personal data protection, so that transferring personal data there can be processed as in the internal EU market.

Technical Principles. The GDPR regulation dramatically changes the legal situation concerning deployment of identification schemes by imposing the requirements having a major impact on the technical reality.

One of the basic rules of security good practices is **data minimality**: the system should not gather more data than it is necessary to achieve its purpose. Any excessive data creates an additional risk: in case of a security breach an intruder gets access to more data. Moreover, additional data may be further processed by a malicious system participant and misused in some way.

GDPR adopts **data minimality** principle as a legal requirement. Data minimality concerns not only data processed explicitly, but also data that are created in an implicit way. Consequently, if a scheme A uses personal data R and for the same purpose a scheme B uses a data collection R', where $R \subsetneq R'$, then one can claim that B violates the data minimality principle. Furthermore, the data subject may claim that their consent to process personal data does not apply to the additional data from $R' \setminus R$. One may conclude that there might be serious legal reasons to claim that the system B is ill defined (regardless of the other, maybe good, features).

Another key principle adopted by the GDPR into the legal system is the **purpose limitation**. Namely:

"personal data shall be collected for specified, explicit and legitimate purposes and not further processed in a manner that is incompatible with those purposes"

The problem is that once a data is created, it becomes very hard to guarantee that it is not processed in a way incompatible with the initial purpose. This concerns in particular the case of wireless identification and third parties that merely eavesdrop the communication channel. Moreover, since an identification scheme may be run by devices that are not controlled by the identification system provider, particular care is needed to ensure that these devices will not process the data created by the identification protocol in a way that is incompatible with the initial identification purpose.

The purpose limitation has to be considered jointly with the **storage limitation** principle, which says that the data should be:

"kept in a form which permits identification of data subjects for no longer than is necessary for the purposes for which the personal data are processed"

As in case of heterogeneous identification systems it is hard to control where and for how long the data concerning identification attempts are stored, a pragmatic solution is to minimize the data created during an identification session. This minimization should concern not only the amount of data but first of all their quality and probative value. A pragmatic strategy in this situation is to design a scheme where the data created through the protocol execution stored by a rogue participant could have been created by the rogue participant without executing the identification protocol. Therefore the responsibility is shifted from the identification system designer as the scheme does not increase the privacy violation risks. Such an approach is in line with the **integrity and confidentiality** principle, which states that

personal data shall be processed in a manner that ensures appropriate security of the personal data, including protection against unauthorized or unlawful processing [...] using appropriate technical or organizational measures.

Indeed, in the case of pervasive and heterogeneous IoT systems the organizational measures against unauthorized and unlawful processing could hardly be effective; the main focus must be on the guarantees provided by the technical properties of the system.

Finally, the GDPR states that not only the above rules must be implemented, but also the data controller must be able to prove compliance with the rules. Namely, the **accountability** principle states that

> *The controller shall be responsible for, and be able to demonstrate compliance with [the principles stated in GDPR]*

So GDPR requests to go beyond the "provable security" known from the literature: apart from showing that a protocol fulfills the properties formulated in a formal security model, the data controller has to prove that the formal model covers all relevant attack scenarios. This might be much harder than proposing a seemingly reasonable model and providing a formal security scheme for a given model.

Particular obligations of a party responsible for a system processing personal data – called the *controller* – are stated in Article 25 of the *Data protection by design and by default* section of GDPR:

> *1. Taking into account the state of the art, the cost of implementation and the nature, scope, context and purposes of processing as well as the risks of varying likelihood and severity for rights and freedoms of natural persons posed by the processing, the controller shall, both at the time of the determination of the means for processing and at the time of the processing itself, implement appropriate technical and organizational measures, ... which are designed to implement data-protection principles ... in an effective manner and to integrate the necessary safeguards into the processing in order to meet the requirements of this Regulation and protect the rights of data subjects.*

The norms that follow from this formulation are among others the following:

1. the controller shall evaluate the risks,
2. the security measures may be proportional to risks and assets protected,
3. the controller shall take into account the state-of-the art during system implementation as well as during the processing time,
4. the controller shall implement the system together with technical and organizational security measures,
5. the controller shall integrate the safeguards into the processing.

A common practice on the market has been quite different: the risk analysis was the problem of the customer, the security measures could be disproportionally low and outdated, the system could be composed from untested components delivered by third parties, and installed in an environment not suited for such a system.

From the point of view of identification systems equally important is the second point of this Article:

The controller shall implement appropriate technical and organizational measures for ensuring that, by default, only personal data which are necessary for each specific purpose of the processing are processed. That obligation applies to the amount of personal data collected, the extent of their processing, the period of their storage and their accessibility. In particular, such measures shall ensure that by default personal data are not made accessible without the individual's intervention to an indefinite number of natural persons.

A designer of an identification system is faced with the problem that, for instance, a malicious participant may retrieve data that are not related to the purpose of identification and post it online.

2.2 Security Reality

In the real world, even if an identification protocol is carefully designed in terms of privacy protection rules (at least in the theoretical sense), there are many reasons why it may fail in practice:

poor implementation: a common source of problems is that a software engineer may misinterpret the system specification, or create a software that contains bugs undetected during the testing phase. High complexity of a scheme, large size of the code, and integrating third party components, make this more likely to happen. Ideally, a scheme should defend itself *by-design* against these kind of problems. There are very few techniques that make mistakes of this kind self-evident for an external observer, however there are some possibilities of advance in this area [4].

leakage: in the case of a cheap or faulty hardware we have to deal with the problem of leaking the secrets used by the cryptographic procedures. This may concern leakages of long term private keys, leakages of ephemeral values, leakages of the internal state of pseudorandom number generator as well as simple weakening such a generator so that it becomes predictable. Unless we take care of the features like forward-security, substantial violations of personal data protection rules might follow. While leakage problems have attracted recently a lot of attention in the research community, most research is concentrated on limited leakage. On the other hand, in case of compromising an operating system, the adversary may get access to complete data.

malicious cryptography: if a device is running as a black box, there is a risk that internally it runs a more sophisticated protocol enabling the attacker to get data in a covert way. The deceitfulness of malicious cryptography methods lies in lack of any change of behavior – of course from the point of view of an external observer unaware of certain secret keys [5] (that are not installed in the devices).

Within this category we concern not only malicious smart cards, but most of all the devices like smart phones that might be attacked and subverted by a malicious software.

rogue Verifier: we have to consider the case when a Verifier is dishonest and, for instance, attempts to sell the data about interactions to a third party. Of course, no protocol can prohibit the Verifier to do it, but, somewhat unexpectedly, a strong protocol may ease such an illegal trade of personal data by providing cryptographic proofs of data validity.

rogue Prover: one can mistakenly assume that a Prover will always protect their personal data and therefore should not be regarded as an adversary attacking an identification protocol. An example showing that this assumption might be wrong is e-voting. An adversary may reward the voter merely for a proof that the voter has logged into an election server to cast a vote. This might be enough for the adversary as in some cases (a referendum) the turnout is crucial for the voting result.

All these situations should be taken into account during risk analysis for a particular identification system. Failure to address some of the problems may result, apart from civil responsibility for damages, in very heavy administrative fines [3].

3 Privacy Threats and Privacy Requirements

The aim of this section is to formulate the privacy goal for identification protocols. We follow a semi-formal approach describing problems and resulting requirements in a legal style – generalizing as much as possible to create a simple rule that would be understandable and acceptable by all stake-holders – not necessarily the information security engineers. The rule should be necessary, in the sense that violating it would endanger privacy in one of the ways described in Sect. 2. In Sect. 4 we shall examine some most popular schemes from the literature. We shall see not only that this rule is violated, but also that there are serious privacy threats corresponding to these violations.

Identification Protocol Purpose. In order to answer whether a given way of processing complies with the GDPR regulation it is necessary define the processing purpose. In the case of an identification protocol it can be stated as follows:

Purpose 1. *If a Prover A executes an identification protocol with a Verifier B aiming to present and prove its identity, then the result should be that B gets convinced that it is talking with A.*

Unless otherwise specified (which may happen in some particular application cases), there are no other purposes of executing an identification protocol. So the following cases shall be considered as violations of the purpose limitation principle from GDPR formulated in Article 25.1:

1. a Prover A may convince a third party E that an interaction between A and B has taken place,

2. a Verifier B may convince a third party E that a Prover A has authenticated itself against B,
3. a third party E may convince itself that an interaction between A and B has taken place – without any help from A and B but possibly with the help of other parties including in particular the system provider, manufacturer of the hardware used by A and B etc.

Note that it does not suffice that the above situations are not features given by an identification scheme (direct or indirect ones). It should be ensured by default that these situations will not occur (Article 25.2). Moreover, the controller providing the identification system is responsible for possible failures to guarantee this (Article 24).

The key danger created by an execution of an identification protocol for violating purpose limitation is creating digital data, sometimes with high cryptographic proof value. These data can be protected against misuse in different ways. In case of the communication channel we may have the following options:

– the data are communicated over an encrypted channel between the Prover and the Verifier,
– the data are sent in plaintext, however the physical properties of the channel practically eliminate the risk of eavesdropping,
– the data are sent in plaintext, but they are useless for violating purpose limitation.

The first approach is difficult in practice as a process of creating a secure channel requires typically the public key (and thereby indirectly the identity) of at least one of the parties. (There are possibilities to overcome this problem – see e.g. [6] – but they are nontrivial and too heavy to be used as a universal solution). The second approach is applicable in some cases. Primary examples seem to be the quantum channels and the small proximity communication channels. However, one can hardly imagine that this strategy can be used as a universal solution.

More complicated is protection of the data available to the devices of the Prover and the Verifier. Again, different protection strategies may be applied:

– the technical properties of the device ensure that the data from the device cannot be leaked or predicted by an external observer,
– the data from the device is useless for violating the purpose limitation principle.

The first strategy is problematic. It requires at least tamper-proof devices, secure operating systems, and secure random number generators (if used by the identification scheme). Accomplishing these goals is hard, costly and practically impossible. Even if a moderate assurance level is sufficient due to low risk level for a given practical application, the analysis of the situation might be a challenging task with a high probability of overlooking certain issues. So the second strategy seems to be a better choice – the only problem is to design proper schemes.

Based on the above discussion we may formulate the following rule that would provide GDPR-compliant purpose limitation. It is based on the concept of moving the burden of privacy features proof from the technical design to the cryptographic protocol:

Rule 2. *If a party A is involved in an execution of the identification protocol, then the data, which is related to the protocol execution and available to A including in particular it internal state [evidence data], shall be useless for proving to a third party that the identification protocol has been really executed by the Prover.*

Remark 1. In the above rule by a *third party* we understand any party for which the proof created by an execution of the identification protocol is not explicitly intended according to the protocol specification. In most cases by a third party we understand all parties except for the Prover and the Verifier.

Remark 2. The evidence data in Rule 2 is primarily the data exchanged over the communication channel – so called *transcript* of a protocol execution. This follows from the fact that generally we cannot protect message sent over wireless channels. Of course, we talk here about the ciphertexts (and not the plaintexts), if the communication is encrypted. However, we may have to deal here with other data provided (leaked) by the protocol participants. Therefore, the risk analysis should determine which data might be available for presentation as an evidence data.

In order to systematize properties of protocols in various scenarios we define the following scopes of the evidence data:

Transcript only: in this case the evidence data is merely the transcript of communication: all messages exchanged between the Verifier and the Prover.

Verifier's data: apart from the communication transcript, the Verifier may add some (or all) values used during a protocol execution – ephemeral values, as well as some long period secrets or values derived from them.

Prover's data: this case is symmetric to the previous one, now the internal knowledge of the Prover is included in the evidence data.

Prover's and Verifier's data: in the last scenario the Prover and the Verifier collude to prove that an interaction between them took place. Consequently they reveal some (or all) of their internal data.

Let us motivate shortly why the last three scenarios deserve consideration. First, a Verifier may offer some services after identification of a customer. However, the Verifier may also earn by selling (strongly authenticated) data about activities of their customers. For the second case we may consider a mobile phone used as identification token. Even if the phone owner is interested in preserving privacy, the app used for running the identification protocol may be rogue. For the last case one can concern a physical access control system, where both the devices granting access and the tokens used as provers are provided by the same malicious manufacturer. Then the system deployed for improving physical security may at the same time become a "Big Brother" system where tracing data may be offered to third parties together with a strong evidence of their authenticity.

Remark 3. A limited version of Rule 2 have been considered in the literature and called *deniability*. The idea is that given a transcript of a protocol execution, one can deny that the transcript corresponds to a real interaction based on the argument that it could be created by a simulation. The definition of deniability has been extended to the cases that we are talking about: for instance, Di Raimondo and Gennaro [7] include the case that the Prover aims to prove to a third party that a given transcript corresponds to a real execution.

Knowledge from Past and Future Executions. Unfortunately, while examining a scheme we are not talking about a single protocol execution but maybe about a whole sequence of interactions, including different parties, executed in the past and in the future of the protocol execution under consideration. In some cases there is a priori knowledge that certain data correspond to genuine interactions between indicated parties, even if this cannot be derived from the evidence data.

The situation becomes even more complex, if the secret keys intended for identification are used for other purposes as well. To ease security analysis, it is helpful to assume that the secret keys are dedicated to a single scheme. On the other hand, it is helpful to reduce storage requirements of IoT devices, and therefore one might be tempted to reuse the same key for different purposes. For instance, the key used for the Schnorr identification scheme might be used for creating Schnorr signatures (such an approach has been indirectly suggested in [8]). Moreover, one can be tempted to use one scheme as a plug-in component in another scheme, just saving space necessary to store the binary code for executing the scheme.

In the above cases it would be desirable to provide a security proof even in presence of another schemes based on the same secret key(s). In general, it would be hard to create such a proof in case of interaction of different schemes - especially if one of the schemes in the environment of the scheme under consideration is yet unknown.

4   Example Identification Schemes and Their Privacy Threats

4.1   Static Diffie-Hellman Scheme

The static Diffie-Hellman protocol is one of the very first identification and key establishment protocols [1] (Fig. 1). Many follow-up protocols based on it have been proposed later (see for instance the survey [2]).

For the sake of simplicity, in the description below and in the description of other schemes based on the Discrete Logarithm Problem (DL) we skip the details that emerge if G is chosen to be a prime order subgroup of $\mathbb{Z}_p$. Consequently, we skip all steps necessary to check that the elements belong to the proper groups.

Discussion. First let us recall the basic property of this protocol:

---

params ← ParGen(1^λ): Let $\mathbb{G} = (q, g, G) \leftarrow \mathcal{G}(1^\lambda)$, s.t. G i a group of order q where
   DL assumption holds, g is a generator of G. Set params $= (q, g, G)$.
KeyGen(): sk $= a \leftarrow_\$ \mathbb{Z}_q^*$, pk $= A = g^a$. Output (sk, pk).
Identification($\mathcal{P}(a, A), \mathcal{V}(A)$: The Prover $\mathcal{P}(a, A)$ and the Verifier $\mathcal{V}(A)$ run the following protocol:
   1. $\mathcal{V}$: chooses $x \leftarrow_\$ \mathbb{Z}_q^*$, computes $X = g^x$, and sends X to the Prover $\mathcal{P}$.
   2. $\mathcal{P}$: computes $Z = X^a$.
   3. $\mathcal{P}$: sends Z to the Verifier $\mathcal{V}$.
   4. $\mathcal{V}$: accepts iff $Z == A^x$.

Fig. 1. The static Diffie-Hellman identification scheme.

Observation 3. *A valid protocol execution transcript of the static Diffie-Hellman identification protocol can be created without knowledge of the secret key a of the Prover. Moreover, one can create such transcripts so that their probability distribution is exactly the same as in case of transcripts coming from genuine executions.*

Observation 3 follows from the fact that a forger can mimic the work of the Verifier. Then instead of waiting for response Z from the Prover, the forger derives Z as A^x and this value is written into the transcript as the response of the Prover. Moreover, if the Prover creates challenges A at random, the forger may do the same. So we may conclude as follows:

Corollary 1. *One cannot claim that a valid transcript of a protocol execution corresponds to a genuine interaction between the Prover and the Verifier, as anybody could create such a transcript with exactly the same probability distribution.*

Unfortunately, in case of a rogue Verifier there is a simple way to create an undeniable proof of interaction with a Prover Alice:

Step 1: the Verifier performs the identification protocol to make sure that he interacts with Alice. However, the Verifier claims to fail to receive Z and therefore restarts the identification procedure.
Step 2: in the second run the Verifier chooses an element μ for which the discrete logarithm is unknown. For this purpose one can apply a standard trick: $\mu = \text{Hash}(T)$, where T is some data like Verifier's signature over the current stock exchange rating. (Note that T is unpredictable by Alice and therefore Alice cannot test that this attack is going on.) Alice returns $Z = \mu^a$ and the Verifier accepts (without checking Z).
Step 3: the Prover may prove to Bob that he has interacted with Alice in the following way:
   – the Prover presents T, r and Z,
   – Bob can recompute μ (and convince himself that the discrete logarithm of μ is unknown),

- now Bob can interact with Alice providing the challenge μ^j for j chosen at random.
If Alice returns Z^j, then Bob may conclude that Z is indeed of the form μ^a and accepts the Verifier's proof.

The above procedure is based on the KEA1 assumption [9]: If the data (g, g^a, μ, μ^a) are created for a random μ with an unknown discrete logarithm, then a party knowing a must have been involved in creating this tuple. So we may conclude as follows:

Observation 4. *The static Diffie-Hellman identification scheme enables the Verifier to create a strong proof of interaction with the Prover. Thereby the protocol fails to fulfill the Rule 2.*

The problem with the static Diffie-Hellman identification is that it can be simulated as long as the challenge X has known discrete logarithm. For the opposite case, the situation is totally different and the Verifier gets a response that can be created exclusively by the Prover.

4.2 Schnorr Identification Scheme

The Schnorr identification scheme from [10] is one of the most known schemes – its non-interactive version is the Schnorr signature scheme (Fig. 2).

---

params $\leftarrow$ ParGen(1^λ): Let $\mathbb{G} = (q, g, G) \leftarrow \mathcal{G}(1^\lambda)$, s.t. G i a group of order q where DL assumption holds, g is a generator of G. Set params $= (q, g, G)$.
KeyGen(): sk $= a \leftarrow_\$ \mathbb{Z}_q^*$, pk $= A = g^a$. Output (sk, pk).
Identification($\mathcal{P}(a, A), \mathcal{V}(A)$: The Prover $\mathcal{P}(a, A)$ and the Verifier $\mathcal{V}(A)$ run the following protocol:
 1. $\mathcal{P}$: chooses $x \leftarrow_\$ \mathbb{Z}_q^*$, computes $X = g^x$ and sends X to the Verifier $\mathcal{V}$.
 2. $\mathcal{V}$: chooses $c \leftarrow_\$ \mathbb{Z}_q^*$, and sends c to the Prover $\mathcal{P}$.
 3. $\mathcal{P}$: computes $s = x + ac \bmod q$ and sends s to the Verifier $\mathcal{V}$.
 4. $\mathcal{V}$: accepts iff $g^s == X \cdot A^c$.

Fig. 2. The Schnorr identification scheme.

Discussion. Let us recall the following argument in favor of this scheme:

Observation 5. *A valid protocol execution transcript of the Schnorr identification protocol can be created without knowledge of the secret key a of the Prover. Moreover, one can create such transcripts so that their probability distribution is exactly the same as in case of transcripts coming from genuine executions.*

Recall that a valid transcript (X, c, s) can be created as follows:

- choose s and c at random,
- compute $X = g^s / A^c$.

Obviously, the probability distribution is exactly the same as in case of genuine executions. So again an eavesdropper cannot convince a third party that a presented transcript is a transcript of a genuine interaction with the Prover.

Unfortunately, again the Verifier may create an undeniable proof of an interaction with the Prover. Namely, in the second step, instead of:

$\mathcal{V}$: chooses $c \leftarrow_\$ \mathbb{Z}_q^*$, and sends c to the Prover $\mathcal{P}$

we have:

$\mathcal{V}$: chooses r at random, computes $c = \mathrm{Hash}(X, r)$ and sends c to the Prover $\mathcal{P}$

Note that the change is not detectable by the Prover as long as the hash function behaves like a random function mapping into $\mathbb{Z}_q^*$.

The evidence of an interaction is a tuple (X, r, s). Namely, if a good hash function is used, then X must be created before c and the simulation above does not work. Moreover, essentially in this way the Verifier converts a communication transcript into a Schnorr signature. So, a third party should believe the evidence provided by the Verifier as long as they believe in existential unforgeability of Schnorr signatures. So we may conclude as follows:

Observation 6. *The Schnorr identification scheme enables the Verifier to create a strong proof of interaction with the Prover based on existential unforgeability of Schnorr signatures. Thereby the protocol fails to fulfill the Rule 2.*

One can defer this attack by a slight modification of the Schnorr protocol:

1. $\mathcal{V}$: chooses $c \leftarrow_\$ \mathbb{Z}_q^*$, creates a cryptographic commitment $c' = \mathrm{Commit}(c)$ and sends c' to the Prover $\mathcal{P}$.
2. $\mathcal{P}$: chooses $x \leftarrow_\$ \mathbb{Z}_q^*$, computes $X = g^x$ and sends X to the Verifier $\mathcal{V}$.
3. $\mathcal{V}$: sends c and an opening of the commitment c' to the Prover $\mathcal{P}$.
4. $\mathcal{P}$: checks that c corresponds to c', computes $s = x + ac \bmod q$ and sends s to the Verifier $\mathcal{V}$.
5. $\mathcal{V}$: accepts iff $g^s == X \cdot A^c$.

We do not further discuss effectiveness of this countermeasure, since we have a substantial problem on the Prover's side. We aim to show the following

Observation 7. *The Schnorr identification scheme enables the Prover to create a strong proof authenticating an interaction transcript. Thereby the protocol fails to fulfill the Rule 2.*

Note that revealing the exponent x does not prove that an transcript (X, c, s) originates from a real interaction with the Prover. Namely, if a transcript (X, c, s) satisfies $g^s = X \cdot A^c$, then $X = g^{s-a \cdot c}$. Consequently, the Prover can compute $x = s - a \cdot c$ even in case when (X, c, s) has been created by the simulation as described above.

The attack presented below enables the Prover to present a proof that X has been created <u>before</u> s and the transcript could not be forged in the way discussed above. For this attack, we reuse a trick used in [4] (the difference is that in [4] the trick was used to protect while now it is used for evil purposes). Namely, the step of creating X is modified to the following form:

1. $\mathcal{P}$: chooses $x_0 \leftarrow_\$ \{0,1\}^l$ and retains g^{x_0};
   alternatively $\mathcal{P}$ may compute $x_0 = \text{PRNG}(seed, i)$, where $seed$ is a secret long period seed of the pseudorandom generator PRNG and i is a value of a counter. Moreover, $2^l \ll q$ (for instance $2^l < q/2^{30}$) while x_0 should still be sufficiently large.
2. $\mathcal{P}$: computes $x_1 = \text{Hash}(A^{x_0})$ and $X = g^{x_0 \cdot x_1}$.

The rest of the protocol is executed according to the original specification of the Schnorr identification scheme.

Later, the Prover can prove to a third party Eve that a transcript (X, c, s) originates from the Prover. The following steps are executed:

1. $\mathcal{P}$ presents $z_0 = g^{x_0}$ and $z_1 = A^{x_0}$,
2. The Prover $\mathcal{P}$ and Eve perform an interactive proof of equality of discrete logarithms for (g, z_0) and (X, z_1).
3. Eve checks that $X = z_0^{\text{Hash}(z_1)}$.

The presented proof shows that the Prover knows x_0 such that $X = g^{x_0 \cdot \text{Hash}(A^{x_0})}$. In order to cheat, the Prover would have to find $x_0 < q/2^{30}$ for a given x, such that

$$x = x_0 \cdot \text{Hash}(A^{x_0})$$

As Hash behaves as a random function it is very unlikely that for a random X such an x_0 really exists. Even if it exists, it might be extremely difficult to find it – presumably there is no other choice than the brute force search. So Eve can conclude that X has been chosen before s and therefore s can be treated as a Schnorr signature.

We do not discuss further the attack and the strength of the proof created by the Prover for a third party. There are two-fold reasons for that. First, it serves as an argument that there might be severe problems to prove that the Prover is not manipulating somehow the step in which they choose x and compute X. Any amendment solving this problem may in turn create new places where the Prover may manipulate the execution and create a proof of interaction.

The second reason is that finally we have to do with the case that the Prover and the Verifier may collude and manipulate the execution so that for an external observer everything looks fine, while evidence data provided by the Prover and the Verifier may strongly authenticate a communication transcript. Preventing such a collusion seems to be a challenging task. On the other hand, we shall see that this effort is very likely to be unnecessary, as there are schemes where this line of attack does not work.

4.3   Wu and Stinson-Wu Identification Schemes

The identification protocols from [11] and [12] are closely related (Figs. 3 and 4). The first impression might be that there are only minor differences between them having no substantial impact on their privacy features. We shall see that this is not the case.

---

params $\leftarrow$ ParGen(1^λ): Let $\mathbb{G} = (q, g, G) \leftarrow \mathcal{G}(1^\lambda)$, s.t. G i a group of order q where
 DL assumption holds, g is a generator of G. Set params $= (q, g, G)$.
KeyGen(): sk $= a \leftarrow_\$ \mathbb{Z}_q^*$, pk $= A = g^a$. Output (sk, pk).
Identification($\mathcal{P}(a, A), \mathcal{V}(A)$): The Prover $\mathcal{P}(a, A)$ and the Verifier $\mathcal{V}(A)$ run the following protocol:
    1. $\mathcal{V}$: chooses $x \leftarrow_\$ \mathbb{Z}_q^*$, computes $X = g^x$, and sends X to the Prover $\mathcal{P}$.
    2. $\mathcal{P}$: computes $Z = \text{Hash}(X^a)$ and sends Z to the Verifier $\mathcal{V}$.
    3. $\mathcal{V}$: accepts iff $Z == \text{Hash}(A^x)$.

Fig. 3. The Wu identification scheme.

---

params $\leftarrow$ ParGen(1^λ): Let $\mathbb{G} = (q, g, G) \leftarrow \mathcal{G}(1^\lambda)$, s.t. G i a group of order q where
 DL assumption holds, g is a generator of G. Set params $= (q, g, G)$.
KeyGen(): sk $= a \leftarrow_\$ \mathbb{Z}_q^*$, pk $= A = g^a$. Output (sk, pk).
Identification($\mathcal{P}(a, A), \mathcal{V}(A)$): The Prover $\mathcal{P}(a, A)$ and the Verifier $\mathcal{V}(A)$ run the following protocol:
    1. $\mathcal{V}$: chooses $x \leftarrow_\$ \mathbb{Z}_q^*$, computes $X = g^x$, $Y = \text{Hash}(A^x)$ and sends X, Y to the Prover $\mathcal{P}$.
    2. $\mathcal{P}$: computes $Z = X^a$ and aborts if $Y \neq \text{Hash}(Z)$.
    3. $\mathcal{P}$: sends Z to the Verifier $\mathcal{V}$.
    4. $\mathcal{V}$: accepts iff $Z == A^x$.

Fig. 4. The Stinson-Wu identification scheme.

First let us point to two positive properties of the scheme of Wu:

Observation 8. *Without knowing the secret of the Prover one can generate protocol communication transcripts for the protocol of Wu with the same probability as for the transcripts generated in the genuine protocol executions. So Rule 2 holds when no further evidence data is provided.*

Generating a transcript is possible by mimicking the steps of the Verifier and replacing the answer Z with the value computed as $\text{Hash}(A^x)$.

The second property is much more important (particularly with respect to the difficulties concerning the Schnorr identification scheme at this point).

Observation 9. *The identification protocol of Wu is immune against attempts to break Rule 2 by the Prover.*

This property follows from the sheer reason that the Prover executes a deterministic algorithm. So there is no place to "inject" anything that may serve as a proof presented to third parties. On the other hand, the Prover can create a protocol transcript by simulation.

On the other hand, the protocol of Wu enables the Verifier to create an evidence that later cannot be denied by the Prover. The situation is somewhat better than in the case of the static Diffie-Hellman protocol, but still raise substantial concerns.

Observation 10. *The Verifier can present a value X for which the discrete logarithm is unknown and store the response Z of the Prover. At a later time the Prover might be forced to present $Y = X^a$ and a proof of equality of discrete logarithms for the pairs (g, X) and (A, Y). The judge then checks whether $Z = \text{Hash}(Y)$.*

The scenario from Observation 10 is not unlikely in practice: there might be several reasons why the Prover cannot refuse the request, e.g. from his employer. Last not least, it is always possible to capture the device of the Prover and perform a test execution with the same challenge.

Now let us turn our attention to the identification scheme of Stinson and Wu. First note the following:

Observation 11. *The properties presented in Observations 8 and 9 hold also for the identification scheme of Stinson and Wu.*

The main difference between the scheme of Wu and Stinson-Wu is that in the later case the device of the Prover can defend itself against being used as an oracle to raise into the power a:

Observation 12. *Assuming KEA1 assumption and the Random Oracle Model for the hash function, the Prover in the Stinson-Wu identification protocol does respond to the challenge X of the Verifier only if X has been generated so that the discrete logarithm of X has been known.*

Proof. By the Random Oracle Model computing the correct value of Y requires knowledge of the argument A^x of the hash function. So we see that the party that has created the challenge has the following pairs (g, A), (g^x, A^x). Then, by the KEA1 assumption, we can conclude that this party can extract x.   □

Note that we cannot assure that the challenge (X, Y) has been created by the Verifier himself – the Verifier can serve only as a man-in-the-middle.

Unfortunately, the above observations are not enough to conclude that the Stinson-Wu identification scheme is fully compliant with the Rule 2. This becomes evident when we consider the following attack scenario:

Attack 13 Phase 1: Eve promises the Verifier to pay for being informed that the Prover Alice executes the identification protocol with the Verifier. For this purpose, Eve generates in advance the following data: $X = g^x$ and $Y = \text{Hash}(A^x)$ for x chosen at random. Then Eve passes the pair (X, Y) to the Verifier. (Of course, the Verifier cannot check that (X, Y) are valid, but one cannot hope that the malicious parties are not trusting each other to some degree. Last not least, it is in Eve's advantage to present a correct pair.) Additionally, Eve presents to the Verifier a ciphertext $e = \text{Enc}_{\text{Hash}(A^x)}(x)$. Even if x is contained inside as a plaintext, it is infeasible to decrypt until the Verifier learns A^x which is the expected answer from the Prover.

Phase 2: Once Alice contacts the Verifier and intends to identify herself, the Verifier presents the challenge (X, Y) obtained from Eve. As (X, Y) is presumably correct, the Prover will respond with X^a. As $X^a = A^x$, the Verifier may now decrypt e and learn x. From this point, the Prover is back in the standard situation for identity verification.

Phase 3: Finally, the Prover can present X^a to Eve as a proof that an interaction with Alice has taken place.

The proof presented by the Prover to Eve is a strong one as it is infeasible to find a preimage of Y for the hash function as well as it is infeasible to solve Computational Diffie-Hellman Problem (CDH) [1] for the tuple (g, A, X). If Eve is not itself pretending to be Alice against the Verifier, then Eve knows that Alice was involved in the interaction.

In the attack scenario above, the Prover might be exposed to a cheating attempt from Eve: first Eve offers money and presents the tuple (X, Y, e) to the Verifier. Then Eve herself pretends to be Alice in an interaction with the Prover. The Prover mistakenly assumes that they talk with Alice.

If the Prover fears such a scenario, then the same trick can be used as before: the Prover executes two identification rounds with Alice, claiming that in the first round the response has been unreadable due to physical distortions. In one round, the Prover uses the data obtained from Eve, while in the another round the Prover executes the protocol according to the specification – thereby checking Alice's identity.

Corollary 2. *The Stinson-Wu scheme violates the Rule 2 in the sense that the Verifier can convince Eve that a session with the Prover has taken place, provided that Eve can present a challenge to the Verifier before the Prover and the Verifier start this identification session.*

4.4   Raimondo-Gennaro Deniable Identification

A generic approach to create deniable identification protocols – together with a broad discussion on deniability model and its role in the design of identification protocols has been presented in [7]. Figure 5 presents an instantiation of such a protocol (in this figure we skip some details concerning specification of the hash functions $\mathcal{H}$, H.)

---

params ← ParGen(1^λ): Let $\mathbb{G} = (q, g_1, g-2, G) \leftarrow \mathcal{G}(1^\lambda)$, s.t. G is a group of order q where DDH assumption holds, g_1, g_2 are generators of G, such that reciprocal discrete-logs of g_1, g_2 are unknown. Let $\mathcal{H}$, H be hash functions. Set params = $(q, g_1, g_2, G, \mathcal{H}, H)$.

KeyGen(): sk $= (x_1, x_2, y_1, y_2) \leftarrow_\$ (\mathbb{Z}_q^*)^4$, $c = g_1^{x_1} g_2^{x_2}$, $d = g_1^{y_1} g_2^{y_2}$, pk $= (c, d)$. Output (sk, pk).

Identification($\mathcal{P}(x_1, x_2, y_1, y_2)$, $\mathcal{V}(c, d)$: The Prover $\mathcal{P}(x_1, x_2, y_1, y_2)$ and the Verifier $\mathcal{V}(c, d)$ run the following protocol:
   1. $\mathcal{V}$: chooses $r \leftarrow_\$ \mathbb{Z}_q^*$, computes $u_1 = g_1^r$, $u_2 = g_2^r$, $\alpha = \mathcal{H}(m, \mathcal{P})$, $v = c^r d^{r\alpha}$, $h_1 = \lceil H \rceil(v)$ and sends (m, u_1, u_2, h_1) to the Prover $\mathcal{P}$.
   2. $\mathcal{P}$: computes $\alpha = \mathcal{H}(m, \mathcal{P})$, $v = u_1^{x_1 + \alpha y_1} u_2^{x_2 + \alpha y_2}$, $h_2 = \lfloor H \rfloor(v)$
   3. $\mathcal{P}$: if $h_1 == \lceil H \rceil(v)$, he sends (m, h_2) to the Verifier $\mathcal{V}$, otherwise he aborts.
   4. $\mathcal{V}$: accepts iff $h_2 == \lfloor H \rfloor(v)$.

Fig. 5. Di Raimondo-Gennaro identification scheme based on DDH. $\lceil H \rceil(v)$ ($\lfloor H \rfloor(v)$) denotes the prefix (resp. the suffix) of $H(v)$ of length k, where k is at most the half of the length of $H(v)$

One can easily see that despite all additional features (see [7]) one can adjust Attack 13 to the case of Di Raimondo-Gennaro identification scheme:

Corollary 3. *The Di Raimondo-Gennaro scheme violates the Rule 2 in the sense that the Verifier can convince Eve that a session with the Prover has taken place, provided that Eve can present a challenge to the Verifier before the Prover and the Verifier start this identification session.*

Final Remarks. The scenario of Attack 13 seems to be a quite important one and realistic from the practical point of view. On the other hand, it seems to be infeasible to create a countermeasure against such attacks in the current setting. The reason is that the Prover may always serve as a man-in-the-middle. As long as the Verifier sends only one message and this message initiates the protocol, this message can be created in advance by Eve. On the other hand, building a protocol where the Prover sends the first challenge may open many doors for breaking Rule 2 by the Prover. Moreover, the protocols where the Prover and the Verifier exchange more than 2 messages are less attractive from the practical point of view.

A pragmatic way to solve the problem might be to allow the Verifier to use its public key. Then one can imagine a protocol where the challenge created by the Verifier contains an implicit proof (checkable by the Prover) that the challenge has indeed been created by the Verifier. However, it should be emphasized that the introduction of an additional public key (and the data created with the corresponding secret key) may create a new room for weaknesses.

References

1. Diffie, W., Hellman, M.E.: New directions in cryptography. IEEE Trans. Inf. Theory **22**(6), 644–654 (1976). https://doi.org/10.1109/TIT.1976.1055638
2. Blake-Wilson, S., Menezes, A.: Authenticated Diffe-Hellman key agreement protocols. In: Tavares, S., Meijer, H. (eds.) SAC 1998. LNCS, vol. 1556, pp. 339–361. Springer, Heidelberg (1999). https://doi.org/10.1007/3-540-48892-8_26
3. The European Parliament and the Council of the European Union: Regulation (EU) 2016/679 of the European Parliament and of the Council of 27 April 2016 on the protection of natural persons with regard to the processing of personal data and on the free movement of such data, and repealing Directive 95/46/ec (General Data Protection Regulation). Off. J. Eur. Union **119**(1) (2016)
4. Hanzlik, L., Kluczniak, K., Kutyłowski, M.: Controlled randomness – a defense against backdoors in cryptographic devices. In: Phan, R.C.-W., Yung, M. (eds.) Mycrypt 2016. LNCS, vol. 10311, pp. 215–232. Springer, Cham (2017). https://doi.org/10.1007/978-3-319-61273-7_11
5. Young, A.L., Yung, M.: Malicious Cryptography - Exposing Cryptovirology. Wiley, Hoboken (2004)
6. Błaśkiewicz, P., et al.: Pseudonymous signature schemes. In: Li, K.-C., Chen, X., Susilo, W. (eds.) Advances in Cyber Security: Principles, Techniques, and Applications, pp. 185–255. Springer, Singapore (2019). https://doi.org/10.1007/978-981-13-1483-4_8
7. Di Raimondo, M., Gennaro, R.: New approaches for deniable authentication. J. Cryptol. **22**(4), 572–615 (2009). https://doi.org/10.1007/s00145-009-9044-3
8. Bender, J., Dagdelen, Ö., Fischlin, M., Kügler, D.: The PACE|AA protocol for machine readable travel documents, and its security. In: Keromytis, A.D. (ed.) FC 2012. LNCS, vol. 7397, pp. 344–358. Springer, Heidelberg (2012). https://doi.org/10.1007/978-3-642-32946-3_25
9. Damgård, I.: Towards practical public key systems secure against chosen ciphertext attacks. In: Feigenbaum, J. (ed.) CRYPTO 1991. LNCS, vol. 576, pp. 445–456. Springer, Heidelberg (1992). https://doi.org/10.1007/3-540-46766-1_36
10. Schnorr, C.P.: Efficient signature generation by smart cards. J. Cryptol. **4**(3), 161–174 (1991)
11. Wu, J.: Cryptographic protocols, sensor network key management, and RFID authentication. Ph.D. thesis, University of Waterloo, Ontario, Canada (2009). http://hdl.handle.net/10012/4501
12. Stinson, D.R., Wu, J.: An efficient and secure two-flow zero-knowledge identification protocol. J. Math. Cryptol. **1**(3), 201–220 (2007). https://doi.org/10.1515/JMC.2007.010

Temporal Pattern-Based Malicious Activity Detection in SCADA Systems (Brief Announcement)

Meir Kalech[✉], Amit Shlomo, and Robert Moskovich

Ben-Gurion University of the Negev, Beersheba, Israel
{kalech,amitsh,robertmo}@bgu.ac.il

Keywords: Cyber-security · SCADA · Temporal pattern recognition

1 Scientific Background

Supervisory Control and Data Acquisition (SCADA) is a system which is used to monitor and control various industrial and infrastructure systems, such as power plants, water disposal and distribution, and other systems which are crucial for our modern way of life. There has been an increasing awareness to the protection of infrastructure systems; more and more reports regarding suspected cyber attacks on such systems have been surfacing in the media. The Stuxnet worm is one of the most famous attacks [4]. Attacks on a SCADA system can cause an enormous damage to an organization or even an entire country, therefore, governments and organizations are trying to increase security by adjusting and improving existing solutions to SCADA and by developing new methods to cope with such attacks.

SCADA is comprised of one or more Human Machine Interface (HMI), while each HMI controls several PLCs (Programmable Logic Controllers). The communications between these components can be done in several ways. In this work, we focus on the MODBUS protocol, which communicates over the TCP/IP protocol. MODBUS protocol is simple, and it defines a set of functions, which are used to read/write data from/to the PLCs registers. The PLCs and the HMI take actions according to the registers' values read/written.

The MODBUS communication is usually highly periodic, which is a key observation made by almost all studies in this field [2,6]. This enables to find patterns in the communication and build effective intrusion detection systems. Indeed, previous work considered the type of the command (Read/Write) [2] but, to the best of our knowledge, no work considered the values of the command's parameters (the content of the information to be read/written) neither the duration time of the parameters.

Ignoring the content and time of the parameters, may provide opportunities to sophisticated attacks, which manipulate the MODBUS packets while remaining undiscovered. For instance, instead of opening and closing a water main

Supported by the The BGU Cyber Security Research Center.

S. Dolev et al. (Eds.): CSCML 2019, LNCS 11527, pp. 316–319, 2019.
https://doi.org/10.1007/978-3-030-20951-3_26

valve every 30 min, an attacker may make these operations occur at a frequency of twice a minute, causing the valve to break. To address this challenge, we propose a machine learning approach to detect temporal patterns in the data payload of the SCADA communication protocols. Our algorithm segments first each register based on its values to states, where each state combines similar values. Then we apply a frequent temporal pattern discovery algorithm based on [5], which finds patterns based on the temporal relations between the registers' states. The discovered frequent patterns are then detected in the whole data and their metrics, such as their time duration and frequency, are fed as features into a classifier that learns malicious activities.

To evaluate our algorithm we use a real MODUBS-SCADA dataset from Ben-Gurion University in Israel. The results show that our algorithm is better than a baseline data-driven algorithm that considers only the mean and standard deviation. In addition, we show that our algorithm is sensitive to the way we discretize the data.

The contributions of this paper are: (1) the use of temporal abstraction and duration time mining to detect malicious activities in SCADA systems, and (2) a rigorous evaluation of the classification framework on real world data.

2 Method Description

SCADA systems tend to repeat themselves within a well-defined time period [2], which leads us to apply a malicious activity detection method based on temporal patterns.

To learn the temporal relations between registers' values we discover temporal relations among the symbolic time intervals (concatenated time series having the same value) that were created from the registers' values [3]. A time interval of an event is defined by start and end times. To represent the relation between two events Allen [1] defines temporal relations. In this paper, we are inspired by this approach to find frequent patters inside the SCADA PLCs' registers by tracking the MODBUS communication. We define an event $\langle X, v \rangle$ as the time interval in which register X holds value v. $e.t_s$ and $e.t_f$ denote the start and end times of the event. Namely, once a register is assigned by a new value, a new event is defined and this indicates the start time of the event. In the next time the register will change its value, the end time of the event will be declared.

In Fig. 1(a) we can see an example for a portion of the raw data which holds the values of three registers along time T. Each row contains a time stamp in the first column and a vector of the registers' values, as captured and updated by a MODBUS packet. Figure 1(b) shows the events discovered. Each color represents an event.

We are interested to identify patterns between the registers' values (events) using Allen's relations. For that we employ the KarmaLego algorithm for TIRPs discovery [5]. Shortly, KarmaLego algorithm consists of two main steps: Karma, in which the entire set of E entities (in the database) are scanned. Through that all the symbols are counted, and each pair of symbolic time intervals (according

T	Reg1	Reg2	Reg3
1	4	34	7
2	4	34	67
3	66	34	67
4	66	12	67
5	66	12	7

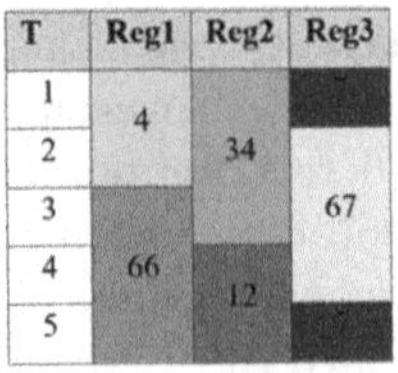

Fig. 1. (a) Raw data - registers. (b) Processed data – events. (Color figure online)

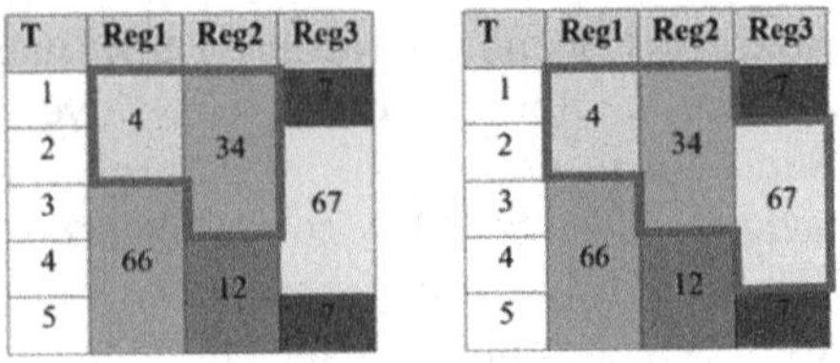

Fig. 2. Patterns discovered by KarmaLego. (Color figure online)

to the lexicographical order) and the temporal relation among them are indexed in an index called the *DharmaIndex*. The DharmaIndex contains all the frequent 2-sized TIRPs ($K = 2$). Later the Lego algorithm extends recursively the frequent 2-sized TIRPs, which results with the entire enumerated tree of TIRPs.

In our algorithm, the entities are the PLC's registers while the symbols are the events defined earlier. Figure 2 shows an example of a temporal pattern discovered by the KarmaLego algorithm for the events in Fig. 1. In the first iteration, the Pattern "Reg1 = 4 *starts* Reg2 = 34" is discovered (the marked red line in the left table). In the next iteration the pattern is extended and a new pattern is discovered: "(Reg1 = 4 *starts* Reg2 = 34) *overlaps* Reg3 = 67" (right table). Using KarmaLego, we discover the patterns which will be fed as features into a machine learning algorithm, as described in the next section. A detailed description of KarmaLego can be found in [5].

The registers' values are continuous and may have many distinct values. This may lead to the number of patterns to explode. Thus, in order to discover frequent temporal patterns, the values are discretized and transformed into symbolic time intervals. For that, in this work we apply three types of discretization: K-Means, Equal Width Discretization (EWD) and Equal Frequency Discretization (EFD). A machine-learning algorithm is then fed by a training set, where each instance in the training set represents a set of features and their class. We define an instance in the MODBUS communication by a time window, where the features are the patterns discovered by the KarmaLego algorithm for that window. Additional features are the vertical support (frequency) and mean duration (the average time) of each pattern within the time window. The class is whether a malicious activity exists in this time window or not. Finally, a malicious activity classifier is trained.

3 Evaluation

The SCADA system at Ben-Gurion University controls the entire computerized systems in the university: security, lights, heating, air-conditioning, etc. This gives us a unique opportunity to test our method with a real SCADA system. We have recorded the entire data from the central HMI station for 5 days. This gave us an access not only to one SCADA PLC, but to all 31 MODBUS/TCP PLCs in the university controlled by the central HMI. The data was recorded using Wireshark and the registers' values were extracted from the MODBUS/TCP packets according to MODBUS/TCP documentation. The total size of the dataset is 18.9 Gb, and it is composed of approximately 20 million packets directed to port 502 (MOSBUS/TCP default port). Unfortunately, we do not have real attacks and thus we injected attacks by extending the periods of time a register holds a certain value.

We used the random forest classifier. In order to evaluate the classification model, we use the standard metrics of Area Under Curve (AUC). Each data point in the results is an average of the thirty classification evaluation runs. Our baseline for comparison considers the mean and standard deviation of the values of each reg-

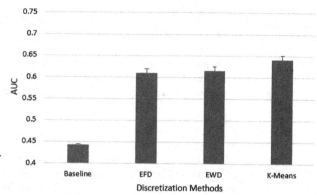

Fig. 3. K-Means outperforms the other methods.

ister during the time window, which are used as features for a classifier. For each time window, the mean values and the standard deviation of each register are calculated and added as features to a training set. Then, a malicious activity classifier is trained with these features.

Figure 3 shows the AUC of the various discretization methods. K-Means performs better than the other discretization methods since K-Means assigns values to the closest bin, rather than just assigning values by width or frequency. The AUC of the baseline is much below the results achieved with our method. These results show that time TIRPs based classification that consider the time are much more effective.

References

1. Allen, J.F.: Maintaining knowledge about temporal intervals. In: Readings in Qualitative Reasoning about Physical Systems, pp. 361–372. Elsevier (1990)
2. Goldenberg, N., Wool, A.: Accurate modeling of Modbus/TCP for intrusion detection in SCADA systems. Int. J. Crit. Infrastruct. Prot. **6**(2), 63–75 (2013)
3. Kam, P., Fu, A.W.: Discovering temporal patterns for interval-based events. In: Kambayashi, Y., Mohania, M., Tjoa, A.M. (eds.) DaWaK 2000. LNCS, vol. 1874, pp. 317–326. Springer, Heidelberg (2000). https://doi.org/10.1007/3-540-44466-1_32
4. Kushner, D.: The real story of stuxnet. IEEE Spectrum **3**(50), 48–53 (2013)
5. Moskovitch, R., Shahar, Y.: Fast time intervals mining using the transitivity of temporal relations. Knowl. Inf. Syst. **42**(1), 21–48 (2015)
6. Zhu, B., Sastry, S., Joseph, A.: A taxonomy of cyber attacks on SCADA systems. In: 2011 IEEE International Conference on Internet of Things, pp. 380–388 (2011)

Anonymous Deniable Identification in Ephemeral Setup and Leakage Scenarios (Brief Announcement)

Łukasz Krzywiecki$^{(\boxtimes)}$, Mirosław Kutyłowski, Jakub Pezda, and Marcin Słowik

Department of Computer Science, Faculty of Fundamental Problems of Technology,
Wrocław University of Science and Technology, Wrocław, Poland
{lukasz.krzywiecki,miroslaw.kutylowski,marcin.slowik}@pwr.edu.pl

Abstract. We present anonymous identification schemes, where a verifier can check that the user belongs to an ad-hoc group of users (just like in case of ring signatures), however a transcript of a session executed between a user and a verifier is deniable: neither the verifier nor the prover can convice a third party that a given user has been involved in a session but also he cannot prove that any user has been interacting with the verifier. Our realization of this idea is based on Schnorr identification scheme and ring signatures. We present two constructions, a simple 1-of-n case and a more advanced k-of-n, where the prover must use at least k private keys. They are immune to leakage of ephemeral keys and with minor modifications this property can be sacrificed for a simpler construction.

1 Introduction

The primary purpose of identification and authentication procedure performed before granting access to certain resources is to check that the applicant – called a *prover* – belongs to a group of users entitled to access these resources. In many cases, there is no need to reveal the real identity of the user and to provide a proof for a future inspection. Nevertheless, in a traditional approach:

- the verifier requests the prover to reveal their identity,
- the prover has to provide a proof of knowledge of a secret related to them, e.g. to sign a challenge presented by the verifier.

This way not only potentially sensitive identity information are introduced into the system, but also a non-volatile cryptographic data of high quality are created.

There are several approaches to anonymity in case of signatures. *Pseudonymous signatures* are related to pseudonymous identity, which is unique per user

This research was initially supported by Polish National Science Centre under grant OPUS no 2014/15/B/ST6/02837 and further funded by Wrocław University of Technology grant S50129/K1102.
Full version of the paper is available in the IACR Cryptology ePrint Archive [1].

S. Dolev et al. (Eds.): CSCML 2019, LNCS 11527, pp. 320–323, 2019.
https://doi.org/10.1007/978-3-030-20951-3_27

and an identification sector, but unlinkable between different sectors. Another approach are *group* or *ring signatures* – they prove membership in a predefined or ad-hoc group, but reveal no identity. In the signature based approaches, an interaction leaves a cryptographic trace that can be used as a proof of interaction against third parties. From the privacy preserving perspective, in the interactive identification process, we require quite opposite feature: the transcript of that interaction should not be used, later on, as a proof that the interaction occured.

This can be achieved by the *deniability* property of the protocol, which is simulatable without any secrets by any party. Anonymous identification can be viewed as an extension to regular identification, where the actual prover is hidden within a group of potential provers. It interactively convinces the verifier, holding the set of the public keys, that it possesses one corresponding secret key.

We consider scenarios, where users do not control the production process of their devices. Malicious producers can leave back doors for randomness leakage or setting. Particularly we consider *Chosen Prover, Leaked Verifier Ephemeral* (CPLVE) model from [2]. Note that anonymous ring authentication of Naor [3] and deniable identification schemes of Stinson and Wu [4], and Di Raimondo and Gennaro [5], are not secure in this model, because they are based on the random ephemeral coined at the verifiers device.

Contribution. The contribution of the paper is the following:

- we propose a k-of-n anonymous and deniable identification scheme;
- we propose a simplified version for case $k = 1$;
- we prove the security of the schemes in the CPLVE model from [2] in the full version of the paper [1].

A case of $k > 1$ can be used when a strong multifactor authentication is required. E.g. for $k = 2$, the user has to use two different keys – one located on an identity card and one located on his laptop. Our proposals are **deniable** in honest verifier setting; **privacy-preserving** due to their anonymous nature and secure in case of **ephemeral leakage or setting**.

2   Proposed Anonymous Identification Schemes Secure in CPLVE

We propose two AIS secure in CPLVE: a general k-of-n scheme and a more efficient 1-of-n scheme. We apply the technique from [6] to immune against ephemeral setup values on provers devices.

Efficient 1-of-n AIS Secure in CPLVE. The construction is depicted in Fig. 1. Assume the prover has a secret key a_j. The anonymity is achieved in as follows: for all public keys for which the prover does not possess the secret key, it simulates Schnorr IS transcripts, selecting c_i values at random. Subsequently it computes missing $c_j = c - \sum_{i \neq j} c_i$ after obtaining challenge c from the verifier and performs IS for his private key in a regular way.

---

params ← ParGen(1^λ):

    Let $\mathbb{G} \leftarrow \mathcal{G}(1^\lambda)$, s.t. CcDH assumption holds; $\hat{e} : G_1 \times G_2 \rightarrow G_T$ be a bilnear map;

    $\mathcal{H} : \{0,1\}^* \rightarrow G_2$ be a hash function. Set params $= (G_1, G_2, G_T, g_1, g_2, q, \mathcal{H}, \hat{e})$.

KeyGen():

    For a key pair i do $\mathsf{sk}_i = a_i \leftarrow_\$ \mathbb{Z}_q^*$, $\mathsf{pk}_i = A_i = g_1^{a_i}$. Output (a_i, A_i).

$\pi(\mathcal{P}(\{a_j\}_J, \{A\}_1^n), \mathcal{V}(\{A\}_1^n))$:

    1. $\mathcal{P}$: for $i \in 1, \ldots, n$ s.t. $i \neq j$ compute: $c_i, s_i \leftarrow_\$ \mathbb{Z}_q^*$, $X_i = g_1^{s_i}/A_i^{c_i}$

    2. $\mathcal{P}$: choose $x_j \leftarrow_\$ \mathbb{Z}_q^*$, $X_j = g_1^{x_j}$, $X = \prod X_i$ and send X to the verifier $\mathcal{V}$.

    3. $\mathcal{V}$: choose $c \leftarrow_\$ \mathbb{Z}_q^*$, and send c to the prover $\mathcal{P}$.

    4. $\mathcal{P}$: compute $c_j = c - \sum_{i \neq j} c_i$, then $s_j = x_j + a_j c_j$, $\hat{g}_2 = \mathcal{H}(X|c)$, $s = \sum s_i$, $S = \hat{g}_2^s$

      and send $S, c_1, \ldots, c_n$ to the verifier $\mathcal{V}$.

    5. $\mathcal{V}$: compute $\hat{g}_2 = \mathcal{H}(X|c)$ and accept iff $c = \sum c_i$ and $\hat{e}(g_1, S) = \hat{e}(X \prod A_i^{c_i}, \hat{g}_2)$.

Fig. 1. 1-of-n AIS secure in CPLVE.

General k-of-n Anonymous AIS Secure in CPLVE. The construction is depicted in Fig. 2. Let $k + z = n$. For a polynomial $L(x)$ of degree $z - 1$, and a set of shares $P = \{(x_i, y_i)\}_1^n$, s.t. $y_i = L(x_i)$ then the following are true:

- each z-element subset of from P can be used to interpolate L;
- a least k shares $(x_j, L(x_j))$ were added to P after L was constructed.

The scheme follows a similar principle of simulating z transcripts and performing honest proofs for the remaining k. To ensure that, the verifier generates a set of k random polynomial points. The prover then inserts z points for the simulated transcripts, interpolates a polynomial and extracts the remaining n challenge values. The verifier finally checks if c values (z simulated and n honest) interpolate a polynomial that still includes the original set of random points.

Security Without CPLVE. Security against ephemeral leakage and setting can be easily removed from the schemes making them insecure in CPLVE model, but more efficient and still secure in scenarios where such attacks are not considered. We modify the 1-of-n scheme (Fig. 1) protocol π in the following way. In step 4. the prover sends to the verifier the value s instead of S, and in step 5. the verifier checks if $g^s = X \prod A_i^{c_i}$ instead of $\hat{e}(g_1, S) = \hat{e}(X \prod A_i^{c_i}, \hat{g}_2)$. Similarly, we modify the k-of-n scheme (Fig. 2) protocol π in the following way. In step 10. the prover sends to the verifier $\{c_i, s_i\}_1^n$ instead of $\{c_i, S_i\}_1^n$, and in step 13. the verifier checks for each $i \in I$ if $g^{s_i} = X_i A_i^{c_i}$ instead of $\hat{e}(g_1, S_i) = \hat{e}(X_i A_i^{c_i}, \hat{g}_2)$. In both cases, this effectively removes the need for pairing-friendly groups, as all operations are performed in G_1 and $\mathbb{Z}_q$. The resulting schemes are *deniable*, *secure* for impersonation, and *anonymous*.

3   Conclusion

We proposed 1-of-n and k-of-n interactive anonymous identification schemes, that support privacy of users *two-fold*:privacy regarded as ability to deny the participation in the protocol interaction and privacy regarded as anonymity within a

Let $I = \{i\}_1^n$, $J = \{j_1, \ldots, j_k\} \subset I$, $Z = \{i_1, \ldots, i_z\} \subset I$, $J \cup Z = I$, $J \cap Z = \emptyset$.

params $\leftarrow$ ParGen(1^λ):

    Let $\mathbb{G} \leftarrow \mathcal{G}(1^\lambda)$, s.t. CcDH assumption holds; $\hat{e} : G_1 \times G_2 \rightarrow G_T$ be a bilnear map;
    $\mathcal{H}_{g_2} : \{0,1\}^* \rightarrow G_2$, and $\mathcal{H} : \{0,1\}^* \rightarrow \mathbb{Z}_q^*$ be hash functions.
    Set params $= (G_1, G_2, G_T, g_1, g_2, q, \mathcal{H}_{g_2}, \mathcal{H}, \hat{e})$.

KeyGen():

    For a key pair i do $\mathsf{sk}_i = a_i \leftarrow_\$ \mathbb{Z}_q^*$, $\mathsf{pk}_i = A_i = g_1^{a_i}$. Output (a_i, A_i).

$\pi(\mathcal{P}(\{a_j\}_J, \{A_i\}_1^n), \mathcal{V}(\{A_i\}_1^n))$:

    1. $\mathcal{P}$: set $X_Z = \{X_i\}_Z$, s.t. $s_i, c_i \leftarrow_\$ \mathbb{Z}_q^*$, $X_i = g_1^{s_i}/A_i^{c_i}$ for each $i \in Z$.
    2. $\mathcal{P}$: set $X_J = \{X_j\}_J$, s.t. for each $j \in J$ compute $x_j \leftarrow_\$ \mathbb{Z}_q^*$, $X_j = g_1^{x_j}$.
    3. $\mathcal{P}$: send $X = X_Z \cup X_J$ to the verifier $\mathcal{V}$.
    4. $\mathcal{V}$: set $P_C = \{(x_i, y_i)\}_1^k$, where each pair $x_i, y_i \leftarrow_\$ \mathbb{Z}_q^*$.
    5. $\mathcal{V}$: compute $\hat{g}_2 = \mathcal{H}_{g_2}(X, P_C)$, send P_C to the provers $\mathcal{P}$.
    6. $\mathcal{P}$: compute the set $P_Z = \{(x_i, y_i)\}_Z$, s.t. $x_i = \mathcal{H}(X_i)$, $y_i = c_i$ for each $i \in Z$.
    7. $\mathcal{P}$: set $P = P_C \cup P_Z$, interpolate a polynomial $L_P(x)$ for points P.
    8. $\mathcal{P}$: compute $\hat{g}_2 = \mathcal{H}_{g_2}(X, P_C)$
    9. $\mathcal{P}$: for each $j \in J$, compute $c_j = L_P(\mathcal{H}(X_j))$, $s_j = x_j + a_j c_j$.
    10. $\mathcal{P}$: for each $i \in I$ compute $S_i = \hat{g}_2^{s_i}$, send $\{c_i, S_i\}_1^n$ to the verifier $\mathcal{V}$.
    11. $\mathcal{V}$: set $\bar{P} = \{(x_i, y_i)\}_1^n$, s.t. $x_i = \mathcal{H}(X_i)$, $y_i = c_i$ for each $i \in I$.
    12. $\mathcal{V}$: interpolate a polynomial $L_{\bar{P}}(x)$ for points $\bar{P}$.
    13. $\mathcal{V}$: accept iff $\forall_{(x_i,y_i)\in P_C} L_{\bar{P}}(x_i) = y_i$ and $\forall_{i \in I} \hat{e}(g_1, S_i) = \hat{e}(X_i A_i^{c_i}, \hat{g}_2)$.

Fig. 2. k-of-n AIS secure in CPLVE.

set of potential provers. The schemes withstand impersonation attacks in the strong CPLVE model. This justifies for implementation on devices, which manufacturing process is not under the sole control of the end-users, and when fair randomness cannot be guaranteed.

References

1. Krzywiecki, L., Kutyłowski, M., Pezda, J., Słowik, M.: Anonymous deniable identification in ephemeral setup & leakage scenarios. Cryptology ePrint Archive, Report 2019/337 (2019). https://eprint.iacr.org/
2. Krzywiecki, L., Słowik, M.: Strongly deniable identification schemes immune to prover's and verifier's ephemeral leakage. In: Farshim, P., Simion, E. (eds.) SecITC 2017. LNCS, vol. 10543, pp. 115–128. Springer, Cham (2017). https://doi.org/10.1007/978-3-319-69284-5_9
3. Naor, M.: Deniable ring authentication. In: Yung, M. (ed.) Annual International Cryptology–CRYPTO 2002 CRYPTO 2002. LNCS, vol. 2442, pp. 481–498. Springer, Heidelberg (2002). https://doi.org/10.1007/3-540-45708-9_31
4. Stinson, D.R., Wu, J.: An efficient and secure two-flow zero-knowledge identification protocol. Cryptology ePrint Archive, Report 2006/337 (2006)
5. Raimondo, M.D., Gennaro, R.: New approaches for deniable authentication. J. Cryptology 22(4), 572–615 (2009)
6. Krzywiecki, Ł.: Schnorr-like identification scheme resistant to malicious subliminal setting of ephemeral secret. In: Bica, I., Reyhanitabar, R. (eds.) SECITC 2016. LNCS, vol. 10006, pp. 137–148. Springer, Cham (2016). https://doi.org/10.1007/978-3-319-47238-6_10

Randomized and Set-System Based Collusion Resistant Key Predistribution Schemes (Brief Announcement)

Vasiliki Liagkou[1,4(✉)], Paul Spirakis[2,3], and Yannis C. Stamatiou[1,5]

[1] Research and Academic Computer Technology Institute, N. Kazantzaki,
University of Patras, 26500 Rio, Patras, Greece
liagkou@cti.gr, stamatiu@ceid.upatras.gr
[2] Department of Computer Science, University of Liverpool, Liverpool, UK
P.Spirakis@liverpool.ac.uk
[3] Department of Computer Engineering, University of Patras,
26500 Rio, Patras, Greece
[4] Department of Informatics and Telecommunications, University of Ioannina,
47100 Koatakioi Arta, Greece
[5] Department of Business Administration, University of Patras, University Campus,
26500 Rio, Patras, Greece

Abstract. One problem that frequently arises is the establishment of a secure connection between two network nodes. There are many key establishment protocols that are based on Trusted Third Parties or public key cryptography which are in use today. However, in the case of networks with frequently changing topology, such an approach is difficult to apply. In this paper we give a formal definition of collusion resistant key predistribution schemes and then propose such a scheme based on probabilistically created set systems. The resulting key sets are shown to have a number of desirable properties that ensure the confidentiality of communication sessions against collusion attacks by other network nodes. Moreover we associate our deterministic key pre-distribution scheme with the theory of set family construction methods showing that the mathematical properties possessed by the sets of such families lead to key sets with the aforementioned desirable properties.

Keywords: Key management · Key pre-distribution ·
Ad-hoc network security · Set systems

1 Introduction

Key predistribution is one of the most effective method for enabling two nodes of a network (especially ad-hoc networks) to establish secure communication. Several proposals exist which deal with key pre-distribution. Here we will focus specifically on probabilistic and deterministic pre-distribution schemes, which have in some way incorporated the use of set systems, and schemes on which these have based their work.

© Springer Nature Switzerland AG 2019
S. Dolev et al. (Eds.): CSCML 2019, LNCS 11527, pp. 324–327, 2019.
https://doi.org/10.1007/978-3-030-20951-3_28

Related Work

Several proposals exist for distributing keys to sensor nodes prior to deployment by using a key pool generated by a polynomial ([1,2,5] and [3]). The authors of [5] propose a key pre-distribution scheme consisting where each node of the network is assigned a random subset of keys from a key pool which is loaded into the memory of each node. The key pre-distribution scheme in [8] follows that of [5]. The difference being that the latter is a probabilistic scheme whereas the former adopts a deterministic approach. A q-composite random key pre-distribution scheme proposed in [2] which address the bootstrapping problem, and it is based primarily on the work described in [5]. Authors in [6] examine also a q-composite scheme and they schemes provide resilience to node captures but at the expense of increased communication overhead.

The interesting point here is that increasing the least number of keys that need to be shared by two nodes in order to establish communication, necessitates a decrease in the key pool size. Du et al. in [4] tried to reduce the size of key ring by assigning larger key ring size to high end sensors and minimum key ring size to low end sensors. Here we try to solve this trade-off between increasing the number of required shared keys and increasing the random key pool size by constructing keys that have properties for preventing *collusion* attacks.

Our Contribution

In this paper we present simple, probabilistic, key ring constructions for use in key management protocols in Mobile Ad-Hoc Networks (MANETs). Our constructions are based on two new key ring properties: (i) the intersection of key rings *is not a subset* of the union of a disjoint set of key rings, and (the stronger, but more difficult to attain, property) (ii) the intersection of key rings is *disjoint* from the union of a disjoint set of key rings. These properties can help towards preventing *collusion* attacks from compromised nodes since they allow honest nodes to always locate communication keys that are not shared with the key rings of compromised nodes. In addition, we present some set system based constructions based on special combinatorial set designs as well as special classes of polynomials. Our goal is to link deterministic key pre-distribution with the theory of set family construction methods showing that the mathematical properties possessed by the sets of such families lead to key sets with the aforementioned desirable properties.

2 A Probabilistic Key Predistribution Scheme and Its Security Properties

In this section we will introduce a simple probabilistic key predistribution scheme and show that it possesses a number of good properties with regard to security. Let $\mathcal{M}$, with $|\mathcal{M}| = m$, denote the set of available keys. During the key predistribution phase, node i selects each key $j \in \mathcal{M}$, independently, with probability p_j and forms its key ring, denoted with $\mathcal{S}_i$. All these sets form a *set system*. In what follows, given a node u, by $\mathcal{S}_u$ we denote its key ring. Below, we define two properties of such set systems that, if obeyed, the key sets they contain have a number of desirable properties:

Definition 1 *(Exclusion property - $\mathcal{E}_{k,l}$). The intersection of the key rings of any set of k nodes is not a subset of the union of the key rings of any set of l nodes, provided the two sets of k and l nodes are disjoint.*

The following property is stronger since it does not allow the intersection and the union of the key sets to have a common element.

Definition 2 *(Isolation property - $\mathcal{I}_{k,l}$). The intersection of the key rings of any set of k nodes is disjoint from the union of the key rings of any set of l nodes, provided the two sets of k and l nodes are disjoint.*

3   Key Rings and Set Systems Based on Combinatorial Designs

In this section we turn our attention to key rings based on combinatorial designs. We, first, define the notion of r-union-freeness (see, e.g., [7]):

Definition 3 *(r-union-freeness). A family of sets $\mathcal{F}$ is called r-union-free if $A_0 \not\subseteq A_1 \cup A_2 \cup \ldots \cup A_r$ holds for all distinct $A_0, A_1, \ldots, A_r \in \mathcal{F}$.*

In our context this property states that for any distinct $r + 1$ sets, any one of them is not contained in the union of the rest r of the sets. This, in turn, implies that the key ring of any node in a communications network always contains some key that is not contained in any set of r of the rest of the nodes, which is important to avoid, e.g., collusion attacks from a set of r compromised nodes (i.e. there is always a key that does not lie in the combined key rings of the compromised nodes). Let us assume, for simplicity, that our goal is to create k-uniform key rings, i.e. key rings with k elements each, with $k > r$. Then, the condition in inequality becomes: $|A_i \cap A_j| < \frac{k}{r}$ for all $i \neq j$.

Let us fix a key set of m candidate keys for the nodes, for a sufficiently (see below) large positive integer m. Let, also, l be an integer l, such as $0 < l < \frac{k}{r}$, which will be the number of elements of the intersection of any pair of key rings. Then we take the following steps:

1. To each pair A_i, A_j we assign a different set of l shared keys out of the pool of the m available keys. (We can, also, let l vary depending on i, j, keeping it, however, in the range $0 < l < \frac{k}{r}$.)
2. For each of the n sets A, $k - l$ keys remain to be determined since the family of sets is k-uniform. We select, for each set, a different set of $k - l$ keys out of the pool of m keys.

To accommodate these two steps, we need $m \geq l \cdot \binom{n}{2} + n \cdot (k - l)$ candidate keys and the resulting key rings are r-union-free.

4   Conclusions

In this paper we have provided a number of key-ring constructions based on two new properties of set families, the *exclusion* and the *isolation* properties as well as combinatorial designs for set systems. Our approach combines the simplicity of probabilistic key management schemes with the strength of the deterministic ones.

With respect to the probabilistic schemes, we provided conditions on the key selection probabilities that dictate when the exclusion and isolation properties hold for the resulting key rings. The key selection algorithm is the simplest one, i.e. each node chooses its key ring by selecting uniformly at random from the pool of candidate keys. Depending on the values of the probabilities, we have shown that the properties hold with high probability.

With respect to deterministic key ring management, we provided some constructions based on set systems that ensure good resulting key ring properties. To this end, we used special classes of polynomials as well as extremal set theory.

As future research, we plan to exploit results from extremal set theory further and combine them with probabilistic schemes in order to combing simplicity with strength in key ring management.

References

1. Blundo, C., De Santis, A., Herzberg, A., Kutten, S., Vaccaro, U., Yung, M.: Perfectly-secure key distribution for dynamic conferences. In: Brickell, E.F. (ed.) CRYPTO 1992. LNCS, vol. 740, pp. 471–486. Springer, Heidelberg (1993). https://doi.org/10.1007/3-540-48071-4_33
2. Chan, H., Perrig, A., Song, D.: Random key predistribution schemes for sensor networks. In: IEEE Symposium on Security and Privacy, Berkeley, California, vol. 197 (2003)
3. Delgosha, F., Fekri, F.: Key pre-distribution in wireless sensor networks using multivariate polynomials. In: 2005 Second Annual IEEE Communications Society Conference on Sensor and Ad Hoc Communications and Networks, IEEE SECON 2005, pp. 118–129. IEEE (2005)
4. Du, X., Xiao, Y., Guizani, M., Chen, H.H.: An effective key management scheme for heterogeneous sensor networks. Ad Hoc Netw. 5(1), 24–34 (2007)
5. Eschenauer, L., Gligor, V.D.: A key-management scheme for distributed sensor networks. In: Proceedings of the 9th ACM Conference on Computer and Communications Security, pp. 41–47. ACM (2002)
6. Gandino, F., Ferrero, R., Rebaudengo, M.: A key distribution scheme for mobile wireless sensor networks: q-s-composite. IEEE Trans. Inf. Forensics Secur. 12(1), 34–47 (2017)
7. Jukna, S.: Extremal Combinatorics: With Applications in Computer Science. Springer, Heidelberg (2011). https://doi.org/10.1007/978-3-642-17364-6
8. Lee, J., Stinson, D.R.: A combinatorial approach to key predistribution for distributed sensor networks. In: WCNC, pp. 1200–1205 (2005)

Author Index

Printed in the United States
By Bookmasters